HOLY MOTHERHOOD

MANCHESTER MEDIEVAL STUDIES

HOLY MOTHERHOOD

GENDER, DYNASTY AND VISUAL CULTURE IN THE LATER MIDDLE AGES

Elizabeth L'Estrange

Manchester University Press

Published by Manchester University Press
Altrincham Street, Manchester M1 7JA, UK
www.manchesteruniversitypress.co.uk

British Library Cataloguing-in-Publication Data is available

Library of Congress Cataloging-in-Publication Data is available

ISBN 978 0 7190 8726 4 *paperback*

First published by Manchester University Press 2008

This edition first published 2016

The publisher has no responsibility for the persistence or accuracy of URLs for any external or third-party internet websites referred to in this book, and does not guarantee that any content on such websites is, or will remain, accurate or appropriate.

Printed by Lightning Source

To my parents, Thomas and Jennifer, with love

In memory of Nanny (Ada Jones), 21 November 1913–19 January 2008

CONTENTS

These can be found between pages 122 and 123.

8 Rohan Workshop, *St Anne with her Three Daughters* (text) and *Holy Kinship* (border), suffrages, *Fitzwilliam Hours*, Cambridge, Fitzwilliam Museum, MS 62, fol. 222r, *c.*1418–30. Reproduction by permission of the Syndics of the Fitzwilliam Museum, Cambridge (© Cambridge, Fitzwilliam Museum)

9 Rohan Workshop, *Mary Cleophas and Mary Salomé with their Sons*, suffrages, *Fitzwilliam Hours*, Cambridge, Fitzwilliam Museum, MS 62, fol. 222v, *c.*1418–30. Reproduction by permission of the Syndics of the Fitzwilliam Museum, Cambridge (© Cambridge, Fitzwilliam Museum)

10 Rohan Workshop, *Nativity of Christ* (border), Gospel of St Luke, *Fitzwilliam Hours*, Cambridge, Fitzwilliam Museum, MS 62, fol. 14v, *c.*1418–30. Reproduction by permission of the Syndics of the Fitzwilliam Museum, Cambridge (© Cambridge, Fitzwilliam Museum)

11 Rohan Workshop, *Birth of Moses*, *Bible moralisée* marginal cycle, *Rohan Hours*, Paris, Bibliothèque nationale, fonds latin, 9471, fol. 129v, *c.*1420 (© Paris, BnF)

12 Rohan Workshop, *Nativity of Christ*, *Bible moralisée* marginal cycle, *Rohan Hours*, Paris, Bibliothèque nationale, fonds latin, 9471, fol. 130r, *c.*1420 (© Paris, BnF)

13 Rohan Workshop, *Marguerite of Brittany at Prayer*, *Omnis te virtus decorat*, *Fitzwilliam Hours*, Cambridge, Fitzwilliam Museum, MS 62, f. 28r, *c.*1418–30, altered after 1450. Reproduction by permission of the Syndics of the Fitzwilliam Museum, Cambridge (© Cambridge, Fitzwilliam Museum)

14 *Holy Kinship*, suffrages, *Hours of Marguerite of Foix*, London, Victoria and Albert Museum, Salting MS 1222, fol. 213r, *c.*1477. Published by kind permission of the Board of Trustees of the V&A (© V&A Images/Victoria and Albert Museum)

15 *Visitation*, Lauds, Anne of Brittany's *Très Petites Heures*, Paris, Bibliothèque nationale, nouvelle acquisition latine, 3120, fol. 40r (© Paris, BnF)

16 *St Claude Presents a Kneeling Girl to St Anne and the Virgin*, *Primer of Claude of France*, Cambridge, Fitzwilliam Museum, MS 159, p. 14, *c.*1500–10. Reproduction by permission of the Syndics of the Fitzwilliam Museum, Cambridge (© Cambridge, Fitzwilliam Museum)

LIST OF FIGURES

PREFACE AND ACKNOWLEDGEMENTS

It is a pleasure to write the acknowledgements for this book and to recall all those who have, in some way or another, helped me arrive at its conclusion. The research for this study began in 1999 with a doctoral thesis in the School of Fine Art, History of Art and Cultural Studies at the University of Leeds. During this time I received the continual encouragement of my supervisors, Anthony Hughes and Eva Frojmovic. Their close criticisms and ability to see this project from a variety of different perspectives were very much appreciated and have continued to influence the way I approach my work. From 2004 I was able to develop this initial project into its present form whilst enjoying the support of a two-year Leverhulme Trust post-doctoral Study Abroad Studentship, during which I continued my research into Books of Hours at the Universities of Liège and Leuven in Belgium. During the final stages of the book I have been supported by an FNRS post-doctoral fellowship in the History of Art department at the University of Liège. Valuable financial assistance for the purchase and publication of additional images and colour plates has come from the Leverhulme Trust, the Chicago Newberry Library's Weiss/Brown Subvention, the Medieval Academy of America's Book Subvention Program, and the Scouloudi Foundation (Institute for Historical Research) in London. These contributions are very gratefully acknowledged.

Working with illuminated manuscripts is a real privilege and the thrill of holding – and beholding – something so old but still so beautiful never diminishes. I am especially grateful to those librarians, scholars and conservators who willingly made their material available for inspection with the minimum of fuss, who checked references, supplied photography, and who often reduced or waived copyright fees. Thanks in particular go to Stella Panayotova and Diane Hudson at the Fitzwilliam Museum in Cambridge, Danielle Shields, Dorothy Clayton and Anne Clarkson at the John Rylands University Library of Manchester, Rowan Watson and Roxanne Peters at the Victoria and Albert Museum, Margaret Lawson at the Metropolitan Museum in New York, Rob Dückers at Emerson College, Pierre-Jean Riamond at the Bibliothèque nationale, and the staff at the British Library and at Bridgeman-Giraudon.

Opportunities to refine my ideas and follow up new leads for this research have come formally at various conferences and, informally, in discussion with colleagues and friends. I am grateful to the following people in particular for sharing their ideas and for their encouragement at the different stages of putting this book together: Monica H. Green who kindly supplied a draft version of her forthcoming book, Kathleen Wilson-Chevalier for putting me on to Anne of France, and Adrian Wilson for sharing his thoughts on the medical aspects of this study. I would also like to thank Ian Moxon, whose help with Latin has been invaluable, and Rosalind Brown-Grant who carefully checked the trickier bits of Old French. Any errors or interpretations are entirely my own. Michael Jones generously shared a wealth of unpublished information on the Breton ducal archives. Hilary Brown and Richard K. Emmerson took the time to read and comment on earlier drafts and their comments were always insightful and constructive. Thanks go to Cathy McClive, in particular, who gave generously of her time and knowledge throughout the writing process. I am also grateful to the anonymous readers and to the editorial team at Manchester University Press for their advice and support in putting this book together. I thank the series editor, Steve Rigby, for his close critical readings of my work along the way, both in terms of structure and in terms of content.

Outside the hushed reading rooms and away from my computer, many other friends have helped me to keep my sanity: my far-flung friends, Kate Bingham, Caroline Braley, Vicki Brett, Shane Blanchard, Rhiannon Daniels, Eva De Visscher, Rachael Morris and Eleanor Wilson have all given me excuses or opportunities to escape now and again. In Belgium, Ingrid Falque (who also helped chase some outstanding references), Ellen Harry, Marie Herbillon and Anne-Catherine Lambrechts have been there for lunches and light-hearted relief on a day-to-day basis, and Christoph Schmid has taught me the value of frequent coffee breaks. Finally, I owe a huge debt to my parents, Jennifer and Thomas, whose belief in and support of my work have never faltered and who gave me the space in which to start and finish this book. It is to them, and with my fondest love, that I dedicate this book.

Note

Bible citations in Latin are taken from the Vulgate. English citations are taken from the Douai-Rheims translation. For Psalms, the Greek numbering is given followed by the Hebrew in parentheses.

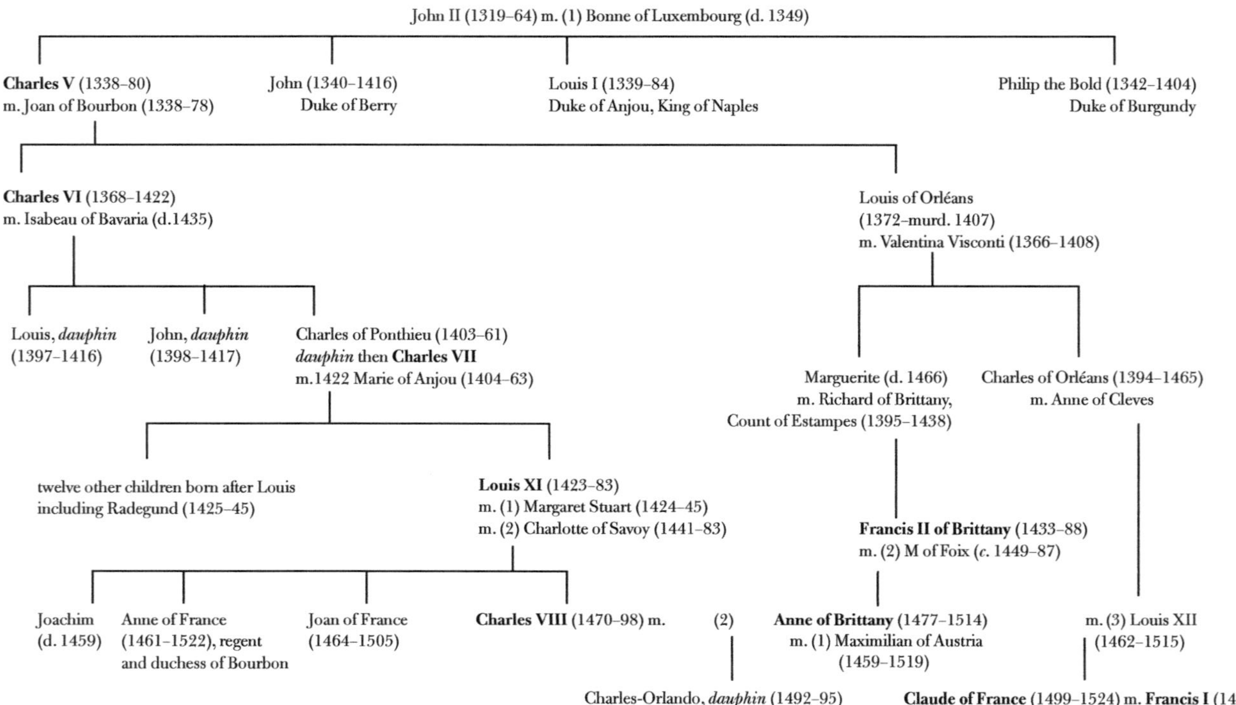

House of France

John II (1319–64) m. (1) Bonne of Luxembourg (d. 1349)

Charles V (1338–80)
m. Joan of Bourbon (1338–78)

John (1340–1416)
Duke of Berry

Louis I (1339–84)
Duke of Anjou, King of Naples

Philip the Bold (1342–1404)
Duke of Burgundy

Charles VI (1368–1422)
m. Isabeau of Bavaria (d.1435)

Louis of Orléans
(1372–murd. 1407)
m. Valentina Visconti (1366–1408)

Louis, dauphin
(1397–1416)

John, dauphin
(1398–1417)

Charles of Ponthieu (1403–61)
dauphin then Charles VII
m.1422 Marie of Anjou (1404–63)

Marguerite (d. 1466)
m. Richard of Brittany,
Count of Estampes (1395–1438)

Charles of Orléans (1394–1465)
m. Anne of Cleves

twelve other children born after Louis
including Radegund (1425–45)

Louis XI (1423–83)
m. (1) Margaret Stuart (1424–45)
m. (2) Charlotte of Savoy (1441–83)

Francis II of Brittany (1433–88)
m. (2) M of Foix (c. 1449–87)

Joachim
(d. 1459)

Anne of France
(1461–1522), regent
and duchess of Bourbon

Joan of France
(1464–1505)

Charles VIII (1470–98) m.

(2)

Anne of Brittany (1477–1514)
m. (1) Maximilian of Austria
(1459–1519)

m. (3) Louis XII
(1462–1515)

Charles-Orlando, dauphin (1492–95)

Claude of France (1499–1524) m. Francis I (1494–154

House of Anjou

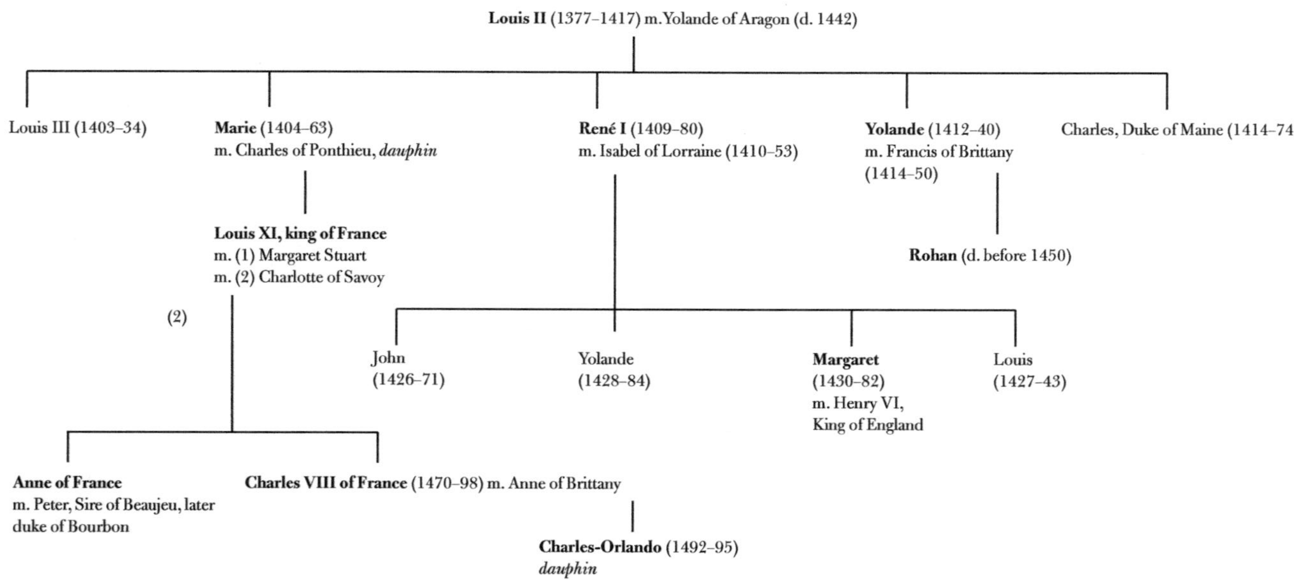

House of Brittany

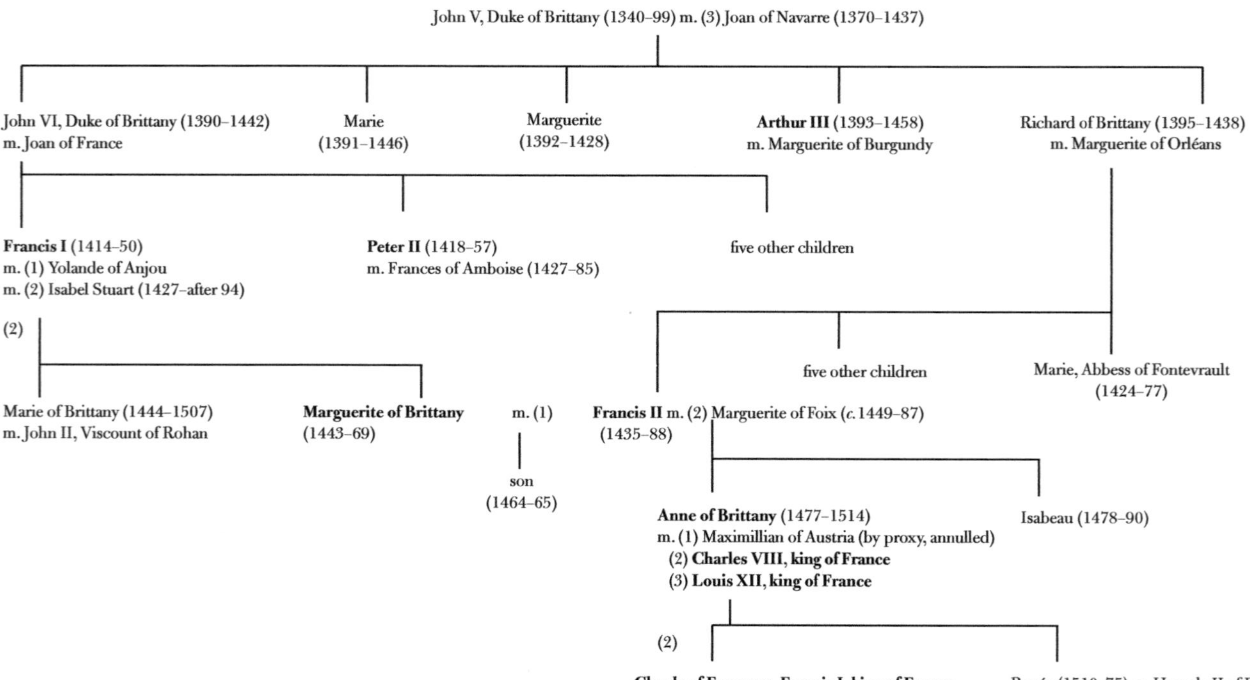

House of Burgundy

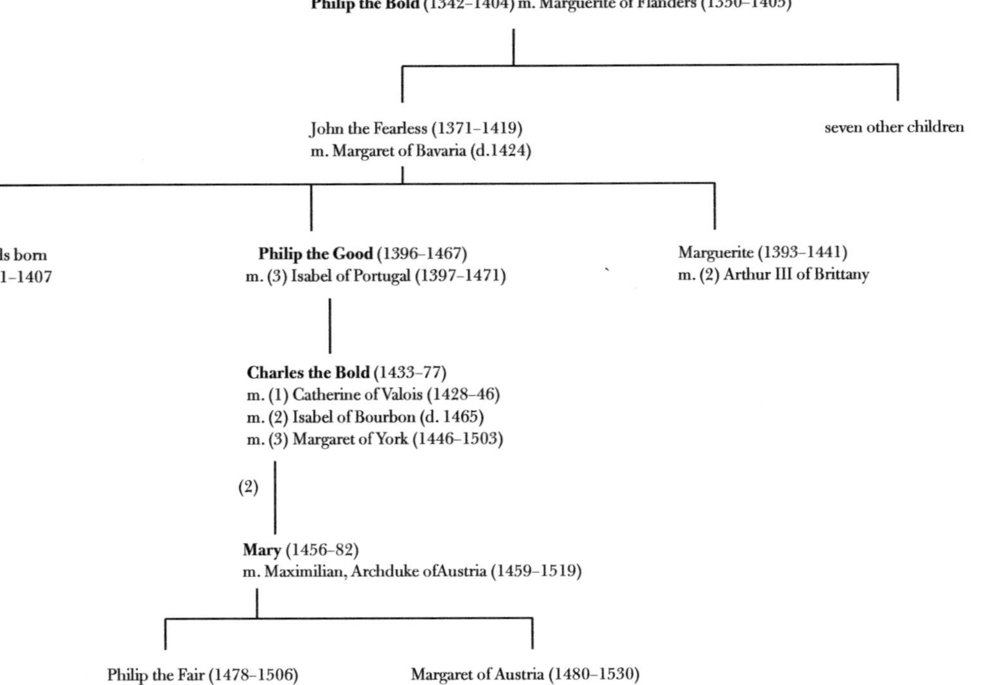

Introduction

In a late-fifteenth-century Book of Hours painted by the Master of James IV of Scotland and held at the John Rylands University Library of Manchester there are two miniatures of the *Birth of St John the Baptist* and the *Birth of the Virgin* (plates 1–2).[1] In each image, the newly-delivered mothers, St Elizabeth and St Anne, rest in bed and are presented with their swaddled child by another woman. Elsewhere in the comfortable domestic interiors, other female assistants clean the floor, and warm sheets before the fire. These miniatures are typical of late-medieval narrative representations of childbearing in that they depict the mother recuperating after the birth in a domestic setting. They show a space in which women care for, and are taken care of by, each other: male figures are absent or marginalised. This female-dominated, post-partum representation of the births of holy or heroic children occurs throughout West European art of the late middle ages, from manuscript painting to sculpture.[2]

Depictions of the births of the Virgin and St John the Baptist are particularly common, not only because of widespread devotion to the saints themselves but also because their births were officially celebrated by the Church and because the saints formed part of the Holy Kinship, the popular cult venerating St Anne and other members of Christ's extended family. The birth scene in the background of the left-hand panel of Rogier van der Weyden's *St John the Baptist Altarpiece* (*c.* 1450–60), for example, shows a woman tending to St Elizabeth who lies in a large bed hung with red curtains. In the foreground, and separated from this domestic space by an architectural frame, the Virgin holds the infant John while the father, Zacharias, is about to write out the child's name (figure 1). Similarly, Jan van Eyck's depiction of St John's birth in the *Turin-Milan Hours* (1380–1450; miniature 1422) shows a well-furnished interior with a number of

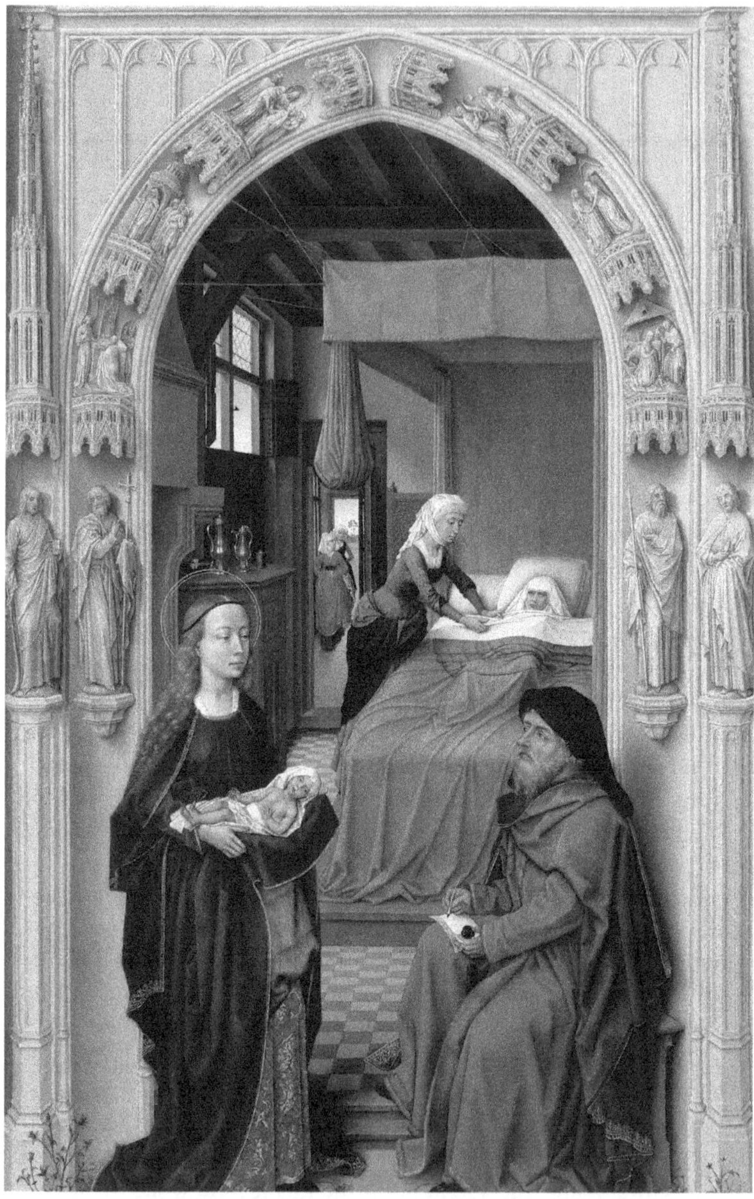

1 Rogier van der Weyden, *Birth of St John the Baptist*, left-hand panel, *St John the Baptist Altarpiece*, Berlin, Gemäldegalerie, *c.*1450–60 (© bpk / Gemäldegalerie, Staatliche Museen zu Berlin. Photo: Jörg P. Anders)

women assisting St Elizabeth, who also lies in a large bed hung with curtains (figure 2). The holy scene is given a familiar touch with the addition of a dog and cat eating in the foreground. Italian frescoes depicting the life of St John the Baptist or the Virgin Mary, such as those painted by Giusto de'Menabuoi in the Baptistery in Padua (*c.*1375; figure 3) and Domenico Ghirlandaio's workshop in Sta Maria Novella in Florence (1485–90), show particularly well-attended lying-ins with a number of female servants bringing food and drink to the mother and bathing the infant. In both the Padua and Florence frescoes, well-dressed visitors, some of whom can be identified as contemporary patrician wives, also enter the rooms to visit the new mother.[3] Such domestic features are also shown in the sculpted relief of St John's birth by Pisano that decorates the Baptistery doors in Florence (*c.*1330–36).

The births of historical or mythical figures were presented in much the same way in illuminated manuscripts. The *Birth of Constantine* was depicted in the background of a miniature illustrating Jean Wavrin's *History of England*: St Helena lies in bed in a secluded room and is presented with her son by a female assistant (*c.*1470–80; figure 4). Likewise, Merlin's mother is shown in a room attended by a number of women in part of a scene illustrating the *Birth and Escape of Merlin* from the prose *Merlin* by Guillaume de La Pierre (1482; figure 5). This domestic, post-partum format was transferred to the woodcut technique that was used to illustrate early printed books, such as the Book of Hours printed by Thielman Kerver in 1498, which shows two women preparing to bathe Mary in a *Birth of the Virgin* scene in the borders of the *Salve Regina* prayer (figure 6); or William Caxton's edition of the *Golden Legend* (1497) where the episode of the Virgin's birth is illustrated with an image of St Anne in bed surrounded by other women.[4]

The appeal of such images for the historian is that they appear to show something about which written sources are usually silent: the private, feminine, space of the childbirth chamber, which separated the parturient or newly-delivered woman from the public, masculine, space of the world outside. Post-partum images of childbirth have thus been invoked by historians to demonstrate the roles women occupied as mothers, care-givers and midwives in the late middle ages, and to recover a 'gendered space' in which women could act for, and by, themselves. Louis Haas for example, has emphasised that the spaces of childbearing belonged to women by referring to 'Renaissance paintings depicting the birth of the Virgin or St John the Baptist [which] commonly place the expectant father outside the room'.[5]

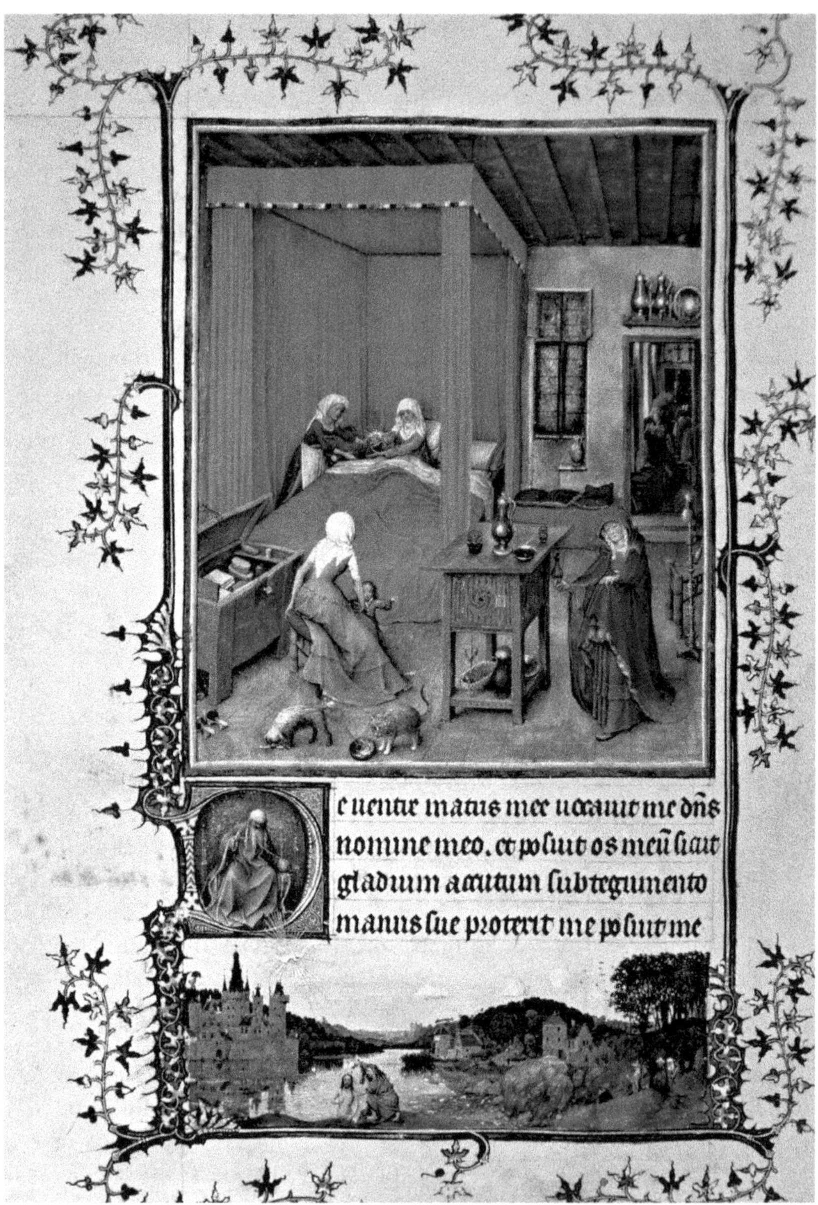

2   Jan van Eyck, *Birth of St John the Baptist and the Baptism of Christ, Turin-Milan Hours*, Turin, Museo Civico d'Arte Antica, Inv. no. 47, fol. 93v, 1380–1450, added 1422 (© Museo Civico, Turin, Italy/The Bridgeman Art Library)

4

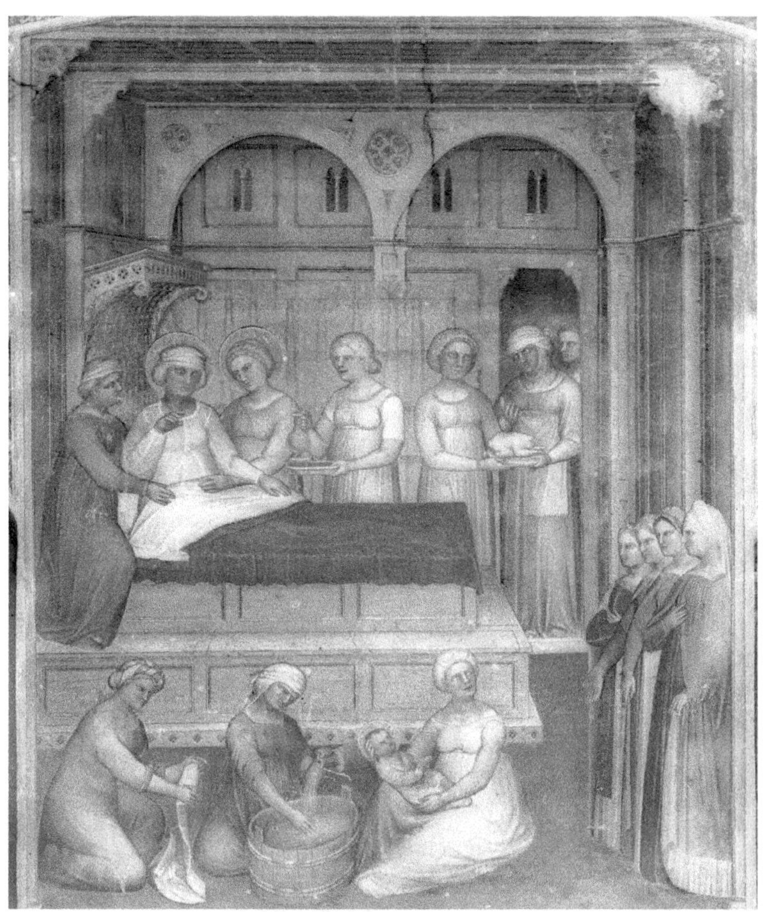

3   Giusto de' Menabuoi, *Birth of St John the Baptist*, Padua, Baptistery, *c*.1375 (© Alinari Archives, Florence)

In an article about the subjugation of midwives in the fifteenth century, Myriam Greilsammer has proposed that, 'The delivery room was one of the few areas where a wife escaped marital authority and expressed her specific womanliness.'[6] She claims that 'a glance at medieval depictions of births strengthens this contention'.[7] Referring to images of the Virgin's birth, she describes the delivery room as 'a bastion of female solidarity, communion, and omnipotence'.[8] Greilsammer's 'glance' at images of childbirth does not, however, sufficiently address the wider context and circumstances in which the images themselves were produced. Similarly, Sylvie Laurent

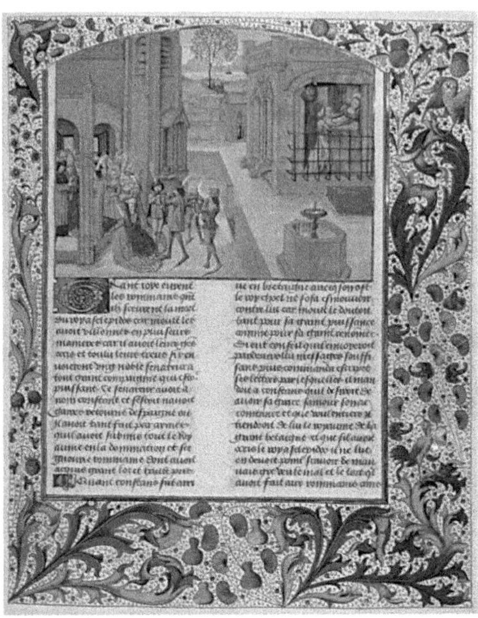

4   *Birth of Constantine* (top right-hand corner), Jean Wavrin's *History of England*, London, British Library, Royal MS 15 E iv, fol. 72r, fifteenth century (© London, British Library)

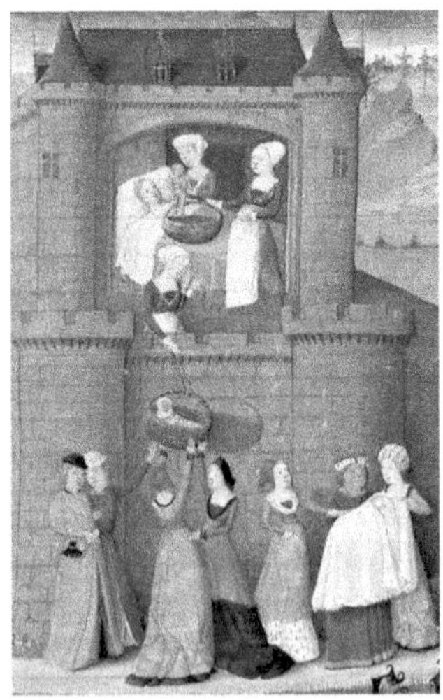

5   *Birth and Escape of Merlin* (detail), *Roman de Merlin*, Paris, Bibliothèque nationale, fonds français, 91, fol. 7r, 1482 (© Paris, BnF)

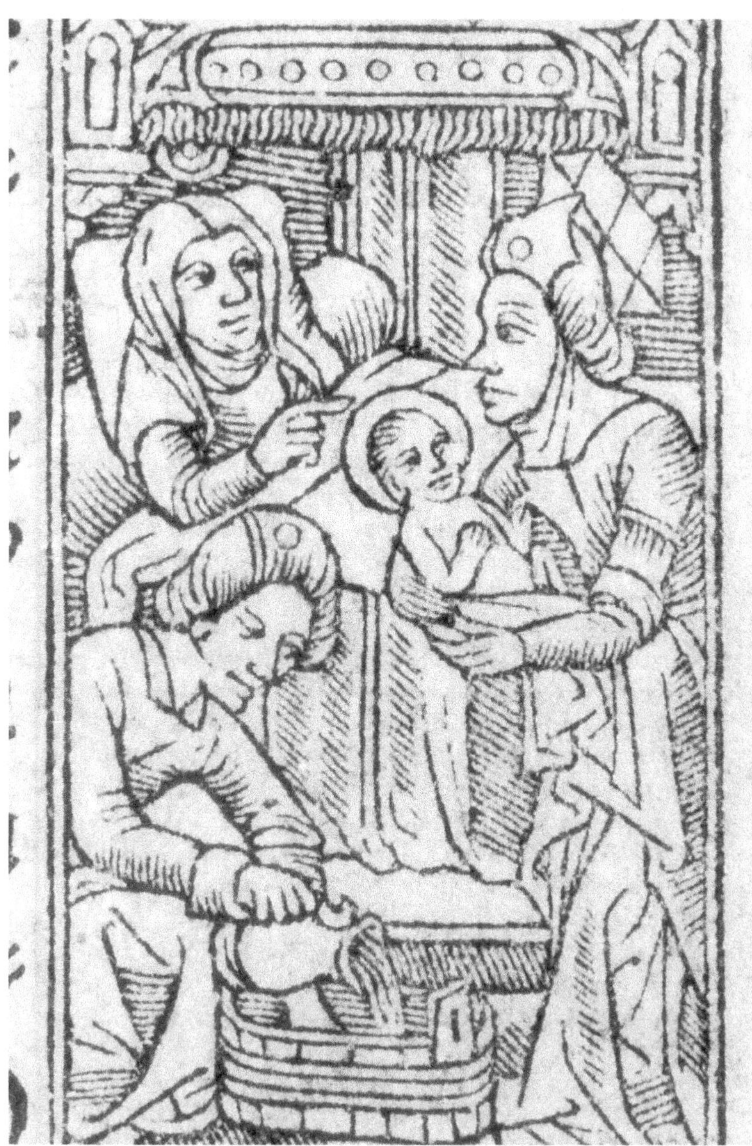

6   *Birth of the Virgin* (border detail), Book of Hours for the Use of Rome (Paris: Thielman Kerver, 1498), Manchester, John Rylands University Library, S15444, p. F3a. Reproduced by courtesy of the University Librarian and Director, The John Rylands University Library, The University of Manchester (© Manchester, John Rylands University Library)

used a number of mainly post-partum birth scenes taken primarily from historical and devotional manuscripts to illustrate her study *Naître au moyen âge*, although she did not consider the original context for which the images were created or who was viewing them.[9] In fact, the front cover of Laurent's book shows the *Birth of the Male Children of Israel*, one of a series of *in partu* birth scenes that illustrated the marginal *Bible moralisée* included in the bespoke *Rohan Hours*, a Book of Hours possibly made for Charles VII (1403–61) and discussed in more detail below (figure 7).

Images of the birth of Julius Caesar often show the medical procedure supposed to have been used to deliver the emperor, but still place it in a domestic setting with female assistants. On the basis of fourteenth- and fifteenth-century illuminations of this event, Renate Blumenfeld-Kosinski has argued that from the beginning of the fifteenth century 'midwives were systematically excluded' from carrying out Caesarean operations.[10] While Blumenfeld-Kosinski was right to document a shift in the gendering of women's obstetrical care around the end of the fourteenth century, it is extremely difficult to use pictorial images of the birth of Caesar taken from historical manuscripts like the *Faits de Romains* as direct evidence for the exclusion of women from surgical procedures.[11] Likewise, the images discussed at the beginning of this Introduction cannot be used unproblematically to access 'normal' medieval childbirth practices, nor can they necessarily be indicative of an audience that is female: plates 1 and 2 of the *Birth of the Virgin* and the *Birth of St John* are found in a manuscript made for an Augustinian canon, a man in religious orders. Nevertheless, as images of women and more specifically of holy mothers, they do raise questions for the art historian seeking to understand not only the role of the female sex in late-medieval society but also the problems of using art as an historical source.[12]

By taking these female-dominated images of successful birth as a starting point for posing questions about genders, spectators, and reception, this study proposes several things. To begin with, it develops a more nuanced interpretation of this iconography than has previously been offered and, through this, a more subtle analysis of 'gendered' spectatorship. It then situates these images in the context of devotion to St Anne, the Holy Kinship, and the idea of *beata stirps* or blessed lineage, in order to consider the significance of narratives of blessed motherhood and holy dynasties in the lives of men and women in the fifteenth century, especially the aristocratic readers and commissioners of manuscripts from the houses of Anjou, Brittany and France. The analysis, therefore, moves beyond Greilsammer's 'glance at medieval depictions of births' to explore the

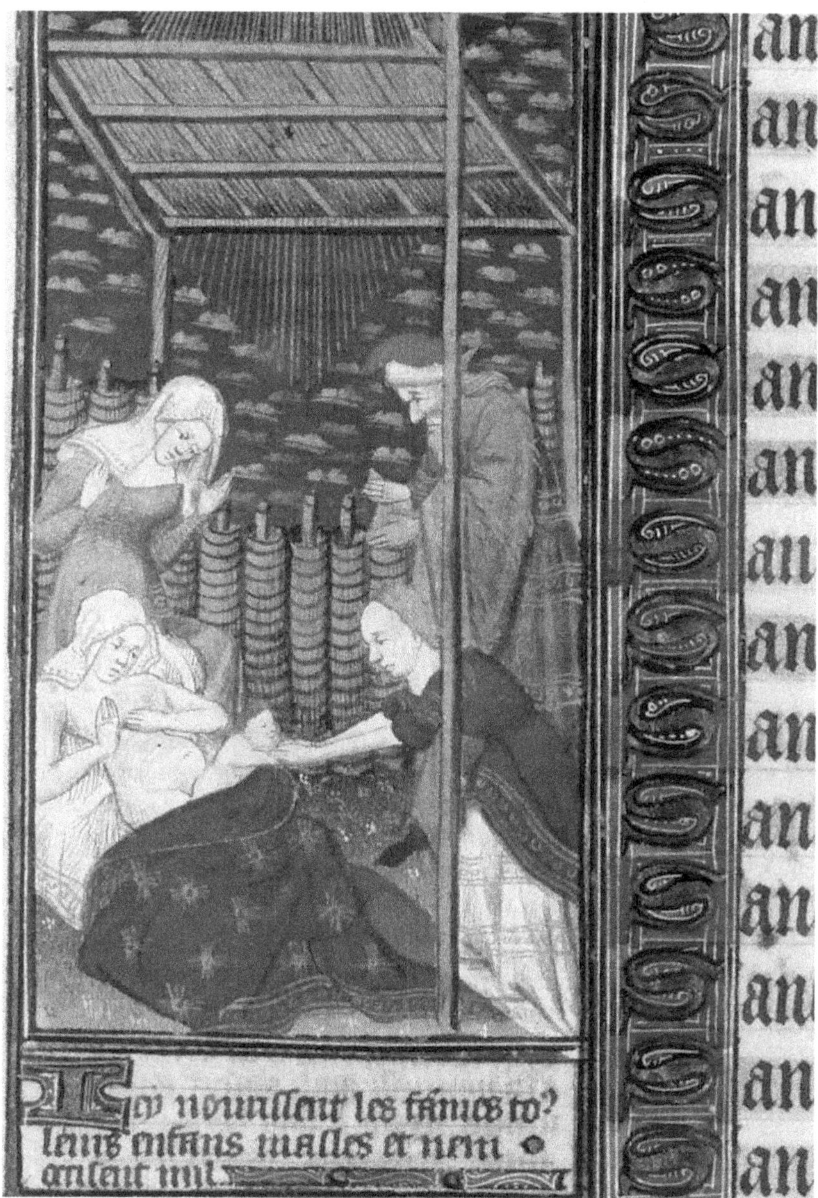

7   Rohan Workshop, *Birth of the Male Children of Israel*, *Bible moralisée*
marginal cycle (detail), *Rohan Hours*, Paris, Bibliothèque nationale, fonds
latin, 9471, fol. 127v, *c.*1420 (© Paris, BnF)

implications of, and possibilities for, using religious images to identify childbirth as a 'bastion of female solidarity, communion and omnipotence'.[13] Particular attention is paid to the commissioners and recipients of images of childbirth: for whom were the images made and in what contexts were they encountered? Is gender alone sufficient a category to understand the appeal and meanings these images had for different viewers? How far can the occurrence of this imagery of holy motherhood in works associated with female viewers be a straightforward indication of women's tastes and patronage? What part did social roles play in the reception of such intimate images of women's social and biological activity? Are male viewers a priori excluded from this type of imagery? Some aspects of the questions posed here have been addressed by scholars working on late medieval visual cultures, the figure of St Anne, and the construction and fluidity of medieval and modern gender roles. This study draws on and adds to these existing approaches in order to offer some answers to these and other questions regarding the place of the female viewer in late medieval visual culture and modern attempts to define her.

The cult of St Anne and the Holy Kinship is central to this enquiry. Devotion to the Virgin's mother, St Anne, was strong in Northern Europe in the fifteenth and sixteenth centuries, where she appeared in art and literature as the matriarch of a family of holy mothers and miraculous births.[14] The main sources for St Anne's and thus Christ's genealogy in the later middle ages were Jacobus de Voragine's *Golden Legend* and the *Proto-Evangelium of James*, supposedly written by Christ's cousin St James the Less.[15] In order to explain a number of biblical and apocryphal references to Christ's brothers and cousins, texts like the *Golden Legend* explained that St Anne had been married three times (the *trinubium*): first to Joachim, by whom she bore the Virgin, and then to Cleophas and Salomé by whom she bore two other children, Mary Cleophas and Mary Salomé (sometimes called Mary Jacobi). Between them these women gave birth to a host of holy children including St John the Evangelist, St James the Great, St James the Less, St Jude and St Simon. St Elizabeth, mother of St John the Baptist, was also related to this kinship by virtue of being the Virgin's cousin. Certain accounts of St Anne's genealogy trace the family tree back even further to explain that St Elizabeth's mother, Hysmeria, was the sister of St Anne; Hysmeria and Anne were, in turn, the children of Erementiana and Stollanus, of the house of Judah, thus reinforcing Christ's own descent from this house, via King David.[16]

The Holy Kinship became an extremely popular subject for manuscript and panel paintings. Whereas some paintings focused solely on St Anne,

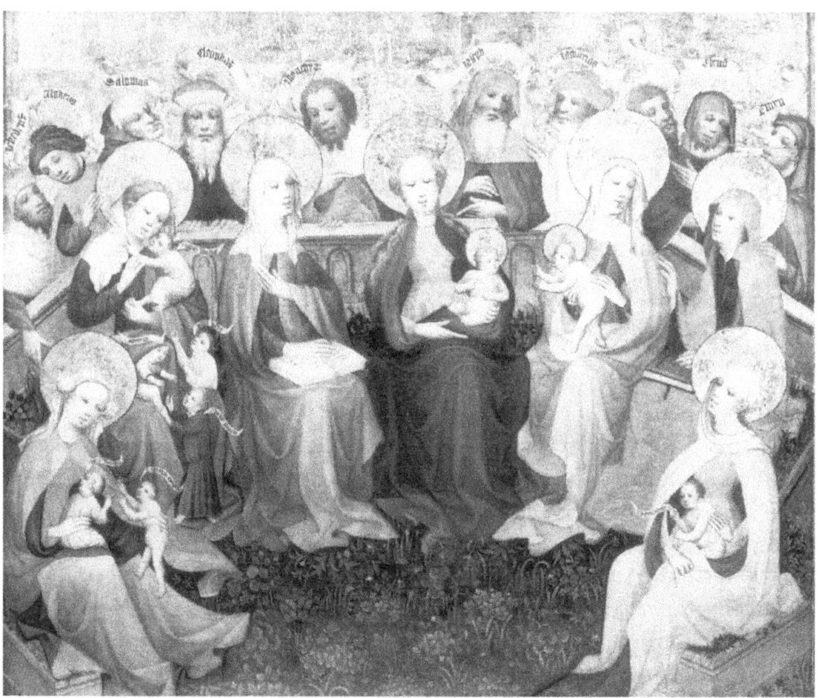

8   Follower of the Master of St Veronica, *Holy Kinship* (central panel), Cologne, Wallraf-Richartz-Museum, Inv. Nr. 59, *c.* 1420 (© Cologne, Wallraf-Richartz Museum/Rheinisches Bildarchiv)

the Virgin and Christ, others celebrated all the family members, as in the *Holy Kinship* painted by the Follower of the Master of St Veronica from early-fifteenth century Germany (*c.*1420; figure 8). In this image it is important to note that the husband-fathers are separated from the main foreground space, and from their wives and children, by a wall. Furthermore, in contrast to the mothers who are all haloed, the men have only scrolls bearing their names fluttering over their heads. This distinction between husbands and wives, both spatially and in terms of holiness, emphasises the marginal role of fathers in the narrative of Christ's family. Although the cult of the Virgin's husband, St Joseph, enjoyed a revival during the fifteenth century when he was rehabilitated from a rather comic figure who believes he has been cuckolded by his young, pregnant, wife, to a more respectable family man, the central aspect in devotion to Christ's family was the holy mothers.[17] Thus despite the inferior status ascribed to the female sex in many late-medieval medical and ecclesiastical writings, this focus on holy motherhood would appear to privilege the social roles of late-medieval lay women. In particular, as Pamela Sheingorn has noted, St Anne and her extended family asserted 'the positive value of marriage and motherhood' and were used as devotional paradigms by, and for, married women.[18]

In fact, St Anne was one amongst a number of biblical or apocryphal mothers who were unexpectedly blessed with children by God. One example already mentioned here is St Elizabeth who, although not the object of a cult in the same way as St Anne, was regularly depicted in devotional images not only in scenes of St John's birth but also in those of the Visitation where, six months pregnant, she greets her kinswoman, the Virgin, who has just conceived Christ. Other examples of blessed mothers who appear in the course of this study include the Old Testament matriarchs Sarah and Hannah. Both women bore sons in old age after a period of infertility. Hannah's song of thanksgiving for her conception in the first book of Samuel was interpreted typologically as a reference to the Virgin's Magnificat, spoken after the Annunciation, thus creating a link between the Old and New Testament women blessed in childbirth.[19]

Art historians have already pointed out that images and stories of holy women and miraculous conceptions seem to have been appropriate ways for lay people to express their own childbearing and parenting interests, especially in the context of illuminated Books of Hours.[20] Alison Stones, for example, claims that the images in a prayer book made for an enigmatic 'Madame Marie', including the *Meeting at the Golden Gate* and the *Birth of the Virgin*, 'emphasis[e] the patroness's interest in themes of motherhood'.[21] Similarly, Anne Rudloff Stanton has argued that the birth scenes and images of holy mothers and their children that illustrate the *Queen Mary Psalter* mean that it may have been commissioned for a royal woman expected to bear children.[22] Kathryn Smith has demonstrated that St Anne had an important role to play in fourteenth-century Books of Hours owned by lay women, particularly as a means to pray for successful conception and safe delivery and as a model for the education of one's children, since St Anne also functioned as an example of a wise mother and educator and was often depicted teaching the Virgin to read.[23] The strong focus on St Anne in the *Bolton Hours*, for example, has led Patricia Cullum and Jeremy Goldberg to suggest that it was made for a mother and her daughter since, through the images, 'the mother is able to provide her daughter with a model of piety and conduct, just as St Anne was herself . . . the very model of the modern devout mother'.[24] The examples noted here thus demonstrate an apparent link between female viewers and images of St Anne.

However, as Ashley and Sheingorn point out in their study of St Anne, there is a 'tendency to essentialize' and 'to assume that symbols have an intrinsic and permanent meaning'.[25] They note, in fact, that although St Anne was associated with female experiences, she was also a figure available to men, who used her to 'express the dynastic impulses of royalty or symbolize the civic liberties of Florence'.[26]

St Anne could also have a place in the joint devotions of a husband and wife and the *Châtillon Hours* (*c*.1430–50) is one example of a couple apparently turning to the saint in an attempt to have to have their childless marriage blessed.[27] The Hours of the Virgin are decorated with images depicting the life of the Virgin Mary rather than the more usual cycle of Christ's infancy. Thus the hour of Prime shows the *Birth of the Virgin* in a cosy domestic interior with St Anne seated in bed while a woman tends to the baby before the fire. Features such as a set of shelves with jugs and bowls, a cradle, cats and even a mouse add to the intimacy of the scene (figure 9).

The manuscript's focus on St Anne continues with a miniature of the mothers and children of the Holy Kinship, showing St Anne with the Virgin, Christ, St Elizabeth and St John the Baptist. The desired outcome of the Châtillons' devotion to St Anne is found at the beginning of the manuscript where two full-page miniatures show the owners, Jacques and Jeanne, in prayer, presented by their patron saints, and surrounded by a host of male and female children respectively that have been referred to as their imaginary descendants (fol 58v–59r; figure 10).[28]

Emphasising a link between female viewers and devotion to St Anne is also problematic because of the wider problem of analysing women's engagement with objects produced within a patriarchal society. Here a patriarchal society is understood as one which, in general, defined the male sex as the norm, and in which the female sex, thought of as inferior, suffered a relative exclusion from access to economic freedom, status, and power.[29] For example, Brigitte Buettner and Sandra Penketh have pointed out that Books of Hours were often given to a woman on the occasion of her marriage and could include prayers and iconography carefully selected by her bridegroom or his family as a means of encouraging her in her new role.[30] For Penketh, '[i]t would be too obtuse to claim that books of hours were bought by men to give to their wives as "code books of behaviour"' but for Madeleine H. Caviness in her study of Jeanne d'Evreux's *Hours* this is entirely feasible.[31] Importantly, Caviness insists on the need to recognise that, when 'dealing with "women's books" . . . we should not assume the female owner/reader exercised the control we normally ascribe to a patron'.[32]

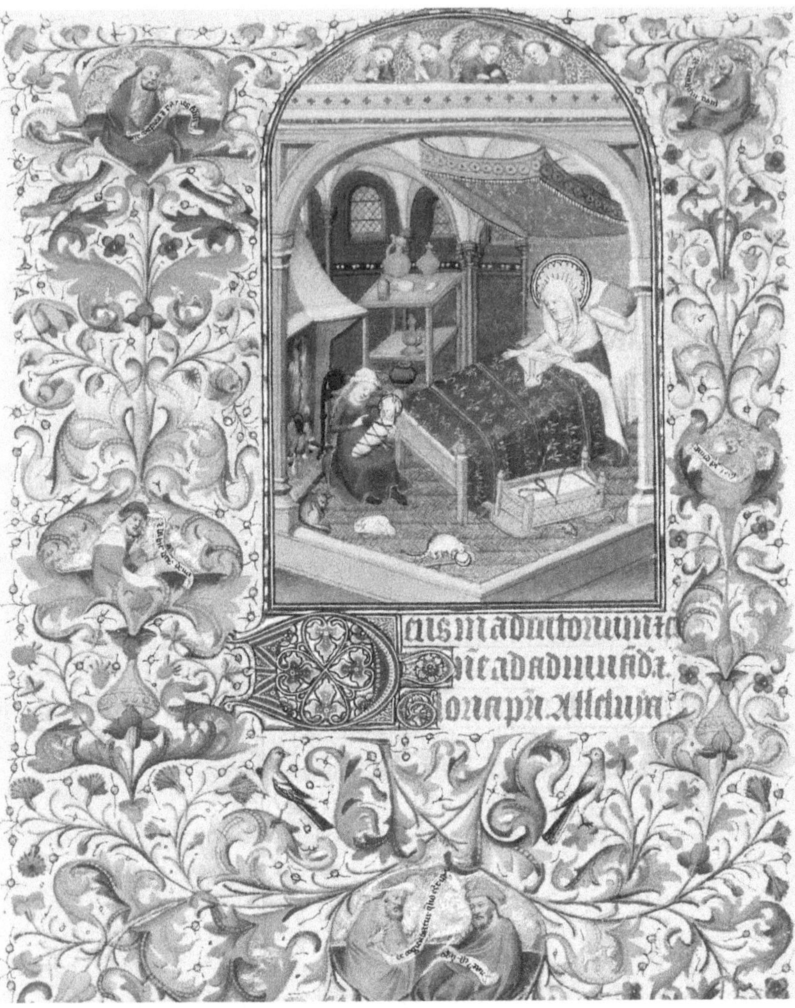

9   *Birth of the Virgin*, Prime, *Châtillon Hours*, Paris, Bibliothèque nationale, nouvelle acquisition latine, 3231, fol. 122r, *c.*1425–50 (© Paris, BnF)

A parallel example from fifteenth-century Italy helps to demonstrate this double bind further. Jacqueline Marie Musacchio has studied the significance and reception of decorated wooden trays and majolica wares given to pregnant women in Italy in the fifteenth and sixteenth centuries.[33] These objects were often decorated with what are in fact secular versions of

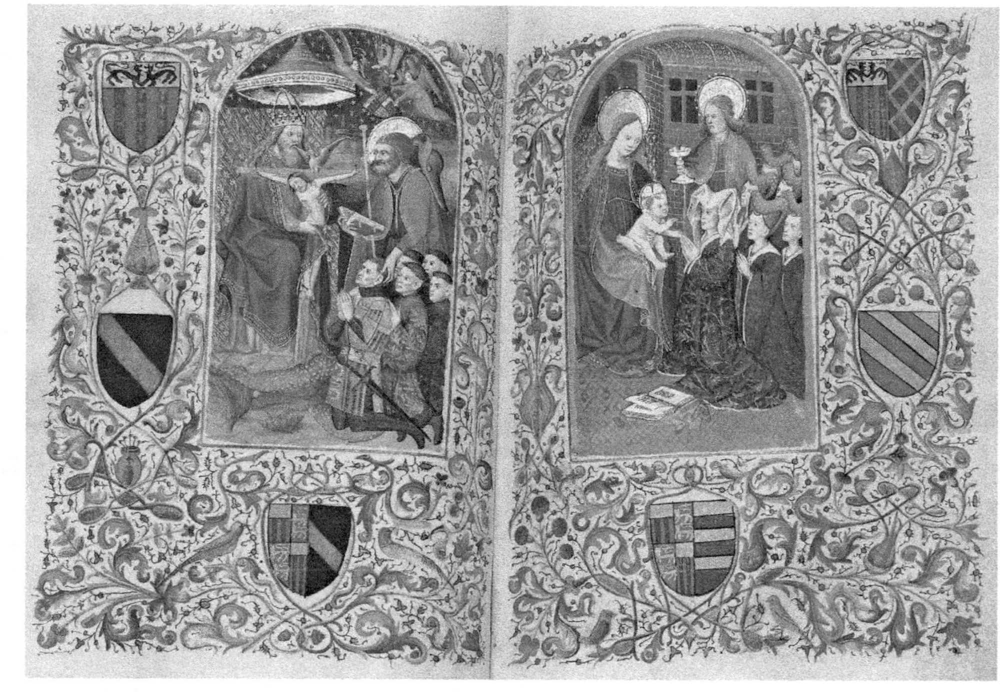

10   Donor portrait of Jacques and Jeanne de Châtillon with imaginary descendants, *Châtillon Hours*, Paris, Bibliothèque nationale, nouvelle acquisition latine, 3231, fols 58v–59r, *c*.1425–50 (© Paris, BnF)

the religious birth scenes described at the start of this chapter. Musacchio points out that although these objects were intended to encourage women to procreate and to celebrate a successful birth, they were actually commissioned and exchanged by Florentine patriarchs for whom the conception of a legitimate heir was a conjugal as well as a civic duty.[34] Musacchio's study thus exposes the tensions inherent in the objects, which depict an apparently 'private' and 'feminine' space, intended for female viewers but executed at the behest of male patrons. The question arises, therefore, of how one can extract the meanings that images of successful childbirth held for the women who received them. Is it in fact possible or even desirable to do so?

The first part of this book deals with such questions by opening the debate in Chapter 1 about what it might mean to 'gender' viewing or visual cultures. In doing so, it takes issue with previous studies of women's viewing and reception in the medieval and early-modern period that often rehearse an 'empowerment versus victim' binary, which precludes a positive assessment of women's agency and spectatorship. In order to move beyond this impasse, the study takes its cue from Jeffrey Hamburger's statement that we should not turn 'a deaf ear or a blind eye to the materials that, no matter how mediated, might tell something of how medieval women shaped, viewed and responded to their own culture'.[35] Using the work of gender theorist Judith Butler, Chapter 1 calls into question the link between maternity and the feminine gender to demonstrate that motherhood or parenting could be considered as a social practice that informed the viewing of certain spectators, male and female, rather than being a stable characteristic of 'women spectators'. This idea helps to develop a methodological approach to the interpretation of images of holy motherhood which draws on Michael Baxandall's influential concept of the 'period eye', in which he explored the socially acquired 'cognitive habits' used by mercantile viewers in fifteenth-century Italy to interpret pictures.[36] Another, culturally relative, *situational* viewing position is thus proposed to show that certain viewers, predominantly, but not exclusively young, lay, aristocratic women, acquired a certain training, via the roles that they played in society, which rendered them sensitive to the domestic, post-partum images of childbirth found in their Books of Hours. The result is an approach that enables an evaluation of the viewing practices of certain people at the social level, without reducing spectatorship to a simple male-versus-female, or power-versus-subjugation template.

The methodology of the first chapter is developed in Chapters 2 and 3 by analysing the social and devotional practices surrounding childbirth, thus fleshing out the culturally relative equipment that defines the 'situational eye'. Chapter 2 demonstrates that people had recourse to a number of popular practices such as pilgrimages and prayers, as well as to written remedies and medical treatises that could assist with conception and labour. These sources reveal the value placed on families and children by both men and women in the fifteenth century, in particular, the lengths to which aristocratic families went in order to secure a legitimate (male) heir. They also reveal the practical care available to a mother, and the importance of the thrice-married St Anne, matriarch of Christ's extended family, in the devotions of couples and especially women wishing to ensure successful childbearing.

Chapter 3 details the ceremonies that followed a birth, notably the lying-in month and the rite of churching, which were provided for with special beds, linens, materials and feasts. As in images of the Virgin's birth, the Visitation or the Holy Kinship, these rituals placed the new mother and her female companions at the centre of attention. Therefore, when such images of holy motherhood are considered in the context of this evidence from material culture, their potential value for the people involved in the precarious processes of pregnancy, childbirth and parenthood, is brought into sharper focus.

The second part of this book puts the methodological approach of the first half into practice empirically and with historical specificity. Chapters 4 and 5 consider in detail a group of fifteenth-century devotional manuscripts associated with aristocratic men and women from the houses of Anjou and Brittany and whose social roles required them to conceive heirs to maintain and strengthen dynastic interests. Three of these manuscripts were written for, and used by, young duchesses of childbearing age. The *Fitzwilliam Hours* and the *Hours of Marguerite of Foix* contain decorative cycles and prayers that emphasise birth and motherhood as well as saints important to the families' dynastic heritage. The *Hours of Marguerite of Foix* and the *Prayer Book* belonging to Marguerite's daughter, Anne of Brittany, include specific, personalised prayers for the conception of a son and for assistance in childbearing. However, following the methodology proposed in Chapter 1, the meaning of these manuscripts and their images is not analysed solely in relation to their female owners since it was not only the women of these families who were concerned with the conception of healthy children. For this reason, other manuscripts containing images of childbirth and associated with male members of the family are also considered. Although many of the manuscripts considered here, such as the *Rohan Hours*, are well-known and have been studied from a stylistic aspect, they have not previously been analysed from the point of view of their maternal imagery and how this relates to the mutating fortunes of their aristocratic owners.

Instead of seeking to identify what Greilsammer called a 'specific womanliness' in images of holy motherhood, this study explores how the social role of parenthood was an inextricable part of fifteenth-century aristocratic patriarchal society, for both men and women. For aristocratic women in particular, it is suggested that, although images of maternity were often produced to reinforce their roles as wives and bearers of legitimate male heirs, the cultural practices available to those women allowed them to read images of holy motherhood in such a way that they could manage the execution of those roles, both devotionally and practically.

Notes

1 Manchester, John Rylands University Library, Latin MS 39; see M. R. James, *A Descriptive Catalogue of the Latin Manuscripts in the John Rylands Library at Manchester* (Manchester: Manchester University Press, 1921), pp. 97–102; and Thomas Kren and Scot McKendrick, *Illuminating the Renaissance: The Triumph of Flemish Manuscript Painting in Europe* (Los Angeles and London: J. Paul Getty Museum/Royal Academy of Arts, 2003), cat. 108, pp. 367–8.

2 For an iconographic analysis of images of the Virgin's birth and childhood see Jacqueline Lafontaine-Dosogne, *Iconographie de l'enfance de la Vierge dans l'empire byzantin et en occident* (Brussels: Palais des Académies, 1964).

3 The presence of the female patron in Giusto's fresco is discussed in Chapter 1. On the presence of Tournabuoni women in Ghirlandaio's frescoes, see Steffi Roettgen, *Italian Frescoes: The Flowering of the Renaissance* (New York, London and Paris: Abbeville Press, 1997), pp. 176–7.

4 Manchester, John Rylands University Library, Inc 12018.1: Jacobus de Voragine, *The Golden Legend*, translated and printed by William Caxton (Westminster, 1497), p. 84a.

5 Louis Haas, 'Women and Childbearing in Medieval Florence', in *Medieval Family Roles: A Book of Essays*, ed. by Cathy Jorgenson Itnyre (New York and London: Garland, 1996), pp. 87–99 (p. 91).

6 Myriam Greilsammer, 'The Midwife, the Priest, and the Physician: The Subjugation of Midwives in the Low Countries at the End of the Middle Ages', *Journal of Medieval and Renaissance Studies*, 21 (1991), 283–329 (p. 321).

7 Greilsammer, p. 321.

8 Greilsammer, p. 321.

9 Sylvie Laurent, *Naître au moyen âge. De la conception à la naissance: la grossesse et l'accouchement (XIIe-XVe siècle)* (Paris: Le Léopard d'or, 1989). See also her later study, 'L'accouchement dans l'iconographie médiévale d'après les miniatures de la Bibliothèque nationale', in *Maladies, Médecines et Sociétés: approches historiques*

pour le présent, ed. by F. O. Touati, 2 vols (Paris: L'Harmattan, 1993), I, pp. 144–52. Subsequent references to Laurent are to *Naître au moyen âge*.

10 Renate Blumenfeld-Kosinski, *Not of Woman Born: Representations of Caesarean Birth in Medieval and Renaissance Culture* (Ithaca and London: Cornell University Press, 1990), p. 91.

11 See the many examples printed in Blumenfeld-Kosinski, such as the *Commentaires de César*, Oxford, Bodleian Library, Douce MS 208, fol. 1r. The paucity of Caesarean section diagrams in medical manuscripts was probably, as Blumenfeld-Kosinski concedes, due to the 'small role obstetrics played in the university curriculum and education' (p. 59). The first medical reference to the Caesarean procedure is Bernard de Gordon, writing in 1303, and it is first fully described by Guy de Chauliac in 1363. However, Caesarean deliveries (on live women, at least) did not become medical practice until the late-sixteenth century. For Chauliac's original text see, Guy de Chauliac, *Inventarium sive Chirurgia magna*, 2 vols, ed. by Michael R. McVaugh and Margaret S. Ogden, Studies in Ancient Medicine 14 (Leiden: Brill, 1997). Kathryn Taglia includes a more nuanced discussion of midwives and the Caesarean procedure in her article 'Delivering a Christian Identity: Midwives in Northern French Synodal Legislation, *c.*1200–1500', in *Religion and Medicine in the Middle Ages*, ed. by Peter Biller and Joseph Ziegler, York Studies in Medieval Theology 3 (York: York Medieval Press, 2001), pp. 77–90.

12 In an article from 1989, Monica H. Green noted that, 'One particularly fruitful form of evidence not yet fully exploited is artistic depictions of childbirth and other medical encounters, though . . . we need to beware mistaking topoi (in this case, iconographic ones) for historical realities. See Monica Green, 'Women's Medical Practice and Health Care in Medieval Europe', *Signs: Journal of Women in Culture and Society*, 14 (1989), 437–73 (p. 475).

13 Greilsammer, p. 321.

14 On the rise in devotion to St Anne and on her cult in general, see the introduction and essays in *Interpreting Cultural Symbols: Saint Anne in Late Medieval Society*, ed. by Kathleen Ashley and Pamela Sheingorn (Athens, GA and London: University of Georgia Press, 1990). See also Ton Brandenbarg, 'St Anne and Her Family', in *Saints and She-Devils: Images of Women in the Fifteenth and Sixteenth Centuries*, ed. by Lène Dresen-Coenders (London: Rubicon Press, 1987), pp. 101–27.

15 Jacobus de Voragine, *The Golden Legend: Readings on the Saints*, trans. by William Granger Ryan, 2 vols (Princeton: Princeton University Press, 1993), esp. II, pp. 149–53; and the *Proto-Evangelium of James*, *The Apocryphal New Testament*, trans. by M. R. James (Oxford, Clarendon Press, 1924).

16 See Brandenbarg, p. 101.

17 St Joseph was portrayed as a comic character in mystery plays, for example, where he fails to understand Mary's pregnancy following the Annunciation. See for example, Theresa Coletti, 'Purity and Danger: The Paradox of Mary's Body and the En-gendering of the Infancy Narrative in the English Mystery Cycles', in *Feminist Approaches to the Body in Medieval Literature*, ed. by Sarah Stanbury and Linda Lomperis (Philadelphia: University of Pennsylvania Press, 1993), pp. 65–93. See also Marjory Bolger Foster, 'The Iconography of St Joseph in Netherlandish

Art, 1400–1550' (unpublished doctoral dissertation, University of Kansas, 1978); Cynthia Hahn, ' "Joseph Will Perfect, Mary Enlighten and Jesus Save Thee": The Holy Family as Marriage Model in the *Mérode Triptych*', *Art Bulletin*, 68 (1986), 54–66; and Rosemary Drage Hale, 'Joseph as Mother: Adaptation and Appropriation in the Construction of Male Virtue', in *Medieval Mothering*, ed. by John Carmi Parsons and Bonnie Wheeler (New York: Garland, 1996), pp. 101–16.

18 Sheingorn, 'Appropriating the Holy Kinship: Gender and Family History', in *Interpreting Cultural Symbols*, ed. by Ashley and Sheingorn, pp. 169–98 (p. 180).

19 I Samuel 2. 1–10. For the story of Sarah and Abraham see Genesis 18.

20 General studies on Books of Hours and their contents include John Harthan, *Books of Hours and Their Owners* (London: Thames & Hudson, 1977); *Time Sanctified: The Book of Hours in Medieval Art and Life*, ed. by Roger Wieck (New York: Brazilier and The Walters Art Gallery, 1988); and Eamon Duffy, *Marking the Hours: English People and their Prayers 1240–1570* (New Haven and London: Yale University Press, 2006). Of the vast amount of literature on women and Books of Hours, standard reference articles remain: Susan Groag Bell, 'Medieval Women Book Owners: Arbiters of Lay Piety and Ambassadors of Culture', in *Women and Power in the Middle Ages*, ed. by Mary Erler and Maryanne Kowaleski (Athens, GA and London: University of Georgia Press, 1988), pp. 149–87; Sandra Penketh, 'Women and Books of Hours' and Martha W. Driver, 'Mirrors of a Collective Past: Re-considering Images of Medieval Women', both in *Women and the Book: Assessing the Visual Evidence*, ed. by Lesley Smith and Jane H. M. Taylor (Toronto and London: University of Toronto Press and the British Library, 1997), pp. 266–80 and pp. 75–93; Anne-Marie Legaré, 'Reassessing Women's Libraries in Late Medieval France: The Case of Jeanne de Laval', *Renaissance Studies*, 10 (1996), 209–29. Studies since 2000 include the articles in the special edition of *Journal of the Early Book Society*, 4 (2001); Jocelyn Wogan-Browne, ' "Reading is Good Prayer": Recent Research on Female Reading Communities', *New Medieval Literatures*, 5 (2002), 229–97; Andrea Pearson, *Envisioning Gender in Burgundian Devotional Art, 1350–1530: Experience, Authority, Resistance* (Aldershot: Ashgate, 2005); and the articles in *Livres et lectures des femmes en Europe: entre Moyen Âge et Renaissance, Lille, 24–26 mai 2004*, ed. by Legaré (Turnhout: Brepols, 2007).

21 Alison Stones, 'Nipples, Entrails, Severed Heads, and Skin: Devotional Images for Madame Marie', in *Image and Belief: Studies in Celebration of the Eightieth Anniversary of the Index of Christian Art*, ed. by Colum Hourihane (Princeton: Index of Christian Art and Princeton University Press, 1999), pp. 47–64 (p. 50).

22 See Anne Rudloff Stanton, 'From Eve to Bathsheba and Beyond: Motherhood in the *Queen Mary Psalter*', in *Women and the Book*, ed. by Smith and Taylor, pp. 172–89.

23 Kathryn A. Smith, *Art, Identity, and Devotion in Fourteenth-Century England: Three Women and Their Books of Hours* (London and Toronto: British Library and University of Toronto Press, 2003), esp. pp. 249–87. On St Anne as a paradigm for wives and mothers see Sheingorn, 'The Wise Mother', *Gesta*, 32 (1993), 69–80.

24 Patricia Cullum and Jeremy Goldberg, 'How Margaret Blackburn Taught her Daughters: Reading Devotional Instruction in a Book of Hours', in *Medieval Women: Texts and Contexts: Essays for Felicity Riddy*, ed. by Jocelyn Wogan-Browne *et al.* (Turnhout: Brepols, 2000), pp. 217–36 (pp. 225, 231).

25 Ashley and Sheingorn, p. 5.

26 Ashley and Sheingorn, pp. 4–5.

27 Susie Nash, *Between France and Flanders: Manuscript Illumination in Amiens in the Fifteenth Century* (London and Toronto: The British Library and University of Toronto Press, 1999), p. 69. The whereabouts of the manuscript was unknown at the time of Nash's publication but it was subsequently acquired by the Bibliothèque nationale (Paris, Bibliothèque nationale, nouvelle acquisition latine, 3231).

28 François Avril and Sylvie Lisiecki, 'Le livre d'heures de Jacques II de Châtillon', *Chroniques de la Bibliothèque nationale de France*, 17 (2002), 7–10 (p. 9).

29 On defining patriarchy, see S. H. Rigby, *English Society in the Later Middle Ages: Class, Status and Gender* (London: Macmillan, 1995), pp. 243–4; and Whitney Davis, 'Gender', in *Critical Terms for Art History*, ed. by Robert S. Nelson and Richard Shiff, 2nd edn (Chicago and London: University of Chicago Press, 2003), pp. 330–1. On sexual difference in the middle ages, see Joan Cadden, *Meanings of Sex Difference in the Middle Ages: Medicine, Science and Culture* (Cambridge: Cambridge University Press, 1993).

30 Brigitte Buettner, 'Women and the Circulation of Books', *Journal of the Early Book Society*, 4 (2001), 9–31 (pp. 16–17); and Penketh, p. 275.

31 Penketh, p. 275; and Madeleine H. Caviness, 'Patron or Matron? A Capetian Bride and a *Vade Mecum* for Her Marriage Bed', *Speculum*, 68 (1993), 333–62.

32 Caviness, p. 356.

33 Jacqueline Marie Musacchio, *The Art and Ritual of Childbirth in Renaissance Italy* (New Haven and London: Yale University Press, 1999).

34 Geraldine Johnson has shown that terracotta reliefs of the Madonna and Child also had a role to play 'in addressing early modern concerns about birth and marriage in particular'. See Geraldine A. Johnson, 'Beautiful Brides and Model Mothers: The Devotional and Talismanic Functions of Early Modern Marian Reliefs', in *The Material Culture of Sex, Procreation and Marriage in Premodern Europe*, ed. by Anne L. McClanan and Karen Rosoff Encarnación (New York: Palgrave, 2001), pp. 135–61 (esp. p. 136).

35 Jeffrey F. Hamburger, *The Visual and Visionary: Art and Female Spirituality in Late Medieval Germany* (New York: Zone Books, 1998), p. 16.

36 Michael Baxandall, *Painting and Experience in Fifteenth-Century Italy: A Primer in the Social History of Pictorial Style*, 2nd edn (Oxford: Oxford University Press, 1972, repr. 1986), esp. pp. 29–40; and *The Limewood Sculptors of Renaissance Germany* (London: Yale University Press, 1980). References to Baxandall's work in subsequent chapters are to *Painting and Experience*.

PART I

Gender, agency and the interpretation of material culture

1

The situational eye: viewing, gender and response in the later middle ages

In 1375 the artist Giusto de' Menabuoi was commissioned to decorate the baptistery in Padua.[1] The commission probably came from Fina Buzzacarini, the wife of Francesco il Vecchio, ruler of Padua. Part of Giusto's decorative cycle depicted the life of St John the Baptist and the *Birth of St John* on the north wall shows a well-attended, post-partum scene that corresponds to the religious birth scenes described in the Introduction (figure 3). St Elizabeth is sitting in bed attended by a group of six women, including the Virgin, who is identifiable by her halo. One of the women holds out a bowl and jug, perhaps for the mother to wash her hands before she partakes of the chicken that two other women bring into the room. In the foreground, three more women are seated on the floor, bathing the infant John. The woman holding the child turns to the right, where another woman stands with three companions. This woman is probably Fina Buzzacarini, with her daughters. Fina appears to acknowledge this privileged access to the holy child by pointing towards herself.[2] Fina's presence in the *Birth of St John the Baptist* with her daughters complements that of the other women and reinforces the all-female space of the childbirth chamber: she pays a visit to this holy mother, as she too was visited during her own childbearing.

It has been suggested that Fina's fourteen-year wait for a son was the motivation behind the choice of subject for the baptistery's decoration. As the wife of Padua's ruler, Fina was aware that, although she had already given birth to three daughters, her husband's sovereignty was under threat without a male heir, especially as her husband had already been the victim of an attempted assassination by his uncle.[3] The birth of a son, Francesco Novello, after a long wait, thus led Fina to identify herself with St Elizabeth who conceived St John after many years of sterility. The *Birth of St John*

25

fresco may, therefore, 'be seen as an appropriate thank-offering for [her son's] safe delivery and prayer for his future safety'.[4]

The patron's interest in childbearing and wifely duties is reinforced elsewhere in the Baptistery. The apsidal chapel housed an altarpiece decorated with the arms of Fina and her husband, also probably by Giusto. Around the central figures of the Virgin and Child are twelve scenes from the life of St John the Baptist, including a scene of his birth that is very similar to the fresco version.[5] Fina's tomb, placed on the west wall, was surrounded by scenes from the life of the Virgin whose mother, St Anne, also conceived after years of sterility.[6] Fina is also shown kneeling before the Virgin and Child and presented by John the Baptist in the votive fresco painted on the west wall of the baptistery. Furthermore, the decorative cycle was organised so as to include what Benjamin Kohl calls a 'rare grouping' of six biblical matriarchs blessed in childbirth, Anne, Elizabeth, Sarah, Rebecca, Rachel and Leah, to the left of the Virgin in the Paradise dome.[7] The privileging, in a commission by a lay woman, of these holy women whom God helped to conceive in old age or after years of sterility suggests that these figures were particularly relevant for the patron whose own social role depended on the production of male heirs.

The Padua Baptistery is just one example that demonstrates a link between lay women's commissioning interests and the stories of miraculous childbirth that gravitate around the figures of St Anne and the Holy Kinship. As noted in the Introduction, illuminated Books of Hours provide other examples of the apparent relevance of narratives of holy motherhood to female readers and viewers. In the *Hours of Marguerite of Foix* (discussed in detail in Chapter 5) for example, the mothers Hannah and Sarah are among those listed in a prayer for a son, while in the manuscript's *Birth of the Virgin* and *Holy Kinship* scenes St Anne appears in her three guises as blessed mother, wise educator and grandmother of Christ (plates 4 and 6). The *Fitzwilliam Hours* also discussed later in this book include not only images of the mothers that made up Christ's extended family but also other saints, like St Elizabeth of Hungary, who were associated with the *beata stirps*, or blessed lineage, of the Angevin dynasty to which the original readers of the book belonged, thus drawing a parallel between the contemporary family, its holy predecessors, and the family of Christ.[8] However, as the following discussion shows, there is a need to analyse further the degree of agency that can be attributed to female viewers in the choice of images of holy motherhood and the meanings that can subsequently be proposed for them. For example, can the Padua frescoes be considered evidence of Fina's commissioning power and personal interests as a wealthy patrician widow, or do they reiterate her place within a patriarchal society for whom the birth of (male) heirs was paramount and where failure to do so could have severe consequences for the male dynastic line?

This type of double-edged question is representative of the 'empowerment' versus 'victim' binary that has characterised not only studies of women's engagement with religious texts and images in the medieval period but feminist approaches to history in general.[9] For the critic interested in analysing women's spectatorship, in particular their use of and response to images of motherhood and childbirth, this double bind results in a methodological impasse. Whereas looking for evidence of a particularly 'feminine' response to images and texts helps to redress the absence of the women from the historical record and to highlight situations in which they attempted to resist or to shape the place allocated to them by patriarchal society, close analysis of the contexts which elicited such resisting or 'empowered' responses reveals that those contexts and responses may well have served, albeit inadvertently, to reassert the prevailing patriarchy. The aim of this chapter is to develop an analytical approach that moves beyond these interpretative double binds and finds a space in which spectatorship can be understood within its sociocultural context without resorting to oppositions such as male–female, positive–negative, or empowerment–victim.

Considering previous critiques of women's responses to religious texts and images paves the way for the methodological approach set out later. In particular, querying the place that women's reproductive capacities have played in constructions of the feminine gender and in analyses of women's reception demonstrates that, although medical and ecclesiastical commentators in the middle ages regarded biological and gender roles as closely intertwined, biological capacity does not a priori inform the responses of female readers and viewers, nor does it necessarily provide a subversive aspect to those responses. In addition, separating out the feminine gender from biological motherhood shows that although both may have had an important role to play in how a viewer interpreted the maternal imagery presented in subsequent chapters, other factors such as class and social positions are equally important.

The example of Fina Buzzacarini serves here as a case in point: rather than being related to her gender or sexuality per se, it can be argued that Fina's identification with St Elizabeth relates instead to her position as a lay, married woman from the patrician classes, for whom society dictated that the birth of a son was essential to ensure her position and that of her husband. The methodological approach developed in the second half of this chapter is, therefore, intended to provide a framework within which the patronage, choices and responses of certain viewers can be assessed at the social level, beyond the empowerment–victim binary and without recourse to biological essentialism. This framework draws its inspiration from Baxandall's influential concept of the 'period eye' and the cognitive habits acquired by the merchant viewer through education and cultural experience. The 'situational eye' proposed here is used in subsequent chapters to show how a combination of social categories and experiences that includes, but is not restricted to, gender, worked to inform the commissioning and interpretation of images of birth and motherhood by certain viewers, in particular those from the aristocracy for whom successful childbearing, and even non-biological parenting, could be a lifetime's concern. Thus, instead of looking for evidence of a particularly 'feminine' response to images of holy motherhood and childbirth or a 'subculture' of women who demanded such imagery, this chapter proposes a strategy for exploring how these images were commissioned, received, utilised and recycled within the constraints and possibilities afforded by the patriarchal society of which the viewers, female but also male, were a part.

Gender, images and response

The application of gender as a category for analysing imagery and response in the field of medieval studies still owes much to the ground-breaking work of scholars such as Judith M. Bennett, Joan W. Scott and, in particular, Caroline Walker Bynum.[10] In *Jesus as Mother*, published in the early 1980s, Bynum posed questions about the rise of feminine metaphors in monastic texts and images from the twelfth century onwards. In the writings of Cistercian monks, notably those of St Bernard of Clairvaux, themes of birth, maternity and marriage proliferate as ways of talking about the Crucifixion, the salvific nature of Christ's blood, and His relationship to humankind. Later, in *Holy Feast and Holy Fast* Bynum claimed that 'feminised' representations of Christ bleeding or 'lactating' at the Crucifixion offered women, especially holy women or those in religious orders, an image of themselves through which they could be empowered within a patriarchal society.[11] Bynum's aim in these early works was to recover the voices of late-medieval female mystics that were subsumed within a society that scripted the female as imperfect, and to find some historical space for them to inhabit within a twentieth-century historiography that still marginalised 'women' as a field of study. However, Bynum's model has been criticised for 'assum[ing] that gender is an essence that appears prior to other categories and informs them, that the feminine mirrors, indeed reduces to, the female reproductive function, that the female body is the originary, foundational site of gender'.[12] Although Bynum was right to note that dominant thinkers of the middle ages equated the female sex with childbearing, her insistence on the similarity between Christ's 'suffering and feeding flesh' and the 'fleshly' nature of women elides the gap between the highly-developed, male-authored metaphors of religious language, the varied material existences of 'women' in the middle ages, and women's access to this kind of imagery.

A similar criticism could be levelled at Christiane Klapisch-Zuber's interpretation of the Christ-child effigies that were placed in the wedding trousseaux of young brides or given to young girls entering convents.[13] In a secular context Klapisch-Zuber claims that these effigies functioned as fertility symbols to encourage young wives in their maternal role.[14] For the female religious, she suggests that nursing, rocking, and dressing these 'dolls', 'allowed the recluse her *primary social function* – the maternal function – and put her *desire and frustrations within limits* [and] allowed these women an experience that their secluded life *condemned* them never to know'.[15] Like Bynum's recovery of the feminised Christ for female mystics, Klapisch-Zuber was working to reclaim the use of these child figures for a feminist history. Since the effigies are almost exclusively associated with women it is entirely plausible that they were offered to women in the ways Klapisch-Zuber suggests. However, although the 'maternal function' may have been the 'primary *social* function' for many *lay, married* women in the middle ages, it was, and is, not a defining aspect of the feminine gender, any more than the 'paternal function' was/is a feature of the masculine gender.

Although fewer than their married counterparts, it should be noted that a number of women in the medieval period entered an enclosed religious life – perhaps, as Margaret Miles has suggested, to avoid the physical demands of wife- and motherhood.[16] Still other women remained single and childless in the secular world for a variety of reasons: economic, religious and sexual.[17] By contrast, other women in privileged enough positions were able to use 'mothering' as a kind of patronage to further their own personal and political causes in a society which excluded them from traditional access to power. For example, taking St Anne as her model, Anne of France (1461–1522), eldest child of Louis XI (1423–83), educated children from influential aristocratic families both before and after the birth of her own daughter Suzanne in order to influence first the future of the French crown and then the duchy of Bourbon.[18] In Chapter 4 it will be shown how Yolande of Aragon and Joan II of Naples also engaged in this sort of political parenting to cement kinship ties and to ensure inheritance claims. Turning to a modern critique of how gender roles are constructed and particularly the role of maternity therein helps to point up the instability of a category like 'women' for (art) historical analysis and, in particular, to highlight the risk of reducing all women to, and explaining their responses via, biological function.

In her seminal study on gender roles, *Gender Trouble*, Butler highlighted the 'political problem that feminism encounters in the assumption that the term women denotes a common identity'.[19] Butler's querying of the category of 'women' thus requires critics to deconstruct their own attempts to recover 'women's' histories since the referent is itself a product of patriarchal hegemonic discourses. She claims that '*women*, even in the plural, has become a troublesome term [. . .] because gender is not always constituted coherently or consistently in different historical contexts, and because gender intersects with racial, class, ethnic, sexual and regional modalities of discursively constituted identities'.[20] Butler's acknowledgement of the variable constructions of gender and the way they intersect with other categories is important here as a way of avoiding a ghettoising of women's engagement with art objects into homogeneous reading or viewing 'communities' and 'subcultures' that are always placed in an antagonistic relationship with 'men'.[21] Thus the viewing subject defined later in this chapter and explored throughout the book is deliberately not restricted to the female sex or the feminine gender: the interpretations proposed here of the images of holy motherhood and childbearing produced in the fifteenth century are contingent not only upon the viewers' roles within a secular society, as husband or wife, for instance, but also on their place within the social hierarchy – in this case as members of the ruling nobility.

Butler's questioning of the place of biological maternity in the construction of the feminine gender is also important here. In *Gender Trouble*, she takes issue with Julia Kristeva's notion of maternity as a pre-cultural essence of woman and thus its subversive potential within the Symbolic. Butler claims that Kristeva's 'naturalistic descriptions of the maternal body effectively reify motherhood and preclude an analysis of its cultural construction and variability'.[22] Butler contends that a woman's desire to give birth, which Kristeva sees as existing prior to culture and thus as potentially disruptive to the patriarchal (cultural) hegemony, 'might attest to maternity as a social practice required and recapitulated by the exigencies of kinship'.[23] For Butler, Kristeva's thesis fails because she sees maternity as essence, a claim which actually reinforces women's subjugation to patriarchy. For the purposes of this study, the idea of maternity as a social practice reveals how women's bodies were appropriated for the socially-driven need to produce male heirs for the survival of dynastic families. In addition, it also reveals how, as a social, performative act, mothering, or perhaps more precisely parenting, could operate as a form of patronage that did not necessarily involve blood children to influence dynastic relations, as in the case of Anne of France noted above.

Finally, Butler's thesis has also been used by David Aers and Lynn Staley to explode Bynum's theory that in the later middle ages women's flesh was equal to the suffering flesh of Christ. In the same way that Butler proposes that the '[paternal] law might well be the *cause* of the very [maternal] desire it is said to *repress*', Aers and Staley challenge the possibility that women might have found a subversive empowerment in identifying with dominant representations of the feminised Christ.[24] They propose that: 'The abjections that [Bynum] explicates as subversive might be better viewed . . . as themselves a product of modes of piety designed to make their practitioners objects of control.'[25] Such an interpretation complicates the idea that maternity, the childbirth chamber, and thus images thereof, were a 'bastion of female solidarity, communion and omnipotence' since maternity, like gender, can be considered a social practice that is not only performed by, but demanded of, the female sex in order to help propagate the heterosexual, patriarchal matrix.[26]

In the light of Butler's approach to gender and maternity, the presence of imagery and texts relating to motherhood and childbearing in manuscripts made for lay women readers appears less than straightforward. It was noted in the Introduction that women may have received books from relatives that were intended to promote and encourage certain behaviours such as good motherhood and wifely chastity.[27] This was particularly true for the aristocracy in the fifteenth century, for whom legitimate heirs were essential to strengthen and maintain territories and titles. Thus Caviness suggested that the manuscript, commissioned for Jeanne d'Evreux by her husband Charles IV and full of marginal grotesques, 'warned [the young queen] to keep her mind on her prayers and to avoid adultery'.[28] As noted previously, the many scenes of holy women and their children in the *Queen Mary Psalter* may also have been intended to provide a model for a royal woman expected to bear children. Therefore, although references in manuscripts to holy motherhood may be indicative of society's expectations of lay women and even of women's own reading habits, it is clear that any attempt on the part of the critic to use such images as evidence of 'female omnipotence' or empowerment is complicated by the fact that these images are the product of a patriarchal society that promoted male superiority and female subjugation.

Following Butler, an emphasis on the construction of gender and maternity by, and for, a patriarchal hegemony seems to leave the critic with little potential to analyse, in a positive way, those occasions when women such as Fina Buzzacarini, or the duchesses discussed below, commissioned or encountered images of holy mothers and female-dominated childbirth scenes. Adopting a position whereby any cultural artefact produced within a patriarchal society inevitably functions to (re)assert and maintain the power of those in control does not sufficiently take into account the way in which people in the fifteenth century viewed themselves and others as gendered and classed bodies in relation to those artefacts. Neither does taking up this position acknowledge the possibilities for individual responses or for acting within the constraints of patriarchy. Some critics have explored ways of moving beyond this impasse, an impasse which has been compounded in the area of visual studies by the influence of psychoanalytic and film theories in which the woman is cast as the passive object of an active male gaze.[29]

A more positive assessment of women's spectatorship in fifteenth- and sixteenth-century Italy has been proposed by Adrian W. B. Randolph whose work looks at the 'ceremonial objects associated with marriage and birth'.[30] Considering *deschi da parto* and other birth wares such as those studied by Musacchio, Randolph considers how these objects were received in patrician households not only by the male patrons by whom they were commissioned but also by the female viewers whose viewership is implied by the domestic context. In doing so, Randolph proposes a gendered viewing strategy that reformulates Baxandall's concept of the 'period eye'. Randolph's approach provides a valuable start in assessing women as viewers in a positive way, especially in relation to maternal imagery. As the following section shows, however, it requires further terminological clarification and a tighter definition of the viewing subject. The remainder of this chapter therefore proposes an alternative modification of the period eye, termed the 'situational eye'. This methodology, while remaining aware of the double binds discussed in the preceding sections, seeks to show how an understanding of viewers' social positions, their expectations, and their training in deciphering pictures can liberate analyses of images and response from the constraints of a male–female, empowerment–victim binary.

The situational eye[31]

Baxandall's concept of the 'period eye' has played a central role in our understanding of viewing and spectatorship in the medieval and early modern period since its first appearance in the 1970s. Baxandall defines the period eye as 'a stock of patterns, categories, and methods of inference; training in a range of representational conventions; and experience, drawn from the environment'.[32] For example, Italian merchants were schooled in mathematics and geometry, and instructions on how to gauge a barrel were included in a mathematical handbook written for merchants by Piero della Francesca.[33] In his paintings, Baxandall claims, Piero would invoke this particular skill in the mercantile viewer, asking him to use it to gauge and interpret volumes and shapes on the picture plane.[34]

In another example Baxandall argues that agents of the period eye were sensitive to nuances in religious paintings through familiarity with the sermons of popular preachers, who expounded at length on events from Christian narrative, such as the Annunciation.[35] However, despite the influence of the period eye on art historical studies, the concept has been criticised by scholars seeking to understand the role that gender played in the reception of visual cultures. Baxandall admits in *Painting and Experience* that his period eye effectively deals only with 'mercantile and professional men, acting as members of confraternities or as individuals, princes and their courtiers, the senior members of religious houses'.[36] It is not, therefore, difficult to conclude that the agent of the period eye is, as Randolph has described it, 'humanistic, mercantile' and 'overwhelmingly male'.[37] Nevertheless, Baxandall's identification of the 'cognitive habits' which a fifteenth-century viewer used to interpret images acknowledges how response was dependent on, and could be influenced by, a combination of socially-acquired skills and experience. Baxandall thus identifies 'subgroups' of the period eye, such as the fifteenth-century physician who was trained to 'observe the relations of member to member of the human body as a means to diagnosis', which would have made him 'alert and equipped to notice matters of proportion in painting too'.[38]

This example of a doctor's visual sensitivities shows how the basic principle of the period eye can be nuanced to take account of different viewers who were members of a particular social group or who had received training in a particular role. However, rather than exploring other subgroups of the mercantile period eye, this study uses Baxandall's principle to propose an alternative viewing strategy or series of 'cognitive habits' that reveals the multivalency of images and the inadequacy of gender alone as a category for analysing spectatorship. In order to do this, it is necessary to consider more closely certain feminist approaches to the period eye to differentiate the reformulation offered here from these existing revisions.

Focusing on the way the period eye privileges the male, mercantile viewer, Randolph and Paolo Berdini have offered differing critiques and expansions of the concept in order to take account of the place of female viewers within fifteenth-century visual culture. Berdini's analysis takes issue with the idea of the universality of the period eye which, he claims, has undergone a 'gender neutralization'.[39] Through the humanistic 'viewing regimes' that inform Baxandall's theory, particularly Albertian perspective, and the writings of Leonardo, Berdini argues that women are assigned a passive role whereby they must be represented with 'downcast eyes and tilted head'.[40] Berdini's interpretation takes its cue from psychoanalytic, especially Lacanian, understandings of the female gaze and Randolph argues that this leaves his 'complementary' critique of the period eye 'caught within a disempowering and anachronistic psychoanalytical frame, in which . . . the male gaze transfixes and objectifies the female form'.[41] In his own work, Randolph has argued for a more active type of female spectatorship by focusing on the context in which certain art objects like birth trays and *dovizie* statuettes were received in their domestic context.

As Musacchio pointed out in her study of birth trays, the production and display of domestic objects promoting and celebrating maternity relates to the private and public concerns of fifteenth-century Florentine men for whom procreation was understood to be a conjugal, as well as a civic, duty. However, Randolph suggests that these objects may also have worked 'allegorically[,] representing motherhood to their female audience in a positive manner, mediating between the pain and perils of childbirth and a maternal desire for healthy offspring'.[42] Thus, he suggests that the 'female spectator who emerges from this analysis complements, very usefully, the most pervasive and familiar spectator of the period', namely Baxandall's male, mercantile viewer.

In developing his notion of a 'gendered period eye', Randolph looks at the way small terracotta figurines of women bearing baskets of fruit and often accompanied by small children functioned in the fifteenth-century Italian household (figure 11). These statuettes, produced by the della Robbia workshop and known as *dovizie*, were based on a (now lost) *Dovizia* statue by Donatello (1429) that originally stood in the Mercato Vecchio in Florence.[43] The figures were painted with words that directly recall Psalm 112, 'in which the "blessed man" is promised "wealth and riches in his house"'.[44] Randolph thus proposes that 'these figurines might, therefore, be seen to produce and perpetuate the notion of an ideal heterosexual family unit' in which the male spectator completes the group: a female viewer is, implicitly, excluded.[45]

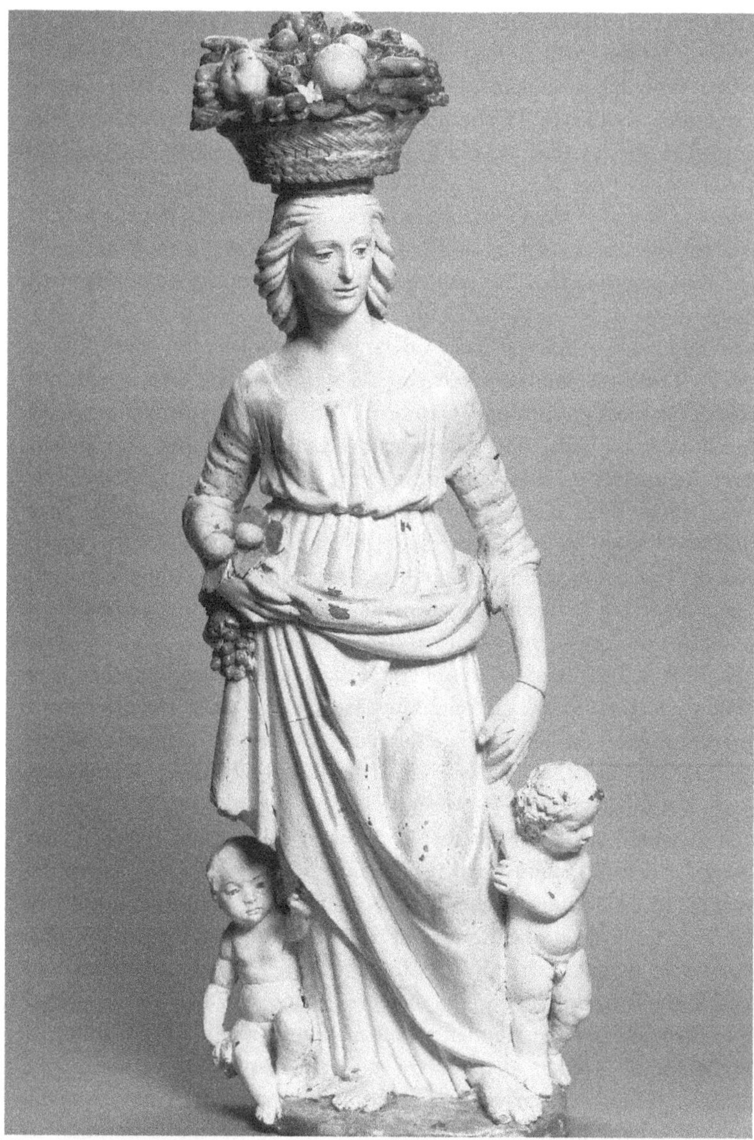

11   Giovanni della Robbia (Italian, 1469–1529?), *Figure of Dovizia (Plenty)*, The Cleveland Museum of Art, *c.*1520–29 (© Ohio, The Cleveland Museum of Art. Gift of S. Livingston Mather, Constance Mather Bishop, Philip R. Mather, Katherine Hoyt Cross, and Katherine Mather McLean in accordance with the wishes of Samuel Mather 1940.343)

However, Randolph goes on to argue that 'given the gendering of urban domains and the coding of domestic spaces as particularly feminine, the configuration that posits a male viewer alone seems facile'.[46] These statues, he suggests, recall Aby Warburg's *ninfa fiorentina*, the basket-carrying, nymph-like figures that are often found in birthing scenes like Filippo Lippi's *tondo* of the *Madonna and Child with Stories from the Life of the Virgin* (1452–53) or the Ghirlandaio workshop's fresco of the *Birth of St John the Baptist* in the church of Sta Maria Novella in Florence.[47] Randolph suggests that the way these figures enter the birth chamber, drapery flowing, so as to 'stress the procreative potential of the female body', and laden with baskets of food, 'appears to bolster the symbolism of birth'.[48] Thus, the similarity between the *ninfa* and the *dovizie* figurines made the statuettes appealing not only to the Florentine patriarch who saw himself as completing the 'heterosexual family unit', but also to the Florentine patrician bride and mother who, 'bringing her experiences, as well as those of her female relatives, to bear on the [figures] might have understood them as mediating between motherhood and civic structures'.[49] The implication is, therefore, that Florentine women viewed objects depicting an idealistic view of maternity in a way that helped them to manage conception, pregnancy and childbearing.

Randolph is aware of the double bind that characterises this analysis of female spectatorship, which 'might just as easily be taken as expressing a misogynist ideal of appropriate feminine automatic response, short-circuiting for the female viewer even the possibility of contemplation, desire, and intellection'.[50] However, he claims that 'the theory of "proximate viewing" as characteristic of women's reception [which] has emerged . . . from feminist and psychoanalytical models [. . .] poses the threat of "confounding" desire and disqualifying women from agency in relation to their material cultural context'.[51] This acknowledged difficulty in assessing women's agency has affinities with Hamburger's approach, noted in the Introduction, on the dangers of turning 'a deaf ear or a blind eye to the materials that, no matter how mediated, might tell something of how medieval women shaped, viewed and responded to their own culture'.[52] The particular value of Randolph's approach, therefore, is his emphasis on the need not to negate women's agency in responding to images simply because those images and responses occur within the context of a patriarchal society.

However, the 'gendered period eye' which he develops further in a subsequent essay on *deschi da parto* remains problematic since it risks being as essentialist as Baxandall's 'universal' or 'masculine period eye', which

Randolph set out to complicate. In particular, his emphasis on women's 'haptic' and 'unstructured' viewing, and the closeness and tactility that this implies, hints at a collapse between subject and object, for which he criticises psychoanalytical interpretational models like Berdini's. For example, he proposes that *deschi*, in the roundness of their form and the way they were meant to be handled, 'challenged the spatial characteristics of the paintings produced for the consumption of the male period eye'.[53] These trays 'can be seen as embodying an alternative "perspective which is not one", a form of unstructured, even tactile viewing that contests the hegemony of the singular and isolated period eye'.[54] While such a contestation is necessary, this critique tends towards dividing women's and men's viewing into separate, homogeneous categories of spectatorship, in particular, reiterating traditional discourses in which the masculine is associated with rationality and order, and the feminine is associated with irrationality and disorder. Randolph admits that 'to describe a portion of women's visual culture is [not] to gender fully the period eye' but it is precisely the idea of a singular 'women's visual culture' that needs to be called into question.

As we have seen above, Butler has queried 'women' as a stable category and challenged an a priori connection between biological sex and gender roles. Whilst acknowledging the excellent scholarship contained in Randolph's reformulation of the period eye, especially concerning fifteenth-century Florence, the following section proposes a more refined version of this concept for the readers and viewers of the French manuscripts discussed in Chapters 4 and 5. This refinement allows us to consider how the social roles and circumstances of these viewers, rather than their biological sex per se, affected their commissioning and reception of images. It should be noted that, as an interpretative strategy, the situational eye could theoretically be used to analyse the reception of different types of images by exploring the cognitive habits relative to their viewers. Here, however, the focus is on how the social practices around childbearing in the fifteenth century rendered certain viewers – often, but not exclusively lay, aristocratic women – sensitive to depictions of holy motherhood. By remaining on the level of the social, the situational eye is a way to analyse narratives and images of holy motherhood in non-essentialist ways and without confounding the agency of female (and male) viewers.

As noted at the beginning of this section, Baxandall's period eye could be described as the sum of the culturally-relative equipment and cognitive habits acquired by the fifteenth-century Italian merchant. These skills were catered to by the painter and allowed the merchant to interpret paintings.

A similar level of sensitivity to images and texts informs the situational eye but it is the exact skills, equipment and experience that differ. For instance, where the merchant was skilled in geometry and was aware of the cost of certain pigments, the agent of the situational eye was especially familiar with narratives of holy motherhood and with the cost and quality of fabrics used to decorate bedrooms. Some of these skills were available to people across the social spectrum; others were the particular privilege of the aristocracy; and others still were more likely to have been acquired by lay women than lay men. However, it is the conjunction of these socially acquired skills and experience that informs the situational eye and which thus allows for a certain flexibility in the definition of the agent. Although many of these agents were women, the concept is deliberately not defined by sex or gender since it will not be assumed that men's and women's interpretations of maternal imagery were necessarily antagonistic. As such, women who were not biological mothers but who perhaps expected to become so – women who assisted at the births of friends and relatives, and even older women or widows who were past their own childbearing years – could be agents of the situational eye. Similarly, as it will be shown for the case of René of Anjou (Chapter 4), men whose social roles required them to be interested in the conception of healthy (male) heirs and who were involved financially or even practically in the preparations or management of a birth, could also acquire the cognitive habits of the situational eye that rendered them sensitive to narratives and images of holy motherhood.

One of the overarching themes informing the situational eye was knowledge of the cult of St Anne and the Holy Kinship, saints efficacious in childbirth, and familiarity with biblical stories of holy motherhood. The *Châtillon Hours*, noted in the Introduction, has an image cycle devoted to the life of the Virgin Mary and shows Jacques and his wife Jeanne with the children that they hoped their devotion, expressed through the manuscript, would help them to conceive (figures 9–10). Members of the aristocracy, whose positions gave them access to patronage and power, could appropriate and exploit the Holy Kinship and its association with miraculous birth in order to help guarantee healthy heirs. Subsequent chapters show how members of the French royal family, including Louis XI, his daughter Anne of France and her sister-in-law Anne of Brittany, drew on the cult of the Holy Kinship and of St Anne in particular. When children were not forthcoming, however, or when a child not biologically one's own could serve as a political pawn, St Anne, the wise widow and educator, could also serve as a model for the kind of adoptive mothering and educating in which Anne of France or Yolande of Aragon engaged. Biological heirs were, however, the best way to guarantee direct dynastic succession and to prevent a title from passing to a different branch of the same family or to another family entirely.

Thus, familiarity with and the commissioning of medical texts that were designed to ensure fertility also informed the situational eye and reveal that some aristocratic men – but also in one case an aristocratic woman – used their power as wealthy patrons to try to guarantee conception and to ensure that their progeny, preferably male, were delivered safely and in good health. Once conception had taken place, other remedies were available to help influence the sex of the child or to assist with labour. The latter remedies, in the form of prayers or 'charms', frequently invoked holy mothers like St Anne, St Elizabeth and the Old Testament matriarch Hannah. These sources, another 'cognitive habit', were likely to have been familiar to and used by women involved in childbearing. Furthermore, Smith's point that devotional manuscripts, especially Books of Hours, could serve as a 'repository of "magical" and protective prayers' foregrounds the idea that, as agents of the situational eye, certain viewers were especially sensitive to the inter-textualities and intervisualities between representations of holy motherhood and remedies available for assisting childbirth, and that they could use this knowledge to help manage the roles expected of them by society.[55]

Other cultural experiences which informed the situational eye were those which followed a birth. The ceremony of lying-in, explored in Chapter 3, placed the new mother at the centre of attention and was intended to provide the best care through the provision of a secluded space, special clothes and fabrics, and restorative food and drink. Evidence from Eleanor of Poitiers' late-fifteenth-century treatise *Les Honneurs de la cour* for example, shows that lay, aristocratic women were skilled in the preparations of these events, particularly in terms of the fabrics required and provision for guests. Such knowledge, it will be shown, informed the viewing of images of holy childbirth which alluded to these rituals through the female-dominated birth chambers and the type of beds and rich fabrics that were portrayed. Lying-in and the subsequent ritual of churching or 'purifying' a new mother can be understood, given their origins in Judaic blood taboos, as controlling and subjugating the post-partum woman. However, participation in these events, which in other ways privileged the new mother would, it will be argued, have rendered post-partum birth scenes and images of the Virgin's own churching or Purification, multiva-lent. To use Natalie Zemon Davis's phrase, both lying-in and churching placed the woman 'on top' in a household, disrupting normalised gender roles and social hierarchies.[56] Thus certain female viewers may have seen in these images not only an encouragement or even an order to procreate but also the possibilities, even as they fulfilled that patriarchally driven injunction, of achieving some recognition and validation for undergoing the physical processes of pregnancy and birth. Furthermore, being able to relate to images of successful, holy, childbirth was important for men as well as women, since they offered an example of God-given birth within a legitimate marriage that signified the continuation of a blessed dynasty.

In the second part of this study, the methodology proposed here and the evidence analysed in the following chapters are brought together to interpret a group of manuscripts related to the houses of Anjou, France and Brittany in the fifteenth century. The two chapters constituting the second half will show the situational eye of the Angevin and Breton duchesses – and also the dukes – who were expected to conceive and give birth for the benefit of their realms was informed by the narratives, practices and ceremonies that surrounded aristocratic births in the fifteenth century. Consideration of certain aspects of these families' fortunes will show how the images could function not only as a positive space through which to manage social roles but also as a reminder of lost children or one's inability to procreate. Such an interpretation is particularly true for some of the duchesses whose ability to bear children was under scrutiny because of a continuing lack of male heirs and because of the presence of a competing mistress. The manuscript case studies thus show how female-dominated images of holy motherhood could function beyond didactic or idealised intentions that were intended to control the responses and behaviour of the female viewer. Whereas such intentions remain possible, it is argued that, through their situational eye, the female owners of these manuscripts were able to use representations of St Anne, miraculous childbirth, and holy dynasties to assert their own positions and to enable them to manage society's expectations of them as wives and mothers.

Notes

1 Cordelia Warr, 'Painting in Late Fourteenth-Century Padua: The Patronage of Fina Buzzacarini', *Renaissance Studies*, 10 (1996), 139–55. Although Fina's patronage of the frescoes is not definitively established, Warr argues convincingly for it based on Fina's other commissions and on her choice of the baptistery for the placement of her tomb. Fina's involvement in the baptistery is also discussed by Benjamin Kohl, 'Fina da Carrara, née Buzzacarini: Consort, Mother, and Patron of Art in Trecento Padua', in *Beyond Isabella: Secular Women Patrons of Art in Renaissance Italy*, ed. by Sheryl E. Reiss and David G. Wilkins (Kirksville: Truman State University Press, 2001), pp. 19–36.

2 Warr, p. 154.

3 Warr, p. 153.

4 Warr, pp. 153–4.

5 Warr, p. 145 and n. 21.

6 Kohl, p. 27.

7 Kohl, p. 28.

8 On *beata stirps* see Gábor Klaniczay, *Holy Rulers and Blessed Princesses: Dynastic Cults in Medieval Central Europe* (Cambridge: Cambridge University Press, 2002).

9 See for example, Ludmilla Jordanova, *History in Practice* (London: Edward Arnold, 2000), pp. 164, 201.

10 See Judith M. Bennett, 'Medieval Women, Modern Women: Across the Great Divide', in *Culture and History 1350–1600: Essays in English Communities, Identities and Writing*, ed. by David Aers (Hemel Hempstead: Harvester, 1992), pp. 147–75; Joan W. Scott, 'Gender: A Useful Category of Historical Analysis', *American Historical Review*, 91 (1986), 1053–75; Caroline Walker Bynum, *Jesus as Mother: Studies in the Spirituality of the High Middle Ages* (Berkeley, Los Angeles and London: University of California Press, 1982); *Holy Feast and Holy Fast: the Religious Significance of Food to Medieval Women* (Berkeley and Los Angeles: University of California Press, 1986); *Fragmentation and Redemption: Essays on Gender and the Human Body in Medieval Religion* (New York: Zone Books, 1991).

11 See Bynum, *Holy Feast*, pp. 260–1.

12 Kathleen Biddick, 'Genders, Bodies, Borders: Technologies of the Visible', *Speculum*, 68 (1993), 389–418 (p. 397).

13 Christiane Klapisch-Zuber, *Women, Family and Ritual in Renaissance Italy*, trans. by Lydia Cochrane (Chicago and London: University of Chicago Press, 1985), pp. 310–29. More context-specific interpretations of these effigies have been offered by Ulinka Rublack, 'Female Spirituality and the Infant Jesus in Late Medieval Dominican Convents', *Gender and History*, 6 (1994), 37–57; and Rosemary Drage Hale, 'Rocking the Cradle: Margaretha Ebner (Be)Holds the Divine', in *Performance and Transformation: New Approaches to Late Medieval Spirituality*, ed. by Mary A. Suydam and Joanna E. Zeigler (London: Macmillan, 1999), pp. 211–39.

14 Klapisch-Zuber, p. 317.

15 Klapisch-Zuber, p. 327; emphasis mine.

16 Margaret Miles, *Image as Insight: Visual Understanding in Western Christianity and Secular Culture* (Boston: Beacon Press, 1985), p. 88.

17 On women in the pre-modern period who did not marry see the introduction to *Singlewomen in the European Past, 1250–1800*, ed. by Bennett and Amy Froide (Philadelphia: University of Pennsylvania Press, 1999).

18 Children educated at Anne's court included Marguerite of Austria, engaged to Anne's brother Charles from an early age, and Suzanne of Bourbon's future husband Charles de Montpensier. See my article 'Ste Anne et le mécénat d'Anne de France', in *Patronnes et mécènes en France à la Renaissance*, ed. by Kathleen Wilson-Chevalier (Saint-Étienne: Publications de l'Université Saint-Étienne, 2007), pp. 135–54.

19 Judith Butler, *Gender Trouble: Feminism and the Subversion of Identity* (New York: Routledge, 1990; repr. 1999), p. 6.

20 Butler, p. 6; emphasis original.

21 The terms 'subculture' and 'reading/viewing communities' are used by Felicity Riddy in her article ' "Women Talking About the Things of God": A Late Medieval Sub-Culture', in *Women and Literature in Britain 1150–1500*, ed. by Carole M. Meale (Cambridge: Cambridge University Press, 1993), pp. 104–27; and, more recently, by Pearson in *Envisioning Gender*.

22 Butler, p. 103. Kristeva's approach to motherhood discloses a very Western, Catholic, and historically transcendent conception of motherhood that does not take into account historical context. See 'Stabat Mater', in *The Kristeva Reader*, ed. by Toril Moi (Oxford: Basil Blackwell, 1986), pp. 160–86; and 'Motherhood According to Giovanni Bellini', in *Desire in Language: A Semiotic Approach to Literature and Art*, ed. by Léon Roudiez, trans. by Thomas Gora, Alice Jardine and Leon S. Roudiez (Oxford: Basil Blackwell, 1980), pp. 237–70. In 'Stabat Mater' Kristeva's contention is, as Moi points out in the introduction to the essay, that with the demise in the cult of the Virgin, 'we are left without a satisfactory discourse on motherhood' and that 'the decline of religion has left women with nothing to put in its place' ('Stabat Mater', p. 160). It is necessary to ask how satisfactory a discourse Mary – as a Virgin mother – can (and did) provide on motherhood and for whom.

23 Butler, p. 115.

24 Butler, p. 115; emphasis in the original.

25 David Aers and Lynn Staley, *Powers of the Holy: Religion, Politics and Gender in Late Medieval Culture* (Pennsylvania: Penn State University Press, 1996), p. 36.

26 Greilsammer, p. 321.

27 Buettner, pp. 16–17; see also Penketh, pp. 275–6.

28 Caviness, p. 355.

29 The idea of woman as the object of an active male gaze has developed from Lacanian models and from the work of film theorists such as Laura Mulvey, whose 'Visual Pleasure and Narrative Cinema', *Screen*, 16 (1975), 6–18 has influenced historians of the medieval and early modern period. See for example Patricia Simons, 'Women in Frames: The Gaze, the Eye, the Profile in Renaissance Portraiture', *History Workshop*, 25 (1988), 4–30; Sarah Stanbury, 'Regimes of the Visual in Premodern England: Gaze, Body, and Chaucer's Clerk's Tale', *New Literary History*, 28 (1997), 261–89; and Regina Stefaniak, 'Correggio's Camera di San Paolo: An Archaeology of the Gaze', *Art History*, 16 (1993), 203–28.

30 Adrian W. B. Randolph, 'Renaissance Household Goddesses: Fertility, Politics, and the Gendering of Spectatorship', in *The Material Culture of Sex*, ed. by McClanan and Encarnación, pp. 163–89 (p. 172); and 'Gendering the Period Eye', *Art History*, 27 (2004), 538–62.

31 An earlier version of the 'situational eye' methodology appeared in my article, 'Anna peperit Mariam, Elizabeth Johannem, Maria Christum: Images of Childbirth in Late-Medieval Manuscripts', in *Manuscripts in Transition: Recycling Manuscripts, Texts and Images*, ed. by Brigitte Dekeyzer and Jan Van der Stock, Corpus of Illuminated Manuscripts 15 (Leuven: Peeters, 2005), pp. 335–46.

42

32 Baxandall, pp. 31–2.

33 Baxandall, p. 87.

34 Baxandall, p. 87.

35 Baxandall, pp. 48–56.

36 Baxandall, pp. 38–9.

37 Randolph, 'Renaissance Household Goddesses', p. 173.

38 Baxandall, p. 39.

39 Paolo Berdini, 'Women under the Gaze: A Renaissance Genealogy', *Art History*, 21 (1998), 565–90 (pp. 566–7).

40 Berdini, p. 568.

41 Randolph, 'Renaissance Household Goddesses', p. 172.

42 Randolph, 'Renaissance Household Goddesses', p. 174.

43 Randolph, 'Renaissance Household Goddesses', p. 163.

44 Randolph, 'Renaissance Household Goddesses', p. 163. The statues are inscribed: *Gloria et divitie in domo tua.*

45 Randolph, 'Renaissance Household Goddesses', p. 172.

46 Randolph, 'Renaissance Household Goddesses', p. 172.

47 Randolph, 'Renaissance Household Goddesses', pp. 175–80. Filippo Lippi's painting is in Florence, Museo Palatino, Pitti Palace.

48 Randolph, 'Renaissance Household Goddesses', pp. 172; 180.

49 Randolph, 'Renaissance Household Goddesses', p. 182.

50 Randolph, 'Renaissance Household Goddesses', p. 174.

51 Randolph, 'Renaissance Household Goddesses', pp. 174–5.

52 Hamburger, p. 16.

53 Randolph, 'Gendering the Period Eye', p. 557.

54 Randolph, 'Gendering the Period Eye', p. 558.

55 See Smith, p. 252.

56 Natalie Zemon Davis, 'Women on Top', in her book *Society and Culture in Early-Modern France* (London: Duckworth, 1975), pp. 124–51.

2

De conceptione ad partum: saints, treatises and prayers for successful childbirth

After a childless first marriage, the French king Louis XI (1423–83) pinned his hopes for an heir from his second marriage with Charlotte of Savoy (1441–83) on his devotion to St Anne and the Holy Kinship. A boy born in 1459 was christened Joachim, after the Virgin's father, but he died when he was only a few months old. Another child, born in 1461, was named Anne after the Virgin's mother.[1] After Anne's birth, Louis gave a wax votive of a child to the church of Notre-Dame de Cléry.[2] However, in their desperation for a male heir, the king and queen made other votive offerings and pilgrimages prior to the birth of the future Charles VIII in 1470. For instance, the queen went on pilgrimage to Puy-Notre-Dame to pay devotion to St Petronilla, the supposed daughter of St Peter.[3] During Charlotte's pregnancy, and two weeks after Charles's birth, Louis went on three pilgrimages to the same church, which also housed a relic of the Virgin's girdle, known for its special powers in assisting with conception and birth.[4] Louis paid 160 *écus d'or* for a silver statue representing his son that was intended for the church's high altar.[5]

Louis XI and Charlotte of Savoy's veneration for St Anne was taken up by their eldest child, Anne of France, whose name was a continual reminder that she had been named after the woman who had miraculously conceived the Virgin Mary. During her own marriage, Anne waited a long time to conceive her only child, Suzanne, and the prevalence of St Anne and imagery relating to the Immaculate Conception in Anne's artistic commissions shows that the story of this devout wife and blessed mother played an important part in her own hopes for an heir and, later, for the protection of Suzanne.[6] It is likely, however, that Anne did not only call upon saintly intervention in her attempts to conceive an heir. Her library contained a number of books of a medical nature and she was the dedicatee of a treatise on the conception and generation of male children specially written for her by the court physician, Bernard de Chaussade.

The measures taken by Louis XI, Charlotte of Savoy, and their daughter Anne of France to secure an heir reveal the overwhelming importance for the aristocracy, particularly royalty, of conceiving legitimate offspring in the fifteenth century. The various forms of assistance to which people, and the nobility in particular, turned – pilgrimage, votive offerings, prayer, medical sources – form part of the culturally-relative equipment or set of 'cognitive habits' which informed the situational eye outlined in Chapter 1. This chapter explores these cognitive habits in more detail by analysing sources designed to ensure successful conception and childbirth. In the same way that Baxandall showed how a certain training in geometry, gestures and religion rendered the mercantile agent of the period eye sensitive to the nuances of fifteenth-century Italian religious painting, so this chapter shows how a training in the sources available to manage conception and childbirth made certain viewers sensitive to the images of holy motherhood and childbirth found in Books of Hours.

The discussion begins by looking at some of the medical ideas about conception and childbirth circulating in the later middle ages. When considered in conjunction with prayers for a safe delivery, these medical texts suggest, as Fiona Harris Stoerz has argued, that 'medieval people exhibited considerable concern for the pain and peril of women in childbirth and made serious efforts to lessen their physical and emotional suffering and ensure their survival, even at the expense of a child'.[7] Thus, although maternity, as Butler has argued, constitutes an exigency of patriarchal kinship, it is important not to assume that the patriarchal society of the later middle ages considered women expendable or that they were physically neglected during childbirth.[8] As Chapter 3 shows, the concern for and care available to women during labour was continued in the lying-in period that followed. Moreover, as indicated previously, it will not be assumed that husbands, fathers and physicians were uninterested in conception and childbirth simply because they were men and were generally excluded from the immediate circle of care-givers during and after a birth.

Evidence for the interest that aristocratic men, as well as women, took in childbearing is demonstrated by two fertility treatises: one written for the Count of Foix and the other for Anne of France. These works show that the conception of heirs was a pressing concern not only for dukes trying to ensure their lineage, but also for duchesses, who were equally interested in the consolidation of family ties or political gains. Rather than seeing a woman's interest in conceiving an heir as a sign of her disempowerment or passive acceptance of her place within a patriarchal society, it can be used to help open up a context in which a woman was able to manage her expectations, and health, and negotiate her social roles. Further evidence that women were able to deal with the roles assigned to them by the society in which they lived in a positive manner is demonstrated through an analysis of the prayers and text-amulets intended to ensure the safe delivery of the parturient woman. Such remedies draw parallels between the woman giving birth and the mothers of the Holy Kinship, as well as invoking other saints efficacious in childbearing. They thus provided a devotional context to the management of labour, one in which God's intervention in childbearing was remembered, and complement other remedies that circulated in herbal and gynaecological texts.

These prayers occurred not only in commonplace medical collections but also in devotional manuscripts and Books of Hours owned by women. As such, they are an important source in suggesting how the owners of the manuscripts discussed in Chapters 4 and 5 viewed and understood their texts and images. On the one hand, the popularity of devotion to the Holy Kinship and the wide circulation of the prayers considered here implies that sensitivity to the themes of holy motherhood were shared by male as well as female viewers from different social backgrounds who were interested in ensuring conception and a successful birth. The contexts in which these childbirth prayers – like the medical treatises – were written, indicate that it is problematic to divide the reception of childbearing images solely along biologically-determined gender lines. Lay women as well as lay men were concerned to procreate for the cultural, rather than biological, reasons of maintaining kinship ties and securing heirs within a patriarchal society. Therefore, in so far as they both participated in the social practices available to help manage childbearing, it would be presumptuous to suggest that they necessarily viewed childbirth or representations of childbirth differently.

Such an idea will be important in the following chapters when considering how men like René of Anjou, as well as women like Isabel Stuart and Marguerite of Foix, viewed their Books of Hours. Nevertheless, given that women were in all probability cared for by members of their own sex during childbirth, it is reasonable to suppose that lay women, especially wives and mothers, were often the agents of this culturally-relative situational eye. It is likely that the prayers for successful delivery, which call upon examples of holy motherhood and which are sometimes found in female-owned Books of Hours, were performed by those women assisting in the childbirth chamber. The sources and analysis offered here, then, contribute towards showing how a certain type of spectator, predominantly, although not exclusively, married women and mothers, viewed and interpreted the idealised images of childbirth and maternity found in Books of Hours.

De generatione: treatises for ensuring conception

Since Monica Green took up the subject of women's healthcare in the 1980s, the study of medieval and early modern obstetrics and gynaecology has developed into a vast field in its own right.[9] The text most usually cited in relation to medieval gynaecology is the so-called *Trotula*, dating from the twelfth century. Although by the end of the twelfth century this was considered to be a single text by a female author from the medical school in Salerno, Green has shown that it is in fact a compilation of three texts of Salernitan origin by different authors who treat women's diseases and cosmetic concerns, and general health problems, in markedly divergent ways.[10] For medieval readers, however, the *Trotula* provided a wealth of advice and information; and by the fifteenth century the text had been translated into the major European vernaculars, including French, English, German and Dutch making it one of the most widely circulated texts on gynaecology.[11]

In addition to the *Trotula*, many other medical treatises dealing with conception and birth circulated in the late middle ages. These were often Latin translations of earlier works such as the writings of Rhazes, a ninth-century Arabic physician, Albucasis's *Surgery* and Avicenna's *Canon of Medicine*. These texts found their way into the West in the central middle ages via southern Italy and had a lasting influence on many later authors. During the thirteenth and fourteenth centuries new works began to appear, such as Albert the Great's *Secrets of Women* and the writings of Bernard de Gordon and Guy de Chauliac, all of which included sections on gynaecology and obstetrics.[12] It is important to note that these works deal with gynaecological conditions in the context of other medical and surgical conditions. Furthermore, they often lack evidence of practical experience of childbirth, being intended for an equally learned male audience.[13] Nevertheless, the fact that older ideas were frequently recycled and copied into small collections available to general healers, as well as into elaborate volumes dedicated to wealthy patrons, suggests that these treatises did have an influence on ideas about the management of conception and childbirth.

Given the often theoretical, rather than practical, nature of texts treating obstetrics and gynaecology, and the fact that they spoke primarily to a male readership, modern scholarship has often opposed male-authored 'medical' treatises to the oral or 'folkloric' culture of the women who actually assisted at the birth.[14] Guy de Chauliac has often been cited as evidence that men were not interested in obstetrics because he claimed in his surgical treatise that, since midwives took care of the delivery, there was no need to discuss it further (*Et quia istud negocium exercetur pur mulieres ut plurimum, non oportet in ipso multum immorari*).[15] However, he goes on to suggest that although some difficult births can be handled by the midwife, it was the surgeon's job to supervise and intervene if necessary. Therefore, as Katharine Park and others have shown, textual and oral sources, physicians and midwives, were not always as polarised as some scholarship has claimed.[16] Furthermore, although there is little evidence from midwives themselves of the practices they employed, studies by Greilsammer, David Harley and Merry E. Wiesner have countered Thomas Forbes's notion that 'the profession of the midwife was in general a lowly one', which produced 'ignorant and superstitious' practitioners who might be equated with witches.[17]

Wiesner has produced evidence for the training and apprenticeship of midwives and the important roles that these women played in fifteenth- and sixteenth-century German cities, not just at births but in other situations like court cases and medical examinations. Helen Lemay suggests that midwives may have worked closely with physicians. She takes the example of Anthonius Guainerius, professor of medicine at the University of Pavia in the fifteenth century who, she claims, was actively involved in treating women for gynaecological problems and consulted with midwives who acted as his assistants.[18] Guainerius also serves as a good example of the overlapping of what might be termed learned medical and devotional or superstitious rituals. In his *Treatise on the Womb*, he recommends to the physician that 'it is good that the legend of blessed Margaret be read, and that [the parturient woman] have relics of the saint on her'.[19]

As the patron saint of women in childbirth St Margaret was a popular figure in fifteenth-century devotion. Her miraculous escape from the belly of a dragon was taken as a symbol of pain-free birth and some versions of her *vita* explain how, at the moment of her martyrdom, she offered up a prayer to protect parturient women.[20] St Margaret featured regularly in the litany of Books of Hours and copies of her *vita* were carried by pregnant women or laid upon the parturient to help ensure a safe delivery.[21] The importance of this saint for women in childbirth is discussed in more detail in Chapter 5, since she was singled out for special attention in the manuscripts of Marguerite of Foix and her daughter Anne of Brittany.

Green has noted that the dedication of Guainerius's treatise to Filippo Maria, Duke of Milan, and its title *Treatise on the Womb* rather than 'On the Diseases of Women' indicates that it was 'motivated . . . by an explicitly male desire for progeny'.[22] However, men were not interested solely in 'learned' treatises: it was noted at the start of the chapter that Louis XI turned to the Holy Kinship in his hopes that Charlotte of Savoy's pregnancy and childbirth would be successful. Furthermore, Guainerius's acknowledgement of the role of St Margaret in facilitating in childbirth suggests that men as well as women were interested in the recitation of the life of St Margaret and that they were also sensitive to representations of this saint and those connected with holy childbirth in devotional books.

A further instance illustrating this lack of a clear distinction between medical and devotional or 'superstitious' advice, or between masculine and feminine spheres, is found in the *Trotula* which advises readers to write the letters of the palindrome *sator arepo tenet opera rotas* in cheese or butter and to give them to the woman to eat to help deliver the child.[23] This palindrome was believed to be invested with powerful properties and appears in other manuscript remedies for childbirth.[24] The retention of the formula in nearly all Latin manuscript editions of the complete *Trotula* ensemble indicates that a 'magical' formula was not necessarily considered incompatible with more practical advice, such as hot herbal baths.[25]

The examples cited here show that the differences sometimes drawn today between medicine, magic and religion were not yet applicable, or at least were less discernible, in the later middle ages. Consequently, it is necessary to exercise caution in the gendering of sources based on a notion that men were associated solely with medical and 'rational' texts and women with oral or 'magical' texts. Although Green has shown that men, rather than women, owned fertility and gynaecological tracts in medieval France, the following consideration of the childbearing problems of the counts of Foix and of Anne of France further demonstrates that sources cannot be gendered in a straightforward fashion and provides evidence that women, as well as men, took active steps to help them become the parents that their social positions required.[26]

The court of Foix in the later middle ages provides an example of the succession problems that could arise from the lack of a male heir, and thus the importance of children to noble families. It also reveals the role of physicians in treating the apparent causes of childlessness at aristocratic courts by addressing the gynaecological and obstetrical problems of their female members. In the late fourteenth century the counts of Foix were beset by inheritance problems, which began when count Gaston Phoebus died in

1391 without a surviving heir.[27] Although his cousin Matthew successfully claimed the title, he too died without any heirs in 1398. The county then passed to Archambauld of Grailly, husband of Matthew's sister Isabel. During this period of instability, the physician Valesco de Tarenta (*fl.* 1382–1426) was practising at the court where he treated a large number of patients, male and female, from across the social spectrum.[28] Among his cases were several patients whom he treated for gynaecological problems, including excessive menstruation and suffocation of the womb. Valesco's own medical writings showed that he had a particular interest in obstetrics and gynaecology, especially retention of the menses which he associated specifically with an inability to become pregnant.[29] This interest, William York argues, was 'a result of his own personal experiences at the court of Foix' where two countesses under his care failed to give birth to surviving heirs: it was therefore 'unlikely that [he] missed the connection between the warfare and decline in prestige in Foix and the lack of direct male heirs'.[30]

The succession of the house of Foix stabilised with the accession of Count Archambauld and his wife Isabel, who were succeeded by their son John. However, it was probably the family's recent history of inheritance problems that later prompted John's son Gaston IV (1426–72) to commission a treatise on fertility, the *Pomum aureum*, or *Golden Apple*, to ensure that his own marriage would be fruitful and his lineage secure.[31]

Gaston married Eleanor of Navarre (1425–79) in 1436 when he was only ten and his wife eleven years old. Given their ages, children would not have been expected immediately.[32] However, the *Golden Apple* dates from 1444 suggesting that Gaston commissioned it before the birth of his first child in the same year and implying that the lack of an heir may already have been giving him cause for concern.[33] The text was written by Pierre Andrieu, master of medicine at the University of Toulouse, who based his work on earlier tracts by Montpellier physicians and on those of other well-known writers such as Avicenna and Rhazes.[34] The treatise is divided into chapters that treat subjects such as the formation of the child in the womb, what factors determine the conception of a male or female child, the signs of pregnancy, how to avoid miscarriage, and managing the birth. As Green's work on this text shows, it was designed to include illustrations drawn from Muscio's descriptions of foetal malpresentations, an inclusion which would have rendered the original manuscript, now lost, a luxury item.[35] Furthermore, despite Andrieu's reliance on older sources, he also shows some innovation in his remedies for treating the woman during and after childbirth.

50

Andrieu's treatise thus not only reveals the aristocracy's pronounced interest in generation but, as Green argues, 'his detailed instructions on how the parturient should be positioned' and his comments on how to dispose of the afterbirth 'suggests Pierre's own experience in (or just outside) the birthing room'.[36] Gaston's engagement of an innovative practitioner like Andrieu and the commissioning of a luxury manuscript therefore bear witness to the importance Gaston ascribed to the conception of heirs and the seriousness with which he took his role as Count of Foix.

Gaston and Eleanor either paid close attention to the *Golden Apple* or they need not have worried: Eleanor bore at least nine children between 1444 and 1466, many of whom survived beyond infancy.[37] However, their daughter Marguerite of Foix (*c*.1449–87) encountered fertility problems in her union with Francis II of Brittany (1433–88), problems which were addressed in the prayer for a son included in her Book of Hours, discussed in detail in Chapter 5. This prayer, which refers to Marguerite's deliverance from sterility and which expresses her hopes for a son, indicates that she was, like her father, acutely aware of the expectation of heirs that came with her social position as a duchess. Although we do not know what medical books, if any, Marguerite owned, her father owned, in addition to the *Golden Apple*, a respectable library of some forty manuscripts to which Marguerite may have had access. Furthermore, she would have been aware of the advice proffered by court physicians such as Andrieu since she and her daughter Anne of Brittany were under the care of the French royal physician Bernard de Chaussade.[38] As noted at the beginning of this chapter, Chaussade had himself written a treatise on generation for another woman suffering from infertility, Anne of Brittany's sister-in-law, Anne of France. The discussion now turns to this treatise, considering it in the context of Anne's own long-awaited birth, and that of her daughter, Suzanne. In this way it will be suggested that Anne did not just passively accept the role demanded of her as an aristocratic wife, but that she exercised a considerable amount of power and agency within the constraints of the society in which she lived.

Anne of France was an active patron of the arts, maintaining and adding to an impressive library of manuscripts and printed works. Anne's library contained, in addition to a number of secular and religious works, texts that offered advice on health matters, such as two books described as 'livre de médicin', a printed copy of works by Albert the Great, and a copy of Rhazes' *Book of Almansor*.[39] It is therefore likely that she commissioned Chaussade's text *On Conception and Generation, Especially of Male Children* herself.[40] The date of Chaussade's treatise, 1488, is crucial to understanding its place in Anne's life.[41] In the preface she is referred to as the famous, first-born, sister of King Charles VIII (fol. 1r: *Karoli octavi francorum regis soror inclita et primogenita*) and as 'duchess and most supremely powerful mistress of the most distinguished Bourbons' (fol. 1r: *ac nobilissimorum borboniorum ducissa et prepotessima domina*). Following the death of her father, Louis XI, in 1483, Anne, as the king's eldest child, ruled as regent during the minority and early years of her brother's reign until his marriage with Anne of Brittany in 1491. Although Anne enjoyed a great deal of power as regent, she was aware that she would have to relinquish this power at some point as Charles VIII gradually asserted his independence. During her regency, therefore, Anne also worked towards securing the duchy of Bourbon for her husband, Peter, who was the third son of Duke John I. When Peter's older brother John II of Bourbon died without any heirs in 1488, Anne persuaded Charles, the next in line to inherit the title, to pass the duchy to Peter: as Cardinal of Lyon, Charles was not in a position to marry and engender heirs for the Bourbon dynasty.[42] By taking control of the Bourbonnais through her husband, Anne hoped to create her own dynasty, independent of the French crown, from which she had been excluded as a woman. The success of her plans nevertheless relied on her ability to conceive and give birth to healthy, preferably male, heirs and although the couple had been married for fifteen years by 1488, the date of both Peter's accession and the treatise, they had yet to produce an heir.[43]

The treatise written for Anne by Chaussade was, therefore, designed to solve a long-standing problem that was beginning to cause her concern. The first part of the text deals with general problems of conception such as the causes of infertility, the difficulties of conceiving, and how to know whether barrenness is the fault of the man or the woman. The second part contains five chapters specifically on the conception of a son. It gives advice such as the best time for conceiving sons, how the strength of the seed facilitates the begetting of sons, and how the nature of one's own womb is beneficial for the engendering of male children. Whereas men's commissioning or writing of gynaecological tracts can be interpreted as evidence of their own interest in securing heirs, or because they were in the service of those who had such interests, Chaussade's text shows that a duchess like Anne of France could also be interested in childbearing for social and political reasons, rather than to fulfil what Bynum and Kristeva imply is a pre-cultural maternal drive. Anne's recourse to and knowledge of medical theories were a result of and facilitated by her social position as a rich and educated woman with commissioning power. She exploited this position and education, combining it with her devotion to St Anne, to help her execute her social role as duchess and thus maintain an influential position in French politics.

Anne's interest in her patron saint derived from her parents, who were particularly devoted to the story of St Anne's miraculous conception of the Virgin and who named their first surviving child after her. St Anne and the iconography of the Immaculate Conception played a major part in Anne of France's own life. Her most famous commission is the *Moulins Triptych* (*c.*1498, France, Moulins Cathedral) showing, on the outer wings, Anne and her daughter Suzanne presented by St Anne, and her husband Peter of Bourbon presented by St Peter, to a central panel of the Virgin of the Immaculate Conception (figure 12). Less well known are the three majestic statues that she commissioned before 1515 from Jean Guilhomet for her residence at Chantelle. These show St Anne teaching the Virgin, St Peter and St Suzanne and are now housed in the Louvre in Paris.[44]

Anne's association with her patron saint, not only as a woman blessed with a child after years of infertility but also, as shown in Chapter 1, as a motherly educator, provides evidence of the importance and relevance of St Anne in the execution of her social roles. Together with her artistic patronage, the commissioning of Chaussade's text indicates how Anne could manipulate the social roles assigned to her, as duchess, wife, and potential mother, not only to execute those duties but also to bring some benefits to her own position by securing for herself and her heirs the duchy of Bourbon. The interest that Anne of France showed in childbearing suggests that the duchesses discussed in Chapters 4 and 5, who were Anne's contemporaries and in some cases her relations by marriage, were also aware of the consequences that the fulfilment of social duties, or failure thereof, could bring. These duchesses are likely to have acquired similar skills and experience to Anne of France that allowed them to take an active part in managing the need to produce heirs using the images and texts relevant to family and childbearing in their manuscripts.

The treatises made for Gaston of Foix and Anne of France are rare examples of personalised fertility tracts written for rich, aristocratic, patrons. Other, less elaborate, manuscripts nevertheless show that the remedies available to the aristocracy were also circulating among the less privileged in the form of commonplace collections that offered all kinds of advice for curing illnesses or resolving undesirable situations from toothache, diseases in animals, sterility and difficult childbirth. For example, an experiment to test for infertility that Chaussade included in Anne's treatise also appears in commonplace books and medical collections from the fourteenth and fifteenth centuries.[45] It is in the context of

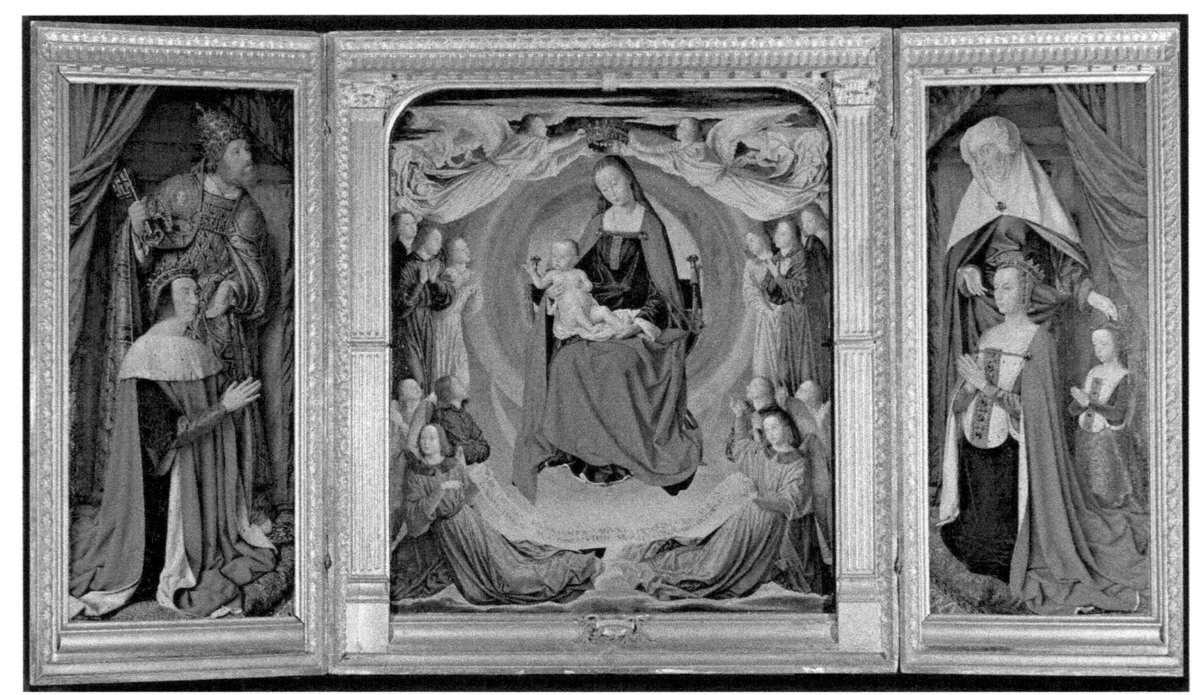

12 Master of Moulins (Jean Hey, *fl. c.*1483–*c.*1529), *The Moulins Triptych* (*The Bourbon Altarpiece*), *c.*1498 (© Moulins Cathedral, Allier, France/The Bridgeman Art Library)

medical miscellanies and, as we shall see, devotional manuscripts, that prayers specifically for assistance in labour are often found. These texts, which invoke St Anne and other holy mothers, form a link between the pilgrimage practices, relic veneration and images of childbirth discussed so far in this study. Furthermore, the frequency with which such remedies are found suggests that they were widely available and that they also contributed to the situational eye of lay women in particular, whether aristocratic or not. It is, thus, likely that a lay woman's knowledge of these narratives and prayers would have been brought to bear when viewing representations of the birth of the Virgin and maternal saints in devotional manuscripts.

Pro dolore partus dic ad mulierum: remedies for facilitating labour

The prayers for labour considered in this section are sometimes referred to in the manuscripts and in the secondary literature as 'charms', perhaps because they fall somewhere between traditional prayers and nonsensical texts.[46] Here the term remedy or prayer is preferred since, as Lea Olsan has noted, 'people often employed charms under the same conditions as they did medical recipes on the one hand and prayers on the other'.[47] These remedies were intended to be said out loud, written on food and ingested, or noted on scraps of paper and laid upon the body. As such, they were largely oral texts, ephemeral and adaptable. Yet their appearance in all kinds of manuscripts and the ways in which they were recorded, suggests that they were considered worth collecting and, more importantly, that they were used. Sometimes the prayers were scribbled onto a blank page or highlighted for the reader with a series of crosses or pointing fingers.[48] People owning such collections probably included those practising some kind of medicine or general healing, suggesting that the prayers would have been known by, or used to treat, a wide variety of people.[49]

Given that literacy in the late middle ages was more prevalent among men than women, and since the prayers for labour are frequently in Latin, this raises the question of whether women had direct access to these texts themselves and whether they would actually have been able to read them. However, as a number of studies have shown, in the fifteenth century lay women often practised a functional, if not more scholarly, literacy and the fact that the texts are usually preceded by a vernacular rubric indicating how the text should be used certainly suggests that they were intended for lay use.[50] Furthermore, the mnemonic structure of some of the prayers suggests that the Latin text could easily be remembered and passed on orally.[51]

Thus, in discussing women's access to the childbirth prayers on a fifteenth-century scroll analysed below, Don C. Skemer notes, of the proposed female owner: 'If not literate in the sense of being able to read Latin with full comprehension, she was probably literate enough to find her way to particular sections of the text (especially the divine names) and to be able to say them aloud.'[52] The fact that some prayers were preserved in devotional manuscripts owned by lay women of childbearing age suggests that women were interested in these prayers or that they expected to use them.[53] Therefore, whether or not women had access to or were able to read these texts as they appear in the commonplace collections, the frequency with which the prayers occur and the fact that they also appear in Books of Hours owned by women, makes it reasonable to suppose that women knew them, along with other popular prayers such as the Hail Mary and the Our Father, as part of an oral, if not literate, culture.

The prevalence of the Holy Kinship and biblical matriarchs is one of the most striking features of many of the prayers for childbirth, providing a link to, and complementing the use of, these figures in works of art that referred to infertility issues, such as Fina Buzzacarini's commission for the Baptistery in Padua or the Marian cycle in the *Châtillon Hours*. However, in the prayers the holy mothers are invoked less for the fact that they were made fertile and more for the generally miraculous and felicitous nature of their childbearing. The first type of prayer considered here is the *peperit* or *genuit* formula, in which the mothers of the Holy Kinship are invoked along with their children:

> Pro dolore partus dic ad mulierum: Anna peperit Samuelem, Elisabet genuit Iohannem, Anna genuit Mariam, Maria genuit Christum. Infans, siue masculus siue femina, exi foras. Te uocat saluator ad lucem. Sancta Maria peperit saluatorem, peperit sine dolore. Christus natus est de uirgine. Christus te uocat, ut nascaris. Exinanite. Exinanite. Exinanite. Postea ter Pater noster.[54]

Through the recitation of the genealogies, the prayer serves to bring the parturient woman and her helpers into the collective of holy mothers blessed by God. The allusion to these stories of miraculous childbirth, together with reference to the Virgin's pain-free delivery of Christ, provide Christian precedents for the mother now giving birth and set up a context in which she can hope to receive divine intervention and be released from the throes of labour. In another version of the *peperit* formula, the third person plural *credimus* indicates that the speakers of the prayer are collectively announcing their belief that Mary gave birth to both man and God and that, through this, the parturient woman will be able to give birth to her child successfully:

> De virga virgine ubi oritur radix Jesse. Anna peperit Mariam, Maria Salvatorem. In nomine domini Jesu Cristi, infans, exi foras, sive sis masculus sive femina. Pater Noster et Ave Maria et Credo. In nomine Patris etc. Sicut vere credimus quod beata Maria peperit infantem, unum verum deum et hominem. Item et tu, ancilla Cristi, pare infantem. In nomine Patris etc.[55]

A connection is implied between the parturient woman and the Virgin Mary not only through the context of the labour itself, but because the woman is referred to as *ancilla domini*, the words with which Mary described herself at the Annunciation in the Gospel of St Luke.[56] Luke's version of events leading to the birth of Christ inspired the depiction of the Annunciation and the Visitation in the middle ages. An Annunciation was the standard image for the first hour of Matins in Books of Hours, where the Virgin's reply to Gabriel's announcement, *ecce ancilla domini*, was often represented on a scroll as in the opening of Matins in the *Fitzwilliam Hours* (plate 3).

As Baxandall argued in *Painting and Experience*, familiarity with representations of the Annunciation and the various stages of Mary's reaction that could be depicted formed part of the cognitive habits of the period eye, an interpretation that can easily be extended to the situational eye, given the frequency with which this event was depicted in Books of Hours and referred to in sermons and devotional literature.[57] Performers of these prayers, as well as the parturient woman herself, could easily have related these texts referring to examples of successful, God-blessed, childbirth, to familiar images of Mary and St Elizabeth at the Annunciation and Visitation, thereby creating a context in which references to these two events, whether visual, textual or performative, provided a way to manage the birth and look towards a successful outcome.

In addition to the biblical mothers noted so far, another mother–child pair was included in one version of the *peperit* formula: St Caecilia and her son St Remigius.[58] St Remigius baptised Clovis, the first King of the Franks, in 497 after he was persuaded to convert to Christianity by his wife Clothilde. In this context, St Remigius also constitutes an oblique reference to another saint efficacious for women in labour, his godson St Leonard, who was said to have delivered a French queen, probably Clothilde, from a difficult labour through the intercession of his prayers.[59] A copy of St Leonard's prayer was included in one of Anne of Brittany's manuscripts that dates from her second marriage to Louis XII.[60] This prayer, which is discussed in greater detail in Chapter 5, created a link between Anne's own hopes for a successful birth after the loss of many children, Frankish dynasty history, her own patron saint St Anne and another biblical mother, Sarah, whose unexpected conception of Isaac is referred to in the prayer. The inclusion of St Remigius and his mother in prayers for childbirth thus not only complements the references to St Anne, St Elizabeth and the Virgin, but it also creates an allusion to St Leonard, an allusion to which a viewer with the relevant cultural training, like Anne of Brittany, could well have been sensitive.

The examples discussed above show that the *peperit* formula is often found in conjunction with the *exi* or *veni foras* formula. This consists of an adjuration to the child, whether male or female, to come forth (*sive masculus, sive feminas, exi foras*) since Christ the saviour calls him or her to the light that s/he may be born (*te uocat saluator ad lucem/Christus te uocat, ut nascaris*). The prayer can therefore be divided into two sections and Marianne Elsakkers has argued that these different parts, 'the slow, narrative sections' of the *peperit* formula, and 'the faster and louder imperative sections' of the *exi* formula, accommodated the different stages of labour and 'may have constituted a rhythmic mnemonic device, a reminder of how to breathe' during, and between, contractions.[61] By reading the texts as a kind of 'work song', Elsakkers's argues that the female helpers took control of, and actively managed, the birth.[62] Similarly, the prayers' collective of holy mothers, and the visual images that they evoked, mirrored and reinforced the group of women gathered in the birth chamber, offering another way for those involved to focus on and to manage the birth itself. This argument is strengthened further when considering that the words of the *exi* formula have their origin in St John's Gospel, being the words with which Christ raised Lazarus from the dead: *Haec cum dixisset, voce magna clamavit: Lazare, veni foras.*[63]

A remedy for childbirth contained in a collection of medical tracts and recipes compiled in the fourteenth and fifteenth centuries advises writing the key words *lazare, veni foras* and *vocat Christus te ad lucem*, on pieces of apple and giving them, in this order, to the parturient woman to ensure her delivery.[64] L. Weston claims that the allusion to Lazarus in the prayers explicitly brings death and mourning into the process of giving birth, in which the mother 'has become more a vessel than a participant'.[65] She suggests that this is disempowering for the parturient woman and her assistants who, instead of 'actively managing the birth . . . become, like sisters of Lazarus, audience rather than actors'.[66]

58

The reference to Lazarus can be read more positively, however. In speaking the words that Christ spoke to Lazarus, the woman or women executing the 'charm' performed a Christ-like role in bringing forth a live child and preserving the life of the mother. Therefore, although the parturient woman and her assistants may have recognised the womb-tomb nexus established by the reference to Lazarus, the quotation refers, on the other hand, to resurrection, to death overturned, and to the giving of life. The prayers' references to miraculous conception, the Virgin's pain-free childbirth, and the resurrection of Lazarus thus mean that the women around the mother could have considered the prayer and themselves in a more active light than Weston suggests. The prayer, its execution, and the women's presence in the room become essential to the success of the birth in hand. Therefore, viewed with the situational eye of the women in the childbirth chamber, the *peperit/exi* prayers offered them a means not only to manage the birth in the best possible way for the parturient woman, but also to exercise their agency in using and interpreting what are nevertheless 'patriarchal' narratives.

The prayers considered thus far show that the standard complement of Holy Kinship mothers, St Anne, St Elizabeth and the Virgin and their children, could be reinforced by references to other mothers and their children, such as Hannah and Samuel and St Caecilia and St Remigius. Hannah's narrative is alluded to again in another type of prayer, the so-called *Arcus* charm:

> Here bygynnes a charme for trauellyng of childe. In nomine patris & filij & spiritus sancti. Amen. Arcus forcium super nos sedebit, virgo Maria natabit, lux & hora sedule sedebit rubus rebus rarantibus natus nator natoribus saxo. Sic memor esto vt sit puer vt puella. Eius exijt foras mater, quum christus natus est, nullum dolorem passa est. Venit homo, fugit dolor. Christus adiutor, adiuro te virga per Patrem & Filium & Spiritum Sanctum vt habeas potestatem coniungendi. Say this charm thris & scho sal sone bere childe, if it be hir tyme.[67]

The line which gives the charm its name, *Arcus fortium super nos sedebit* recalls a line from the song of thanksgiving uttered by the matriarch Hannah after the long-awaited birth of her son Samuel: *Arcus fortium superatus est* (The bow of the mighty men are broken, and they that stumbled are girded with strength).[68] Olsan claims that the 'verbal similarity' between the two texts make it likely that the words of the *Arcus* charm were intended to refer to this miraculous birth.[69] Furthermore, in biblical exegesis, Hannah's song was interpreted as a type of the Virgin's Magnificat, the words Mary spoke at the Annunciation, when she agreed to the Incarnation.[70] Given her appearance, as a woman blessed in childbirth, in a variety of sources connected with childbearing, from the *peperit* remedies, to the Padua Baptistery and the *Queen Mary Psalter*, Hannah and her story can be said to form part of the cognitive habits of the situational eye. Listeners and performers of the *Arcus* formula may therefore easily have noted this allusion to her in the text. Her importance as a role model informing the situational eye is further evidenced by her inclusion, along with other Old Testament matriarchs, in Marguerite of Foix's prayer thanking God for the end of her infertility. The discussion of this text below will show that Marguerite, the speaker of the prayer, situated herself at the end of a list of women made fertile in the hopes that, like these women, she too will be appointed a son.

Whereas certain of the remedies for labour involve the incanting or ingesting of powerful words, other special prayers, written out on parchment, were intended to be carried about the person or laid on the afflicted body. These amuletic objects often provided protection against 'menacing demons, sudden death (including in childbirth), and a host of specific misfortunes'.[71] In some cases, the prayers have survived via the instructions for making them into amulets that were recorded in manuscripts; in other cases the amulet itself has survived in the form of a length of rolled parchment.

An early fifteenth-century French scroll studied by Skemer (now in a private collection), 'was designed to provide both general and specific protection through a series of component texts to a noble or bourgeois woman, married and of child-bearing years'.[72] To help the woman in labour it was necessary to place the text beneath her right breast so that God might liberate her (*ponat hec breue sub dextra mammula et illico deo auxiliante liberabit se*).[73] Skemer argues that the childbirth 'charm is located near the mid-point of the various texts, so that it would be perfectly positioned to provide protection during childbirth when the amulet roll had been unrolled and placed text-down, curling over the woman's abdomen'.[74] The scroll thus worked through a combination of God's intervention and the physical proximity of the text to the appropriate place on the woman's body.

One remedy for delivering a woman in labour recommends tying a text to the parturient woman's right side to bring out the child, whether alive or dead (*ceste lyez entre le destre de deyns et tantost istera lenfant vif u mort*).[75] Like the prayers already considered, this text includes references to the mothers of the Holy Kinship, St Caecilia and St Remigius, and Lazarus, thus constituting another example of the texts and contexts through which these holy narratives of birth and resurrection contributed to the cognitive habits of the situational eye.

Surviving prayer scrolls often claim to derive their measurement, and thus their power, from their association with the length of Christ's body or other relics.[76] A much rubbed English scroll in the Wellcome Library in London, dating from 1500, is decorated with a series of images relating to the Passion and is covered on both sides with protective prayers.[77] When placed about a labouring woman's stomach, the scroll will ensure that she is 'safe delyvyrd wythowte parelle [peril] and the chylde shall have crystendome and the mother puryfycatyon'.[78] Another, incomplete, inscription on the same scroll suggests that it was associated with the power of the Virgin's belt or girdle.[79] Relics of the Virgin's girdle, and also that of her chemise, were widely venerated throughout Europe in the fifteenth century particularly by women hoping to ensure their fertility or an uncomplicated delivery. These scrolls thus function in a similar way to actual relics conserved in local churches or to images in Books of Hours that claimed to represent a scaled version of Christ's body or his wounds. For example, the Privy Purse expenses of Elizabeth of York, mother of Henry VIII, show that she 'paid 6s. 8d. to a monk for a girdle of Our Lady' to ensure her safe delivery.[80] The church of Puy-Notre-Dame to which Louis XI made pilgrimages around the time of the birth of his son Charles also housed a relic of the Virgin's girdle. In September 1495, Louis's daughter-in-law Anne of Brittany borrowed this relic 'in order to enhance the fertility of her union with Charles VIII'.[81] The church of Notre-Dame in Chartres boasted a chemise worn by the Virgin at the Annunciation which, Gail McMurray Gibson notes, was used during royal pregnancies to bless a tunic that was then presented to the queen or dauphine.[82]

Like these relics, the parchment scrolls were intended to provide a pain-free childbirth after the fashion of the Virgin's own experience and, like the medical treatises and the prayers for incantation already discussed, they add to the cognitive habits of the situational eye. In particular, their use of the same narratives of holy motherhood reinforces the idea that knowledge of and participation in these practices also informed people's viewing and the significance of childbirth-related images that appeared in Books of Hours. Furthermore, the prayers and amulets invoking holy mothers were bolstered by those which invoked St Margaret, patron saint of women in labour. A French roll, dating from the end of the fifteenth century for example is 'chiefly comprised of a vernacular life of St. Margaret'.[83] In addition 'there are three brief Latin and French prayers appealing for the intercession of St. Margaret, St. Geneviève, and the Virgin Mary; and an eight-line Latin prayer related to childbirth (*Pro muliere parturiente*)'.[84] Thus not only was it likely that knowledge of remedies for delivery brought the images of St Anne and the Holy Kinship found in Books of Hours into sharper focus but it was also likely that it allowed images of St Margaret to be invested with special meaning as well.

The protective prayers on scrolls related to the length of Christ's body, such as the Wellcome example, often invoke another holy mother–child pair, St Julitta and her son St Quiricus, martyred under the emperor Diocletian.[85] In the context of their use during labour, these two saints complement the other mothers and children, like St Caecilia and St Remigius, St Anne and the Virgin, and Hannah and Samuel already discussed.[86] St Julitta and St Quiricus also appear in a prayer written around an image of the Cross in the fourteenth-century *Carew-Poyntz Hours*.[87] Although the prayer itself does not specifically mention childbearing, it does offer protection from an undesirable or sudden death: as the other prayers preserved on scrolls indicate, this often included death in childbirth. In fact, the manuscript's prayers for bodily health are, quite literally, closely bound up with its images of maternity and parenthood. The book contains, for example, a prayer to the Virgin's parents, St Anne and St Joachim which is 'accompanied by a bas-de-page drawing of the Finding of Moses (fol. 30v), another subject concerned with a childless woman miraculously granted offspring': other scenes include the *Meeting at the Golden Gate* and the *Birth of the Virgin*.[88] Since the prayer forms indicate that the *Carew-Poyntz Hours* were made for a female reader, this manuscript foregrounds the idea that prayers for childbirth formed part of the cognitive habits of the situational eye and, more specifically, that certain female viewers in particular acquired the culturally-relative equipment to see links between, and to use to their advantage, images and narratives of holy motherhood.

Other manuscripts owned by lay women and married couples further show how knowledge of childbirth prayers informed their situational eye and suggests that they used images of the Holy Kinship and other saints associated with successful childbirth as important aids in managing their roles of wife/husband and (potential) parents. The fourteenth-century *Neville of Hornby Hours*, for example, contains prayers for a woman suffering from the pain of labour, including the recommendation to say a prayer in honour of God, the Virgin, and St Julitta and St Quiricus.[89] This manuscript is also illustrated with portraits of a husband and wife in some of the miniatures depicting the Virgin's early life, such as her Presentation in the Temple. Smith notes that a miniature of St Anne teaching the Virgin 'illustrates two prayers in honour of the mother of Mary, the first in Anglo-Norman, the second in Latin, both of which praise St Anne for her miraculous fecundity'. One of these prayers 'extols [St Anne] for humbly enduring the shame and stigma of barrenness' for which she was rewarded with the Immaculate Conception.[90]

A Book of Hours personalised for Hawisia De Bois (*c.*1325–30) contains two Anglo-Norman prayers offering succour in childbirth.[91] The first is a prayer for general protection of the type found on the scrolls discussed above. It is to be said in honour of the Five Joys of the Virgin and will protect the speaker from a number of situations including death in childbirth.[92] The second prayer has a rubric claiming it is specifically to protect parturient women (*Feme que ceste oreison dirra a sun enfantement ne perira*).[93] Another copy of this prayer is preserved in a liturgical manuscript where it has an even more specific rubric claiming that it was said by St Thomas Becket's mother during her labour and that any other woman who says it before she gives birth will not die.[94]

The story of St Thomas's birth was also included among those of other holy children in the *Queen Mary Psalter*, a manuscript which, Stanton has argued, was made for an aristocratic woman who was expected to become a mother herself. St Thomas and his mother thus join the ranks of the other holy mothers discussed here by providing devotional precedents for the woman in labour and those seeking to help her. St Thomas Becket's effectiveness in difficult childbearing situations is further indicated by some of the miracle cases attributed to him. In one example William of Oxford, husband of Alienor who was suffering in labour, 'tied some Becket relics round her neck, upon which she immediately gave birth to a son'.[95] Although the rubric relating the childbirth prayer in Hawisia's Book of Hours to Thomas Becket is not included in her manuscript, the saint does appear in the suffrages along with other saints known for their efficacy in childbearing such as St Leonard, St Anne and St Margaret.[96] Hawisia's manuscript thus provided a number of resources that offered assistance during labour. A similar combination of relevant saints, images and prayers in the female-owned manuscripts discussed in Chapters 4 and 5 suggests that these Books of Hours also functioned as places through which the owner managed her social role as a mother, from conception to birth and beyond.

In addition to being simply included in Books of Hours, there is another way in which childbirth prayers are linked to the contents and images of these devotional manuscripts. In one childbirth prayer in a British Library manuscript, the words 'Jeremiah was born of Celica' appear amongst the list of miraculous births: *christus natus fuit de virgine Maria. Maria de Anna, Iohannes de Elizabeth, Ieremias Celica*.[97] Although Celica might appear to be a corruption of Cilinia or Caecilia, the mother of St Remigius who appeared in the *exi* formula charms discussed above, Olsan notes that 'a female "Celica" seems to have been substituted for the Vulgate's "Helcia", subverting the patriarchal lineage of the Prophet in Jeremiah 1:1'.[98] The inclusion of Jeremiah in a childbirth charm is, moreover, particularly appropriate given that Jeremiah was a prophet whom God sanctified in his mother's womb.[99] In addition, the opening words of the Book of Jeremiah also formed part of the sanctoral for the feast of the Nativity of St John the Baptist.[100] The sanctoral for St John's birth is a conflation of Old and New Testament writings that contains many allusions to childbirth. As a liturgical text, it is most frequently found in breviaries belonging to confirmed religious rather than in Books of Hours that were owned by lay people.[101]

However, the feast of St John's nativity constituted an important day in the liturgical calendar since it was one of only three births, the other two being Christ's and the Virgin's, celebrated by the church. Lay people were, therefore, aware of the importance of St John's nativity, which was singled out in red or gold in the calendars of Books of Hours and where it might also be illustrated with an image of his birth. Where a breviary or Book of Hours did include the sanctoral of St John's birth, this too was often illustrated with an image of his birth, as in the John Rylands manuscript discussed at the beginning of this book (plates 1–2) or in the so-called *Burgundy Breviary* which was made for Duke John the Fearless of Burgundy (1371–1419) and his wife Margaret of Bavaria (1424) (figure 13). The miniature of St John's birth in this manuscript conforms to the model of comfortable domesticity described in the Introduction. St Elizabeth lies in bed and a woman stands to one side holding the infant; at the foot of the bed is Zacharias, a scroll issuing from his mouth indicating that he is in the process of naming his son.

The reference to Jeremiah both in the childbirth prayer and in the sanctoral for St John's birth, and the illustration of his birth in Books of Hours, thus opens up a specific relationship between the spaces and management of childbirth and the official liturgy of the church. The situational eye of reader-viewers with an interest in the conception and bearing of children, such as Duke John and Duchess Margaret, would have been sensitive to this intersecting of sources, allowing them to discern intertextualities and intervisualities between their manuscripts, popular devotional practices,

64

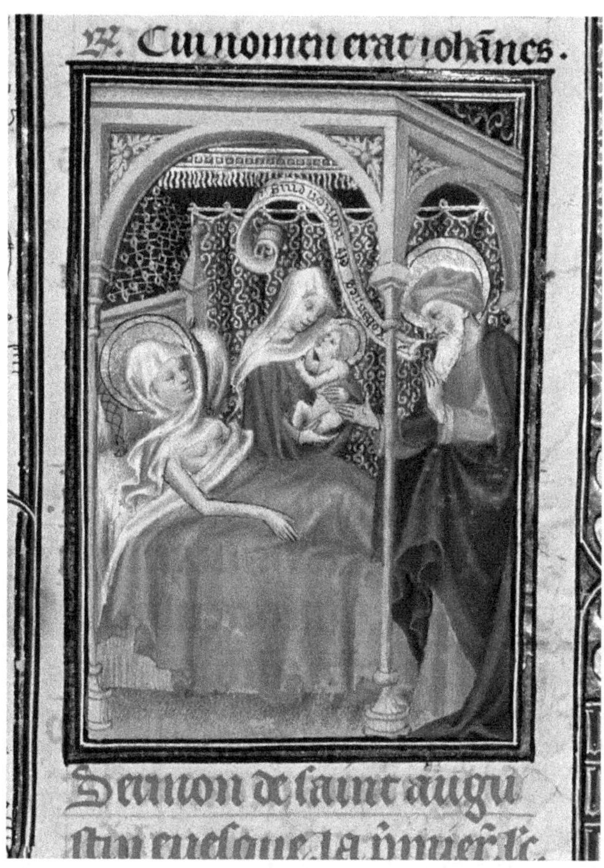

13   Master of the Breviary of John the Fearless, *Birth of St John the Baptist* (detail), sanctoral, *Breviary of John the Fearless*, London, British Library, Harley MS 2897, fol. 315r, *c.*1413–19 (© London, British Library)

official church liturgy and the various remedies available for facilitating childbirth. By looking, in Chapter 3, at the way the domestic features included in images of holy childbirth alluded to contemporary practices employed in the birth chamber, it is possible to emphasise further the situational eye's sensitivity to the interrelationship between manuscripts, images, texts and cultural practices. Together, this evidence helps to demonstrate the way that idealised images of holy motherhood could function as aids to the execution of pregnancy, birth and parenting as social roles that were required of certain viewers.

The material considered in this chapter has fleshed out one aspect of the culturally-relative equipment that informed the situational eye, equipment that would have been brought to bear on images of motherhood and maternity by those viewers with an interest – dynastic, political or otherwise – in conception and childbearing. By highlighting, on the one hand, similarities between medical treatises for infertility and remedies for labour and, on the other, connections between the narratives invoked in the prayers and the images found in Books of Hours, it has been possible to point up the way sources are interrelated. Equipped with the cognitive habits to notice such relationships, the viewers of images and the readers and performers of texts, prayers, and remedies relating to conception and birth were able to understand and use them to provide help and relief in childbearing.

Analysis of the interest that the French royal family and the counts of Foix showed in the engendering of children has indicated the importance of heirs for aristocratic families as a means of gaining or maintaining political influence. Both men and women from the nobility took active measures to treat, or to avoid, infertility as the works of the physicians Valesco and Andrieu at the court of Foix attest. Their works reveal a practical interest in childbearing both on the part of the physician and on the part of the family that was related to the problems of inheritance and succession. Similar problems also occurred at the French court and the examples of King Louis XI of France, Charlotte of Savoy and their daughter Anne of France demonstrate that divine intervention could be sought for the conception and protection of children in the form of pilgrimages, votive offerings and devotion to the Holy Kinship, especially to St Anne. In particular, Anne of France's attempts to conceive the child necessary for the continuation of an independent Bourbon dynasty shows that asking for God's intercession through devotion to the Virgin's mother, witnessed in the *Moulins Triptych*, was not incompatible with seeking advice from university-trained physicians in the form of a medical treatise. The title of Chaussade's treatise for Anne, *On Conception and Generation, Especially of Male Children*, indicates that she was acutely aware of the need for a son to secure her own Franco-Bourbon lineage.

Anne's need for an heir, and thus her interest in both medical treatises and the cult of St Anne, was driven by political interests in which she sought to maintain for herself a certain level of power and influence within a patriarchal, aristocratic system that had, on the one hand, allowed her to rule as regent of France but, on the other, had excluded her from succeeding her father as its monarch. Thus, her interest in conceiving an heir should not be condemned simply as submission to or acceptance of her role in patriarchal society. It should, instead, be understood as a means through which she could manipulate the role granted to her by that society to her best advantage. By reading the evidence at the social level, it is apparent that Gaston of Foix and Anne of France's interest in childbearing was part of the performance of their social roles within the aristocracy of the later middle ages.

In addition to personalised medical treatises, help for conception and birth was available to both men and women from a variety of other, but not necessarily mutually exclusive, sources. The importance of childbearing in the lives of people lower down the social scale is witnessed by the frequency with which prayers for labour are found in medical collections, miscellaneous compilations, and in devotional manuscripts. These remedies suggest an interest in the care and survival of the parturient woman and complement medical remedies and devotional acts like pilgrimage. The consistent recurrence of St Anne, St Elizabeth and the Virgin in prayers for labour indicates that the mothers of the Holy Kinship were not only important in asking for help in the conception of heirs, as the examples of Louis XI and Anne of France show, but that their invocation also played a central role during labour itself.

These holy mothers were complemented, in some sources, by invocations to other saints such as St Margaret, St Leonard and St Thomas Becket through their *vitae* or their relics. The fact that women were cared for by other women during labour suggests that the cognitive habits relating to these remedies and their saints, although not unavailable to men, were acquired in particular by the female assistants involved in the childbirth chamber. It has been argued that the collective of holy mothers invoked in the prayers implied both the inclusion of the parturient woman in these miraculous narratives and mirrored the group of women caring for her. Whereas the *peperit* formula may have served as practical breathing advice, and thus as a way for the parturient and her companions to manage the labour, the reference to Lazarus in the *exi* formula indicates the pivotal role of the female performer in delivering the child. The prayers thus show that women involved in childbearing, either as the parturient or as a carer, could use and appropriate patriarchal narratives for the execution of their social roles without necessarily being disempowered. Furthermore, the inclusion of prayers for childbearing in Books of Hours owned by lay women, coupled with images of the Holy Kinship for instance, suggests that the manuscripts, like the remedies, were part of the means available to women to manage their social roles.

Thus, although it is still important to remember, as noted in the preceding chapters, that female viewers could be offered images and models for identification by those seeking to control their behaviour for the benefit of patriarchal society, it is equally important to consider the possibilities for women to have responded and used those images and models for their own ends. The evidence presented here suggests that, viewed from within their social roles as wives and mothers, women could understand St Anne and other holy mothers as figures who provided practical and devotional assistance, ensuring not only the execution of their wifely duties but also their deliverance – corporeal and spiritual – during what could be a physically demanding time. In Chapter 3, the analysis is extended to the care given to and the ceremonies attended by women after the birth and the way these relate to images of the Virgin's birth and her Purification in Books of Hours. This evidence adds to the cognitive habits informing the situational eye, further demonstrating the values that women, and often men, of a certain social status could discern in images of holy motherhood.

Notes

1 A girl, Louise, was born between Joachim and Anne, but did not survive more than a few months. See Pierre Pradel, *Anne de France, 1461–1522* (Paris: Publisud, 1986), p. 10; n. 5.

2 Pradel, p. 10; n. 3; and Jean Cluzel, *Anne de France: fille de Louis XI, duchesse de Bourbon* (Paris: Fayard, 2002), p. 21.

3 Cluzel, p. 28.

4 Legaré, 'Charlotte de Savoie's Library and Illuminators', *Journal of the Early Book Society*, 4 (2001), 32–87 (p. 39).

5 Legaré, 'Charlotte de Savoie's Library', p. 39.

6 On Anne's patronage and her devotion to St Anne, see my article, 'Anne de France'; and Élodie Lequain 'Anne de France et les livres: la tradition et le pouvoir', in *Patronnes et mécènes*, ed. by Wilson-Chevalier, pp. 155–68.

7 Fiona Harris Stoerz, 'Suffering and Survival in Medieval English Childbirth', in *Medieval Family Roles*, ed. by Itnyre, pp. 101–20 (p. 102).

8 Butler, p. 115.

9 For work on women's healthcare in the middle ages up until 2005, see the article by Green, 'Bodies, Gender, Health, Disease: Recent Work on Medieval Women's Medicine', *Studies in Medieval and Renaissance History*, 2 (2005), 1–49. See also her book *Women's Healthcare in the Medieval West* (Aldershot: Ashgate, 2000); and article 'From "Diseases of Women" to "Secrets of Women": The Transformation of Gynecological Literature in the Late Middle Ages', *Journal of the Medieval and Early Modern Society*, 30 (2000), 5–39. Green's latest book on women's gynaecological healthcare is *Making Women's Medicine Masculine: The Rise of Male Authority in Premodern Gynaecology* (Oxford: Oxford University Press). I would like to thank her for sharing a chapter of this book with me before its publication.

10 Green, ed. and trans., *The* Trotula: *A Medieval Compendium of Women's Medicine* (Philadelphia: University of Pennsylvania Press, 2001), pp. 51-5. See also John Benton, 'Trotula, Women's Problems and the Professionalization of Medicine in the Middle Ages', *Bulletin of the History of Medicine*, 59 (1985), 30-53.

11 Green, *Trotula*, pp. 59-61.

12 See Peter Biller, 'Childbirth in the Middle Ages', *History Today*, 36 (1986), 42-9. See also Green, 'Women's Medical Practice', p. 462.

13 Although obstetrics was not treated as a separate subject until the early sixteenth century with the publication of manuals like Eucharius Rösslin's *Der Swangeren Frawen und Hebammen Rosegarten* (1513), it should, nevertheless, be noted that separate works on midwifery and gynaecology existed in antiquity. Some of these survived (such as Soranus's *Gynecia*, rediscovered in the nineteenth century) and others did not (such as the writings of Demetrius the Herophilean); see *Soranus' Gynecology*, trans. by O. Temkin (Baltimore: Johns Hopkins Press, 1956). Thanks to Adrian Wilson for clarifying this point.

14 See, for example, Grethe Jacobsen, 'Pregnancy and Childbirth in the Medieval North: A Topology of Sources and a Preliminary Study', *Scandinavian Journal of History*, 9 (1984), 91-111.

15 See Chauliac, I, p. 388. For references to Chauliac and midwives, see Laurent, p. 172; and Thomas G. Benedek, 'The Changing Relationship Between Midwives and Physicians During the Renaissance', *Bulletin of the History of Medicine*, 51 (1977), 550-64 (p. 551).

16 See Chauliac, I, pp. 388-9; Green, *Making Women's Medicine Masculine*, esp. Chapter 2. 'Men's Practice of Women's Medicine in the Thirteenth and Fourteenth Centuries'; and Katharine Park, 'Medicine and Magic: The Healing Arts', in *Gender and Society in Renaissance Italy*, ed. by Judith C. Brown and Robert C. Davis (London: Longman, 1998), pp. 129-49; Helen Lemay, 'Anthonius Guainerius and Medieval Gynecology', in *Women of the Medieval World: Essays in Honour of John H. Mundy*, ed. by Julius Kirshner and Suzanne F. Wemple (Oxford: Basil Blackwell, 1985), pp. 317-36; and 'Women and the Literature of Obstetrics and Gynecology', in *Medieval Women and the Sources of Medieval History*, ed. by Joel T. Rosenthal (Athens, GA and London: University of Georgia Press, 1990), pp. 189-209.

17 Thomas Forbes, *The Midwife and the Witch* (New Haven and London: Yale University Press, 1966), p. 112. For counter-arguments, see Greilsammer; Merry E. Wiesner, 'Early Modern Midwifery: A Case Study', in *Women and Work in Preindustrial Europe*, ed. by Barbara Hanawalt (Bloomington: Indiana University Press, 1986), pp. 94-113; and David Harley, 'Historians as Demonologists: The Myth of the Midwife-Witch', *Social History of Medicine*, 1990 (3), 1-26.

18 Lemay, 'Literature of Obstetrics', p. 193; and 'Anthonius Guainerius', pp. 320-1.

19 Lemay, 'Literature of Obstetrics', p. 197; see also Park, p. 138.

20 Wendy Larson, 'Who is the Master of this Narrative? Maternal Patronage of the Cult of St Margaret', in *Gendering the Master Narrative: Women and Power in the Middle Ages*, ed. by Mary C. Erler and Maryanne Kowaleski (Ithaca and London: Cornell University Press, 2003), pp. 94-104.

21 Edina Bózoky, 'From Matter of Devotion to Amulets', *Medieval Folklore*, 3 (1992), 91–107. In the 1920s a birthing bag which had been in the same family for generations and used by locals to facilitate labour was opened up to reveal a wealth of objects including a life of St Margaret claiming to protect women from death in childbirth. See A. Aymar, 'Le sachet accoucheur et ses mystères. Contribution à l'étude du folklore de la Haute-Auvergne', *Annales du Midi*, 38 (1926), 385–401; and Louis Carolus-Barré, 'Un nouveau parchemin amulette et la légende de sainte Marguerite patronne des femmes en couches', *Comptes Rendus de l'Académie des Inscriptions et Belles-Lettres*, 1979, 256–75.

22 Green, 'Women's Medical Practice', p. 461.

23 See, for example, the occurrence of this remedy in a French redaction of the *Trotula* in Paris, Bibliothèque nationale, fonds français, 1327, fols 1r–117r (fol. 77v); and see Green, *Trotula*, pp. 100–1.

24 The Aurillac birthing bag noted above included a parchment inscribed with a series of magic symbols including the words *sator arepo tenet opera rotas* written out in a square. Around the edge of this square are the words *Hanc figuram mostra mulierum in partu et peperit* (Show this figure to a woman in labour and she will give birth). See the copy printed in Aymar; and see Carolus-Barré, p. 259. On the use of the Sator formula in childbirth, see *A Manual of the Writings in Middle English, 1050–1500*, X (part XXV *Works of Science and Education*), ed. by George R. Keiser (New Haven: The Connecticut Academy of Arts and Sciences, 1998), pp. 3673, 3873; and Herbert L. Bodman, 'The Sator-Formula: An Evaluation', in *Laudatores Temporis Acti: Studies in Memory of Wallace Everett Caldwell*, ed. by Mary Francis Gyles and Eugene Wood Davis (Chapel Hill: University of North Carolina Press, 1964), pp. 131–41.

25 See Green, *Trotula*, p. 236; n. 50.

26 Green, 'The Possibilities of Literacy and the Limits of Reading: Women and the Gendering of Medical Literacy', in Green, *Women's Healthcare in the Medieval West*, pp. 1–76.

27 William Henry York, 'Experience and Theory in Medical Practice during the Later Middle Ages: Valesco de Tarenta (*fl.* 1382–1426) at the Court of Foix (France)' (unpublished doctoral dissertation, Johns Hopkins University, 2003), pp. 28–31.

28 On Valesco's patients, see York, pp. 170–6.

29 See York, pp. 181–91. He notes that over half of the sixth book of Valesco's most famous work, the *Philonium*, was concerned specifically with women's illnesses.

30 York, pp. 179; 181.

31 The original manuscript is lost but a copy survives in Paris, Bibliothèque nationale, fonds latin, 6992, fols 79r–90v.

32 The minimum age for procreation recommended by jurists and physicians was twelve for girls and fourteen for boys.

33 Green, *Making Women's Medicine Masculine*, pp. 249; 261; 274.

34 E. Wickersheimer, *Dictionnaire biographique des médecins en France au Moyen Âge*, 2 vols and supplement (Geneva: Droz, 1979), II, p. 612. Andrieu's work is discussed by Green in *Making Women's Medicine Masculine*.

35 Green, 'Reuse, Renew, Recycle: Fetal Images and Obstetrical Innovation, 1300–1400', paper presented at the Society for the Social History of Medicine, Annual Conference, University of Warwick, UK, 28–30 June 2006.

36 Green, *Making Women's Medicine Masculine*, p. 261.

37 H. Castillon, *Histoire du comté de Foix, depuis les temps anciens jusqu'à nos jours*, 2 vols (Toulouse: Cazaux, 1852), II, p. 474.

38 See Wickersheimer, I, p. 73. Chaussade also served Anne of France's mother Charlotte of Savoy and the young Margaret of Austria (1480–1530), who spent her early years at the French court as the fiancée of Charles VIII.

39 For the books in Anne's library, see 'Inventaires des Livres qui sont en la librairie du chasteau de Molins', in *Les Enseignements d'Anne de France, duchesse de Bourbonnois et d'Auvergne, à sa fille, Susanne de Bourbon*, ed. by A.-M. Chazaud (Marseille: Laffitte Reprints, 1978), pp. 231–58. For the medical texts see items 67, 80 and 145 from the library at Aigueperse; and items 45, 164 and 208 from the library at Moulins.

40 *Tractatus de conceptione et generatione praecipue filiorum*, Paris, Bibliothèque nationale de France, fonds latin, 7064, fols 1r–82v.

41 The manuscript is dated at Amboise, 1488 at the end of the manuscript (fol. 82v).

42 Albert Châtelet, *Jean Prévost: le Maître de Moulins* ([Paris]: Gallimard, 2001), p. 87.

43 A son, Charles, born in 1475 two years after their marriage, did not survive; see Pradel, p. 31.

44 Paris, Louvre, Département des Sculptures, Jean Guilhomet, also called Jean de Chartres, St Peter (R.F. 1159); St Anne Educating the Virgin (R.F. 1158), and St Suzanne (R.F. 1160), before 1515; see also L'Estrange, 'Anne de France'.

45 In Chaussade's text (fol. 16v) it is recommended to take the 'seed' of the man and the woman and throw each into a vase of clean water; whoever's seed floats on the top of the water is the infertile partner. Similar examples occur in Lincoln Cathedral Library Manuscript A. 5.3, fol. 303r, published by Margaret Ogden, *The Liber de Diversis Medicinis in the Thornton Manuscript*, Early English Text Society, original series 207 (London: Oxford University Press, 1938) and in London, British Library, Royal MS 17 A viii, fol. 65r.

46 The term 'charm' is problematic and the linguistic and quasi-magical features of such texts warrant more discussion than is possible here. For a discussion of charms and their definition, see Susan Eastman Sheldon, 'Middle English and Latin Charms, Amulets and Talismans from Vernacular Manuscripts' (unpublished doctoral dissertation, University of Tulane, 1978), esp. pp. 28–31; other literature on 'charms' includes Douglas Gray, 'Notes on Some Middle English Charms', in *Chaucer and Middle English Studies in Honour of Rossell Hope Robbins*, ed. by Beryl Rowland (London: George Allen & Unwin, 1974), pp. 56–71; Tony Hunt, *Popular Medicine in Thirteenth-Century England: Introduction and Texts* (Cambridge: D. S. Brewer, 1990); and Lea Olsan, 'Latin Charms in British Library MS Royal 12 B. XXV', *Manuscripta*, 33 (1989), 119–28 and 'The Arcus Charms and Christian Magic', *Neophilologus*, 73 (1989), 438–47.

47 Olsan, 'Latin Charms', p. 119.

48 For example, London, British Library, Sloane MS 3160, fols 129v –41v.

49 Gray, p. 59.

50 On types of literacy see, for example, Wogan-Browne, '"Reading is Good Prayer"', esp. pp. 244–6.

51 See Marianne Elsakkers, 'In Pain You Shall Bear Children: Medieval Prayers for a Safe Delivery', in *Studies in the History of Religions*, ed. by Anne-Marie Korte (Boston, Leiden, and Cologne: Brill, 2001), pp. 179–209.

52 Don C. Skemer, 'Amulet Rolls and Female Devotion in the Late Middle Ages', *Scriptorium*, 55 (2001), 197–227 (p. 205).

53 The *Neville of Hornby Hours* (London, British Library, Egerton MS 2781) for example contains prayers for assistance in childbirth. This manuscript is discussed below.

54 'For suffering in childbirth, say to the mother: Hannah bore Samuel, Elizabeth brought forth John the Baptist, Anna brought forth Mary, Mary brought forth Christ. Child, whether you [be] male or female, come forth. The saviour calls you to the light. Holy Mary bore the saviour, she bore him without pain. Christ was born of a virgin. Christ calls you so that you may be born. Make empty the mother's womb. Say afterwards three times Our Father'. My translation; Latin printed in Elsakkers, p. 183; I have altered the layout of the text and added to the punctuation.

55 London, British Library, Sloane MS 3564, fols 55r–v. The charm is also printed in Hunt, p. 93, n. 135. 'From the rod, the Virgin, where springs the root of Jesse. Anna bore Mary, Mary bore the Saviour. O child, in the name of the Lord Jesus Christ, come forth, whether you be male or female. Our Father and Ave Maria and Credo. In the name of the Father, etc. Thus we truly believe that the blessed Mary bore a child, truly both God and man. And so too you, servant of Christ, will bear a child. In the name of the Father etc.' My translation.

56 Luke 1. 38.

57 See Baxandall, pp. 49–57.

58 See for example Paris, Bibliothèque nationale, fonds français, 1802, fol. 17r; BL, Royal 17 A. viii, fol. 103r (Olsan, 'Latin Charms', p. 123); BL, Sloane 3160, fol. 169r; and BL, Sloane 3564, fols 55v–56v. Both Sloane prayers are included in Hunt, pp. 92; 97. See below (n. 75) for Sloane 3564.

59 St Leonard of Limousin (d. 599, sometimes known as St Leonard of Noblat). See Louis Réau, *Iconographie de l'art chrétien: l'iconographie des saints*, 3 vols (Paris: Presses Universitaires de France, 1958), III, p. 799. Voragine, in *The Golden Legend*, states that 'Leonard is said to have lived about the year AD 500', and that he was brought up at the royal court of Clovis. The implication is, therefore, that the queen in question was Clovis's wife Clothilde (r. 493–511). See Voragine, II, p. 244.

60 Chicago, Newberry Library, MS 83, fols 49v–52v.

61 Elsakkers, pp. 203–4 and n. 79.

62 Elsakkers, p. 205.

63 John 11. 43: And when he had said these things, he cried with a loud voice: 'Lazarus, come forth.' See also Olsan, 'Latin Charms', p. 123.

64 London, British Library, Royal MS 12 B xxv, fol. 61v. 'divide pomum in iij partes, scribe in prima parte *lazare*, in 2a parte *veni foras*, in 3a *vocat christus te ad vitam*, et da mulieri partes per ordinem ad comedendum et sine dubio pariet ante horam nonam'.

65 See L. M. C. Weston, 'Women's Medicine, Women's Magic: The Old English Metrical Childbirth Charms', *Modern Philology*, 92 (1994-5), 279-93 (p. 292); and G. Storms, *Anglo-Saxon Magic* (The Hague: Martinus Nijhoff, 1948), p. 283.

66 Weston, p. 292.

67 This Latin version taken from that printed in Ogden's edition of the *Thornton Manuscript*, p. 56. The text is also found in BL, Royal 17 A viii, fols 47r-v, from which Olsan provides this translation: 'The bow of the mighty will preside over us. The Virgin Mary will swim. The day and the hour are set ready. *rubus rebus rarantibus natus nator natoribus saxo scilicet*. Let this be remembered so that her boy or girl comes forth. A Man came. Pain fled. Christ is our Help: I adjure you rod, through the Father, Son and Holy Spirit, that you have the power to bring forth water.' Olsan reads 'scilicet' for Ogden's 'sic' ('scik' in Royal 17 A viii). In the final line of the Latin she reads 'comningendi' whereas Ogden and I expand 'cōiūgendi' to 'coniungendi'. With this latter reading it is possible to translate 'ut habeas potestatem coniungendi' as 'that you should have the power of joining [i.e. performing intercourse, penetrating]' which takes into account the play on *virga* (rod/penis) and *virgo* (virgin) in the previous line.

68 I Samuel 2. 4; Olsan, 'The Arcus Charms', p. 440. The debates about the original meaning of the *Arcus* charm are too complex to warrant inclusion here but it has been used to interpret and reconstruct an Old English version of the charm which appears in London, British Library, Harley MS 585; W. L. Braekman, 'Notes on Old English Charms II', *Neophilologus*, 67 (1983), 605-10. For further examples of the *Arcus* charm see Keiser, p. 3874.

69 Olsan, 'Arcus', p. 440.

70 See Luke 1. 46-55.

71 Skemer, p. 199.

72 Skemer, p. 205. In addition to Skemer's article see also Laurent, pp. 194-8; Curt F. Bühler, 'Prayers and Charms in Certain Middle English Scrolls', *Speculum*, 39 (1964), 270-8; and W. J. Dilling, 'Girdles: Their Origin and Development, Particularly with Regard to their Use as Charms in Medicine, Marriage, and Midwifery', *Caledonian Medical Journal*, 9 (1912), 337-57 and 403-25.

73 Skemer, p. 205.

74 Skemer, p. 205.

75 BL, Sloane 3564, fols 55v-56v: Iam nova pronies celo dimittur alto + christe + maria + Iohannes + Elizabet + remigius + celina lazare veni foras adiuoro te creature dei utrum sis puer an puella. In nomine patris et cetera exi de utero christe te appellat qui te creavit et redemit et in seculum iudicabit amen ceste lyez entre le destre de deyns et tantost istera lenfant vif u mort [. . .]. See also Hunt, p. 92.

76 See, for example, London, British Library, Rotulus Harley 43 A 14 and New York, Pierpont Morgan Library, Glazier MS 39. Both are discussed by Bühler.

77 London, Wellcome Library, MS 632.

78 Wellcome, MS 632, verso side, about 19cm down. Text printed in S. A. J. Moorat, *Catalogue of Western Manuscripts on Medicine and Science in the Wellcome Historical Medical Library: MSS written before 1650 AD* (London: [no pub.], 1962), p. 492; hereafter *Cat. Well.*

79 The inscription reads: *Thys parchement ys oure lady seynt mary sengter by vertu of thys holy sengter our savyor Jhesu criste and of hys dere mother oure lady seynte.* The Catalogue notes that *sengter* may mean cincture. See *Cat. Well.*, pp. 492–3.

80 Keith Thomas, *Religion and the Decline of Magic* (Harmondsworth: Penguin, 1971; repr. 1991), p. 31. See also Gail McMurray Gibson, *The Theater of Devotion: East Anglian Drama and Society in the Late Middle Ages* (Chicago: University of Chicago Press, 1989), p. 64; and Bühler, p. 274.

81 Legaré, 'Charlotte de Savoie's Library', p. 39. Further examples of the Virgin's girdle existed in Brittany, Constantinople and Assisi, in the church of Notre-Dame in Paris and at Westminster Abbey. See Laurent, p. 57; and Brendan Cassidy, 'A Relic, Some Pictures and the Mothers of Florence in the Late Fourteenth Century', *Gesta*, 30 (1991), 91–9 (p. 93; n. 17). Florentine trecento paintings of the *Madonna del Parto* show her holding a belt or girdle and Cassidy suggests that they were images 'to which expectant mothers and their families might direct their prayers to ease the travails of childbirth and for the safe delivery of a child'. See Cassidy, pp. 91–3; 97.

82 Gibson, *Theater of Devotion*, p. 64.

83 New York, Pierpont Morgan Library, M1092, dated 1491. See Skemer, p. 205.

84 Skemer, p. 205.

85 See Bühler, pp. 274–5.

86 See for example the prayer from a scroll conserved in Pierpont Morgan, Glazier 39; printed in Bühler, pp. 273–5.

87 Cambridge, Fitzwilliam Museum, MS 48, *c.*1350–60, fol. 2b. See the description in M. R. James, *A Descriptive Catalogue of the Manuscripts in the Fitzwilliam Museum* (Cambridge: Cambridge University Press, 1895), hereafter *Cat. Fitz.*; and the entry in the catalogue accompanying the museum's 2005 exhibition, *The Cambridge Illuminations: Ten Centuries of Book Production in the Medieval West*, ed. by Stella Panayotova and Paul Binski (London: Harvey Miller, 2005), no. 83. See also Smith, p. 256.

88 Smith, p. 264.

89 BL, Egerton 2781, fols 24r and 26v. See Smith, pp. 255–6.

90 Smith, p. 264. See also the further examples detailed by Smith, p. 264.

91 *De Bois Hours*, New York, Pierpont Morgan Library, MS M. 700.

92 *De Bois Hours*, fol. 130v.

93 *De Bois Hours*, fol. 141v.

94 London, British Library, Harley MS 1260, fol. 176v: *Cest oroison la mere seint thomas de caunterbirz fiste. Et el la dist devaunt son enfauntement. Et fem qe la dirra ia de son enfaunt ne perra.*

95 Ronald C. Finucane, *The Rescue of the Innocents: Endangered Children in Medieval Miracles* (New York: St Martin's Press, 1997), p. 20.

96 Smith, esp. pp. 252–4.

97 BL, Royal 12 B xxv, fols 61v–62r; see Olsan, 'Latin Charms', p. 122.

98 Olsan, 'Latin Charms', p. 123.

99 Olsan, 'Latin Charms', p. 123.

100 Jeremiah 1. 4–5: *Priusquam te formarem in utero novi te et antequem exires de ventre sanctificavi te. Et prophetam in gentibus dedi te.* (Before I formed thee in the bowels of thy mother, I knew thee; and before thou camest forth out of the womb, I sanctified thee, and made thee a prophet unto the nations).

101 James H. Marrow, 'History, Historiography, and Pictorial Invention in the *Turin-Milan Hours*', in *In Detail: New Studies of Northern Renaissance Art in Honor of Walter S. Gibson*, ed. by Laurinda S. Dixon (Turnhout: Brepols, 2001), pp. 1–14 (p. 2).

3

The lying-in month and the rite of churching: post-partum rituals and the material culture of childbearing

In 1430 Marguerite of Burgundy (1393–1441), wife of the future duke of Brittany Arthur III (1393–1458), wrote a letter to her sister-in-law Isabel of Portugal (1397–1471), wife of Philip the Good, duke of Burgundy (1396–1467), advising the duchess on the preparations she should make for the period of her lying-in, for her child's baptism, and for the day of her churching.[1] The advice was timely and may even have been sent for a specific pregnancy since Isabel had married Philip in January 1430 and on 30 December of the same year she gave birth to a son, Antoine (d. 1432).

Marguerite's letter details the number and types of beds that Isabel should have in her room, which must itself be hung with canopies and green silks and fine fabrics from Rheims. She also specifies that the room must be lit by two candles and that the windows should remain shut for eight days after the birth.[2] A dressing room (*la chambre à parer*) should be set aside, as close to this first room as possible, and should be furnished with a large canopied bed. This room would be used to receive visitors on the day of the child's baptism and here they should be offered wine and sweetmeats.[3] The child's room should be decorated with fabrics the same colour as those used in the mother's room, and should be hung with tapestries featuring her coat of arms (*et toute icelle chambre tendue de tapis à vos armes*). The infant's cradle should be painted with motifs of the mother's choosing, as well as with an image of the Virgin holding the Christ Child.[4] On the day of her churching, the duchess should be dressed in ducal insignia (*en habit royal*) and led from her bed to the church by the highest ranking lord present and afterwards she should hold court, if she is able (*vous debvez tenir salle, se vous pouvez nullement*).[5]

This chapter considers how the post-partum practices of lying-in and churching described by Marguerite form another part of the cultural training that informed the situational eye. Together with the sources discussed in Chapter 2, those analysed here are key to understanding how the viewers that are discussed in Chapters 4 and 5 responded to the images of holy mothers and childbearing in their manuscripts.

The rituals of lying-in and churching for which Marguerite of Burgundy offered such precise advice have their origins in Levitical blood taboos, which required the separation of the newly-delivered woman from the community followed by her purification.[6] In discussing these rites, some anthropologists and historians like Arnold Van Gennep and William Coster have emphasised the notions of pollution, cleansing and reintegration that are inherent in these ceremonies. Such approaches tend to reinforce the notions of inferiority that the medieval church and medieval medicine assigned to women's bodies.[7] However, others such as Adrian Wilson and Paula M. Rieder have analysed lying-in and churching from the point of view of the different people involved, stressing the tensions in and multivalency of these practices.[8] In particular, they have shown that lying-in and churching offered mothers valuable care, recognition and a chance for celebration during and after what was a physically demanding time. Therefore, from the point of view of the newly-delivered woman and her companions in particular, the ceremonies of childbirth offered a space in which social/gender roles were not only confirmed but could also be inverted in so far as they made a lay woman the focal point of the household and the main actor in a religious ceremony.

It is likely that the tensions and disruptions inherent in the lying-in and churching ceremonies had a bearing on how certain viewers interpreted images of childbirth and related scenes such as the Virgin's Purification in the Temple. Analysing the interrelationships between post-partum practices and manuscript miniatures highlights the multivalent potential of both and shows how they could function beyond any original didactic or controlling intention. Seen in the context of lying-in and churching, images of childbirth in devotional manuscripts could symbolise, for both the men and women involved, the dangers of childbirth, the happy or even sad outcome of birth, and also the upsetting of traditional gender hierarchies that childbearing entailed.

The first part of this chapter considers how familiarity with the arrangements for lying-in nuanced certain viewers', especially lay aristocratic women's, reception of images of the birth of the Virgin and St John the Baptist, in which mother and child are cared for by other women in comfortable, often richly decorated, surroundings. The different arrangements noted by Marguerite of Burgundy in her letter to Isabel of Portugal indicate some of the prominent features of the lying-in of aristocratic women, in particular the importance of fabrics and furniture in the decoration of the bedrooms, and certain practical arrangements like the darkening of the room, and the provision of food and drink for visitors. Although, as noted at the beginning of this study, images of holy childbirth cannot be taken as straightforward evidence for what went on in the childbirth chamber in the fifteenth century, many images, including those in the manuscripts owned by the Angevin and Breton duchesses discussed later, do allude to luxurious, well-assisted lying-ins through the domestic details represented. The images thus have affinities with evidence relating to material culture such as Marguerite of Burgundy's letter or Eleanor of Poitiers's treatise *Les Honneurs de la cour.*

The second part of this chapter discusses how the rite of churching validated a woman's social role as wife and mother, and how women could bring their understanding of this ceremony to bear on the images of holy motherhood in their Books of Hours. On the one hand, churching reinscribed normalised gender roles for women by affirming their social positions as wives and mothers, subject to priestly and marital authority. Churching was bound up with notions of sexual fidelity and unmarried mothers could find it hard to be churched.[9] On the other hand, churching was the only rite provided by the church exclusively for a sexually-active woman. The mother was singled out in a special ceremony in which she entered the church's sanctuary, a sacred space normally reserved for the clergy. She would, therefore, have experienced the ceremony as elevating her above her normally inferior position within a patriarchal society. In particular, the close association between the churching ceremony and the Virgin's Purification, which was also celebrated in the corporate feast of Candlemas, indicates that a new mother could situate herself in relation to the ultimate mother and obtain divine blessing, specifically for herself, for having carried and given birth to a child. Images of the Virgin's Purification in Books of Hours thus become another means through which women could negotiate and manage their social roles. Central to the development of this idea is Zemon Davis's 'women-on-top' theory in which she highlights the potential of images to disrupt the normal social order.

The previous chapters have shown that, although the gendering of healthcare in the fifteenth century would have made lay women particularly sensitive to the presence of holy mothers in childbirth prayers and in illuminated manuscripts, it did not exclude men from taking an active interest in using devotional and medical sources to ensure successful conception and the birth of (male) heirs. In the same way, although the ceremonies of lying-in and churching were operated for and by lay women, they did not exist independently of men. Placing a woman's childbearing and lying-in in the context of the rest of the household and community demonstrates how men were also implicated in the events and celebrations surrounding a birth. By this token, it is reasonable to suggest that husbands and fathers were also receptive to the all-female space and elaborate preparations depicted in manuscript miniatures of the birth of saints even if they were absent from the birth chamber. Therefore, although those women involved in childbearing remain the prime agents of the situational eye, men are not excluded from this viewing position.

Il y avoit un grand ciel, de drap de damas vert . . .: lying-in after childbirth

In medieval and early-modern Western Europe, a mother remained secluded for up to six weeks following the birth of a child. A period of post-partum seclusion was stipulated in Leviticus and Green notes that this time also 'corresponded approximately to the duration of the lochial flow from the uterus after childbirth'.[10] The lochial flow, or post-partum bleeding was, like menstrual bleeding, associated with leprosy and other diseases; thirteenth-century penitentials advised the avoidance of sexual intercourse before purification and during menstruation through fear of disease or sickly children.[11] In Northern Europe in the fifteenth century, lying-in aver-aged about a month although the length and elaborateness could vary depending on the household's means and the level of help available. Evidence about lying-in for the fifteenth century is more forthcoming for aristocratic women than for their counterparts in the lower echelons of society. However, sources such as diaries and accounts from the sixteenth and seventeenth centuries suggest that lying-in was a practice to which all Christian women adhered to a certain extent and it is reasonable to assume that this was also the case in the preceding centuries.[12]

Care for the newly-delivered mother was provided by those female assis-tants, relatives, friends or hired midwives, who had assisted during the labour and who remained on hand to attend to the mother and organise the baptism of the child, which usually took place a few days after the birth.[13] Records from medieval Italy show that a woman's mother might attend the birth and the lying-in, and that midwives and *guardadonne* were paid to assist for several days or even weeks after the birth.[14] In Burgundy, the accounts for the lying-in of Isabel of Portugal reveal the presence of a wet-nurse, a nurse to rock the cradle, a lady-in-waiting, and a night nurse just to look after the child.[15] In her treatise on the customs and rules governing the degrees of estate at the Burgundian court during the reign of Philip the Good, Eleanor of Poitiers includes discussion of the importance of furnishings in the birth chamber, a point which will be returned to below.[16] She also reveals certain aspects essential to the care of the new mother, such as keeping the room warm and dark. Eleanor noted that after the birth of Philip's granddaughter, Mary of Burgundy, in 1456, Isabel of Bourbon's room had a fire that was always lit according to the weather, rather than as a mark of estate, and that the child's room had a fire, in front of which the cradle was placed.[17] Like Marguerite of Burgundy's letter to her sister-in-law, Eleanor's treatise also notes that the *chambre de madame* was kept dark after the birth: she describes two candles burning brightly on the buffet since the shutters of the room were not opened until fifteen days after the birth.[18]

The practice of swaddling the infant was of particular benefit to the new mother since it has the effect of sending the child to sleep, thus providing the mother and her companions with valuable time to rest.[19] Although Eleanor's treatise is silent on swaddling, the *Trotula* mentions it briefly, along with the bathing of the infant, in the section 'On the Regimen for the Infant' and it can be presumed that it constituted an important part of neonatal care.[20] That swaddling was popular in fifteenth-century Italy, at least, is indicated by the fact that coins were sometimes placed in the swaddling clothes of children about to be baptised.[21] Domestic help, paid or otherwise, the darkening of the room and the bathing and swaddling of the child were all aspects designed to aid the mother's recovery from the birth and to provide the best care for her and the child. In these arrangements, as Wilson notes, 'women had worked out what was best for them'.[22]

Another way in which the lying-in ceremony provided care for the newly-delivered mother was the special attention given to the provision of food and drink. Other women and sometimes men paid visits during the lying-in period bringing gifts for the mother and child and these guests had to be provided for. For fifteenth-century Italy, the accounts of Ser Girolamo da Colle show the purchase of poultry and sweetmeats during the lying-in of his wife Caterina. These foods served both to help keep up the mother's strength and to provide refreshment for the women helping with the birth and post-partum care.[23] Musacchio notes that poultry was often purchased during childbearing since it was considered easy for the mother to digest.[24] Sugar-coated delicacies were served to those guests who came to visit the new mother: the accounts of several Italian household show that additional purchases sometimes had to be made if guests exceeded the expected numbers.[25] Sweetmeats or *dragée* were also offered to the guests visiting Isabel of Bourbon. According to Eleanor of Poitiers there was a little low table in the corner of Isabel's *chambre de parement*, on which were placed the jugs and cups for serving drink to those who came to visit the duchess, after they had partaken of the sweets on the dresser.[26] Later, Eleanor comments that the guests were served a spiced wine (*hippocras*) and that provision for this must be made by women of all estates.[27] Hippocras was probably similar to the restorative 'caudle' that, Wilson and Becky Lee note, was served at births in England in the middle ages and early modern period.[28] In addition to providing nourishment for the mother, then, the caudle or spiced wine drink also served a 'ceremonial and social function' since it was drunk by the women visiting the new mother.[29]

Turning to depictions of the birth of the Virgin and of St John the Baptist, we find allusions to the practical arrangements for childbirth detailed here. For example, in the *Birth of the Virgin* in the John Rylands Book of Hours mentioned in the Introduction, a woman warms a sheet before the fire while another hands the swaddled child to St Anne (plate 2). In the *Châtillon Hours*, a woman sits in front of an open fire holding the Virgin who is wrapped in swaddling clothes; in the background a number of jugs and small vessels are arranged on an open dresser (figure 9). One of the attendants in the *Birth of St John the Baptist* in Giusto de' Menabuoi's Padua Baptistery cycle carries a jug on a tray and another one hands a chicken on a plate to her companion (figure 3). Referring to another painting by Giusto, of the *Birth of the Virgin*, Musacchio notes that the presentation of a roasted bird to St Anne 'help[ed] women relate to the religious stories on a more personal level' and that a 'mother viewing such a painting might remember the poultry she was brought during her own confinement and [thus] feel a closer bond with the holy figures because of it'.[30]

The Padua *Birth of St John* also shows the bathing of the child, a feature frequently found in manuscript illuminations of birth scenes. For example, in the miniature of the *Nativity of Christ* at the hour of Prime in René of Anjou's *Paris Hours*, discussed in more detail below, a female attendant fills a bathtub and the Virgin reaches out to test the temperature of the water (plate 5). A border miniature of the *Birth of the Virgin* in the *Hours of Marguerite of Foix*, shows several women attending St Anne, crowding round her bed and, in the foreground, a woman bathing the child over a tub (plate 6). Therefore, although the inclusion of features such as a fire, a bath, plates of food, and female attendants are part of the standard representation of post-partum birth scenes, it is likely that a viewer who was aware of these actual practices was able to bring the otherwise generic, domestic, details of the image into sharper focus. For those women who were involved in childbirth as mothers and carers, the successful, post-partum, female-dominated images of the Virgin and St John's birth may well have recalled the care which they had organised, experienced, or which they expected to undergo one day.

In *Painting and Experience*, Baxandall described the agents of the 'period eye' as being 'on their mettle' in front of pictures, able to discern nuances, some of which are lost to us today.[31] The letter from Marguerite of Burgundy to Isabel of Portugal, and the treatise written by Eleanor of Poitiers, who served as a lady-in-waiting to Isabel's daughter-in-law, Isabel of Bourbon, show that certain female viewers from the aristocracy were also 'on their mettle' in front of objects from material culture, and that they were trained to be highly sensitive to materials, furnishings and degrees of estate. According to Eames, those versed in courtly manners could interpret the 'nuances of social distinction . . . conveyed by such details as the number and position of beds in a suite of rooms and by the type of fur used for the coverlets . . . though it is evident that on occasion the degree of honour claimed could disturb spectators'.[32] Thus Christine de Pizan, another 'viewer' trained in courtly manners, criticised a merchant's wife in her *Livre des trois vertus*, whose elaborate lying-in rivalled that of the French queen.[33]

Eleanor's and Marguerite's descriptions of childbearing are key to proposing how aristocratic women like the duchesses considered in the following chapters understood the post-partum images in their prayer books. For example, when the images are read in conjunction with descriptions of aristocratic lying-ins, the details they include in terms of beds and fabrics, give them an air of estate, one entirely suitable for a blessed mother and her special child and, by extension, an aristocratic woman and her baby. The following section, therefore, examines in detail the evidence for lying-in found in sources like Eleanor of Poitiers' treatise, demonstrating the particular sensitivities of the aristocratic situational eye and in turn opening up more nuanced readings of images of holy childbearing. Although Eleanor wrote the *Honneurs de la Cour* from within the Burgundian court, she frequently refers to practices at the court of France and describes certain rules that applied to the French queen.[34] Moreover, the advice sent by Marguerite of Burgundy to Isabel of Portugal differs little from Eleanor's advice, even though Marguerite was keen to stress at the end of her letter that she only knows about the customs of Brittany (*Et ce que j'en scais, ce n'est que selon la façon de Bretaigne*).[35] It is probable, therefore, that Eleanor and Marguerite's cognitive habits regarding degrees of estate, beds and fabrics, were also acquired by the Angevin and Breton duchesses discussed in Chapters 4 and 5.

Eleanor gives a detailed description of the furnishings and preparations for Isabel of Bourbon's lying-in after the birth of her daughter Mary of Burgundy in 1456. Three chambers were prepared for the birth, the *chambre de parement*, the *chambre de madame*, and the *chambre de l'enfant*. The *chambre de madame* where Isabel of Bourbon lay contained two large beds separated by an aisle at the end of which was a large high-backed chair.[36] Eleanor is careful to note that the number of *traversaines*, the long curtains that hung in the aisle between the two beds, was governed by rules of estate. The queen of France had four of these curtains but Isabel of Bourbon and her mother-in-law Isabel of Portugal, duchess of Burgundy, only had three.[37] The *chambre de madame* was hung entirely in green: the beds were covered by a canopy of green damask fringed with green silk with curtains of green half-satin.[38] The colour green was a mark of estate, reserved for the queen of France and other *grandes princesses*, ever since Isabeau of Bavaria chose to lie-in in this colour, rather than the customary white.[39] Eleanor notes that countesses and other *grandes dames* should not, however, use green in their lying-in room.[40]

Other types of fabrics and their colours used for the lying-in room were also of marked importance. In describing them, Eleanor employed specific words that reveal individual aspects of the beds and their furnishings, such as *courtine* (a curtain or some other kind of hanging), *traversaine* (a curtain that hung at the foot and round the middle of the bed), *ciel* (a canopy fitted to the ceiling), *franges* (borders or fringes), and *gouttieres* (pelmets or valances). She also distinguishes between fabrics like *soye* (silk), *damas* (damask), *demy satin* (half-satin), *samyt* (samite, a rich velvet silk fabric originally from Syria, often woven with gold or silver thread), *tapis* (floor and wall coverings), and *veloux* (velours or velvet). The fur she specifies for some of the bed covers is *menu vair*, or miniver, an expensive type of fur that comes from the northern grey squirrel. For example, the room prepared for the child, Mary of Burgundy, contained two large beds which were hung with purple and green damask silk, and with curtains of the same colour in samite.[41] In the dressing room (*chambre de parement*) where Isabel would receive visitors, the bed was hung with crimson satin and there were carpets of red silk.[42] Eleanor's eye for detail reveals that ermine and a fine violet cloth were used on the duchess's beds and these fabrics extended to the floor; beneath these, were two beautiful sheets of fine gauze, which were longer than the covers.[43]

Marguerite of Burgundy also placed an emphasis on the fabrics that Isabel of Portugal should use during her lying-in, such as sheets woven in Rheims (*toille de Rheims*) and those of white linen (*toille de lin blanche*).[44] Isabel should also have, she notes, four small cushions, for which she gives specific dimensions, the material from which they should be made, and the manner in which they should be decorated, embroidered with pearls and with large stuffed buttons at the four corners after the latest fashion (*de la plus belle et nouvelle façon*).[45]

The ability of Eleanor and Margaret to make distinctions between fabrics, colours and lengths of material is indicative of their social status and education, in the same way that Baxandall's medically-trained viewer was 'alert and equipped to notice matters of proportion in painting'.[46] Turning to manuscript illuminations of holy births demonstrates how Margaret, Eleanor and other aristocratic women could have easily applied this training to discern allusions to material furnishings in these images.

Eleanor noted that red hangings were used for the *chambre de parement* at the court of Burgundy; such hangings were depicted in both the *Birth of St John the Baptist* panel in Rogier van der Weyden's altarpiece and in Jan van Eyck's depiction of the curtains surrounding St Elizabeth's bed in the *Turin-Milan Hours* made for the duke of Berry (figs 1–2). In the *Châtillon Hours*, St Anne's bed has a green and blue canopy and a blue coverlet embroidered with gold fleur de lys (figure 9). Like the colours used to dye fabrics, the inks and gold leaf used to illustrate manuscripts were expensive and the way they were used highlighted the wealth and status of the person by, or for whom they were commissioned. In the *Birth of the Virgin* miniature in Jean Mansel's *Fleur des histoires*, St Anne's bed is hung with dark green curtains and covers; behind the bed is a rich blue panel sewn with gold (figure 14). Since this manuscript was made for Edward IV, the richness of St Anne's bed and surrounding fabrics was probably not lost on the king, whose wardrobe accounts detail a wealth of beds, bedding and covers.[47] The accounts show that for the visit of a Burgundian entourage several lengths of red worsted were used to make *costers* (ornamental hangings for a wall or a bed) and *celours* (bed canopies). Green *sarsinet* (a fine silk material), was used to make two *travasses* or curtains to divide a room, and they were also decorated with five ounces of green silk ribbon.[48] When Edward's daughter Elizabeth of York gave birth to Margaret Tudor in 1489, the room was hung with rich tapestries and the queen was provided with 'a bed made up of a wool-stuffed mattress, a featherbed, a down-filled

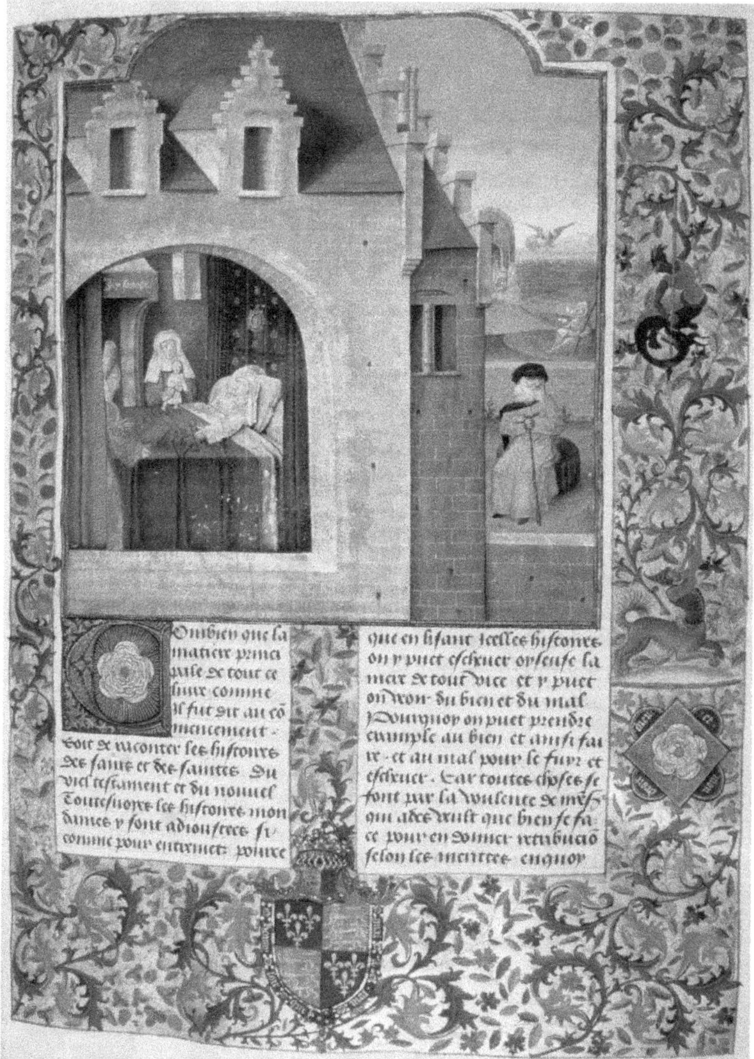

14 *Birth of the Virgin*, Jean Mansel, *Fleur des histoires*, London, British Library, Royal MS 18 E vi, fol. 82r, fifteenth century (© London, British Library)

bolster and four down pillows, finest linen sheets and pillow cases, a linen quilt, and a coverlet of ermine and cloth of gold' and a chronicler noted that the queen's room was hung with 'riche Clothe of blew Arras, with Flourdelissis of Golde'.[49] The furnishing of bed chambers was, therefore, an important part of aristocratic society and the rules of estate and, since it had a particularly special role to play during childbearing, it was something that lay women at court were particularly attuned to notice.

The furnishings employed by noble families during childbirth were carefully orchestrated to demonstrate paternal wealth and power to those visiting the new mother.[50] By suggesting that mothers, in particular, saw in images of holy childbearing allusions to the actual practices that they experienced, and that they found these images empowering or positive, raises questions about their agency as viewers. It risks implying women's passive acquiescence to their role as providers of heirs for a patriarchal society. For instance, Musacchio has pointed out that in fifteenth-century Italy the special purchases made for the birth chamber, and the visiting of the new mother, were part of the 'politicized nature of childbirth' and that the exchanges of gifts were 'determined by lineal, political, and social ties, and they were paid for by men'.[51] However, simply assuming that cultural activities asserted patriarchal power and subjugated, or even bypassed, women completely risks ignoring how those activities were viewed by the people who were apparently being subjected to them. As discussed in Chapter 2, women such as Anne of France were keen to execute their social roles as duchesses and mothers in order to consolidate and manipulate their own positions within the constraints of a hierarchical, male-dominated, system. Thus it is possible that aristocratic women positively interpreted and received those practices that were designed especially for them as mothers, especially if those practices were intended to give them care and respite and to emphasise their social standing. This interpretation can be developed further by looking at the example of Isabel of Bourbon in *Les Honneurs de la cour*.

Eleanor of Poitiers's description of the room in which Isabel of Bourbon's visitors were received indicates that it was rife with dynastic symbolism relating to Isabel's father-in-law. The room contained all the richest plate, crystal and gold belonging to Duke Philip, such as pots, cups and goblets of gold. The dresser was hung with a cloth of crimson and gold, bordered with black velvet. Embroidered in gold on this border was the *fusil*, a lozenge-shaped heraldic device used by the duke.[52] The presence of Philip the Good's objects and his device thus asserted a male presence in a space from which men were otherwise excluded, at least for part of the time. These objects also framed Isabel's childbearing as an event essential to the maintenance of the dynasty and prestige of the Burgundian court. Isabel's husband Charles was Philip's only son, and Isabel was Charles's second wife, his marriage to Catherine of Valois (1428–46) having been without issue. The decoration of Isabel's room was, therefore, intended to impress those who visited the duchess during her lying-in, to demonstrate the duke's position, and to celebrate the birth of the child on whom the long-term hopes of the duchy rested.[53]

To a certain extent, such lavish decoration, especially one emphasising male lineage, might seem, like the exchanges of gifts between Italian men, to bypass, or ignore the woman who has given birth. Furthermore, Eleanor's account is concerned primarily with the fabrics and matters of estate, not with Isabel herself. However, it is worth noting that the lying-in rooms of Isabel of Portugal, mother of Charles the Bold (1433–77), were furnished with chairs and tapestries displaying the heraldry of both of their houses.[54] Marguerite of Burgundy told Isabel of Portugal that her room should be hung with green tapestries showing her coats of arms, and that other fabrics should be embroidered with such devices as would please her.[55] For the birth of Prince Arthur in 1486, the chamber of Elizabeth of York, wife of Henry VII of England, included a pallet or couch with 'a canopy of crimson satin embroidered with gold crowns, the queen's arms and other devices'.[56] The inclusion of a woman's own arms in her lying-in chambers meant that her lineage was privileged, rather than ignored. Similarly, as the following chapters demonstrate, women could choose to place their own heraldic devices at strategic positions in their manuscripts to emphasise their roles as duchesses, queens and mothers.

The use of personal emblems thus opens up the possibility of a space in which an aristocratic lay woman could exercise agency in her interpretation of her prescribed social and gender roles. The following section explores how, through this agency gained through the situational eye, women interpreted lying-in and also the images of this practice in their manuscripts, as a reversal or upsetting of traditional gender roles. That such an interpretation was possible is suggested by the disruption that a birth and the subsequent lying-in could entail and, above all, by the re-centring of the household – be it aristocratic or not – around the new mother so that she was placed 'on top'. In order to analyse the subversive potential of the events associated with childbearing and to suggest how women exercised agency in their interpretation, it is necessary to look not only at women's interaction with those events and ceremonies but also at the ways in which men were implicated in these practices. Furthermore, consideration of men's relationship to the lying-in ceremony is key to proposing how the images of childbearing in Books of Hours functioned for both male *and* female readers and, therefore, to moving beyond sex-bound active–passive interpretations.

Men's involvement in the practices surrounding childbirth is most often witnessed through financial records and accounts. Although a husband might be excluded from the childbirth chamber during labour, concern for his wife and child meant that he needed to provide them with the best affordable care. In addition to purchasing special foods and linens like Ser Girolamo, husbands could also be responsible for choosing a midwife or a wet-nurse.[57] Men in late-medieval England recorded having sent gifts of food and drink to neighbours who were lying-in. For example, Lee notes that John Wallop gave two swans to Alice, countess of Kent; in other cases men provided the wine for the caudle: one John Watts, for example, sent a gallon of sweet wine to Margaret de Wauton.[58]

This evidence, together with that for fifteenth-century Italy and Burgundy, shows that childbearing was an expensive business, not only for the father but also for the friends of the new parents. Such costs were deemed necessary, however, not only to ensure good care for the mother and child but as a means to demonstrate wealth and status to friends and neighbours. Therefore, whereas for the woman lying-in offered a period of respite, for the husband it could be a time of expense. Lying-in could disrupt the household in general and in particular a man's normal routine, both within and outside the marital chamber, as he had to modify any usual expectations or habits. During her lying-in, the social expectations placed upon a woman were momentarily suspended: a woman of the lower classes was released her from physical household duties, meaning that the husband was expected to play a greater role in the everyday management of the household.[59] Furthermore, the woman was neither pregnant, nor was she expected to have sex with her husband. This suspension of the marital debt probably provided welcome relief for those women who, if they were able to conceive, could spend a great many of their childbearing years pregnant.[60] Men, however, sometimes saw this suspension differently and Wilson cites evidence from the sixteenth and seventeenth centuries in which husbands remarked on their banishment from the marital bed.[61] In fact, lying-in could also impinge upon a man's routine even if the woman in question were not his own wife. For instance, the husband of Gertrude Scurtebiers, wet-nurse to Charles the Bold, was recompensed to the sum of 4 *soldi* a day for the inconvenience of his wife's absence.[62]

A man's involvement in arrangements for lying-in thus meant that he too could have picked up on the domestic features represented in images of holy childbirth. Viewed with the husband's situational eye, images of women gathered round the well-furnished bed of the new mother, perhaps presenting her with food, could have, on the one hand, symbolised the interruption that childbearing caused to normal routines and reminded him of the cost that the lying-in month and the visitors could entail. The images thus functioned, perhaps, as visual parallels to popular texts like the *Quinze Joies de Mariage* and the *Batchelor's Banquet* which satirised the practices and celebrations of childbearing.[63] On the other hand, husbands and fathers could also have viewed the images as symbols of their responsibility towards society and their family, both in terms of providing an heir and terms of providing for the festivities. Chapter 4 argues that for aristocratic male viewers like René of Anjou (1409–80), who were less affected on a day-to-day basis by the disruption of their wife's childbearing and lying-in than members of the lower classes, comfortable, quasi-aristocratic images of the *Birth of the Virgin* or the *Nativity of Christ* symbolised a parallel between their own family and that of Christ, and referred to the potential that a birth signified for the future of the dynastic house.

The various meanings embodied in the lying-in ceremony, and the allusions to this practice found in manuscripts, do not have to be mutually exclusive; a viewer's interpretation could have oscillated between different interpretations at different times in their life. Thus, Chapters 4 and 5 suggest that the female viewers of the *Fitzwilliam Hours* and the *Hours of Marguerite of Foix* derived different meanings from the manuscripts' images of holy childbirth, depending at what points in their lives they encountered them: for example, at the beginning of their marriages, after a child had died, or during pregnancy. Thus, although men and women might have acquired different cognitive habits that affected their sensitivity to images of childbirth, there was sufficient overlap in those habits – such as ways of ensuring the best care for the mother or hopes for the dynasty – that allowed them to draw similar, rather than conflicting, meanings from the images. However, it is still important to look further at the ways in which childbearing could disrupt gender hierarchies, placing women 'on top', in order to counteract the empowerment–disempowerment thesis discussed in Chapter 1 and to show how female viewers could actively interpret the images of holy motherhood that they encountered.

By making women the centre of attention, Wilson has argued that the ceremony of childbirth in the early modern period disrupted normalised gender relations to the extent that it 'placed the woman "on top" amidst *all* families'.[64] His reading of the ceremony takes its cue from Zemon Davis's 'Women on Top' essay. Here, Zemon Davis analysed images of the disorderly woman, countering the view of some feminists by suggesting that this topos 'did not always function to keep women in their place. On the contrary it was a multivalent image.'[65] In particular, she argued that representations of scenes such as Phyllis riding Aristotle and Delilah cutting Samson's hair that were painted on fifteenth-century Italian birth trays, or *deschi da parto*, show how the subjection of women in marriage 'might be reversed temporarily during the lying-in period'.[66] As objects closely associated with female viewers and childbirth, *deschi* provide a good way of teasing out further meanings of the lying-in ceremony and its relationship to the images in Books of Hours.

As Musacchio has examined in her study of Italian birth wares, *deschi da parto* were frequently illustrated with images of women dominating men taken from secular narratives such as Petrarch's *Triumph of Love* and *Triumph of Chastity*.[67] For instance, a tray from the workshop of Apollonio di Giovanni is decorated on one side with two naked boys playing with poppy seed capsules; the other side is decorated with a painting illustrating Petrarch's *Triumph of Chastity* in which Cupid, shown as a young man, is bound and processed on a cart presided over by an imposing female figure (figures 15–16). Like similar depictions on marriage chests or *cassoni*, images of the world turned upside down were intended to keep women in their place, promote marital fidelity and to encourage wives in their procreative capacity.[68] Thus, in the example shown here, Musacchio has argued that the image of the poppy seed capsules were symbols of fertility designed to encourage the woman to conceive. The reverse scene of the *Triumph of Chastity*, she claims, 'must have been intended as a warning to the pregnant woman to remain chaste in her marriage and ensure the paternity of her children'.[69]

While this interpretation remains valid, another one can also be proposed whereby the iconography of the *Triumph of Chastity* or the *Triumph of Love*, in which female characters dominate, was read by the pregnant woman who received the tray as more than an admonition to fidelity and a reaffirmation of gender roles. Viewed from the woman's perspective, with a situational eye informed by the dangers of childbearing and the expectations of a patriarchal society, the topsy-turvy imagery of *deschi* could have come to function as an allegory of lying-in. In representations of the 'woman on top', the mother could have seen a version of the disrupted gender roles in her household occasioned by her childbearing, with all the special preparations and benefits that made her and her child the centre of attention. By this token, Apollonio's image of Chastity itself becomes

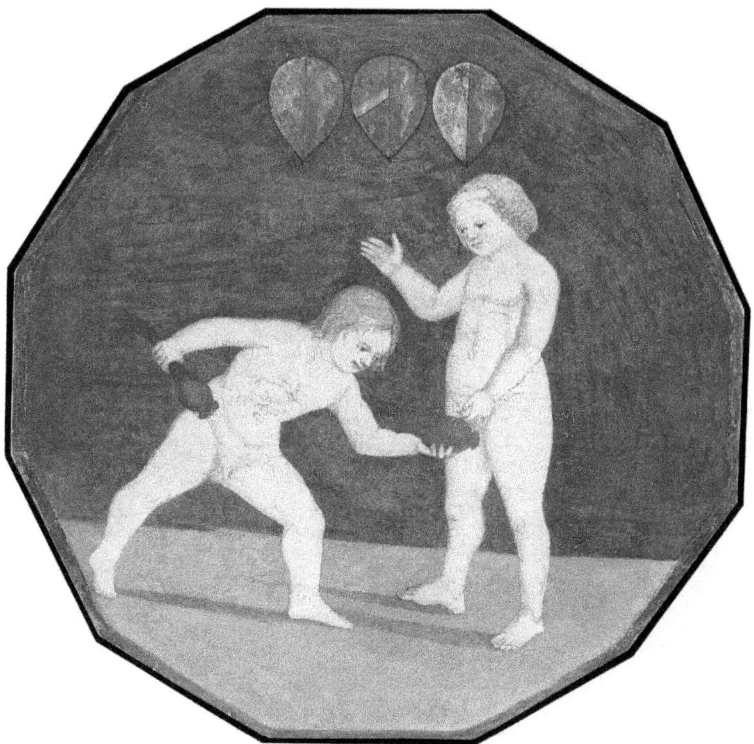

15   Apollonio di Giovanni (workshop), *Two Boys Playing with Poppy Seeds*, *Desco da parto*, North Carolina Museum of Art, Raleigh, Gift of the Samuel H. Kress Foundation, *c.*1450–60 (© Raleigh, North Carolina Museum of Art)

multivalent, triumphing in more ways than one. Whereas for the men involved in the purchasing and giving of *deschi* the ostensible meaning of the *Triumph of Chastity* was to promote wifely fidelity, for the woman receiving the tray it could have functioned differently. Lying-in was in itself a period of chastity, of abstinence, in which the wife's, rather than the husband's, physical needs came first. Thus the 'warning' to remain chaste that was inherent in the *Triumph* image could, at the same time, be a symbol of the woman's exemption from the marital debt, and the chastity imposed on the husband during her lying-in.

This interpretation of *deschi*, from the mother's point of view, can even be extended to the conventional images of lying-in that decorated birth trays. In their representation of lavishly decorated bedrooms, rich fabrics

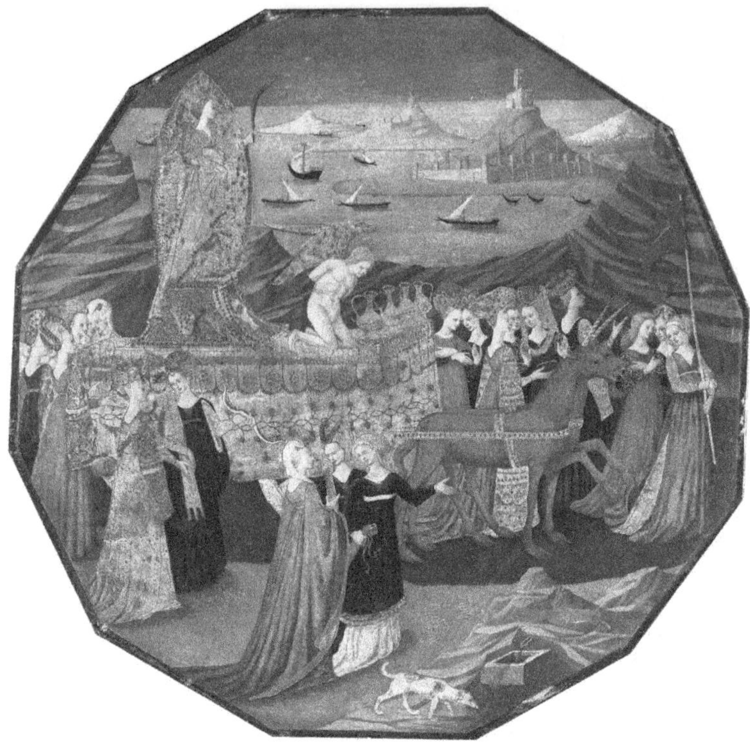

16   Apollonio di Giovanni (workshop), *Triumph of Chastity*, *Desco da parto*, North Carolina Museum of Art, Raleigh, Gift of the Samuel H. Kress Foundation, *c*.1450–60 (© Raleigh, North Carolina Museum of Art)

and dishes of food, these secular images alluded directly to the material preparations for childbirth from which the new mother and her helpers would benefit.[70] Although secular, the images on *deschi* bear many similarities to those images of holy childbearing found in Books of Hours. The lay women who received and looked at this type of imagery on *deschi da parto* and in devotional manuscripts could thus have interpreted it as a validation of their roles as wives and mothers in a patriarchal society – a role so important that it placed them at the centre of attention in their household, just as the mother and her companions were the central figures on the *deschi* or in post-partum scenes in Books of Hours.

However, in the same way that the lying-in period was only temporary, this interpretation of the images may also be unsustainable, resulting in, and inevitably supporting, the reassertion of the normalised gender hierarchy and thus the consequent subjection of women within patriarchy that was implied in the critiques of Butler and Aers and Staley. Zemon Davis's idea of multivalency is, therefore, important since she argues that images were available for interpretation in different ways, at different times and by different viewers. In particular, the fact that *deschi* retained an important place in a household's furnishings, often visibly displayed, suggests that the subversive meanings with which they could be invested remained available and did not automatically disappear with the end of lying-in.[71] By the same token, the post-partum images found in manuscripts could also have retained their multivalency since these books were themselves cherished, added to, and meditated upon. Thus it is possible that a female viewer, by the act of re-viewing an image of the Virgin's birth or a similar secular image on a *deschi*, could be reminded of a happy childbearing and the gender reversal that she had experienced during the lying-in ceremony.

An insistence on the multivalency of images also reveals other, perhaps less positive, meanings that should not be ignored in the enthusiasm to seek out evidence of how women were able to negotiate the patriarchal society in which they lived in a way that best suited their needs. Viewed or reviewed prior to a birth, images on *deschi* or in Books of Hours of successful, luxurious (holy) confinement scenes could function, for a mother- or even father-to-be, as a meditative space through which they could manage the real possibility of a complicated birth and pray for a successful outcome in a setting appropriate to their means and status. Such images could also function in the commemoration of a lost child, or even the inability to conceive. The difficulties around conception and of giving birth to healthy children meant that some of the duchesses discussed below viewed the images of successful childbirth in their manuscripts in a variety of ways, at different times during their lives: as a means to anticipate the successful outcome of a pregnancy, as a sharp reminder of society's expectations of them and/or of their inability to succeed in this, the death of an infant, or as a reminder of a successful delivery. Images of holy childbirth thus provided a way for these lay, aristocratic, women better to perform, as Butler would have it, their social roles as wives and mothers by offering legitimate, God-given examples of motherhood that also alluded to the contemporary lying-in ceremony and its attendant benefits in which the woman was given the best possible care and attention.

Pour le jour que vous devez relever: the post-partum rite of churching

Whatever a Christian woman's social status, a successful birth and its attendant celebrations were continued when the mother made her way to church surrounded by her female friends, relations, and the midwife who had assisted at the birth.[72] Modern interpretations of the mother's post-partum attendance at church have often reflected the purification-versus-thanksgiving debate that surrounded the ceremony in the early sixteenth century.[73] The origins of the rite, in Levitical blood taboos, and the purity-pollution binary that performance of the rite implied, cannot be ignored and did form part of the central meaning of churching for certain of its participants. However, in her study of the rite in Northern France in the later middle ages, Rieder points out that although churching 'served to support and maintain the patriarchal order of medieval society' it 'had different meanings to different audiences at different times'.[74] Rieder's interpretation of churching therefore has similarities with Zemon Davis's insistence on the multivalency of the 'woman on top' image discussed in the previous section. Thus, on the one hand, churching established and maintained a social and gender hierarchy in which the clergy dominated the laity, and men dominated women. On the other, it had the potential to disrupt the normal order since it privileged a sexually-active woman in an ecclesiastical context.

It is likely that the woman being churched after nine months of pregnancy and a successful birth viewed her position in the ceremony differently to that of the presiding, celibate, male priest. Therefore, as with the lying-in ceremony and its visual representations, it is important to explore the multivalency of the churching ceremony and its visual equivalent, the Virgin's Purification in the Temple. Rieder, for instance, suggests that because of the link between churching, Mary's Purification, and the feast of Candlemas, images of the Purification in illuminated manuscripts 'offer some insight into the way medieval people conceived of the custom of churching'.[75] It is more interesting, however, to turn this idea around to explore how knowledge and experience of churching rites were brought to bear on the interpretation of post-partum images of childbirth as well as other images of holy motherhood like the Virgin's Purification. In particular, considering how churching was viewed through the situational eye of the women involved is key to suggesting how they found spaces, within the constraints of patriarchy, in which to exercise their agency and manage the roles that they occupied. The following section explores some of the tensions in the churching ceremony and suggests that newly-delivered mothers and the company of women attending the ceremony viewed churching as a continuation of the destabilising of traditional gender roles begun with the lying-in ceremony and that this could have extended to their viewing of related images in their Books of Hours.

Historians' access to the ritual of late-medieval churching and the meanings it held for the participants is complicated by the paucity and bias of sources. Liturgical sources, in the form of service books, show how the rite was to be carried out from an ecclesiastical point of view and do not indicate how the woman, priest and congregation participating in the ceremony were expected to understand it. In aiming to understand churching better, Rieder draws on other sources such as letters of remission, judicial proceedings, and statutes that comment on those aspects of churching which came into conflict with secular and ecclesiastical law. She argues in particular that the placing of the rite in liturgical books, near the rites for marriage, baptism, prayers for the sick, and for lepers, reveals the multiple meanings of the ceremony for the church.[76] Proximity to marriage and baptismal rites relates churching to the institution of marriage as the proper context for procreation; the placement of the rite amongst prayers for the sick calls attention to the healing and purificatory aspects of the ceremony.

Turning to the accounts of churching contained in Marguerite of Burgundy's letter and Eleanor of Poitiers's treatise reveals details about the material arrangements that churching entailed amongst the nobility, such as the participants, the procession to the church and the gifts offered. Evidence from the post-Reformation period is also valuable when analysing reception of the ritual in the later middle ages: the fact that women continued to seek out churching after the Reformation, when it was considered by Puritans to be a popish purification ritual, suggests that the female participants considered churching to be a celebratory aspect of popular culture rather than a subjugation to ecclesiastical and patriarchal law.

The Church considered women who had just given birth to be polluted not only by the lochial flow, or post-partum bleeding, that followed a delivery, but also by semen and by the sin of lust, which they were supposed to have enjoyed during conception.[77] In some French and English rites the notion of pollution/purification is evident in the way the priest met the new mother at the door of the church, sprinkling her with holy water.[78] This act of cleansing not only allowed the new mother to enter the church and thus to rejoin the Christian communion, from which she had been absent during her lying-in, but it also signified that she could now resume sexual relations with her husband without fear of engendering deformed or leprous children.[79]

Notions of purification and submission to God's law are certainly present in the psalms used in many European rites, such as Psalm 50(51) (*Miserere me*) which asks for mercy, and Psalm 120(121) (*Levavi oculus*) which asks for cleansing from sin and restoration to the joy of salvation.[80] The introductory rite from Boulogne begins with Psalm 23 (24) which states that 'those who desire entrance into the sanctuary of the Lord must be innocent and pure of heart'.[81] The woman's supposed sexual pollution had an important role to play in the maintenance of the hierarchical relationship between priest and laity, man and woman since, without it 'the meaning of celibate purity and the consequent power of the clergy could be called into question'.[82] Yet at the same time as the rite emphasised the priest's moral and spiritual superiority over the laity and in particular a man's superiority over a woman, it also threatened that superiority by providing a personal ceremony for a lay, sexually-active, woman.[83]

It is within this contradiction, around what Rieder calls the 'insecure borders' between fixed categories and roles, that women could have understood the churching ceremony as something other than purification. Thus, although the purification-cleansing aspect of churching was no doubt obvious to those people participating in or witnessing the rite, it was not necessarily the central or sole meaning given to the ceremony by the female participants. For instance, it is possible that female participants found Psalm 120(121), with its references to the lifting up of one's eyes, and to the Lord being one's shade, highly significant if they had come to the church veiled.[84] The veil, along with the group of women accompanying the mother, signified a continuation of the enclosure and protection of the birth chamber, an enclosure authorised, rather than dictated, by God. Furthermore, the fact that churching took place in the community, and in the company of the women who had assisted at the birth, allowed for a public celebration not only of the mother's survival but also of the care and support that lay women offered to each other during childbirth: according to Gibson, 'the awesome Latin psalms and blessings, the holy water and burning candles, sanctified not only the body of the new mother, but the entire body of attending women'.[85] Furthermore, as Wilson has pointed out, the continued popularity of churching among women in the early modern period suggests that ideas of pollution were less relevant to the mother herself and to those who came into contact with her than ones of blessing and thanksgiving.[86]

Like lying-in, churching acknowledged and celebrated the nine months of carrying a child and the several hours of labour. One of the prayers for childbirth found on the Wellcome scroll discussed in Chapter 2 indicated that it would ensure the child's baptism and bring the mother 'to puryfy-catyon'. During the lying-in period, the mother had been the centre of attention with the aim of ensuring as full a recovery as possible by absolving her from her physical duties and nourishing her with special foods. Seen from the mother's point of view, then, churching was an integral part of, and an end to, the 'ceremony' of childbirth. It symbolised the success of the lying-in period: by coming to church with those who had assisted at the birth, a mother showed that she had received the appropriate care to assist her in her recovery, even if the child did not survive.

Once the woman had been brought into the church, she was led by the priest into the sanctuary, a sacred space normally reserved for the clergy.[87] She approached this space alone, rather than as part of a collective body, for example as a member of the parish, for communion, or with her husband, for marriage. The woman's privileged position in the sanctuary was one 'that neither the clergy nor the gendered structure of medieval society generally recognized as appropriate'.[88] From the woman's point of view, her presence here had the potential to sustain the destabilisation of gender roles begun in the lying-in room by continuing to place the woman 'on top' within a society that otherwise maligned the female sex as inferior and less important than the male. That women perceived this part of the ritual as one of privilege and a reversal of the normal order is indicated by the meaning attributed to the blessed bread or *pain bénit*. In late-medieval France, *pain bénit*, was distributed at the end of the mass as a substitute for communion. Thus, although not communion in itself, the blessing and sharing of bread still served to unite the local community, especially since it was often made by members of that community.[89] Furthermore, although churching did not include communion, certain ecclesiastical statutes issued between the thirteenth and fifteenth centuries, and analysed by Rieder, indicate that some women interpreted the *pain bénit* they received from the priest in the sanctuary as if it were in fact the consecrated host.[90] A statute from Chartres in the mid-fourteenth century 'warned women taking bread after their purification not to fall to their knees before it, nor strike their breasts and say "Confiteor" as they received it'.[91] In another, from 1403, Bishop Simon de Boucy of Soissons ordered priests 'to tell [the women] that they are giving them only plain bread; otherwise, they would allow them to commit idolatry'.[92]

The fact that steps were taken to clarify the meaning of blessed bread indicates that the giving and receiving of it was perceived by both priest and woman as potentially disruptive. For the clergy, it signified a dangerous slipping between signifier and signified, between bread as a symbol of community, and bread transformed into the consecrated body of Christ. For the new mother, receiving blessed bread in the privileged physical and spiritual context of the churching ceremony called normalised, hierarchical social and gender roles into question. Given that the laity normally only received communion once a year, the singling out of a woman and giving her blessed bread in the sanctuary could well have been understood by her as an alternative or additional communion, thus reiterating the special value and disruptive potential of the service, that derived from childbearing itself.

Understanding the subversive and multivalent potential of the churching ceremony reveals that a woman could also have discerned such potential in her reception of images of the Virgin's Purification where she saw the Virgin, like herself, in close proximity to the altar and the priest. A woman's churching mirrored the Virgin's own appearance in the Temple forty days after the birth of Christ. On the one hand, the fact that the Virgin did not need to be purified put a distance between her and other mothers but, on the other, Mary's insistence on coming to the Temple like ordinary women made her a more accessible figure for Christian mothers. The rite therefore also brought them close to God's own mother who had also submitted to Levitical law.

Images of the Virgin's Purification were frequently depicted in Books of Hours at the hour of Nones, where they were sometimes conflated with the episode of Christ's Presentation in the Temple.[93] As in the examples from the *Fitzwilliam Hours* and the *Hours of Margaret of Foix*, Mary is depicted in the Temple in the company of other women, who bring offerings; she is also shown close to the altar and to the priest (figures 17–18). In fact, evidence from Eleanor of Poitiers' treatise shows that aspects of aristocratic women's churching bore some relationship to the images of the Virgin's Purification. For instance, Eleanor describes how a princess being churched should make an offering of a candle containing a piece of gold or silver, and how she should also bring a loaf of bread and a carafe of wine. These gifts are, she says, to be carried by the women accompanying her, just as the female servants in the *Purification* images noted here carry baskets with the Virgin's offerings.[94] Therefore, in the same way that it has been suggested lay women understood post-partum images of childbirth as allusions to the comfort and disruption of the lying-in period, it is also possible that they viewed images of the Purification as evidence not only of their participation in official church law but also of their proximity to the Virgin, in many other ways a seemingly unattainable figure. Furthermore, the paradox inherent in the Virgin's own, unnecessary, churching also

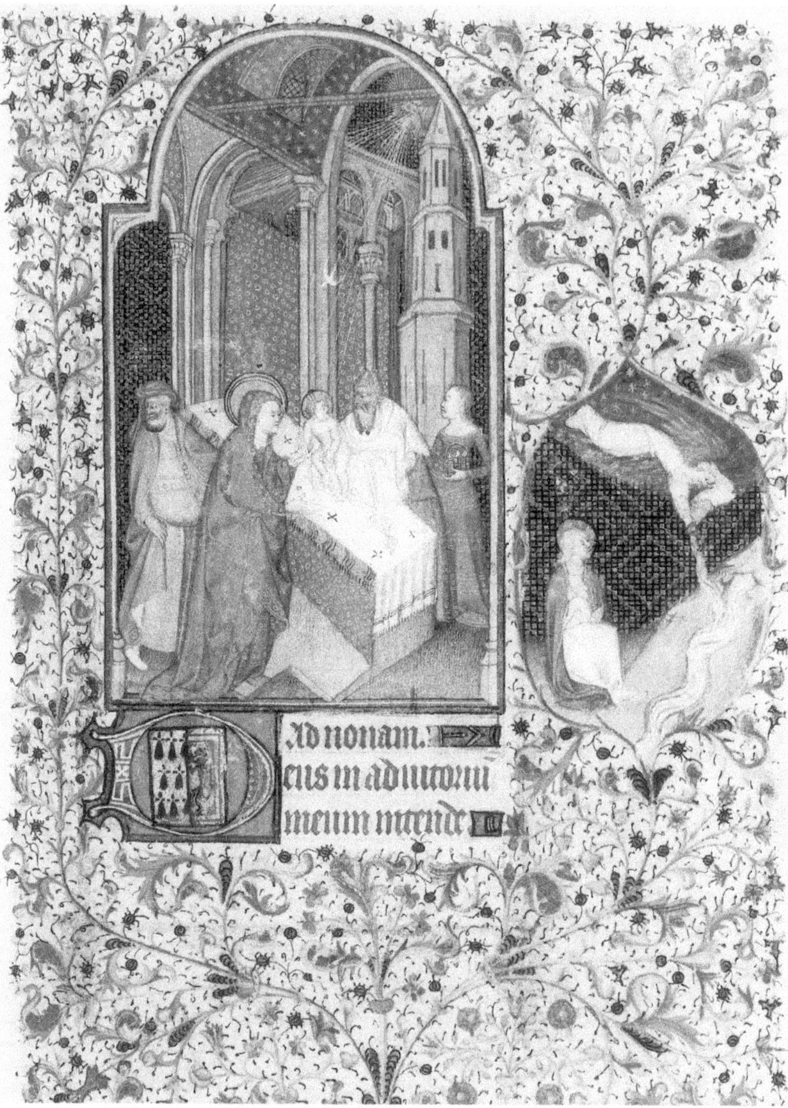

17   Rohan Workshop, *Presentation of Christ in the Temple* (*Virgin's Purification*), Nones, *Fitzwilliam Hours*, Cambridge, Fitzwilliam Museum, MS 62, fol. 81r, *c*.1418–30. Reproduction by permission of the Syndics of the Fitzwilliam Museum, Cambridge (© Cambridge, Fitzwilliam Museum)

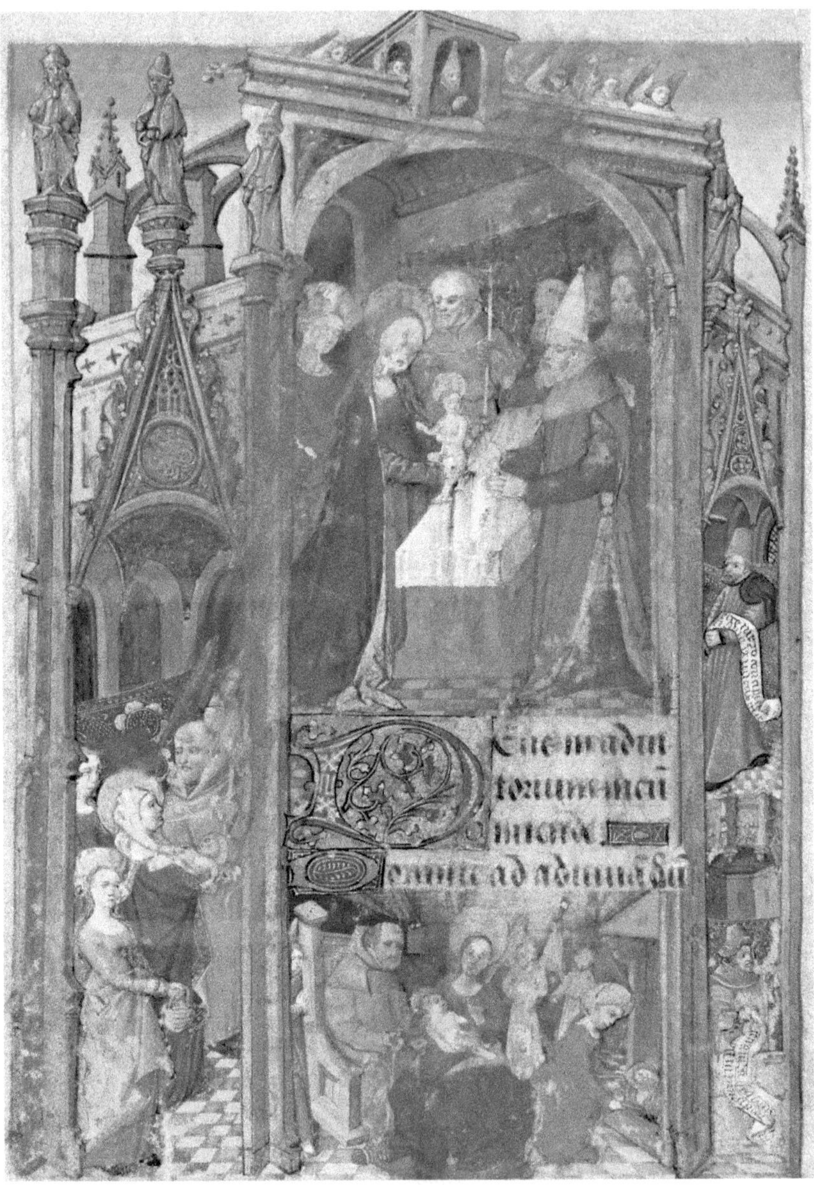

18   *Presentation of Christ in the Temple (Virgin's Purification)*, Nones,
Hours of Marguerite of Foix, London, Victoria and Albert Museum, Salting
MS 1222, fol. 78v, *c.*1477. Published by kind permission of the Board of
Trustees of the V&A (© V&A Images/Victoria and Albert Museum)

underlined the tensions inherent in the contemporary rite, as a simultaneous act of purification, healing, and celebration, where traditional gender roles were renegotiated.

In so far as it was a reincorporation, churching was a public event, taking place, like the Virgin's Purification, in the community and in front of witnesses. At all levels of society it could become a cause for celebration (*la feste des relevailles*) especially if the child was also doing well.[95] In aristocratic circles, in particular, churching provided another opportunity for the public display of the family's power, which complemented the preparations made for the lying-in and for the baptism which took place a few days after the birth, and without the mother.[96]

The churching of Elizabeth Woodville (mother of Elizabeth of York, the wife of Henry VII) in 1465 was an event that was visible to the public and involved male members of the royal household. An account of the ceremony was recorded by Gabriel Tetzel who, like Eleanor of Poitiers and Marguerite of Burgundy, was also particularly sensitive to the formalities and display of the event.[97] For instance, he remarks that on the way to the church the queen was preceded by 'a great company of ladies and maidens' and a procession of musicians and the king's choir 'forty-two of them, who sang excellently'.[98] As in the visits to the lying-in room, it is the mother who remains central to the proceedings and as Marguerite of Burgundy's letter to Isabel of Portugal suggests, women were even instrumental in defining and transmitting information about certain details of the ceremony. Marguerite advises Isabel that on the day she leaves her bed (*le jour que vous devez relever*) she must be assisted by two baronesses who will draw back the covers of the bed. The highest-ranking lord there should then take Isabel by the arms, lead her from her bed, and accompany her to and from the church.[99] As noted above, Marguerite advises Isabel that she should be dressed in ducal insignia (*en habit royal*) and Eleanor notes that women attend their churching richly ornamented (*ornées richement*).[100] Although she remarks that less festivity and more simplicity is preferable (more *honneste*), it is still a happy time for all those involved and one can make reasonably merry, each according to his or her estate (*peut on faire chere raisonnable, selon l'estat de chacun*).[101]

The importance of quality hangings to decorate childbirth chambers was demonstrated earlier in this chapter and in the following it will be argued that the allusions to these in images of holy motherhood provided a way to indicate the status not only of the holy families but also to draw parallels between them and the families of the manuscripts' readers. However, Eleanor's description of churching is interesting because in its emphasis on simplicity, and perhaps therefore humility, it draws a direct parallel between the humble status, both spiritual and material, of the Virgin at her purification and that of the aristocratic woman. In the same way that the Virgin brought herself down to the level of ordinary women in acquiescing to the purification rite despite the fact that her virginity remained intact, so could the aristocratic woman eschew rich trappings and gifts and bring herself down to the level of the Virgin's material poverty, indicated by her offering of two doves. The proximity that the rituals and images of lying-in and churching establish between the Virgin and other holy mothers and the female readers of the manuscripts form an important point for discussion in the subsequent chapters.

The evidence presented here indicates that the ceremony of lying-in offered suitable post-partum care for a newly-delivered mother and that the rite of churching provided a context within the official liturgy whereby thanks could be given for a mother's deliverance from childbirth. The lying-in ceremony could entail much preparation and expense for families across the social strata and for aristocratic families in particular it was an opportunity for self-promotion and public display. This display reinforced the importance of childbearing for the patriline and thus reveals the way women's bodies were appropriated for what Butler called the 'exigencies of kinship'. However, this is not the sole interpretation possible: the benefits that the lying-in ceremony brought to the mother herself should not be overlooked. A mother who could expect to enjoy a well-attended lying-in was not only provided with nourishing foods and bed-rest but she and her child, if it survived, also became the centre of attention. The refocusing of the household and the family's interests, spaces and finances on the mother placed the woman 'on top' in a way that upset the usual routine.

Knowledge of the lying-in ceremony and awareness of the way it disrupted the normalised gender roles of patriarchal society were important cognitive habits informing the situational eye. They are thus central to understanding how lay women involved in childbirth received and interpreted generic images of miraculous births and holy motherhood in their manuscripts as more than simple admonitions to wifely chastity and encouragement to ideal motherhood. A further cognitive habit explored in this chapter was the sensitivity to fabrics and furnishings for the lying-in chamber. The purchasing of special fabrics and linens for a birth also marked the mother out for special attention and, in some cases, was used to indicate her degree of estate. Eleanor of Poitiers' treatise demonstrates that aristocratic women were especially familiar with different types of fabrics, their colours, cost and usage. By this token, it has been suggested that an aristocratic viewer, especially a woman involved in childbearing, would have noted the rich colours and attention to details of furnishings of estate in images such as the *Birth of the Virgin* and the *Purification*.

The ceremony of churching, which followed the lying-in period, is a complicated rite that on the one hand appears to reinforce the victim-empowerment binary explored earlier. At an ecclesiastical level, churching underlined women's inferior place in social and gender hierarchies and stressed their physical impurity following childbirth. The rite thus promoted notions of male (clerical) superiority in which the woman always remains subjected. However, from the participating woman's point of view, the ceremony also embodied other meanings: it gave recognition to the dangers of childbearing, honouring the role of motherhood, and it sanctioned the female-orientated 'ceremony' of childbirth which it concluded.[102] In particular, by privileging a sexually-active woman and making her the centre of her own ecclesiastical rite in one of the most important parts of the church, it had the potential to bring the prevailing social and gender hierarchies into question by placing the woman 'on top'. As Rieder acknowledges, 'While medieval women and men would never have described the subversion of gender roles and identities as an alternative meaning of churching, they could surely have perceived the possibilities inherent in the flexibility of the ritual actions and objects used in the rite.'[103]

Given the pressure on young fifteenth-century lay women to bear children and the difficulties associated with conception and birth, churching, like the lying-in ceremony and the prayers discussed in Chapter 2, offered a lay woman a means to negotiate and manage the roles assigned to her by society by providing practical support and acknowledgement. While to some people in the fifteenth century, and even to modern critics, these ceremonies reinforced the subjugation of the female sex, it is important to note their multivalency and to recognise the benefits that they held for the participants. The danger otherwise lies in dismissing the ceremonies as part of the inevitable, controlling, forces of patriarchal society together with any possibility for women to exercise agency or opinion within that society.

Combining the material discussed in the previous chapters with the nuanced interpretations of lying-in and churching offered here, the second part of this book turns to an in-depth analysis of manuscripts owned by aristocratic lay women who were, or who became, wives and mothers. These chapters demonstrate how the cognitive habits analysed thus far informed these women's reception of the images and prayers in their manuscripts. Placing the manuscripts and their contents in the context of the childbirth ceremony available to aristocratic women, it is argued that these women viewed images of holy birth and motherhood as allegorical versions of their own childbearing through which they could pray for God's intervention for a successful delivery and recovery, and find an acknowledgement of the value of their role as childbearers within a patriarchal society.

Notes

1 Jacques Paviot, '*Les États de France (Les Honneurs de la cour) d'Éleonore de Poitiers*', *Annuaire-Bulletin de la Société de l'Histoire de la France*, 1996, 75–125 (pp. 120–1). See also his article, 'Les Honneurs de la cour d'Éléonore de Poitiers', in *Autour de Marguerite d'Écosse: Reines, princesses et dames du XVe siècle, Actes du colloque de Thouars (23 et 24 mai 1997)*, ed. by Geneviève and Philippe Contamine (Paris: Champion, 1999), pp. 163–79. All subsequent references to Paviot are to '*Les États*'.

2 Paviot, p. 124.

3 Paviot, pp. 122; 124.

4 Paviot, pp. 122–3.

5 Paviot, p. 125.

6 In Leviticus 12 it was specified that a mother should wait forty days after the birth of a boy and eighty days after the birth of a girl before being purified.

7 See Arnold Van Gennep, *The Rites of Passage*, trans. by Monika B. Vizedom and Gabrielle L. Caffee (London: Routledge & Kegan Paul, 1960), esp. pp. 46–7; William Coster, 'Purity, Profanity, and Puritanism: the Churching of Women, 1500–1700', in *Woman and the Church*, Church History 27 (Oxford: Basil Blackwell, 1990), pp. 377–87.

8 See, for example, Adrian Wilson, 'The Ceremony of Childbirth and its Interpretation', in *Women as Mothers in Pre-Industrial England: Essays in Memory of Dorothy McLaren*, ed. by Valerie Fildes (London: Routledge, 1990), pp. 68–107; and Paula M. Rieder, *On the Purification of Women: Churching in Northern France, 1100–1500* (New York: Palgrave Macmillan, 2006). For an overview of interpretations of the rite throughout history, see also Peter Rushton 'Purification or Social Control? Ideologies of Reproduction and the Churching of Women after Childbirth', in *The Public and the Private*, ed. by Eva Gamarnikow *et al.* (London: Heinemann, 1983), pp. 118–31.

9 Rieder, *Purification*, pp. 139–41.

10 See Green's entry under 'Childbirth and Infancy' in the *Dictionary of the Middle Ages*, Supplement I, www.gale.com/pdf/samples/sp806428.pdf (Accessed 26 July 2006), pp. 108–13 (p. 111) where she also notes that 'Jewish and Muslim women likely had similar [lying-in] practices, though little work on their traditions has so far been published'.

11 See Rieder, *Purification*, pp. 67–9.

12 For the early modern period Wilson suggests that lying-in had 'much scope for flexibility' and it was an event that crossed social boundaries. See Wilson, 'Participant or Patient? Seventeenth-century Childbirth from the Mother's Point

of View', in *Patients and Practitioners: Lay Perceptions of Medicine in Pre-Industrial Society*, ed. by Roy Porter (Cambridge: Cambridge University Press, 1985), pp. 129–44 (p. 139).

13 Musacchio, p. 39; Wilson, 'Participant or Patient?', p. 138; Becky Lee, 'A Company of Women *and* Men: Men's Recollections of Childbirth in Medieval England', *Journal of Family History*, 27 (2002), 92–100 (p. 96).

14 Musacchio, p. 53; and Haas, pp. 91–3.

15 Monique Sommé, 'Le Cérémonial de la naissance et de la mort de l'enfant princier à la cour de Bourgogne au XVe siècle', in *À la cour de Bourgogne: le duc, son entourage, son train*, ed. by Jean-Marie Cauchies (Turnhout: Brepols, 1998), pp. 32–48 (p. 38).

16 A complete edition of Eleanor's treatise, in the original French only, has been published by Paviot. An extract with a freely arranged English translation is included in Penelope Eames, *Furniture in England, France and the Netherlands from the Twelfth to the Fifteenth Century* (London: Furniture History Society, 1977), pp. 257–73.

17 Paviot, p. 100.

18 Paviot, p. 100. The darkening of the room was a feature that had particular benefits for the mother since in the nineteenth century it was discovered it that it helped to prevent her from developing eclampsia; see Wilson, *The Making of Man-Midwifery: Childbirth in England 1660–1770* (London: UCL Press Ltd, 1995), p. 29.

19 Wilson, *Man-Midwifery*, p. 29.

20 Green, *Trotula*, pp. 106–9.

21 Musacchio, pp. 47, 56.

22 Wilson, *Man-Midwifery*, pp. 26–9.

23 Musacchio, pp. 40–1.

24 Musacchio, p. 40.

25 Musacchio, pp. 41–2.

26 Paviot, p. 100.

27 Paviot, pp. 105; 108.

28 Lee, 'A Company of Women *and* Men', p. 96; Wilson, 'Participant or Patient?', pp. 135–8. The fourteenth-century mystic Margery Kempe imagined carrying a flask of 'pyment' or spiced wine in her vision of assisting at the birth of St John the Baptist. See *The Book of Margery Kempe*, ed. by Barry Windeatt (Harlow: Longman, 2000), p. 76. Wilson ('The Ceremony of Childbirth', pp. 73–4) notes that the fortifying and restorative effects of the caudle means it was also prepared for sick people. Thus Margery Kempe also prepares a 'good cawdel' for the suffering Virgin in her vision of the Crucifixion, *The Book of Margery Kempe*, p. 352.

29 Wilson, 'Participant or Patient?', pp. 135–8.

30 Musacchio, pp. 40–1. The painting in question is on the outer wing of a private altarpiece, *c.*1367, London, National Gallery (NG701).

31 Baxandall, p. 37.

32 Eames, p. 77.

33 Christine de Pizan, *Le Livre des Trois Vertus*, ed. by Charity Cannon Willard (Paris: Champion, 1989), pp. 184–6. In the *Book of the Knight of the Tower* the author advises his daughters not to follow the example of the king and queen of Cyprus whose overly elaborate post-partum festivities displeased God and resulted in the smothering of the child. See *The Book of the Knight of La Tour-Landry*, ed. by Thomas Wright, Early English Text Society, extra series 33 (London: N. Trüber, 1868), pp. 110–11.

34 Paviot, p. 80. See also Bernard Chevalier who cites Eleanor's treatise in discussing Marie of Anjou's *gésine*: 'Marie d'Anjou, une reine sans gloire, 1404–1463', in *Autour de Marguerite d'Écosse*, ed. by Contamine and Contamine, pp. 81–98 (p. 90).

35 Paviot, p. 125.

36 Paviot, p. 98.

37 Paviot, p. 99.

38 Paviot, pp. 98–100.

39 Paviot, p. 106.

40 Paviot, p. 106.

41 Paviot, p. 100.

42 Paviot, pp. 100–1.

43 Paviot, p. 99.

44 Paviot, p. 121.

45 Paviot, p. 121: 'Item, debvez avoir quatre petits coussinetz, grands d'un pied et d'un tour de large, et de deux pieds de long ou moins de veloux, . . . et brodéz de perles à telles devises qu'il vous plaira. Et chascun coussinet doibt avoir aux quatre coings quatre gros bouttons estofféz de la plus belle et nouvelle façon.'

46 Baxandall, p. 39.

47 *The Wardrobe Accounts of Edward IV*: Part XXIX. Full text published online by the Richard III Society: www.r3.org/bookcase/wardrobe/ward19.html (Accessed 19 April 2007).

48 *Wardrobe Accounts*: Part XXIX.

49 Phillis Cunnington and Catherine Lucas, *Costume for Births, Marriages and Deaths* (London: Adam and Charles Black, 1972), p. 17; and Kay Staniland, 'Royal Entry into the World', in *England in the Fifteenth Century: Harlaxton Symposium*, ed. by Daniel Williams (Woodbridge: Boydell, 1987), pp. 297–313 (p. 309).

50 See Staniland, p. 312. See also Musacchio, p. 46; and Sommé, pp. 37–8.

51 Musacchio, p. 46.

52 Paviot, pp. 99–101: 'Le . . . dressoir et les degréz estoient tous chargéz de vaisselles de cristal, garnies d'or et de pierreries. Et si en y avoit de fin or, car toute la plus riche vaisselle du duc Philippe y estoit, tant de pots, de tasses, comme de couppes de fin or, autres vaisselles et bassins, lesquels on y met jamais qu'en tel cas. Entre autre vaisselle, il y avoit sur le dit dessoir deux drageoirs d'or et des pierreries dont l'un estoit estimé à quarente mil escus, & l'autre à trente mil. Sur ledit dressoir estoit tendu un dorsset de drap d'or cramoisy bordé de veloux noir. Et sur le velour noir estoit brodé de fin or la devise de Monseigneur le duc Philippe, qui estoit le fusil.'

106

53 The child, Mary of Burgundy, though not the son that the duchy needed to ensure the Burgundian line, did, however, inherit the duchy of Burgundy. But it passed to the Austrian empire when she married Maximilian I in 1477.

54 Sommé, p. 37.

55 Paviot, p. 121.

56 Staniland, p. 309.

57 Musacchio, p. 53; Lee, 'A Company of Women *and* Men', p. 97. See also Klapisch-Zuber, pp. 132–64.

58 Lee, 'A Company of Women *and* Men', p. 96.

59 See David Cressy, *Birth, Marriage, and Death: Ritual, Religion, and the Life-Cycle in Tudor and Stuart England* (Oxford: Oxford University Press, 1997), p. 44.

60 For example, as noted above, Eleanor of Navarre had at least nine children in 22 years with Gaston of Foix; Elizabeth of York had eight children between 1486 and 1503.

61 Wilson, *Man-Midwifery*, p. 27.

62 Sommé, p. 38.

63 In the *Quinze joies de mariage* (*c*.1400) or the post-Reformation *Batchelor's Banquet* (1603), female-orientated childbearing customs were criticised by a hen-pecked husband running round after his wife and her companions. See Cressy, *Birth, Marriage and Death*, p. 55.

64 Wilson, 'The Ceremony of Childbirth', p. 86, emphasis original.

65 Zemon Davis, p. 131.

66 Zemon Davis, p. 131; n. 37.

67 Musacchio, p. 64ff.

68 On marriage *cassoni* see Cristelle L. Baskins, *Cassone Painting, Humanism, and Gender in Early Modern Italy* (Cambridge and New York: Cambridge University Press, 1998).

69 Musacchio, p. 55; text accompanying figure 39; and p. 130.

70 See the many examples reproduced in Musacchio, such as the Florentine birth tray now in the Ca' d'Oro, Venice (figure 18).

71 On the place that birth trays and other objects to do with childbearing retained in the home after the birth, see Musacchio, p. 14.

72 See Wilson, 'Participant or Patient?', p. 139; Cressy, 'Purification, Thanksgiving and the Churching of Women in Post-Reformation England', *Past and Present*, 141 (1993), 106–46 (pp. 112–13); and Gibson, 'Blessing from Sun and Moon: Churching as Women's Theater', in *Bodies and Disciplines: Intersections of Literature and History in Fifteenth-Century England*, ed. by Barbara A. Hanawalt and David Wallace (London and Minneapolis: University of Minnesota Press, 1996), pp. 139–54 (p. 149). The principal analysis of the rite is found in Adolph Franz, *Die kirchlichen Benediktionem im Mittelalter*, 2 vols (Frieburg: Herder, 1909; repr., Graz: Akademischer Druck u.-Verlagsanstalt, 1960).

73 In addition to Coster and Cressy, 'Purification' noted above, see also Lee, 'The Purification of Women After Childbirth: A Window onto Medieval Perceptions of Women', *Florilegium*, 14 (1995–96), 43–55; Joanne M. Pierce, ' "Green Women" and Blood Pollution: Some Medieval Rituals for the Churching of Women after Childbirth', *Studia Liturgica*, 29 (1999), 191–215.

74 Rieder, *Purification*, pp. 2, 5. See also her article 'Insecure Borders: Symbols of Clerical Privilege and Gender Ambiguity in the Liturgy of Churching', in *The Material Culture of Sex*, ed. by McClanan and Encarnación, pp. 93–113.

75 Rieder, *Purification*, p. 125.

76 Rieder, *Purification*, p. 84.

77 Rieder, *Purification*, p. 64.

78 Rieder, 'Insecure Borders', p. 95; n. 8.

79 Rieder, *Purification*, p. 120. Although, as noted above, the medieval Christian church took its cue regarding blood taboos from Jewish laws, Cathy McClive has argued that the biblical texts were not originally misogynistic but were concerned with the optimum conditions for healthy procreation. See Cathy McClive, 'Engendrer durant les menstrues: devoir conjugal et interdit sexuel à l'époque moderne', in *Le désir et le goût: une autre histoire (XIIIe–XVIIIe siècles), actes du colloque international à la mémoire de Jean-Louis Flandrin, Saint-Denis, septembre 2003*, ed. by Odile Redon, Line Sallman and Sylvie Steinberg (Paris: Presses Universitaire de Vincennes, 2005), pp. 245–63.

80 Pierce, pp. 198–9.

81 Rieder, *Purification*, p. 85.

82 Rieder, *Purification*, p. 99; and 'Insecure Borders', p. 99.

83 Rieder, 'Insecure Borders', p. 93; *Purification*, pp. 100–1.

84 On the veil, which appears to have become a point of contention between female participants and the clergy in the post-Reformation period, see Coster, p. 384; and Cressy, 'Purification', pp. 312–33.

85 Gibson, 'Blessing', p. 149.

86 Wilson, *Man-Midwifery*, p. 29.

87 Rieder, 'Insecure Borders', p. 104; see also *Manuale et processionale ad usum insignis ecclesiae eboracensis*, ed. by W. G. Henderson, Surtees Society 63 (London: Whittaker and Co, 1875), pp. 213–14.

88 Rieder, *Purification*, p. 100.

89 Rieder, *Purification*, pp. 95–6.

90 Rieder, 'Insecure Borders', p. 105.

91 Rieder, 'Insecure Borders', p. 105.

92 Rieder, 'Insecure Borders', p. 105 and n. 27.

93 Dorothy C. Shorr, 'The Iconographic Development of the Presentation in the Temple', *Art Bulletin*, 28 (1946), 17–31.

94 Paviot, p. 111.

95 Women too sick to attend a public churching could receive the ceremony privately at home, although this would presumably be less cause for celebration. See Rieder, pp. 111; 113.

96 On baptism, see Staniland. Eleanor of Poitiers also includes descriptions of arrangements for the baptism of aristocratic children, including Philip the Fair. See Paviot, pp. 105–6, and 108–11.

97 *The Travels of Leo Rozmital: Through Germany, Flanders, England, France, Spain, Portugal, and Italy, 1465–1467*, trans. and ed. by Malcom Letts, Hakluyt

Society, second series, 108 for 1955 (Cambridge: Cambridge University Press, 1957), pp. 45–6.

98 *Rozmital*, pp. 45–6.

99 Paviot, p. 125.

100 Paviot, pp. 111; 125.

101 Paviot, p. 111.

102 Rieder, *Purification*, pp. 100–1.

103 Rieder, 'Insecure Borders', p. 108.

PART II

Manuscript case studies from the houses of Anjou, Brittany and France

4

Holy mothers, sainted monarchs and *beata stirps*: the *Fitzwilliam Hours* and Books of Hours for the house of Anjou

The first part of this study has proposed a methodological and material context, within which the reception and meanings of images of holy motherhood can be approached. Through the concept of the situational eye, it has been suggested that both lay men and women of a certain social status were trained, like the agent of Baxandall's period eye, to be receptive to religious stories and visual representations relating to miraculous conceptions and blessed mothers. Exploring in detail the cognitive habits and culturally-relative experience informing the situational eye has shown that images of St Anne and narratives of holy births were closely linked to practices and cultures associated with conception, childbearing and family in the fifteenth century. Therefore, it has been argued, lay women's identification with holy mothers like St Anne and St Elizabeth did not necessarily simply reiterate their subjugation within a society that relied on their ability to conceive male heirs for the continuation of the patriline. Instead, by viewing images of the Holy Kinship through the lens of the socially-constructed situational eye, the critic can see how a female viewer could be acutely aware of the limitations of her gender role and of the expectations placed up on her, but could also manage those expectations for her own benefit through the models presented in the images. For example, Anne of France appropriated the Holy Kinship for her own personal and political purposes through identification with St Anne, her daughters and their miraculous stories of childbearing and blessed lineage. This chapter and the following show how such an understanding of maternal and dynastic imagery can be applied to a group of prayer books associated with the houses of Anjou and Brittany – two influential families in the politics of fifteenth-century France.

These two chapters centre on three manuscripts which were commissioned and owned by lay, aristocratic, female readers. Between them, these manuscripts contain a number of images and texts associated with holy motherhood, blessed dynasties and miraculous conceptions: the *Fitzwilliam Hours*, owned by a succession of Angevin and Breton duchesses, the Book of Hours belonging to Marguerite of Foix, duchess of Brittany, and the prayer book belonging to her daughter, Anne of Brittany.[1]

It has been shown that the skills or experiences regarding the reception of narratives of holy motherhood and the ceremonies of contemporary childbearing were more easily acquired by lay women than lay men. A focus on manuscripts owned by women who were expected to bear children as part of their duties as aristocratic wives therefore provides a historically-specific way of interpreting the wider significance of maternal imagery for certain female viewers in the later middle ages. However, as discussed in the preceding chapters, the situational eye as an interpretative strategy does not assume that the agent is gendered masculine or feminine since evidence shows that men also expressed anxieties about the birth of children, took active steps to secure their lineage, and celebrated a birth with suitable attention to detail. Therefore, in order to demonstrate that lay men could also be sensitive to narratives of holy, miraculous childbearing, the analysis of the female-owned *Fitzwilliam Hours* in this chapter is placed in the context of manuscripts owned by male members of the house of Anjou. Doing so aims to avoid a ghettoising of 'women's' viewing or reading into a separate category from 'men's', by showing that the commissioning and political interests of aristocratic men and women were often closely related. By putting the situational eye into practice, the evidence presented here offers further answers to the questions posed at the beginning of this book regarding the gendering of female-dominated imagery and how it can be employed by (art) historians to understand better the lives and viewing interests of women in the middle ages.

The *Fitzwilliam Hours*: commission and provenance

This chapter centres on the *Fitzwilliam Hours* and its place in the artistic commissions of the house of Anjou in the first part of the fifteenth century. Like those of Berry and Burgundy, the house of Anjou was a *maison cadette* of the house of France and during the late fourteenth and early fifteenth century, the dukes of Anjou, as *princes de sang royal*, were closely involved in governing the kingdom of France.[2] The *Fitzwilliam Hours* were probably commissioned by Duchess Yolande of Aragon (d. 1442), wife of

Duke Louis II of Anjou (1377–1417). The manuscript is discussed here in relation to three others commissioned by or associated with the house of Anjou in the early fifteenth century: the *Rohan Hours*, now in Paris, and two Books of Hours acquired by René of Anjou, now conserved in Paris and London.[3] Although all these manuscripts have previously been studied together for their stylistic relationships, the *Fitzwilliam Hours* has never been placed at the centre of an enquiry and the subtleties of the manuscript's contents have not been explored in detail. Moving beyond a simply stylistic approach, this chapter reveals the particular cognitive habits informing the Angevin situational eye by analysing the contexts in which these manuscripts were commissioned, acquired and read. Starting with Yolande of Aragon and her commission of the *Fitzwilliam Hours*, it is argued that the Angevin dukes and duchesses and their protégés were attuned to the social expectations placed upon them as rulers, advisers and (potential) parents, and that they drew on themes of holy motherhood, blessed lineage (*beata stirps*) and dynastic connections with the house of France to assert and execute their positions as members of one of France's leading families.

The *Fitzwilliam Hours* was produced by the Rohan workshop, which was active in France during the first half of the fifteenth century (*c*.1410–40).[4] The manuscript is well known among art historians for the cycle of marginal images illustrating the *Three Pilgrimages* of Guillaume Deguileville and the *Apocalypse* of St John, which occurs throughout the volume. This profuse illustrative programme, coupled with the size of the volume and its integrated portraits, indicates that the manuscript was an expensive, bespoke volume.[5] Internal heraldic evidence and the portrait at the opening of the *Obsecro te* prayer on fol. 20r (plate 7) show that the manuscript was once in the possession of Isabel Stuart (1427– after 1494), daughter of James I of Scotland, and Lady Joan Beaufort, who became the second wife of Duke Francis I of Brittany (1414–50) in 1442.

Isabel's ownership of the *Fitzwilliam Hours* is discussed in detail in Chapter 5, but the volume dates from some time before Isabel's marriage, since her portrait and the arms of Brittany impaling Scotland on many of the pages are later additions.[6] The female forms, such as *peccatrix*, and *famula et serva tua*, found in the *Creator celi* prayer indicate that the original owner was certainly a woman (see fols 137r–140r). The profusion of Marian and maternal imagery throughout the manuscript would, following existing studies of female-owned manuscripts discussed at the beginning of this study, indicate that the owner was perhaps a lay woman who had, or who was expected to bear, children. The inclusion of two marginal images on folios 139v and 140r of a woman dressed as a widow or a nun and praying at an altar, on which Christ appears, is a further suggestion of female ownership (figure 19).

It is widely agreed that Isabel Stuart inherited the *Fitzwilliam Hours* from her husband's first wife, Yolande of Anjou (1412–40), whose mother, Yolande of Aragon, was a patron of the Rohan Master and his workshop.[7] Yolande of Aragon's involvement with the *Fitzwilliam Hours* is implied, in particular, by the inclusion of Angevin saints in the suffrages (short, intercessory prayers), and the incorporation of the marginal *Apocalypse* and *Pilgrimage* cycles – works which were especially popular among people in her entourage. The precise dating of the manuscript has, however, been a matter of debate, polarising scholarly opinions about whether Yolande originally commissioned the manuscript for herself or for her daughter.[8] Those arguing for a later date, of around 1430, have proposed that Yolande commissioned the manuscript for the marriage of her youngest daughter to the future Francis I of Brittany in 1431.[9] Others, maintaining that the manuscript seems stylistically much earlier (between 1415 and 1418), have suggested that Yolande of Aragon was herself the original owner and that she passed it to her daughter on her marriage.[10]

Camille has thus argued that the manuscript was produced around 1418 and that the miniatures of the woman dressed in black in the *Creator celi* and *Suscipiat pietas* prayers represent Yolande of Aragon in mourning for her husband, who died on 29 April 1417, a idea since followed up by Anne-Marie Legaré and Richard K. Emmerson.[11] Although it is impossible to recover with absolute certainty the early history of the *Fitzwilliam Hours*, the following section shows how the saints included in the manuscript's suffrages reveal the likelihood that Yolande of Aragon was its original commissioner and that she commissioned it as a statement of her, and her family's, status and power. Establishing the specifically Angevin aspects of the *Fitzwilliam Hours* and the way the manuscript celebrates Yolande's family heritage is an important step in analysing how the manuscript later functioned for her daughter Yolande of Anjou.

An Angevin Holy Kinship: Yolande of Aragon and the suffrages of the *Fitzwilliam Hours*

Yolande of Aragon was the only surviving child of King John I of Aragon (1350–96). Since inheritance laws prevented her from succeeding her father, the crown of Aragon passed instead to her uncle, Martin I (1356–1410). The marriage between Yolande of Aragon and Louis II of

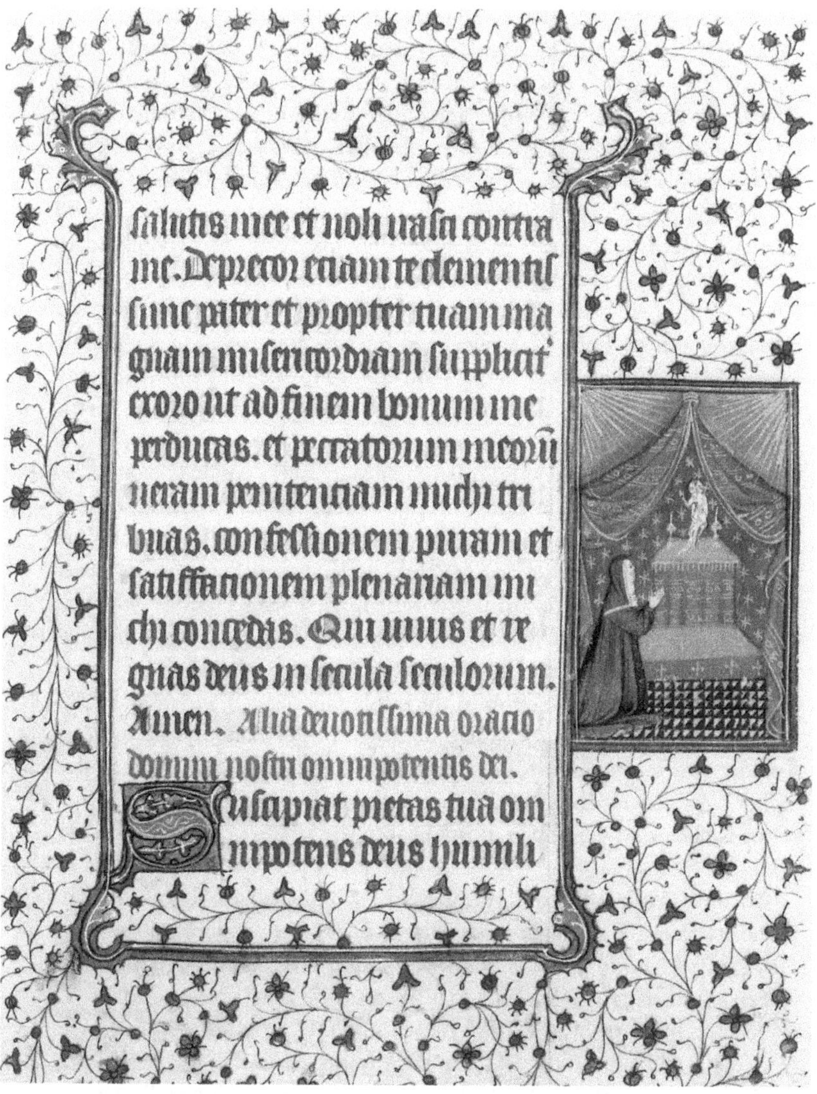

19   Rohan Workshop, Woman habited in black kneeling before an altar, *Suscipiat pietatis*, *Fitzwilliam Hours*, Cambridge, Fitzwilliam Museum, MS 62, fol. 140r, *c.*1418–30. Reproduction by permission of the Syndics of the Fitzwilliam Museum, Cambridge (© Cambridge, Fitzwilliam Museum)

Anjou in 1400 was intended as a means of resolving the on-going dispute between the houses of Anjou and Aragon over the kingdoms of Naples and Sicily.[12] Through this marriage Yolande acquired the title of Queen of the Four Kingdoms: Sicily, Naples, Jerusalem and Aragon. Although these titles remained open to dispute and were often held in name only, Yolande and her family, nevertheless, styled themselves kings and queens.[13]

Yolande played an important role in governing the duchy of Anjou during Louis II's absences in Italy.[14] After his death, she continued to defend Angevin rights to the kingdom of Naples and to the throne of Aragon, supporting the campaigns of her sons Louis III (1403–34) and René in southern Italy. Given her own background, Yolande was highly aware of the importance of marriage and children, especially sons, in resolving political and territorial problems. She thus took an active interest in the upbringing and marriages of her own children and those of others, like the future Charles VII and her granddaughter Margaret of Anjou (1430–82), to enhance the position of the house of Anjou on the French political scene.[15] Yolande's intention to marry her eldest son Louis to Isabelle, the daughter of John V of Brittany (1340–99), may have been intended as a way to break the support of the house of Brittany for the English king, Henry V, who was contesting the rights of Charles VI's sons to the French crown. The marriage never took place and Louis eventually married Marguerite of Savoy but Yolande continued to support the future Charles VII and to foster ties with the dukes of Brittany.[16] The marriage of her daughter Yolande to Francis, heir to the duchy of Brittany, in 1431, is likely to have been aided by her close relationship with Francis's uncle and (later) successor, Arthur III of Richemont, whom she brought into the French royal circle in the 1420s.[17]

Yolande's support for and relationship with the house of France took its authority from the Angevin dukes' status as *princes de sang* and she carefully sought to bring the two houses even closer together through the union of her eldest daughter Marie (1404–63) and the third son of Charles VI (1368–1422) and Isabeau of Bavaria (d. 1435), Charles of Ponthieu, who were engaged from 1414.[18] Charles came under Yolande's protection and tutelage, a protection which intensified when the boy unexpectedly became dauphin in 1417. The union between Charles and Marie reinforced the existing links between the two houses and allowed Yolande and, later, her son René to exploit their royal connections to the maximum. Later in her life, Yolande had a similarly formative role in the upbringing of her granddaughter, Margaret of Anjou, future queen of England who lived with her for eight years.[19] Yolande, therefore, embraced a number of social roles during her lifetime: as duchess, ruler, mother and counsellor. These roles were all referred to in the *Fitzwilliam Hours* through the saints included in the manuscript's suffrages. In particular, the saints provide examples of leadership, mothering, wise parenting (both biological and social), and of the blessed lineage, or *beata stirps*, of the Angevin and French dynasties. All these elements combined to provide models from which Yolande could derive her own authority in directing and influencing the future of the houses of France and Anjou.

A discussion of the blessed lineage of the houses of France and Anjou needs to be placed in the wider context of the tendency to 'sanctify' noble families in the middle ages. In his study of dynastic cults in medieval Europe, Gábor Klaniczay has noted that the 'very number of saintly princesses among the offspring of the interrelated ruling families of Central Europe was enough to give contemporaries the impression that sanctity was a hereditary trait specific to certain dynasties'.[20] Furthermore, he claims that this impression was strengthened by 'the Church's rounding out of the cult of the Virgin Mary with the cult of St Anne and of the Holy Family', which created a 'cultural milieu decidedly conducive to the triumphant revival of the archaic "*beata stirps*" concept'.[21]

One family that could boast such a blessed lineage was the Hungarian house of Arpad whose members included St Stephen (d. 1038) and his son St Emeric (d. 1031), St Ladislas (d. 1095) and St Elizabeth of Hungary (1207–31).[22] In the thirteenth century, the head of the Neapolitan Angevins, Duke Charles I of Anjou (1226–85), sought to link his own family to this holy dynasty by marrying one of the daughters of the Arpadian king, Bela IV.[23] Although Charles was not successful in his bid, he began working on other ways to 'soothe the critics of his ruthless and calculating power play with appeals to the saintliness of his dynasty'.[24] For instance, he drew on the revived cult of Charlemagne, king of the Franks and Holy Roman Emperor, who had been canonised in 1165. Prophecies about the second coming of Charlemagne were circulated widely throughout the high to late middle ages and some of them went as far as to name the new emperor as Charles, son of Charles (*Karolus fili Karoli*). As such, candidates for the new Charlemagne were found amongst rulers named Charles, especially those with fathers of the same name.[25] After the death of his brother, the pious Louis IX, in 1270, Charles I campaigned vigorously for his canonisation. In fact, during Louis's canonisation process, Charles made wider claims for the sanctity of the entire family, including his mother Blanche of Castile (1188–1252). He described Blanche as a 'holy soul' and a 'holy root who has brought forth holy branches' a reference not only to Louis IX but also to his two brothers, Robert of Artois and Alphonse of Poitiers, who he thought might also be candidates for sainthood.[26] Although Charles I died before Louis IX's canonisation in 1297 he had, nevertheless, set in motion the fashioning of an Angevin holy family that elevated the place of this royal house on the European political scene. Together with the prophecies concerning the new Charlemagne, the cult of Louis IX and his devotion to the relics of the Passion were harnessed by later kings of France and influenced Valois devotional trends for decades to come. It is shown below how René of Anjou demonstrated his loyalty to his royal cousins through a similar veneration of Passion relics.

Charles I finally saw his attempts to associate his lineage with that of the Arpadian dynasty when his son Charles (*c.* 1243–1309) married Mary of Hungary (*c.*1257–1323), the great-niece of St Elizabeth, in 1270. The second son born of this marriage, Louis of Toulouse, was later canonised, so consolidating the sanctity of both the Franco-Angevin and Arpadian families. The inclusion of St Elizabeth, St Louis of Toulouse and St Louis IX in the suffrages of the *Fitzwilliam Hours* thus strongly suggests the commissioner's interest in the idea of a Franco-Angevin *beata stirps*, something to which Yolande of Aragon would have been sensitive. In fact, Yolande's situational eye would certainly have been informed by the narratives of Angevin lineage not only through her position as duchess of Anjou, but also through her Aragonese heritage since St Elizabeth's half-sister Jolantha (a variation of the name Yolande), had married King James I of Aragon from whom Yolande was directly descended.[27] This personal connection to the Hungarian *beata stirps*, therefore, added authority to Yolande's position within the Angevin dynasty. The attention given in the *Fitzwilliam Hours'* suffrages to the Frankish queen Radegund and St Anne and her daughters, further reinforces the owner's concern with familial ties and, in particular, with consolidating connections between the houses of France and Anjou. Considering how the dynastic saints included in the suffrages relate to Yolande of Aragon's role in the politics of early fifteenth-century Anjou and France provides strong evidence to suggest that this duchess was the commissioner and initial owner of the *Fitzwilliam Hours*.

Suffrages or *memoriae* are a series of short, intercessory prayers usually found towards the end of Books of Hours. Many of the saints included in the suffrages were common to all Books of Hours, and included petitions to popular figures such as St Michael the Archangel, St Christopher, and Roman virgin martyrs like St Catherine and St Barbara. However, the inclusion of unusual or geographically-specific saints in the suffrages is often indicative of the patron's particular devotional interests. The following section considers those saints among the *Fitzwilliam Hours'* fifty-odd suffrages that suggest the patron's interest in Franco-Angevin *beata stirps* and the maternal saints of Christ's lineage.

The first of these is that of St Anne, whose *vita* made her an important devotional figure for people suffering from fertility problems, or for older married women and widows. The accent in the *Fitzwilliam Hours'* suffrage is upon Anne's broad appeal as a thrice-married woman, mother, grandmother and educator. The prayer refers to her as 'fortunate Anne' (*felix Anna*) and highlights her status as a married woman, wife of Joachim, and how she deserved to be the mother of the Virgin.[28] In the accompanying text miniature she is depicted with all three of her daughters: the Virgin, whom she had with St Joachim, and St Mary Salomé and St Mary Cleophas born of St Anne's subsequent marriages. All three women hold palms and an old man with a crutch follows behind them (plate 8).[29] St Anne appears as a guiding figure, turning back towards her daughters, whose own stances and dress imitate those of their mother. A marginal image on the same folio reiterates St Anne's place in the Holy Kinship by showing her kneeling, her hands clasped in prayer, before the Virgin and Child who are seated on the ground. The haloes on the figures emphasise the holy status of this intimate family group but a sense of humanity is retained in the humility pose of the Virgin and the way Christ reaches out His hand to His grandmother.

The unusual inclusion of a suffrage to St Mary Cleophas and St Mary Salomé, immediately following that of St Anne, reinforces this focus on the female lineage of the Holy Kinship.[30] As noted in the Introduction, these holy daughters of St Anne – half-sisters of the Virgin – were also the blessed mothers of saintly sons. The miniatures accompanying the prayer show them both with their holy offspring. The text miniature shows St Mary Cleophas with her four sons, who were said to include St James the Less and St Simon; in the border miniature, St Mary Salomé is shown accompanied by her two sons, St James the Great and St John the Evangelist (plate 9). In both miniatures the artist has used the same format as in the miniature of St Anne and her daughters on the preceding folio. Both Maries wear a blue and gold cloak over a red tunic and they both turn back towards their children who follow behind them holding palms. The four miniatures on these two pages thus provide several models of blessed motherhood, holy dynasty and successful procreation. They draw attention not only to the social roles expected of lay women as childbearers and as guiding figures for their children but also as key players in Christ's dynastic family. As such, the figures of St Anne and her daughters would have been extremely pertinent for Yolande of Aragon. Following her husband's death in 1417, the widowed Yolande was, like St Anne, the matriarch of an illustrious family which had long claimed holiness. She was also acting as a wise counsellor to her own children as well as to the future Charles VII. Yolande's social roles could thus easily have led her to identify with St Anne and the mothers of the Holy Kinship, just as her great-granddaughter Anne of France would do several decades later.

Dynastic and maternal themes are given further prominence in the *Fitzwilliam Hours* through the suffrage to the Frankish queen, St Radegund (d. 587). Seven scenes, more than those accorded to other saints in the manuscript, are dedicated to this saint (fols 224v–230v), indicating that she was of particular importance to the manuscript's commissioner. According to Camille, St Radegund provides additional evidence for Yolande of Aragon's ownership of the *Fitzwilliam Hours* since one of the variations of the saint's name was 'Aragone'.[31] St Radegund was the reluctant wife of King Clothaire, son of the first Frankish king, Clovis.[32] Unhappy in her marriage, this queen of France escaped from her husband and joined the Benedictine order, founding the abbey of Sainte-Croix in Poitiers.[33]

It might seem odd that Yolande of Aragon – who took an active role in secular life by asserting her own regal heritage and her sons' rights to the kingdoms of Naples and Aragon – should identify with a queen who gave up her royal status, fleeing her husband to become a nun. However, Véronique Day has pointed out that St Radegund's nobility and resolve of purpose made her 'a regal model of determination and success'.[34] As someone who was 'concerned with the affairs of her monastery as well as the affairs of state and the development of the kingdom' she earned the title 'mère de la patrie' and '[i]n the fifteenth century she continued to stand as a mother figure for the community'.[35] St Radegund was credited with several miracles both before and after her death, leading to an influx of pilgrims to the Poitou region, which adjoined that of Anjou, and made her a popular saint among families with royal connections. She thus represented a strong female figure, of noble birth, whose interest lay in devotion to God, in caring for others and in ruling her property.[36] Such characteristics were close to Yolande's own interests and St Radegund's connection with the Frankish kings and her devotion to the True Cross, which the French kings also shared, made her an appropriate model for Yolande's patronage of the dauphin, Charles.

The images of St Radegund in the suffrages of the *Fitzwilliam Hours* show her at different stages in her life and performing various acts of piety.

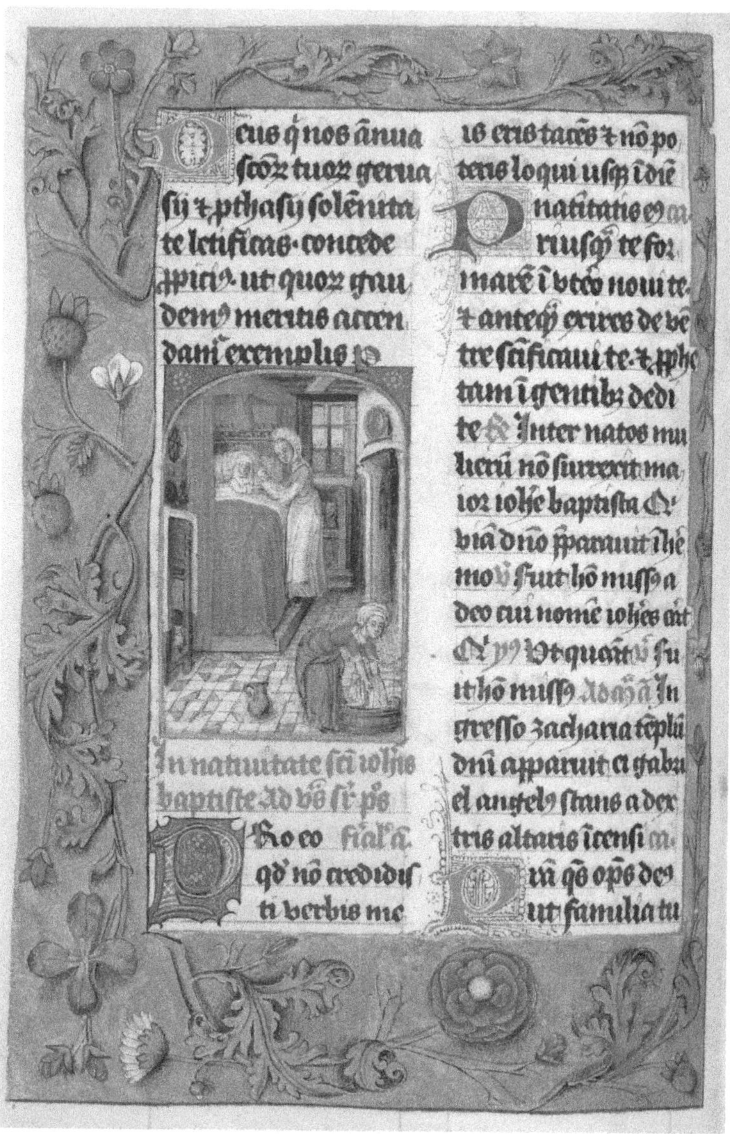

cus q̃ nos ãnua
scoz tuoz geuia
sij ꝓtſiaſij ſolẽnita
te letiſicas · concede
ꝓpici9 · ut quoz ẽnu
dem9 meritis accen
dam̃ exemplis ꝓ

In natiuitate ſc̃i iol̃is
baptiſte Ad uñ ſr̃ p̃s
Ro eo ſial̃ ã
q̃ nõ credidiſ
ti uerbis me

16 cris tacẽs 7 nõ po
tens loqui uſꝗ ĩ diẽ
natiuatie eo ꝓi
priuſꝗ te foz
mare ĩ utro noui te
7 anteꝗ exires de ue
tre ſc̃iſicaui te · 7 ꝓphe
tam̃ ĩ gentib; dedi
te 3 Inter natos mu
lierũ nõ ſurrexit ma
ioz iol̃e baptiſta Q̃
uia dño ſparuit i l̃e
mo ũ ſuit hõ miſſ9 a
deo cui nome ioł̃es ãt
Q̃ p9 Ut quoũ9 ſu
it hõ miſſ9 λoẽ ã In
greſſo zacharia tẽplũ
dñi apparuit ei gabri
el angel9 ſtans a dex
tris altaris ĩcenſi ca
rũ q̃o oꝑs deī
ut familia tu

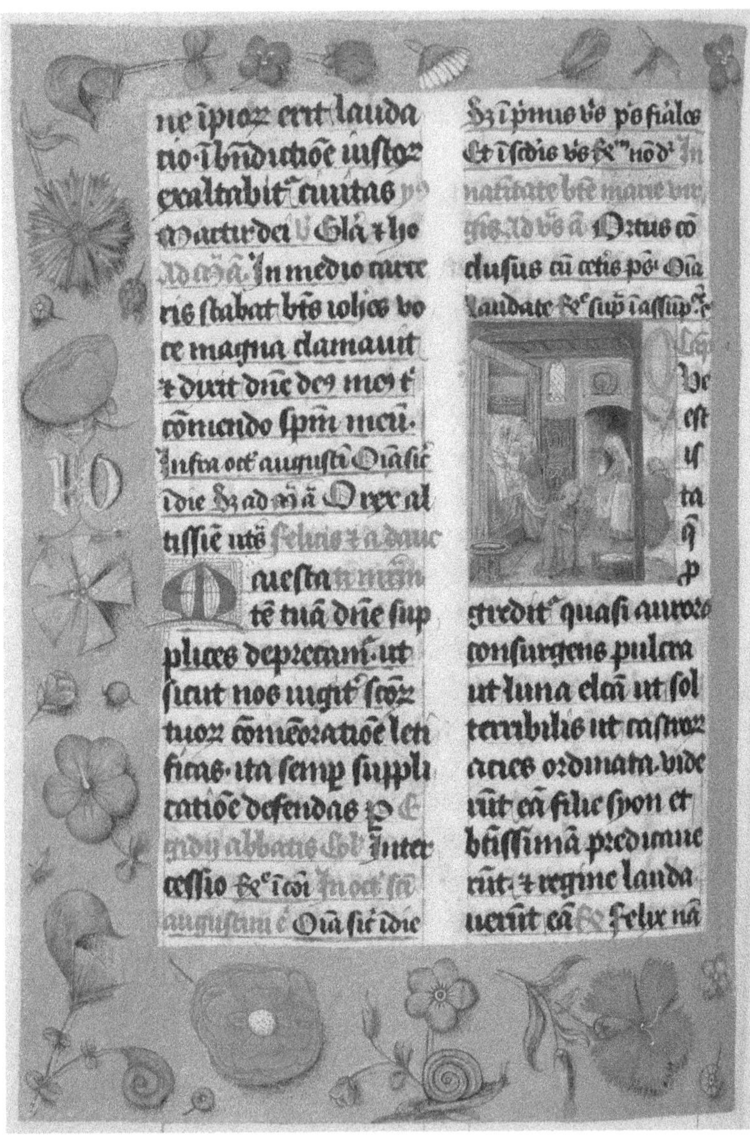

2   *Birth of the Virgin*, sanctoral, Book of Hours, Manchester, John Rylands University Library, MS 39, fol. 197v, *c*.1480–90. Reproduced by courtesy of the University Librarian and Director, The John Rylands University Library, The University of Manchester (© Manchester, John Rylands University Library)

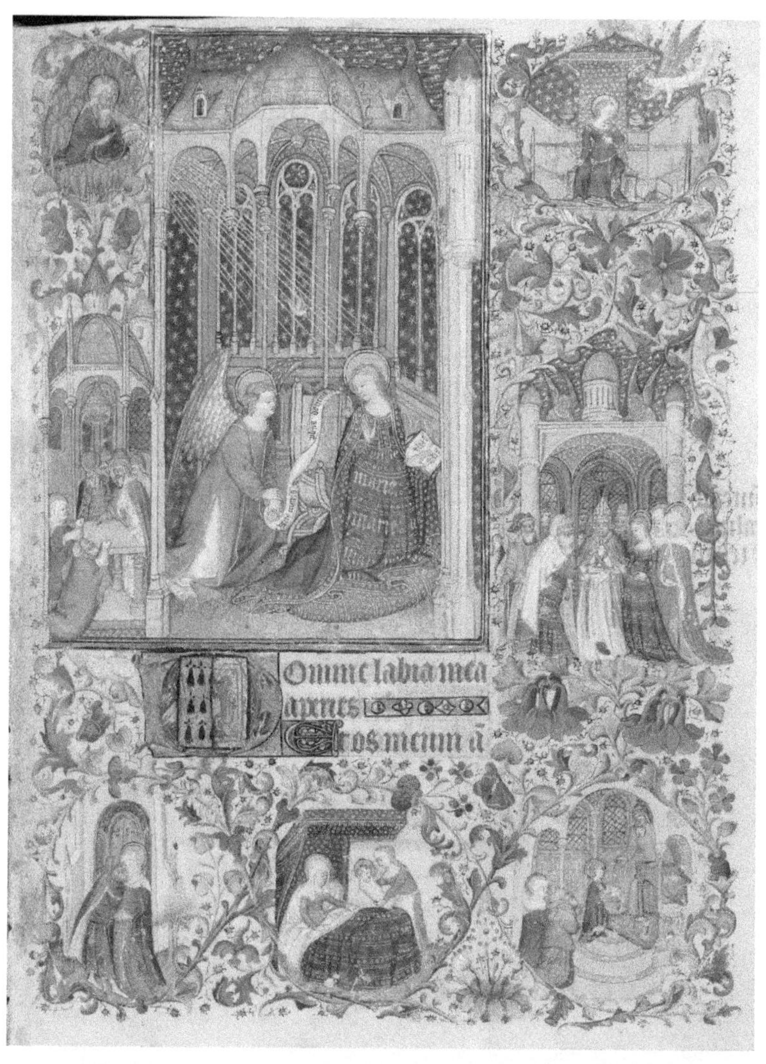

3   Rohan Workshop, *Annunciation*, Matins, *Fitzwilliam Hours*, Cambridge, Fitzwilliam Museum, MS 62, fol. 29r, *c.*1418–30. Reproduction by permission of the Syndics of the Fitzwilliam Museum, Cambridge (© Cambridge, Fitzwilliam Museum)

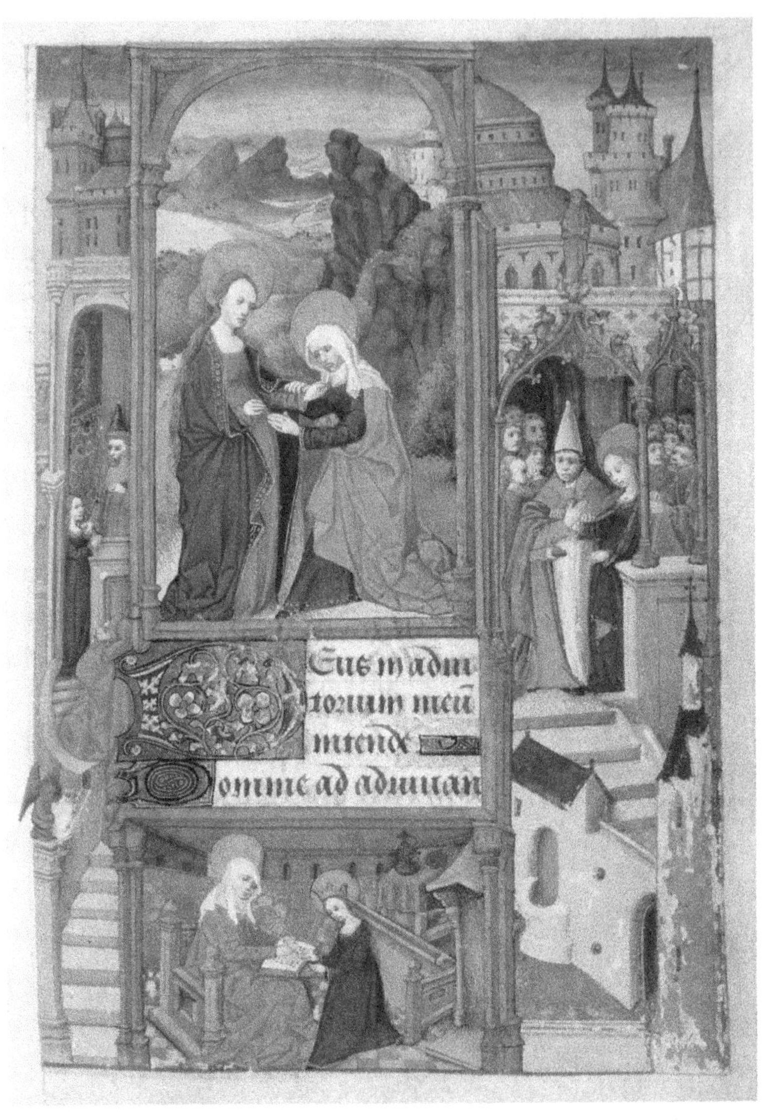

4   *Visitation* with *St Anne teaching the Virgin*, Lauds, *Hours of Marguerite of Foix*, London, Victoria and Albert Museum, Salting MS 1222, fol. 47r, c.1477. Published by kind permission of the Board of Trustees of the V&A (© V&A Images/Victoria and Albert Museum)

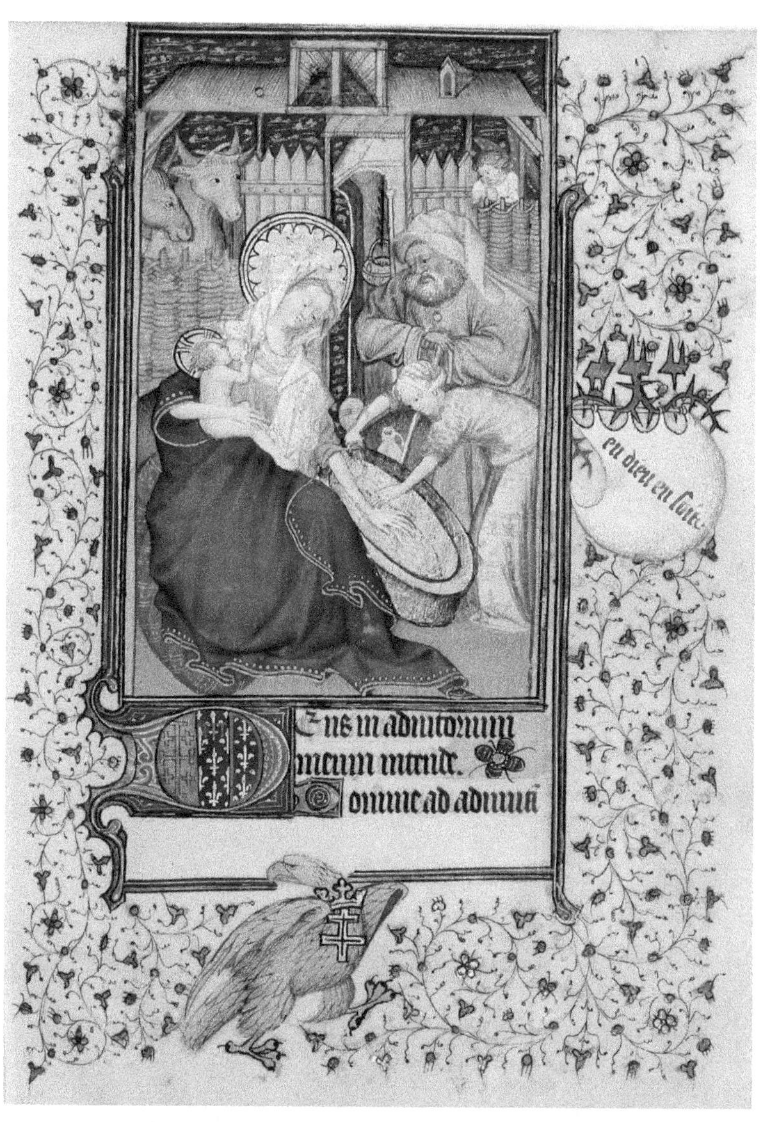

5   Rohan Workshop, *Nativity of Christ*, Prime, *Paris Hours of René of Anjou*, Paris, Bibliothèque nationale, fonds latin, 1156A, fol. 48v, *c*.1434 (© Paris, BnF)

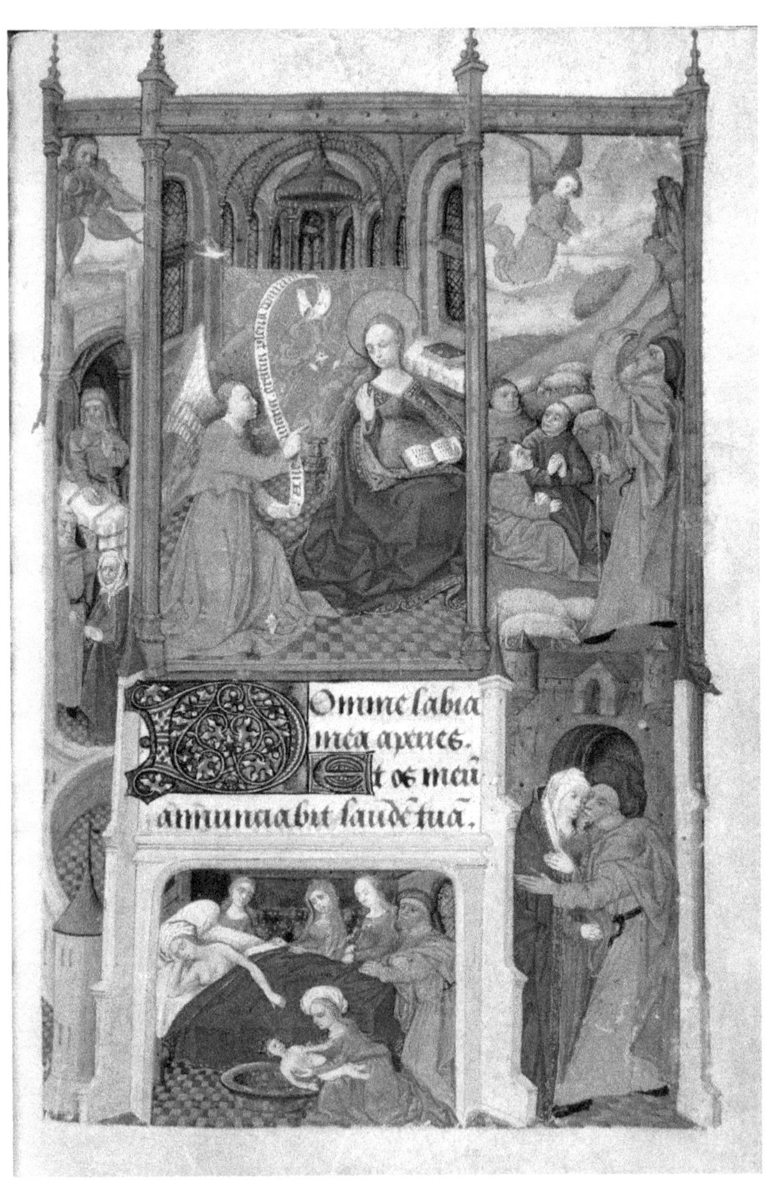

6   *Annunciation* with *Scenes from the Life of the Virgin*, Matins, *Hours of Marguerite of Foix*, London, Victoria and Albert Museum, Salting MS 1222, fol. 33r, *c.*1477. Published by kind permission of the Board of Trustees of the V&A (© V&A Images/Victoria and Albert Museum)

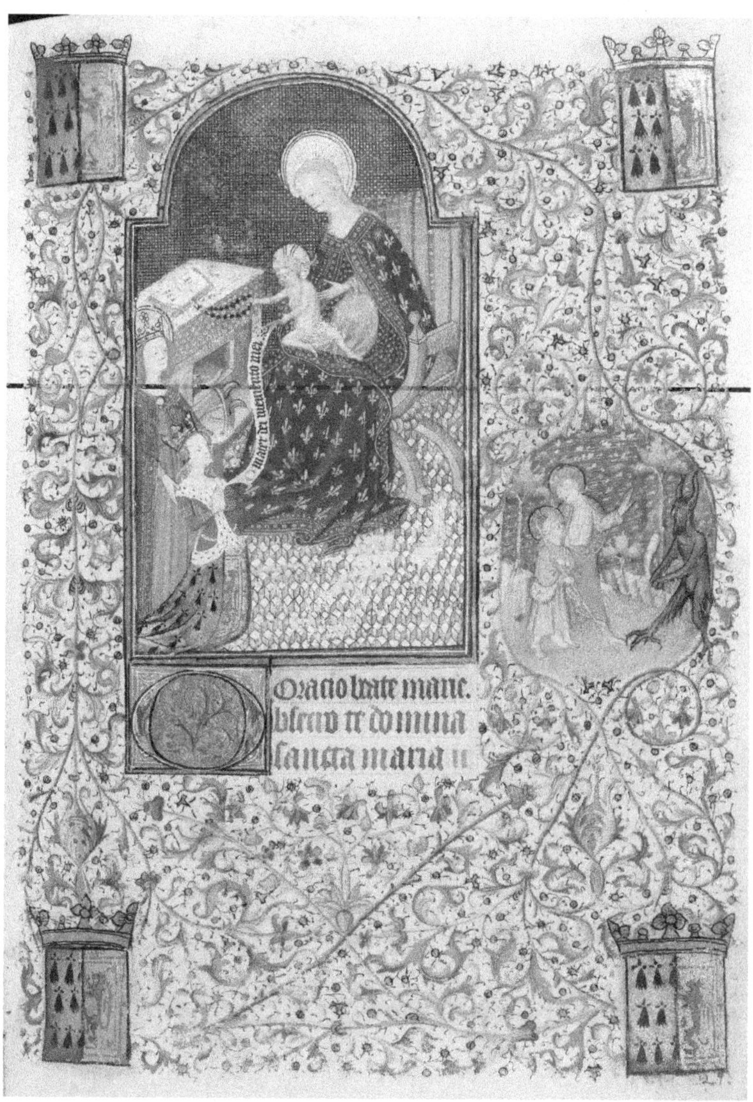

7   Rohan Workshop, *Isabel Stuart presented by St Catherine to the Virgin and Child, Obsecro te, Fitzwilliam Hours,* Cambridge, Fitzwilliam Museum, MS 62, fol. 20r, *c.*1418–30, altered after 1442. Reproduction by permission of the Syndics of the Fitzwilliam Museum, Cambridge (© Cambridge, Fitzwilliam Museum)

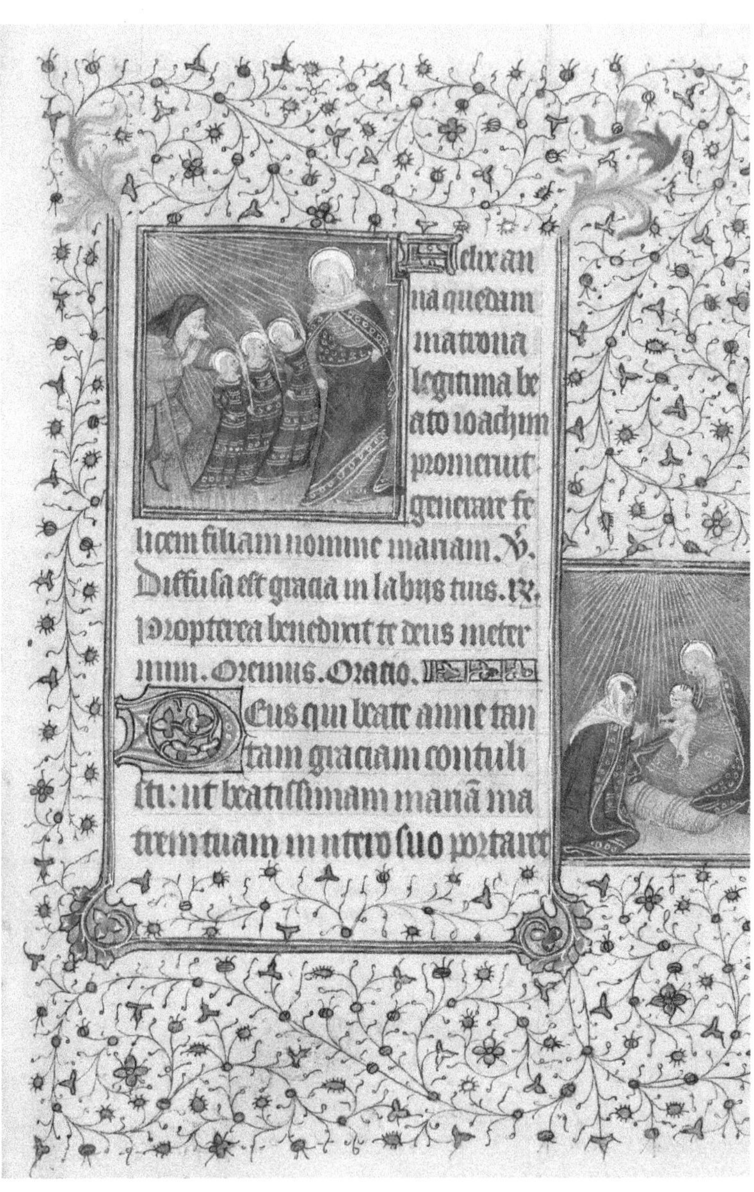

8   Rohan Workshop, *St Anne with her Three Daughters* (text) and *Holy Kinship* (border), suffrages, *Fitzwilliam Hours*, Cambridge, Fitzwilliam Museum, MS 62, fol. 222r, *c.*1418–30. Reproduction by permission of the Syndics of the Fitzwilliam Museum, Cambridge (© Cambridge, Fitzwilliam Museum)

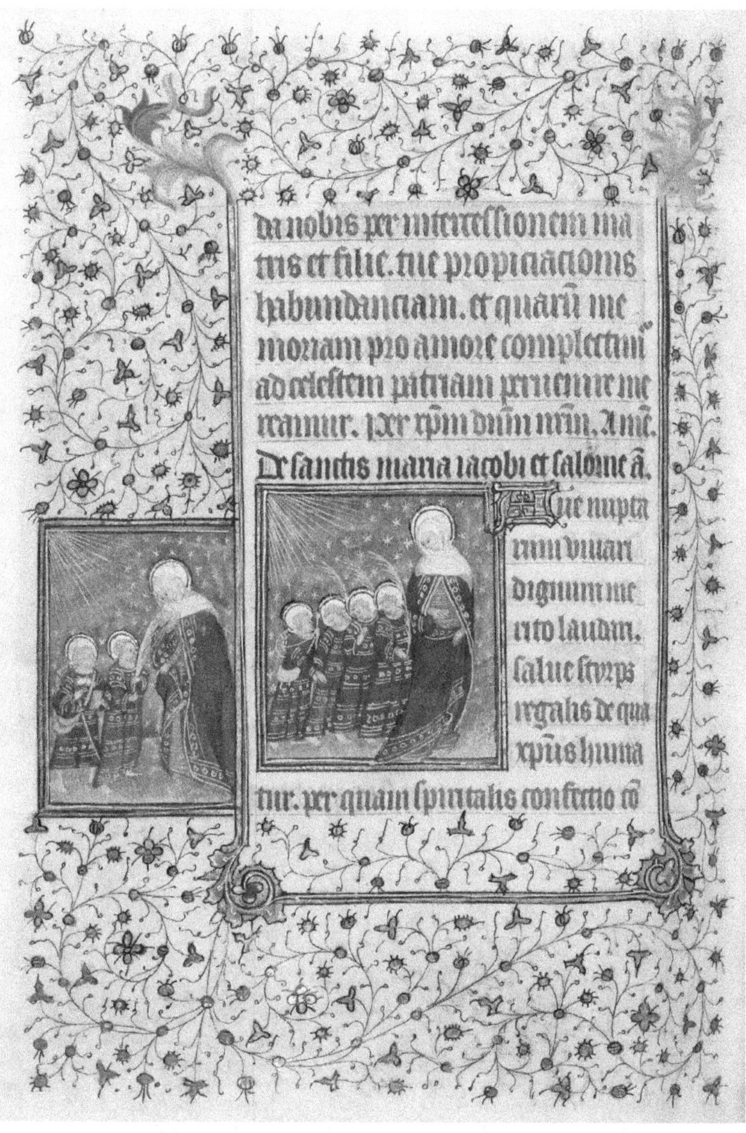

9   Rohan Workshop, *Mary Cleophas and Mary Salomé with their Sons*, suffrages, *Fitzwilliam Hours*, Cambridge, Fitzwilliam Museum, MS 62, fol. 222v, *c*.1418–30. Reproduction by permission of the Syndics of the Fitzwilliam Museum, Cambridge (© Cambridge, Fitzwilliam Museum)

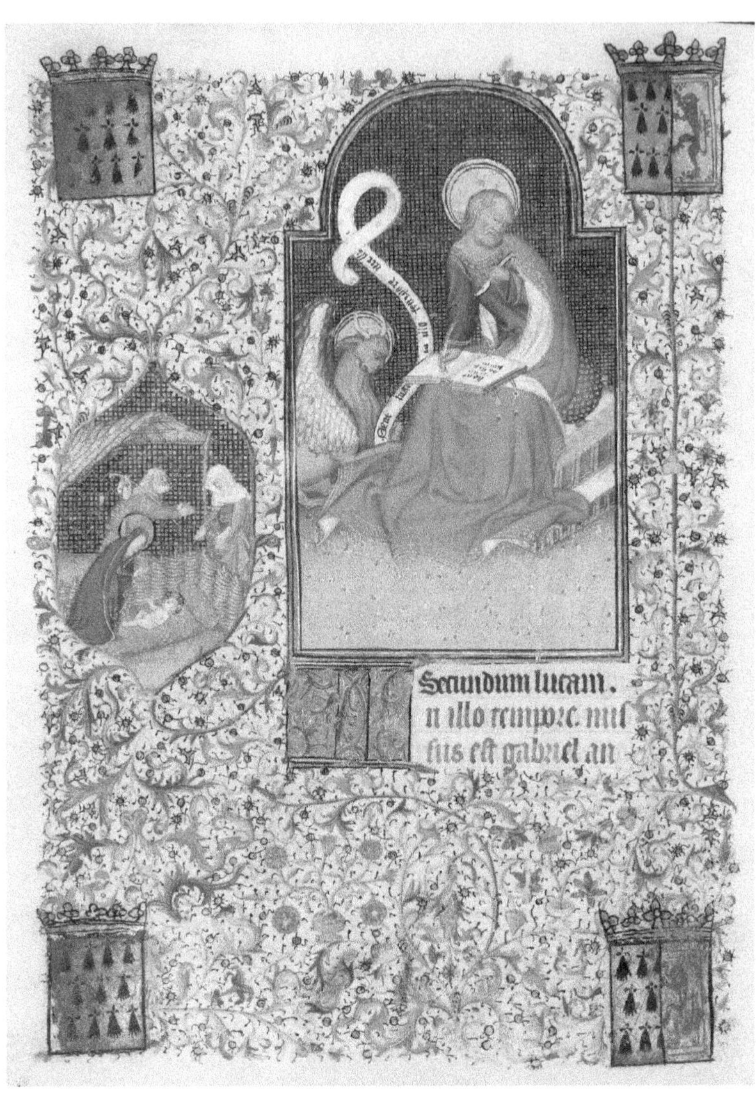

10   Rohan Workshop, *Nativity of Christ* (border), Gospel of St Luke, *Fitzwilliam Hours*, Cambridge, Fitzwilliam Museum, MS 62, fol. 14v, *c*.1418–30. Reproduction by permission of the Syndics of the Fitzwilliam Museum, Cambridge (© Cambridge, Fitzwilliam Museum)

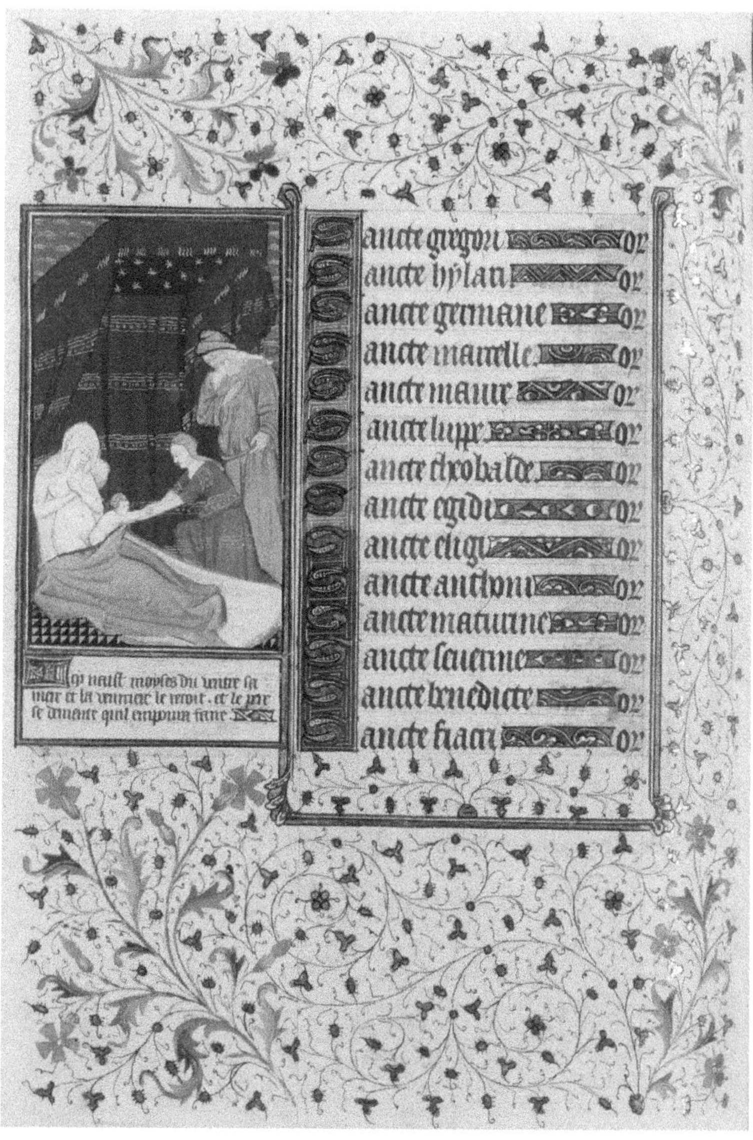

11　Rohan Workshop, *Birth of Moses*, *Bible moralisée* marginal cycle, *Rohan Hours*, Paris, Bibliothèque nationale, fonds latin, 9471, fol. 129v, *c.*1420 (© Paris, BnF)

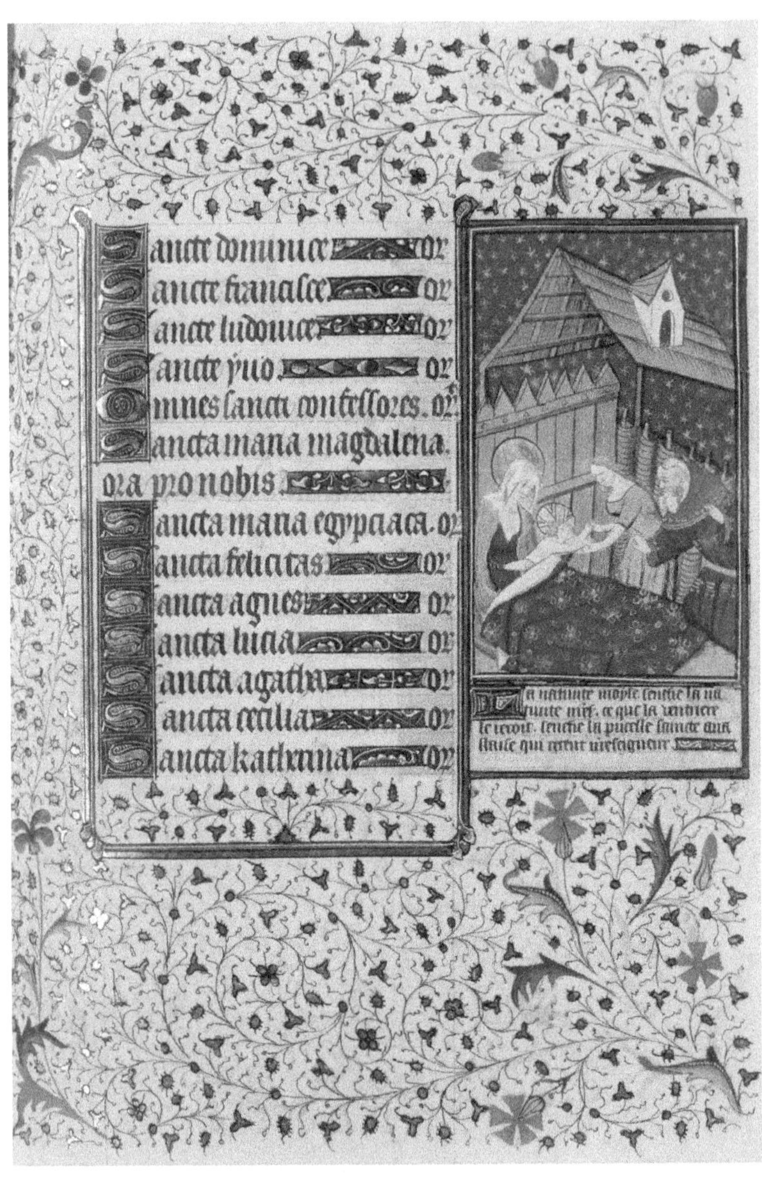

12   Rohan Workshop, *Nativity of Christ*, *Bible moralisée* marginal cycle, *Rohan Hours*, Paris, Bibliothèque nationale, fonds latin, 9471, fol. 130r, *c.*1420 (© Paris, BnF)

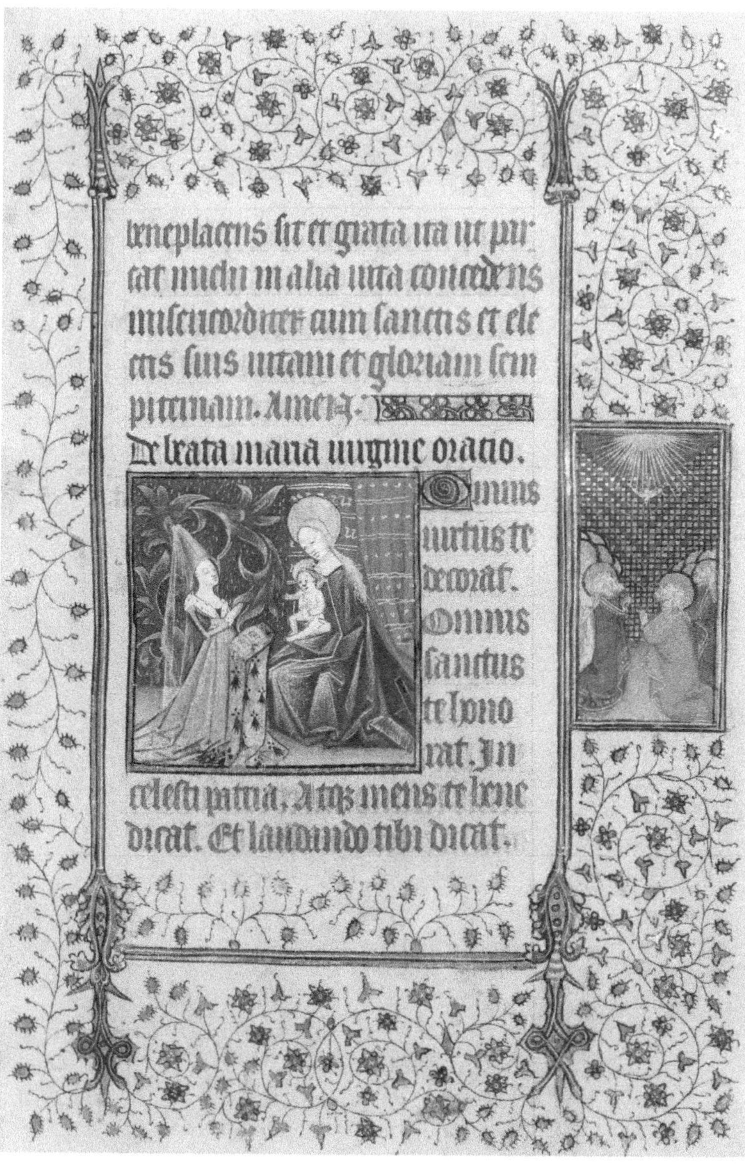

13　Rohan Workshop, *Marguerite of Brittany at Prayer*, *Omnis te virtus decorat*, *Fitzwilliam Hours*, Cambridge, Fitzwilliam Museum, MS 62, f. 28r, *c.*1418–30, altered after 1450. Reproduction by permission of the Syndics of the Fitzwilliam Museum, Cambridge (© Cambridge, Fitzwilliam Museum)

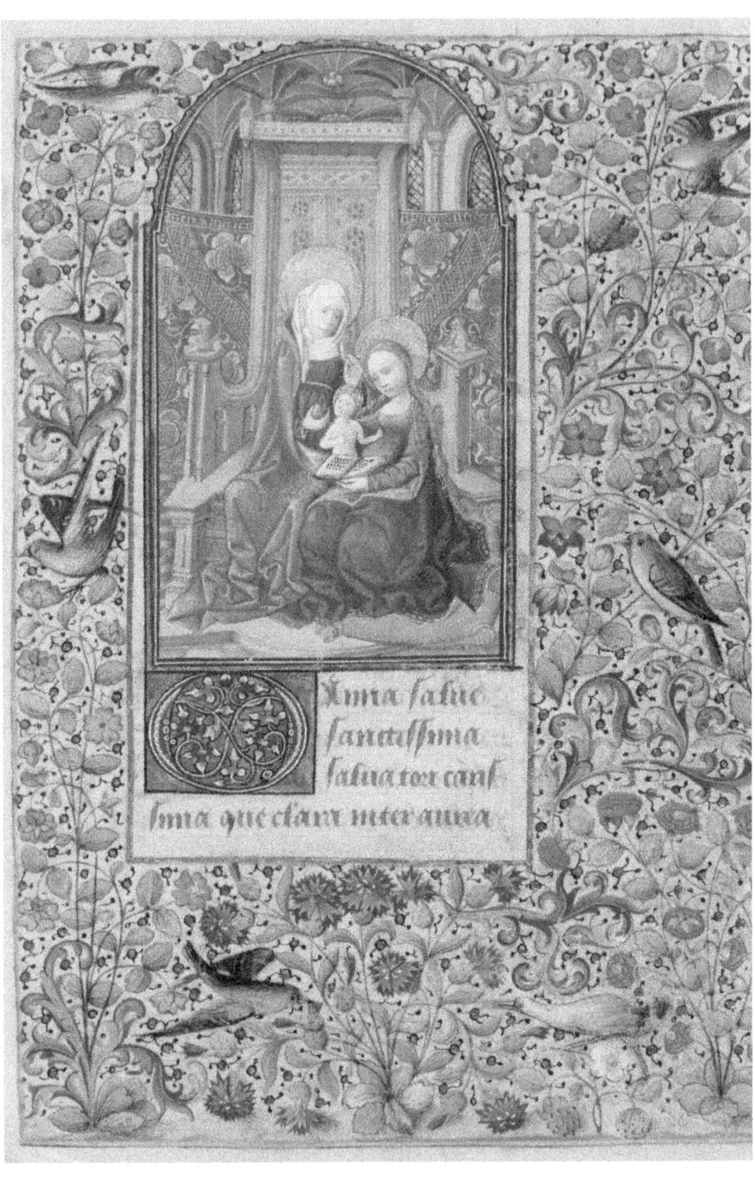

14   *Holy Kinship*, suffrages, *Hours of Marguerite of Foix*, London, Victoria and Albert Museum, Salting MS 1222, fol. 213r, *c.*1477. Published by kind permission of the Board of Trustees of the V&A (© V&A Images/Victoria and Albert Museum)

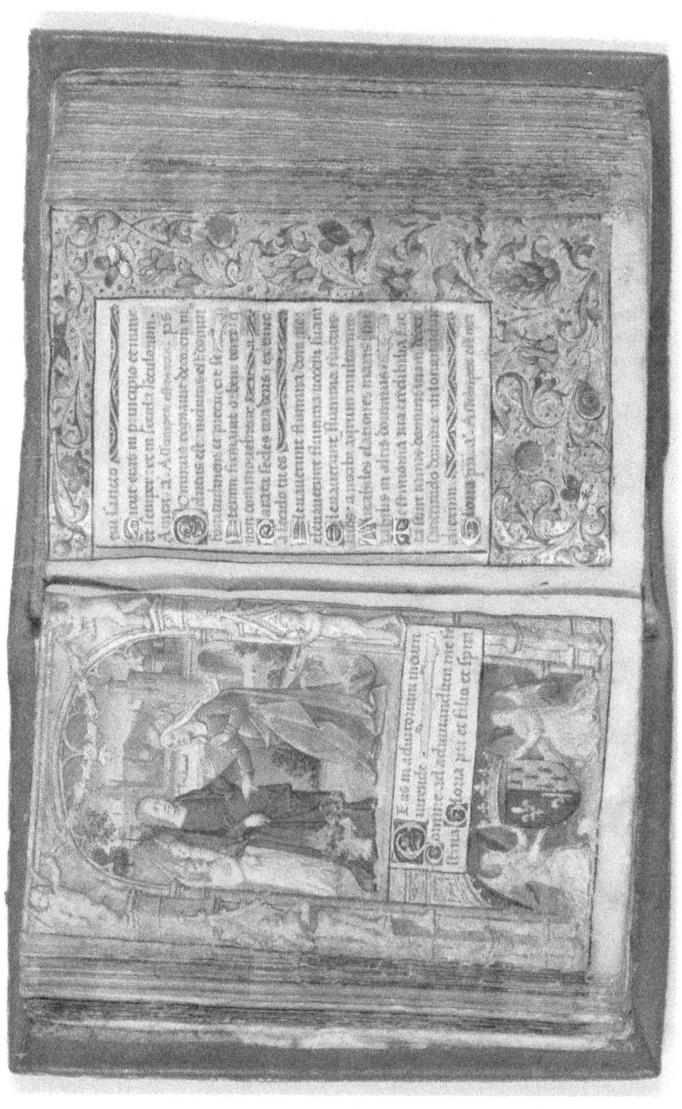

15 *Visitation*, Lauds, Anne of Brittany's *Très Petites Heures*, Paris, Bibliothèque nationale, nouvelle acquisition latine, 3120, fol. 40r (© Paris, BnF)

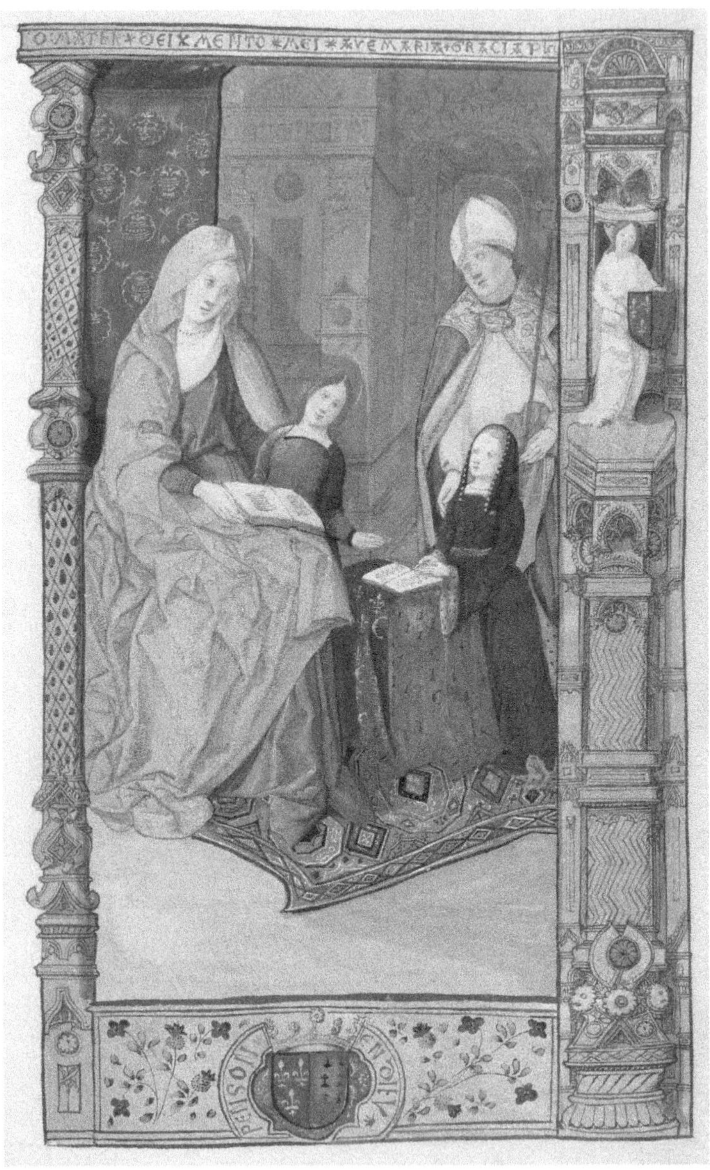

16   *St Claude Presents a Kneeling Girl to St Anne and the Virgin*, *Primer of Claude of France*, Cambridge, Fitzwilliam Museum, MS 159, p. 14, *c*.1500–10. Reproduction by permission of the Syndics of the Fitzwilliam Museum, Cambridge (© Cambridge, Fitzwilliam Museum)

She appears twice as a young girl on her betrothal and marriage to Clothaire (fol. 224v) and is then shown bringing bread to some cripples and interceding on behalf of prisoners (fol. 225r). On fol. 226r she is depicted kneeling before a nimbed bishop with an abbess standing behind her (figure 20), perhaps in the act of receiving her nun's habit. She is subsequently shown as a nun, visiting the sick and kneeling to Christ (fol. 226v). Despite having given up her status as queen of France, St Radegund is shown crowned and haloed in all the miniatures, and the fleur de lys, symbol of the house of France and also part of the arms of Anjou, are retained on her clothes throughout, even on her nun's habit.

Through this continual stress on St Radegund's queenly provenance and her Frankish connections, this holy female saint offered a figure of identification for Yolande of Aragon, who was herself a queen and protector, and mentor of the French dauphin. The presence of St Radegund in Yolande's Book of Hours thus not only *reminded* Yolande of her social roles but, since the inclusion of this suffrage was probably a choice on Yolande's part, the saint also helped her to *construct* and perform that role – one that allowed her, as an aristocratic woman, to influence both the succession of the French crown and the destiny of her own family. Thus, although St Radegund was not a biological mother herself, in her role as an abbess protecting her flock, she showed how 'mothering' or 'parenting' was a social, performative, skill, transferable to children other than one's own.

Yolande may also have drawn on other aspects of St Radegund's *vita* as a means of justifying her role as guardian of the French dauphin. In 569, St Radegund's abbey received a relic of the True Cross from Bishop Eufronius of Tours and the saint thus became influential in promoting the cult of this instrument of the Passion.[37] By the time the *Fitzwilliam Hours* were made, devotion to the Passion of Christ had become a major interest of the French kings, fuelled, in particular, by St Louis IX's veneration for a relic of the Crown of Thorns, for which he built the Sainte-Chapelle in Paris in the thirteenth century. St Radegund embodied a Frankish, queenly, exemplar that also complemented specific Valois devotional interests. A revival of St Radegund's cult in the fifteenth century that has been attributed to Yolande's protégé Charles VII, who baptised his first daughter Radegund, intensified royal connections with the relics of the Passion and was used to further anti-English sentiment at the height of England's claims to the French throne.[38] Charles's interest in this saint may have been inspired by the devotions of his patroness, Yolande.[39] Moreover, Charles's devotion to St Radegund also indicates that a saint invested with maternal values and qualities, other than the Virgin, could appeal to a male, as well

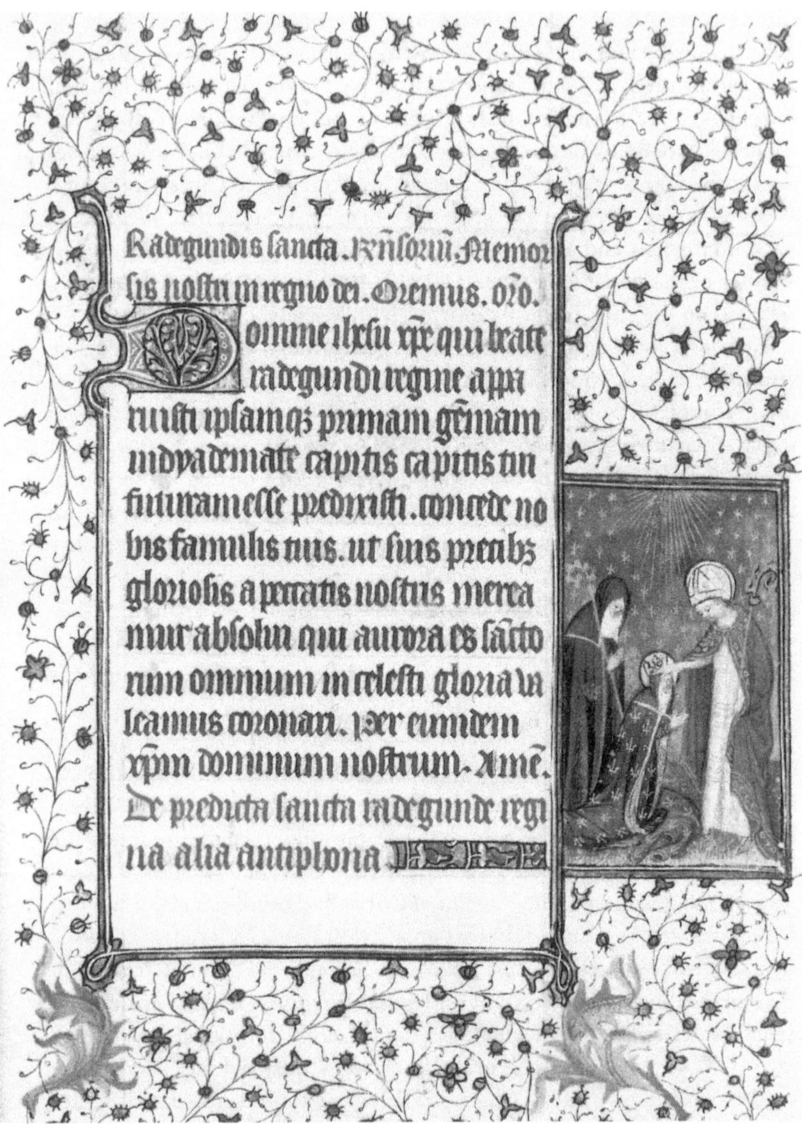

20   Rohan Workshop, *St Radegund Kneeling before Bishop*, suffrages, *Fitzwilliam Hours*, Cambridge, Fitzwilliam Museum, MS 62, fol. 226r, *c*.1418–30. Reproduction by permission of the Syndics of the Fitzwilliam Museum, Cambridge (© Cambridge, Fitzwilliam Museum)

as to a female, devotee through her affiliation with good government and the house of France.

Yolande's protection of the dauphin and the way she manipulated his devotional interests is discussed in further detail below in the context of the *Rohan Hours* – another lavish manuscript which she probably commissioned for her son-in-law. Here, however, further analysis of suffrages in the *Fitzwilliam Hours* reveals how Yolande actively promoted herself and her family through saints from the French and Hungro-Angevin *beata stirps*. Viewed together, these saints evoke a holy dynasty that complements that of St Anne and the Holy Kinship.

St Elizabeth of Hungary, daughter of the Hungarian king Andrew II, became a key figure in the construction of the Angevin *beata stirps* through Charles II of Anjou's marriage with her great-niece, Mary of Hungary. Her presence in the *Fitzwilliam Hours'* suffrages (fols 224r–v) not only indicates the commissioner's interest in celebrating the Angevin dynasty but it also adds another dimension to the manuscript's emphasis on holy mothers. In 1221, St Elizabeth married Louis IV, Crown Prince of Thuringia. The couple had three children and although the marriage was happy, Elizabeth became increasingly drawn to a religious life. She began by carrying out charitable works, engaging, in particular, with the poor and needy and in 1226, while her husband was away, she effectively managed a famine crisis.[40] St Elizabeth's desire for communion with the poor and for a simple religious life was finally fulfilled following Louis's death on the way to the Holy Land in 1227, when she left the court and founded a hospital for the impoverished and worked there performing manual labour.[41] The hospital and its chapel were dedicated to St Francis, who had been canonised in 1228, the year they were founded. In 1235, Elizabeth became the first royal Franciscan tertiary (a lay member of the order) to be canonised.[42]

The illuminations accompanying the suffrage to St Elizabeth in the *Fitzwilliam Hours* emphasise her extraordinary piety. In the text miniature she is shown haloed, kneeling in prayer to a celestial apparition of Christ. In the border miniature she is again haloed and is depicted standing at the door of a building, perhaps intended to represent her hospital. She is assisted by two maids distributing bread to a widow or a nun and a lame man (figure 21). St Elizabeth's aristocratic background, coupled with her charitable works, made her, like St Radegund, an appealing saint for noble women.[43] In the same way as the representation of St Radegund with the fleur de lys of France on her nun's habit served as a constant reminder of the saint's royal, Frankish lineage, the representation of St Elizabeth of Hungary in the *Fitzwilliam Hours* in the manner of St Anne, with a rich cloak of blue

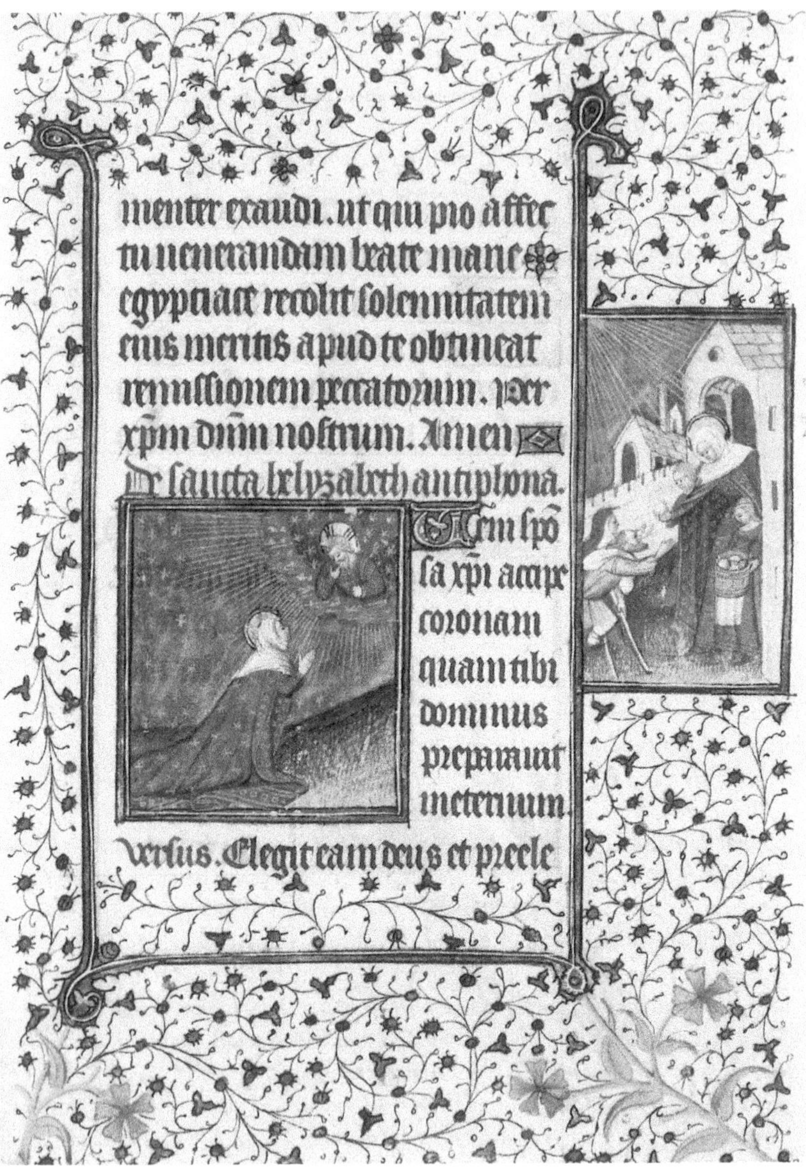

21   Rohan Workshop, *St Elizabeth of Hungary*, suffrages, *Fitzwilliam Hours*, Cambridge, Fitzwilliam Museum, MS 62, fol. 224r, *c.*1418–30. Reproduction by permission of the Syndics of the Fitzwilliam Museum, Cambridge (© Cambridge, Fitzwilliam Museum)

and gold and the headdress of a widow, kept this holy mother saint anchored in the rich, aristocratic and secular world to which Yolande of Aragon belonged. Therefore, despite her extreme piety and poverty, St Elizabeth could still serve as a model for the queen, duchess and mother, Yolande.

This may have been for several reasons. First, Yolande could not only relate to St Elizabeth's reputation as a queen and mother within the Angevin dynasty but also, as noted above, to the saint's relationship to her own Aragonese heritage. Second, St Elizabeth's presence in the suffrages also served to complement that of St Anne and her daughters by underlining the role of women, rather than men, in *beata stirps*. Klaniczy notes that the thirteenth century saw a 'feminisation' of royal cults in central Europe, and that 'the role women had been playing in the biological perpetuation [of *beata stirps*] from time immemorial had acquired a spiritual dimension'.[44] As a wife, mother, widow and saint, Elizabeth of Hungary thus appears as a latter-day parallel to St Anne, reaffirming the importance of the female sex as the source of blessed dynasties and in the transmission of noble sanctity. Yolande of Aragon's knowledge of St Elizabeth as an Angevin saint probably also included familiarity with her saintly female descendants. For example, St Elizabeth's daughter, the Blessed Gertrude (d. 1297), who also lived a life of poverty and piety as a nun, and her nieces St Cunegond (d. 1292) and St Margaret (d. 1270), added to the 'feminisation' of the Arpadian *beata stirps*.[45] Viewed through Yolande's situational eye, the proliferation of holy women emanating from St Elizabeth's lineage added another dimension to her similarity with St Anne, who was also the matriarch of a line of blessed women.

By 1417, Yolande of Aragon's situational eye was informed by her social roles as queen, duchess wife, mother, widow and political adviser within a Franco-Angevin context. Through the specific cognitive habits she acquired as duchess of Anjou, as the matriarch of a family of *princes de sang*, and as mother-in-law and protector of the French dauphin, she was likely to have seen the female saints considered thus far, St Anne, St Mary Cleophas, St Mary Salomé, St Radegund and St Elizabeth, as a coherent group of tangible, holy women rulers and mothers from whom she could derive authority. By turning to the suffrages of St Louis of Toulouse and St Louis IX it is possible to show how Yolande was also able to use these male saints to promote her own personal and familial ambitions, especially to reinforce those specific links between the houses of Anjou and France, which she was establishing through her support of the dauphin and his marriage to her daughter Marie.

St Louis IX, like St Radegund, St Elizabeth and, as we shall see, St Louis of Toulouse, was an aristocrat with a religious calling. Although

St Louis IX was widely venerated in fifteenth-century France, his presence among other royal saints in the *Fitzwilliam Hours* suggests that he had a particular role to play in the commissioner's devotional interests. As the brother of Charles I of Anjou, he served as another lynchpin on which the Anjou's claims not only to dynastic sanctity, but also their status as *princes de sang*, hung. Married to Marguerite of Provence, Louis combined his religious vocation with his responsibilities as king, fathering eleven children while living a life of piety and charity.[46] Most notably, St Louis brought relics of the Crown of Thorns and the True Cross to France, for which he built the Sainte-Chapelle in Paris, thus instigating the veneration of future French kings for relics of the Passion.

In the *Fitzwilliam Hours*, St Louis IX is shown in the border miniature seated at a table where he appears to be sharing his meal with a group of beggars (figure 22). The miniature draws attention to Louis's kingly and holy status by depicting him crowned, haloed, and wearing a blue cloak with gold fleur de lys. These features are retained in the second miniature on the same page where he kneels to a bishop at the door of a church. Behind him stand three figures also dressed in blue robes decorated with the fleur de lys of France. These three 'princes' might have been intended as a reference to Louis's brothers, Robert of Artois, Alphonse of Poitiers and Charles I of Anjou. As noted above, Charles I had argued for the sanctity of all three of his three brothers and tried to promote himself as a reincarnation of Charlemagne. Thus, the presence of the brothers in the miniature would have worked to assimilate the entire family to the good works and sanctity of St Louis IX in the same way that Yolande of Aragon was working to bring a later Anjou generation closer to the house of France.

Through the images and prayers to St Louis IX in the *Fitzwilliam Hours*, Yolande of Aragon may also have thought about Louis's mother, the pious, politically-astute widow, Blanche of Castile. Blanche was an extremely important figure in Louis's life and it has already been noted that she was considered something of a saint after her death. When Louis succeeded to the throne in 1226 aged only eleven years old, Blanche ruled as regent and after his majority she continued to advise her son throughout the rest of her life, ruling again as regent during Louis's absence on crusade in 1248.[47] Blanche's influential role on Louis as a parent and adviser no doubt led to the king's interest in advising his own children. He wrote a conduct guide for his eldest daughter Isabel some time after her marriage to the king of Navarre in 1255, and an educative treatise for his eldest son Philip.[48] A later duchess of royal blood, Anne of France, drew on the exemplar of Louis's conduct manuals when she composed the *Enseignements*

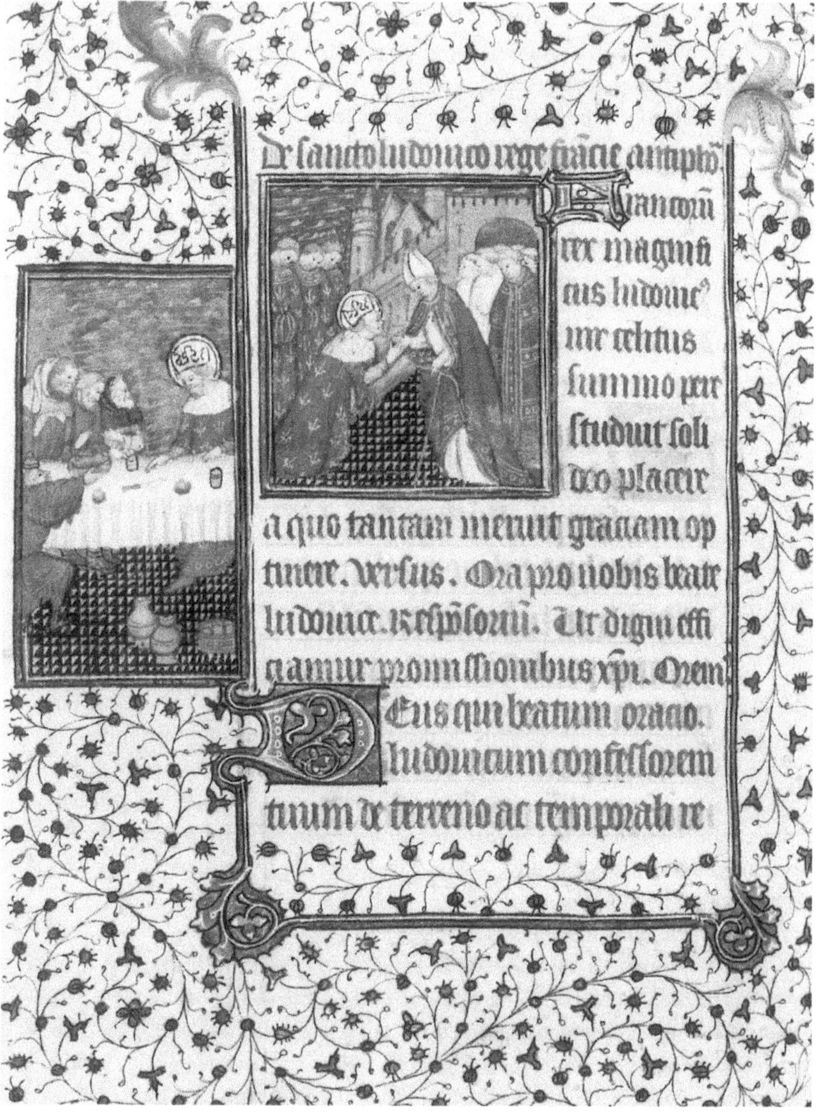

22   Rohan Workshop, *St Louis IX*, suffrages, *Fitzwilliam Hours*, Cambridge, Fitzwilliam Museum, MS 62, fol. 220v, *c*.1418–30. Reproduction by permission of the Syndics of the Fitzwilliam Museum, Cambridge (© Cambridge, Fitzwilliam Museum)

for her own daughter Suzanne.[49] Both Louis and his mother could, therefore, have been taken as models for good parenting by Yolande of Aragon. Despite not being the dauphin's mother, Yolande was, like Blanche, in charge of a future king of France. In fact, she looked after the dauphin's political interests in the place of his own parents who had started to distance themselves from their son, favouring an English succession and eventually disinheriting him with the Treaty of Troyes in 1420.[50] In the context of the *Fitzwilliam Hours*, and viewed by Yolande of Aragon's situational eye, the various facets of St Louis IX's life come together to create a model of Franco-Angevin sanctity, good parenting, and wise rule.

The last saint to be discussed from the *Fitzwilliam Hours*' suffrages is Louis of Toulouse, named after his holy great-uncle and the most important figure in the Angevin's claim to dynastic sanctity. The union of St Elizabeth's great-niece, Mary of Hungary, with St Louis IX's nephew, Charles II, brought together the saintly Arpadian *beata stirps* and the Capetian blessed lineage. From this marriage an Angevin saint proper emerged, St Louis of Toulouse (1274–97).[51] Louis was the second son of Mary and Charles II and from an early age he had felt drawn to the Franciscan order. This choice did not please his family, especially after the death of his older brother, Charles Martel (1271–95), whose rights he was expected to take up.[52] Rather than take on his brother's inheritance as future duke of Anjou, king of Naples and Sicily, and titular king of Hungary, Louis abdicated in favour of his younger brother, Robert, in 1296. Despite taking Franciscan vows with the approval of the Pope, Louis was then forced to take the bishopric of Toulouse in order to appease his father. However, after his death in 1297 his father and brother 'petitioned vigorously for his canonization which Pope John XXII finally promulgated on 7 April 1317'.[53] He thus became proof that the Angevin dynasty was itself 'capable of *bringing forth* "holy branches" [and] could boast dynastic saintliness in its own right'.[54] Although less widely venerated than his royal namesake, St Louis became the patron saint of the house of Anjou and the first son of Marie of Anjou and Charles VII, born in 1423, was baptised Louis, ' "en remembrance de saint Loys de Marseille" '.[55] The inclusion of the little-known St Louis of Toulouse in a manuscript already related by maker and circumstance to the house of Anjou, therefore, lends support to the argument that it was commissioned by Yolande of Aragon and that the decorative and textual programme was designed to speak to her interests and to those of her family.

Louis's Franciscan calling, his abdication and his investiture as Bishop of Toulouse are all depicted in the *Fitzwilliam Hours*' miniatures accompanying his suffrage (fols 219v–220r). In the border scene of folio 219v he is shown haloed and kneeling, dressed in a blue cloak decorated with gold fleur de lys; he receives the Franciscan habit from a group of monks at the door of a monastery (figure 23). On the same page, in the miniature accompanying the text, he is again shown haloed, this time wearing his habit and giving his cloak with the fleur de lys to a beggar. On the following folio he is then depicted as a bishop, wearing a mitre and a cloak decorated with fleur de lys. Looking away to the left he holds out, to the right, his crown, symbolising his renunciation of his titles. As in the case of St Radegund (figure 20), the retention of the fleur de lys on Louis's cloak means that it is the saint's royal status rather than his religious vocation per se which is prominent. Through her own Aragonese descent and her marriage into the house of Anjou, Yolande could claim direct kinship ties with St Louis and his family. She could, thus, draw authority from their sovereignty over Naples, a kingdom which her husband and then her sons spent the first decades of the fifteenth century trying to reclaim with Yolande's support and approval.

The suffrages of the *Fitzwilliam Hours* contain a rich number of references to narratives of holy parents, independently-minded lay women, and blessed lineages with which Yolande of Aragon's situational eye would have been familiar. Taken together, these elements strongly suggest that Yolande of Aragon was the commissioner and original owner of the *Fitzwilliam Hours* and that she used these saints in the execution of her social roles as wife, mother, widow, duchess, queen, adviser and regent for the duchy of Anjou, and as the protector and mother-in-law of the French dauphin. The suffrages to St Anne and her daughters St Mary Salomé and St Mary Cleophas draw attention to the special place of women in Christ's blessed lineage. This Holy Kinship was complemented by the inclusion of the queen, wife and mother, St Elizabeth of Hungary, who was the most important saint among a number of other holy men and women in the Hungro-Angevin *beata stirps*. St Louis of Toulouse consolidated the sanctity of the dukes of Anjou, combining the Franco-Angevin line with that of St Elizabeth of Hungary. The number of images given over to St Radegund implies a particular devotion to this Frankish queen on the part of the commissioner. Like St Radegund, Yolande became a 'mother' to others in her counselling and protection of the future Charles VII, who in turn took up devotion to the cult of this saint. St Louis IX also offered a model of good parenting, one that also recalled the achievements of his mother, Blanche of Castile, as regent and adviser to the king of France.

The *Fitzwilliam Hours* appears to relate specifically to Yolande's personal and political interests around 1417 and Emmerson has suggested that,

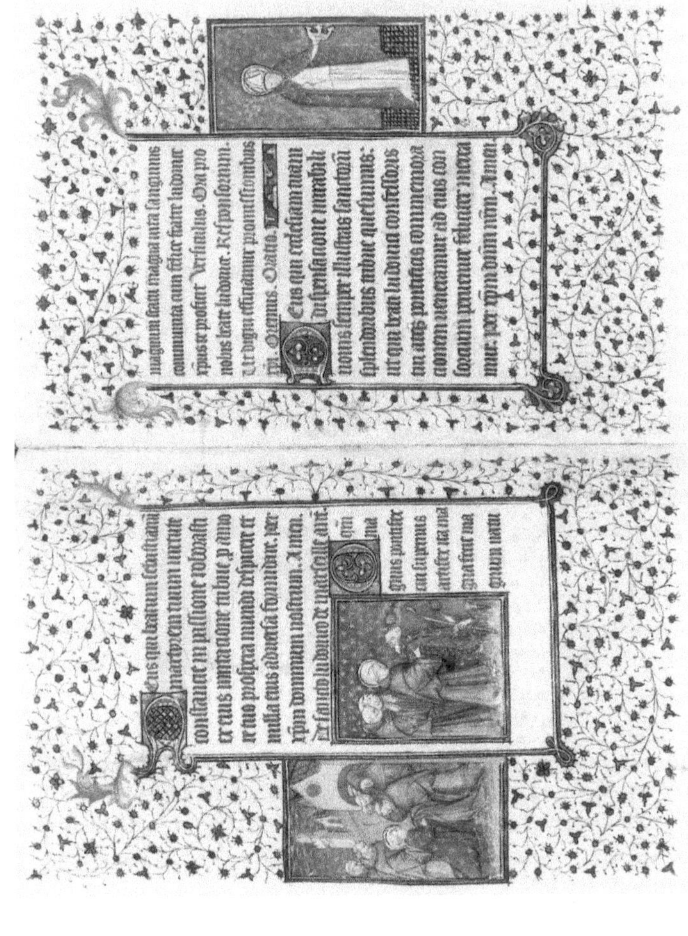

23 Rohan Workshop, *St Louis of Toulouse*, suffrages, *Fitzwilliam Hours*, Cambridge, Fitzwilliam Museum, MS 62, fols 219v–220r, *c.*1418–30. Reproduction by permission of the Syndics of the Fitzwilliam Museum, Cambridge (© Cambridge, Fitzwilliam Museum)

following Louis II's death in this year, her 'decision to commission this lavish manuscript during this critical time may represent an urgent act of devotion and penitent petition to God'.[56] Furthermore, in the same year as Louis's death, Yolande's protégé Charles of Ponthieu became dauphin: her support of the child who was now heir to the French crown and her soon-to-be son-in-law thus acquired an additional boost in the form of a celebration of the illustrious past of both the French and Angevin houses.

The focus on saints from both these families, together with the portrait of the older woman dressed as a widow, would suggest that Yolande commissioned the manuscript for herself rather than for the marriage of her daughter Yolande to the future duke of Brittany in 1430. However, the saints discussed here would not have been irrelevant had the manuscript been commissioned for the younger Yolande, who probably owned it, in any case, around the time of her marriage. Like her mother, she too would have been aware of the relevance of these dynastic saints and could have brought the cognitive habits of her family history to bear on her reading and viewing of the *Fitzwilliam Hours*.

Turning to other aspects of the manuscript's decorative programme, particularly its marginal *Apocalypse* and *Pilgrimage* cycles, its Marian imagery, and donor portraits, reveals further how the manuscript related to Angevin tastes and interests in the early fifteenth century. It thus allows additional consideration of Yolande of Aragon's involvement in the commission of the manuscript as well as a means to explore how her daughter Yolande of Anjou viewed the book once it came into her hands.

Model mothers: the *Fitzwilliam Hours* and Yolande of Anjou

The *Fitzwilliam Hours* are decorated throughout with scenes from Deguileville's fourteenth-century allegorical poems of the *Pilgrimage of the Life of Man*, the *Pilgrimage of the Soul* and the *Pilgrimage of Jesus Christ*, and with scenes from the *Apocalypse* of St John. Both texts provided a wealth of material for artists and illuminators and were popular among the courtly elite in the late middle ages.[57] Members of the Angevin court were especially familiar with both *Apocalypse* and *Pilgrimage* texts and the inclusion of these cycles in the *Fitzwilliam Hours* relates to Angevin taste at the end of the fourteenth and the beginning of the fifteenth centuries.[58] For example, Louis I of Anjou (1339–84) commissioned a monumental *Apocalypse* tapestry cycle for his chapel at the castle at Angers, the designs for which were based on an *Apocalypse* manuscript lent to him by his brother Charles V.[59]

Deguileville's *Pilgrimage* series was also popular among the courts of France: the four brothers, King Charles V, John, the duke of Berry, Louis I of Anjou and Philip, the duke of Burgundy, all owned copies of Deguileville's text.[60] The *Pilgrimage of the Life of Man* was particularly popular at the Angevin court, especially among female readers in Yolande of Aragon's entourage. Louis I's copy, which was adorned with his and his wife's arms passed into the hands of Marguerite of Savoy, wife of his grand-son Louis III of Anjou. Yolande of Aragon's daughter Marie also owned a copy as did several aristocrats connected to Yolande's court.[61] In 1465 René of Anjou's second wife Joan of Laval commissioned a prose copy of the work and his daughter Margaret, who had been brought up by Yolande of Aragon, may well have taken copies with her to England on her marriage to Henry VI.[62] The *Fitzwilliam Hours' Apocalypse* and *Pilgrimage* cycles thus strengthen the argument that Yolande of Aragon was the manuscript's com-missioner and suggest that she was aligning herself with, or even promoting, the court's interest in these texts. These Angevin tastes are also likely to have informed the situational eye of Yolande's younger daughter so that when she came into possession of the *Fitzwilliam Hours* she saw the inclusion of the cycles as referring to her family's patronage of, and association with, these devotional texts.

The particular way in which the *Fitzwilliam Hours' Pilgrimage* cycles are integrated into the rest of the manuscript's decorative and textual con-tents suggests that it was designed to engage its lay, female, reader(s) in an interactive way. To begin with, the first *Pilgrimage* cycle in the *Fitzwilliam Hours* is that of *Jesus Christ*, which in other manuscript examples usually occurs after those of *The Life of Man* and the *Soul*.[63] This order means that the *Pilgrimage of the Soul*, which deals with the after-life, coincides in the *Fitzwilliam Hours* with the Office of the Dead. The *Pilgrimage of Jesus Christ* thus starts on the same page as the opening of the Gospel sequences (fol. 13r). According to Camille, the artists have omitted some of the more obscure episodes in Deguileville's text in order to synchronise the series with the episodes of Christ's early life referred to in the Gospel sequences. This synchronisation not only encouraged the reader to make connections between the main text and the marginal sequence, as Camille noted, but it also gave the story of the Virgin's conception of Christ, her marriage and motherhood, a prominent place right at the beginning of the *Fitzwilliam Hours*.[64] It is, therefore, interesting to analyse how Yolande of Anjou's sit-uational eye led her to interpret these images of holy motherhood specifically in relation to her position as the new wife of the heir to the duchy of Brittany.

Yolande of Anjou married Francis of Brittany in 1431. This alliance strengthened the allegiance between the royal fiefdom of Anjou, ruled by Yolande's brother Louis III, and the independent duchy of Brittany. The Breton dukes had long maintained their sovereignty and wished to avoid being swallowed up in the kingdom of France; throughout the fourteenth century they had supported English attempts to claim the French throne. By the time of Yolande and Francis's union, however, the house of Brittany was divided between support for English and French claims. The union organised between Yolande and Francis may well have been intended to unite the pro-French branch of the house of Brittany with the supporters of Charles VII. Through her marriage, Yolande was, therefore, participating in the political interests of the house of Anjou, specifically those of her mother and of her sister Marie, now queen of France. Part of her role as the wife of the future duke of Brittany would be the conception of male heirs: the first Treaty of Guérande signed in 1365 to resolve the Breton succession wars had introduced a form of Salic law into the house of Brittany preventing the duchy from being inherited by a woman while there was a male heir elsewhere in the house.[65]

The following section thus proposes how Yolande of Anjou received and understood the *Fitzwilliam Hours*, its maternal and dynastic imagery, as a gift from her mother. In line with the methodology expounded previously, the aim is not to assume that Yolande passively accepted these images as an encouragement to being a good wife by becoming a mother but to suggest that she could have actively interpreted them to her own advantage. Thus, through her situational eye, acquired as a noblewoman and, specifically, as an Angevin duchess and daughter of Yolande of Aragon, it will be suggested that the younger Yolande interpreted the *Fitzwilliam Hours* as a marker of her social status, and used its images of her holy ancestors and of God-given motherhood to negotiate her own place within the houses to which she belonged and to ask for God's protection in the roles that she was expected to execute.

The *Pilgrimage of Jesus Christ* starts on the same page as the first Gospel sequence, from the opening of St John (fol. 13r): 'In the beginning was the Word.' This text and those of the following Gospels are brought together with the *Pilgrimage of Jesus Christ* through the border miniatures that show how the Word became flesh through the Virgin. On folios 13v–14r the borders are decorated with an *Annunciation* and with a scene of an angel presenting a kneeling Joseph to the Virgin (figure 24). In both images the Virgin holds a book, a sign not only of her piety but also of the Incarnation of the Word, and of the fulfilment of Old Testament

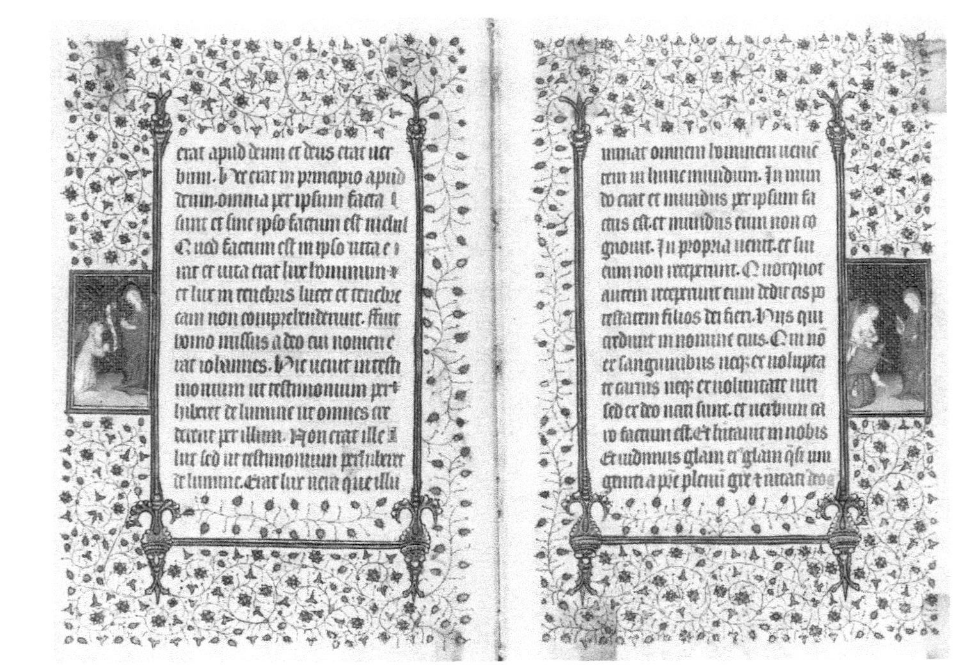

24   Rohan Workshop, *Annunciation*, and *Joseph Presented to Mary*, Gospel of St John, *Fitzwilliam Hours*, Cambridge, Fitzwilliam Museum, MS 62, fols 13v–14r, *c.*1418–30. Reproduction by permission of the Syndics of the Fitzwilliam Museum, Cambridge (© Cambridge, Fitzwilliam Museum)

prophecies, such as that of Isaiah 7. 14, 'Behold a virgin shall conceive', which she was often depicted reading. The two border scenes face each other across the open page, forming a complementary pair which 'recall[s] Mary's double role as both Mother of God and wife of a humble, and understandably confused, husband'.[66] Therefore, on the one hand, the pictures depict divine subject matter, calling attention to Mary's elevation above other women by showing the moment she was chosen to bear the son of God and by showing her in a hierarchical relationship to her husband. On the other hand, the inclusion of Joseph and the juxtaposition of the two images serve to anchor Mary's God-given motherhood in the secular world of marriage that would be recognisable to contemporary lay people.

The reference to Mary's earthly family also complements the other images of saintly married women and mothers in the manuscript, like St Anne and St Elizabeth of Hungary. For lay, aristocratic women like Yolande of Aragon and her daughter, this combining of secular, noble and holy elements in the pictures helped to bridge the gap between their social roles as wives and (potential) mothers and the ideal figure of the Virgin by providing a human context to the holy stories. In a similar way, the invocation of St Anne, St Elizabeth and the Virgin in prayers for childbirth also drew attention to Christ's human, rather than divine, lineage by creating a link between these women's childbearing and that of the woman for whom the prayer was being said.

The humanising aspects of the Marian scenes in the *Fitzwilliam Hours* are continued in the *Nativity* scene, which accompanies the following Gospel of St Luke. The Gospel opens with a large miniature of the Evangelist with a *Nativity of Christ* in the borders (plate 10). The border scene serves to illustrate not only the *Pilgrimage* but also the account of Christ's birth given in this Gospel, so continuing the theme of the Incarnation begun with St John's Gospel a few pages earlier. Furthermore, the colours used to depict Joseph and Mary, red and blue respectively, form a visual link with the blue tunic and red cloak of the Evangelist in the main miniature thus reinforcing the connection between the narrative of St Luke's Gospel and that told in the margins. The Virgin kneels in adoration before the Christ Child, who lies on a red cloth. The stable in which Christ was said to have been born is suggested by the wattle fence and canopy and by the fact that Christ lies on the ground; the rich colours and the haloes, however, indicate the special nature of this birth. In contrast to the Virgin, the figures of Joseph and another woman are placed behind the fence, thus separating them from the holy mother and child. Joseph's gesture towards the woman, as if welcoming her or imploring her help, and the way the woman gestures with both hands over the fence towards Mary and Christ, provide a secular aspect to this birth scene in the same way that popular late-medieval plays also often gave the biblical stories human and contemporary touches by having Joseph send for a midwife to help his wife in labour, or having Mary visited by her mother and sisters.[67]

As the previous chapters showed, the situational eye of aristocratic women like Yolande of Aragon and her daughter Yolande of Anjou would have been informed by the practice of women assisting each other during childbirth and lying-in. They could, therefore, have interpreted the inclusion of a female figure here as alluding to that practice and giving the holy birth an earthly, contemporary touch. For Yolande of Aragon, a viewer particularly interested in the *beata stirps* of the house of Anjou, these allusions worked to draw a parallel between the births of holy figures and the births of members of the Angevin blessed dynasty. Also aware of her family's illustrious, sainted past, Yolande of Anjou would also have been able to read the *Fitzwilliam Hours*' prayers to, and images of, Angevin saints and holy motherhood as references to her own ancestral heritage and as an encouragement to participate in this *beata stirps* through the conception of children within her marriage to Francis of Brittany.

Viewed through the younger Yolande's situational eye, the features of the *Fitzwilliam Hours*' illuminations brought her close to the images in the same way that Musacchio suggested that contemporary details on *deschi da parto* helped Italian viewers feel closer to holy scenes.[68] Furthermore, it was shown in Chapter 3 how the birth imagery on *deschi* and in manuscript miniatures placed the woman 'on top'. It was thus argued that these generic images could function not only to (re)assert women's place in the social hierarchy but as a symbol of the instability of that hierarchy, especially during childbearing. Yolande and the other female viewers of the images of holy motherhood in the *Fitzwilliam Hours* could, therefore, have discerned the multivalency of the images, interpreting them as both an encouragement to perform their roles correctly, and as continual reminders of the way that performance could also upset the established norm by making them and their bodies the centre of attention. Starting with the illuminated page at the beginning of Matins, the following discussion analyses in more detail how Yolande of Anjou's situational eye nuanced her viewing of the maternal imagery in the *Fitzwilliam Hours*.

The opening of the hour of Matins shows an *Annunciation* surrounded by scenes from the life of the Virgin (plate 3). These border images begin on the left-hand side with the refusal of Anne and Joachim's offering in the

Temple. In the *Golden Legend*, Joachim was said to have been turned away from the Temple for his childlessness, which was considered to be a punishment from God.[69] It is perhaps, therefore, significant that here both parents are shown, kneeling at the altar, each offering a lamb. In the same way that the inclusion of Joseph was earlier shown to add a human, secular touch to the narrative of the Incarnation, the presence of both Anne and Joachim at the refusal of their offering secures the story of the Virgin's birth in the context of a legitimately married couple, and the following image shows Joachim and Anne embracing at the Golden Gate after having heard, separately, the archangel's annunciation of the Virgin's birth.[70] The parents of the Virgin also appear together in the scene at the bottom right of the page watching their daughter climb the steps of the Temple, where she spent her early life. The scene on the right-hand side of the folio depicts another secular aspect of Mary's life, her marriage to St Joseph.

Bringing St Joachim and St Joseph into the images in their social roles as husbands and fathers again serves to link the holy, yet secular, families with those of the contemporary viewers and to stress marriage as the proper context for childbearing. However, it is worth noting that despite the place given to St Joseph and St Joachim on this page, only St Anne and the Virgin are depicted with haloes. As in the image accompanying the suffrages to St Anne and her daughters discussed above (plates 8–9), and in the *Holy Kinship* by the Follower of the Master of St Veronica noted in the Introduction (figure 8), such a focus draws attention to the special role of women, rather than men, in the establishment of Christ's dynasty. Thus for Yolande of Aragon as for her daughter, the images on this page functioned as a way of aligning themselves and their own blessed family with the narratives of Christ's *beata stirps*. As an older woman, mother and educator, Yolande of Aragon might have been particularly drawn to the miniature of the *Virgin's Presentation in the Temple* in constructing her role as an educator. Smith has argued that in some Books of Hours owned by women such images of the *Presentation*, like those of St Anne teaching the Virgin, were designed to encourage their owners 'to imitate the concern of the Virgin's parents for the religious, literate and moral education of their children'.[71]

For Yolande of Anjou, receiving this book from her mother around the time of her marriage, this page also contained many subtle allusions. In its celebration of the sanctity of marriage, the God-given gift of children, the role of women, in particular, in generating a holy lineage and educating their children, the page could become a space through which she could visualise, and pray for assistance in, the execution of her social role, not only as the future duchess of Brittany and potential mother to its heirs but also in continuing the Angevin *beata stirps* so celebrated elsewhere in the manuscript. Paying particular attention to the roundel of the *Birth of the Virgin* with reference to the material discussed in Chapter 3, demonstrates how Yolande of Anjou's situational eye would have rendered her especially sensitive to the maternal themes on this page.

The depiction of the Virgin's birth at the bottom of the Matins page fits the schematic, simplified representations of the birth of famous or holy figures discussed at the beginning of this book. A haloed St Anne sits in a canopied bed, the blue and gold fabric of the canopy and the cover providing a direct visual link to the figures of the Virgin elsewhere on the page. A woman holding the swaddled, haloed Mary presents her to her mother. Yet, as with the *Nativity* scene discussed earlier from the *Pilgrimage of Jesus Christ* (plate 10), the presence of the additional woman serves to secure this special, holy birth in the contemporary world of the viewer where women in childbirth were assisted by female friends and relatives.

During their nine-year marriage, Francis and Yolande had one child, a boy named Rohan, who probably died early in early childhood, since he did not succeed his father in 1450.[72] Although there is no evidence for how Yolande's lying-in chamber was hung after the birth of this child, Eleanor of Poitiers's treatise discussed above showed that aristocratic women from Burgundy and France were schooled in the furnishings of estate. For example, she states that the *chambre de parement* of Isabel of Bourbon, duchess of Burgundy, included a bed with a large canopy that was worked with fine and very rich gold embroidery (*brodé de fin or, moult riche*).[73] The presence of a canopy or *celour* was, Eames notes, 'a necessary adjunct for beds of the seigneurial classes' from the fourteenth century onwards, functioning as 'a barometer of power'.[74] Yolande's situational eye would thus have been attuned to the depiction of the Virgin's birth since the bed in which St Anne lies has a large canopy and rich blue covers that are densely embroidered with gold. The white sheets and pillows on St Anne's bed also recall Eleanor's description of the fine gauze (*crespe*) sheets that trailed to the floor, and the bolsters (*carreaux*), which were used in the *chambre de madame*, of the duchess of Burgundy.[75]

When Yolande's niece, Yolande of France, gave birth in 1453, the room was described as having a canopy which covered both beds, fringed at the front with black, white and red borders, and from which were hung blue damask and blue taffeta curtains.[76] Although Yolande of Anjou had died by the time of Yolande of France's lying-in, she would have been familiar with similar furnishings from her own childbearing. Furthermore, she may also have attended one of the many lying-ins of her sister, Marie, or other aristocratic women in her entourage.[77] Evidence from the accounts of Yolande's brother René further shows that Angevin bedrooms were furnished with canopied beds and rich fabrics.[78] Thus, although the *Birth of the Virgin* roundel is very simple and generic, Yolande could have discerned within it certain features that related to her own life as a duchess. The canopy on the bed and the allusion to gold embroidery gives St Anne's lying-in an air of estate and brought this holy mother closer to the secular world which Yolande inhabited. Furthermore, the depiction of a female assistant presenting a healthy child to its mother refers to the care afforded to new mothers during their lying-in, as expounded above. The fact that this woman is not haloed means that she appears as a servant, thus calling attention to a hierarchy of status to which Yolande would also have been sensitive.

In the late middle ages, popular devotional techniques, exemplified in texts like the *Meditations on the Life of Christ*, encouraged the devotee to meditate on images in order to imagine him- or herself at important moments in the lives of the saints. Using the miniatures on this page as aids to a spiritual meditation would have further enhanced this bringing together of the two worlds, by allowing Yolande visualise herself at the Virgin's birth.[79]

The conflating of holy and aristocratic statuses in this tiny miniature of the *Birth of the Virgin* means that, in viewing the manuscript as duchess of Anjou and future duchess of Brittany, Yolande could have found within it, and the page on which it occurs, a number of different meanings during her life. On her marriage, for instance, she may have used it as a focus for her role as potential mother to the duchy's heirs, following in the footsteps of her mother who had given her the book and who, the manuscript suggests, had modelled herself on a number of holy mothers, including St Anne. As Chapter 2 has shown, knowledge of St Anne's place in prayers to ease labour is likely to have been part of the cognitive habits informing an aristocratic woman's situational eye. During her pregnancy, this image of St Anne receiving her child could also have functioned as a space through which Yolande could visualise her own childbearing and manage any fears over the birth, by making a connection between the image, the narrative of St Anne, and specific prayers and remedies for labour. God willing, she too would give birth to a healthy child and enjoy the special arrangements available to her as an aristocratic woman both during and after the birth.

The narrative of the conception of the Virgin that surrounds the *Annunciation*, and other references to miraculous childbirth in the *Fitzwilliam Hours*, may have had a more specific, personal, resonance for Yolande. It is impossible to say whether Yolande had other, unsuccessful pregnancies during her marriage, but the death of Rohan and the fact that no other children survived is likely to have given the duke and duchess cause for concern, as a similar situation would for a later duke, Francis II and his wife Marguerite of Foix. If conception was not proving to be easy, the narrative of St Anne and St Joachim's sterility added another level of significance to Yolande's reading of this opening page of Matins. It revealed the possibility of God's intervention in helping a woman conceive and give birth to a healthy child against all odds – a child who, in addition, was sainted and who would be a key figure in a blessed dynasty.

Other illustrations in the *Fitzwilliam Hours* provided Yolande with further examples of God's intervention in matters of conception. It has already been noted that the *Pilgrimage* cycle of Christ's life allowed additional images of the *Annunciation* and *Nativity* to be included in the *Fitzwilliam Hours*, and that the cycle was organised to coincide with the 'Nativity' Gospel of St Luke. Following the hour of Matins, the opening of the hour of Lauds is illuminated with a large miniature of the Virgin's visit to her cousin St Elizabeth, who conceived St John the Baptist, like St Anne, after years of sterility. The two women greet each other in a landscape and each places a hand on the other's stomach, thus depicting the moment when both women felt their child move in the womb.

Like the *Annunciation* at Matins, the *Visitation* is a standard illustration at Lauds but the depiction of two holy women who had conceived saintly children through God's will, nevertheless, serves as a complement to the scenes of miraculous conception portrayed at Matins and alluded to in the suffrages to St Anne and her daughters. Furthermore, as noted above, St Elizabeth appeared with St Anne and the Virgin in prayers for safe delivery in childbirth. Thus, in so far as the *Visitation* looked forward to the births of St John the Baptist and of Christ and, by extension, the births of contemporary children, this image offered the young Yolande of Anjou a way to think about, negotiate, and pray for conception and successful delivery.

Another image of holy motherhood, the Virgin and Child at the opening of the *Obsecro te* prayer, provided an additional possibility for Yolande of Anjou, and her mother before her, to envisage themselves in close proximity to Christ's family. The *Obsecro te*, in which the speaker appeals to the Virgin's status as a 'mother of God' and 'mother of orphans', addressing 'the Virgin directly, in plaintive tones and in the first person', was a particularly popular place for female donor portraits in Books of Hours.[80] The *Obsecro te*'s donor image was modified when the manuscript passed into the hands of Yolande of Anjou's successor, Isabel Stuart. Although Isabel's ownership of the manuscript is discussed in more detail in Chapter 5, it is worth turning now to the portrait of Isabel presented by St Catherine, since Camille argues that this miniature originally showed Yolande of Aragon, the manuscript's commissioner, presented by St Radegund (plate 7).[81] Considering this portrait even in its current state can still help to suggest how Yolande of Aragon and her daughter Yolande of Anjou engaged with the book and its maternal themes in the context of their own lives.

In the *Obsecro te* miniature in the *Fitzwilliam Hours*, the human and divine figures occupy separate visual and spatial planes. The main space is taken up by the proportionally large Virgin and Child while the much smaller St Catherine and Isabel are restricted to the left-hand corner of the framed image from where they look across an open space towards the edge of the miniature and beyond. The two groups of figures are linked, however, by a scroll with the words *O mater Dei memento mei* (O mother of God, remember me) that extends from the tip of Isabel's hands and is caught by the Christ Child, whose other hand grasps a rosary. The scroll is a symbol of both visual and textual meditation: praying to the Virgin, saying the words of the *Obsecro te*, represented by the scroll, is a way to ask for her remembrance and intercession; meditating on the painted image of oneself at prayer was another means of ensuring a successful petition and of concretising the prayer with a heavenly vision.

Since evidence points to Yolande of Aragon's original ownership of the *Fitzwilliam Hours*, it seems reasonable to suppose that the *Obsecro te* image originally showed Yolande of Aragon, thus placing this wise, mature woman and mother in a privileged position with the ultimate holy mother and her child. The gold fleur de lys on the Virgin's blue cloak marked her with the symbol of royal, but also Angevin, status and drew a visual link between the Virgin and the saints of royal provenance depicted with the same symbol in the suffrages. Camille argues that Yolande would have been depicted with St Radegund, the saint privileged in the suffrages. If so, and the saint appeared dressed in the fleur de lys of France as she does in the suffrages, Yolande's queenly and saintly provenance would have been made explicit.

For the younger Yolande, this page would have offered her a double vision of motherhood, by presenting her with a portrait of her own mother in a posi-tion of piety in front of the Mother of God. Viewed with Yolande of Anjou's situational eye, this miniature and the manuscript as a whole functioned as a tangible link not only between her and the Virgin mother but also between Yolande and her own mother. Given the elder Yolande's success on both the familial and political front, the manuscript could have come to serve as a guide for the younger Yolande to the good execution of her position as an Angevin duchess and as the wife of the heir to the duchy of Brittany.

As a young duchess beginning her married life, Yolande of Anjou could have been particularly sensitive to another aspect of the *Obsecro te* prayer's decoration. The border roundels that accompany the pages of this prayer illustrate part of the *Pilgrimage of Jesus Christ* cycle that began at the Gospel sequences earlier in the manuscript. Folio 21v has a border image depicting the episode when Christ raised Lazarus from the dead. It was shown previously that prayers for assistance in childbirth often included the words *veni* or *exi foras* that Christ used to call Lazarus from the tomb. Therefore, an illustration of Lazarus's resurrection within the context of a prayer to the Virgin's motherhood may well have sharpened the significance of this petition for the younger Yolande and, later, for Isabel Stuart, since both women inherited the manuscript at a time when they were especially concerned with childbearing. Viewed with the situational eye informed by knowledge of popular prayers for labour, the presence of the Lazarus image in the *Obsecro te* gives the prayer an added significance as an aid in praying for assistance or relief in pregnancy and childbirth.

Other prayers in the *Fitzwilliam Hours* provided opportunities to focus on Mary's motherhood and, in particular, to celebrate the human aspect of her relationship with Christ. For example, the miniatures accompanying the suffrage to the Virgin show Mary reclining inside a fenced enclosure with the Christ-Child cosily supported on her lap (figure 25). In the margins of the same page, the Virgin leans tenderly over her son as she supervises Him in a type of wheeled baby-walker. On the following page Mary sits on the ground while Christ plays in a little playpen (fol. 205v). The inclusion of the baby-walker and playpen give the images an intimate, homely touch, making both the Virgin and Christ less hierarchical and more accessible figures. Mary's role as a mother is also brought to the fore through the images accompanying the popular prayers of the *Five Joys of the Virgin* and the *Doulce Dame de miséricorde* (also called the *Fifteen Joys*), which focus on the delights experienced by Mary as mother of Christ.[82]

Like the suffrage miniatures, those accompanying these prayers emphasise the human aspect of Christ's Incarnation and depict Mary's life within a context that would have been recognisable to Yolande of Aragon and her daughter Yolande of Anjou. Both prayers open with a full-page miniature of the Virgin and Child (*Five Joys*: figure 26; *Doulce Dame*, fol. 192r). In the

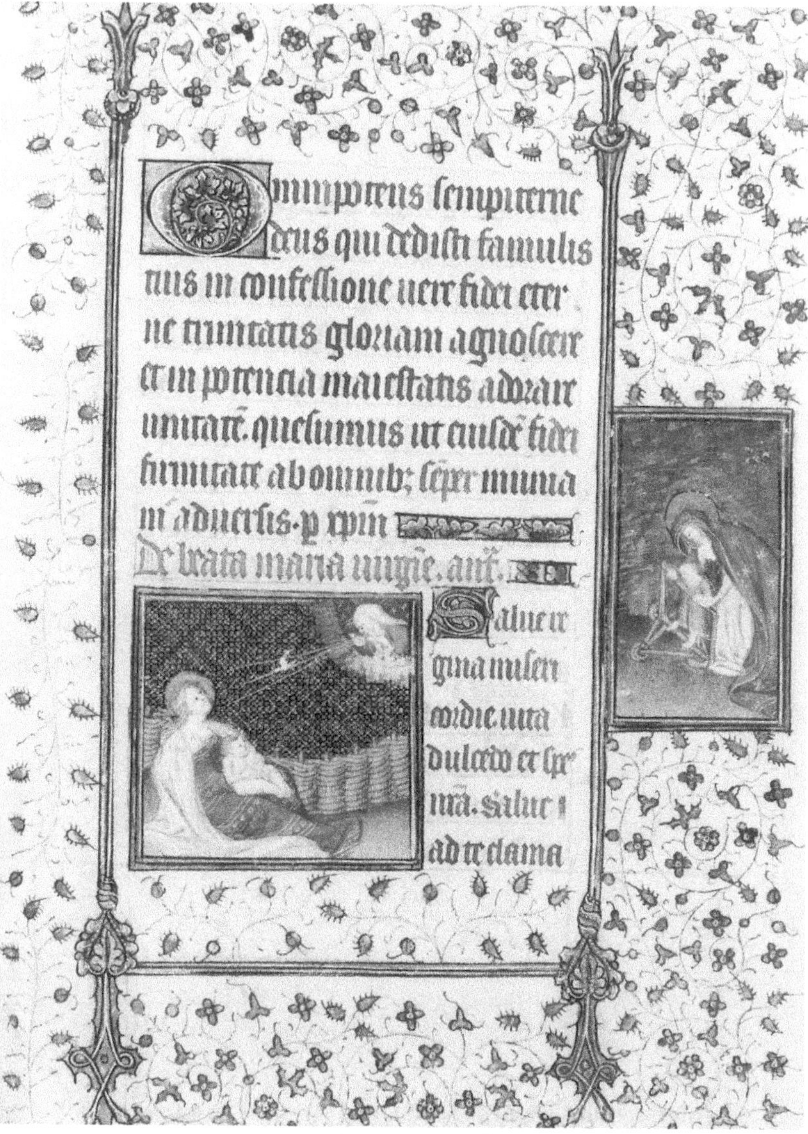

25   Rohan Workshop, *Virgin and Child* (text) and *Virgin Supervising Christ in a Baby Walker* (border), suffrages, *Fitzwilliam Hours*, Cambridge, Fitzwilliam Museum, MS 62, fol. 205r, *c.*1418–30. Reproduction by permission of the Syndics of the Fitzwilliam Museum, Cambridge (© Cambridge, Fitzwilliam Museum)

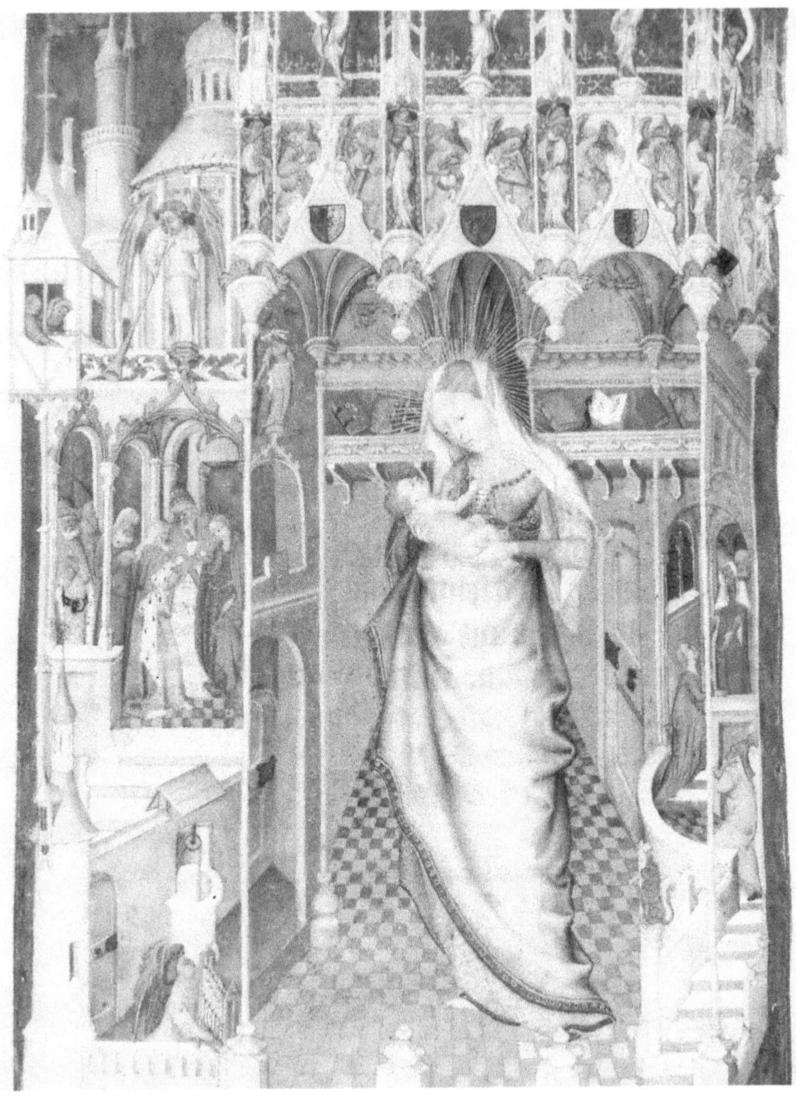

26   Rohan Workshop, *Virgin and Child, Five Joys of the Virgin, Fitzwilliam Hours*, Cambridge, Fitzwilliam Museum, MS 62, fol. 141v, *c.*1418–30. Reproduction by permission of the Syndics of the Fitzwilliam Museum, Cambridge (© Cambridge, Fitzwilliam Museum)

Doulce Dame prayer the Virgin and Child are seated in front of a cloth held up by two angels; one of the angels holds a pot of flowers and the other a harp, which Christ reaches out to take; God the Father appears at the top of the page. In the border of this folio the Virgin is depicted weaving at a frame: this was said to be the Virgin's occupation in the Temple before her marriage. The subsequent border miniatures from this *Doulce Dame* prayer depict other moments from the Virgin's life, including those specifically mentioned in the prayer such as the Annunciation, the Visitation and the Nativity (fols 193r–194r).

The *Five Joys* opens with an image of the Virgin holding the Christ-Child and standing within an elaborate architectural frame. A series of prophets stand on pedestals and emphasise the Virgin's fulfilment of Old Testament prophecies. The church-like building and the figure of blind Synagogue on top of a niche on the left-hand side of the frame indicate that the Virgin is also Ecclesia or Mother Church. The individual scenes incorporated into the border of this miniature show two events which were also depicted in the borders at the opening of Matins: on the left her marriage to Joseph and, on the right, her Presentation in the Temple where she mounts the steps to greet the High Priest. Although not part of the *Five Joys*, these episodes were important events leading up to the conception of Christ and, as in the Matins page, help to tell the story of the Virgin's life.

On the following folios, the border scenes include other images of the Virgin weaving, an *Annunciation* and intimate images of the Virgin holding and suckling Christ, and teaching Him to read (figure 27). Such images highlight Christ's human nature as a child needing nourishment, care and instruction from His mother. In the miniature of the Virgin teaching Christ, the holy pair is seated on the ground and the Christ-Child holds the end of a scroll; His mother holds the other end and gestures towards her son as an indication that she is instructing Him. Like the more frequently-found theme of St Anne teaching the Virgin to read, this miniature draws attention to the role of secular women as educators of young children. Yolande of Aragon was particularly good at executing this role as mentor to the dauphin and later to Margaret of Anjou. By handing her daughter her manuscript she may have been encouraging the younger Yolande to follow in her footsteps.[83] Through her situational eye, Yolande of Anjou would have seen the emphasis in these prayers on the human, secular, aspects of the Virgin's life, especially marriage and childbirth, as providing a model for her own role as a young, aristocratic wife – a model which would have been relevant as she prepared for conception, pregnancy and birth and, after the birth itself, as she began her role as a mother.

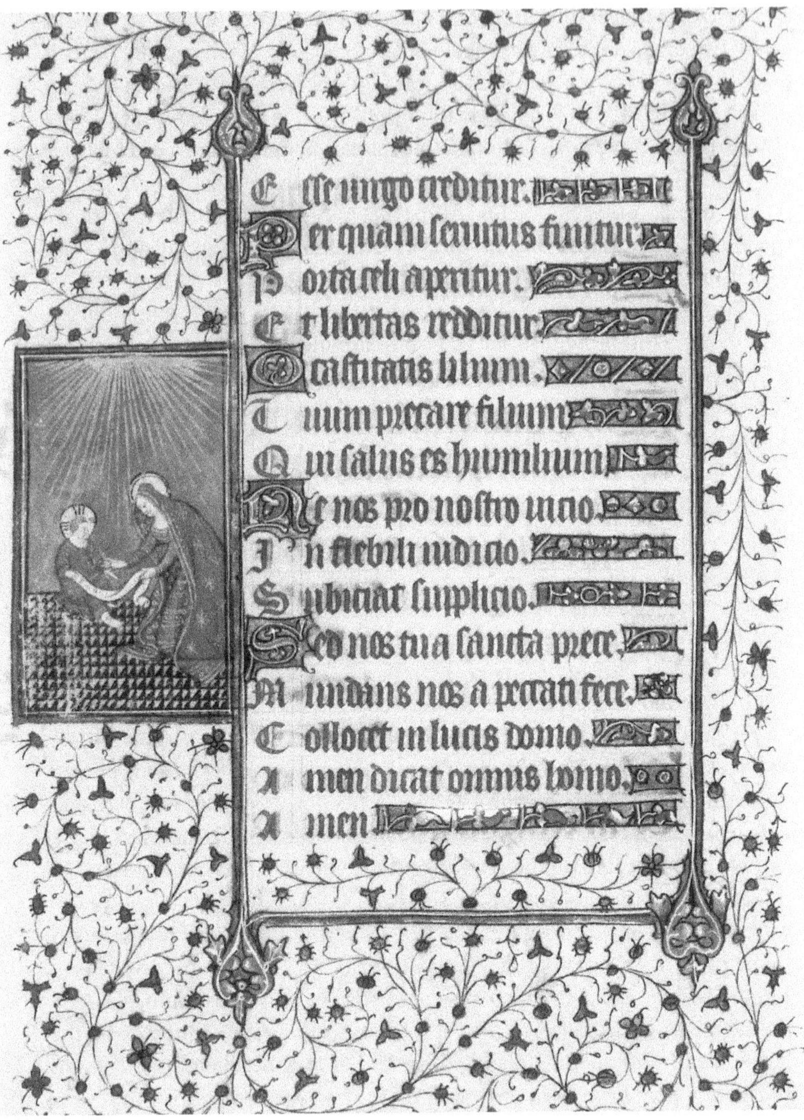

27   Rohan Workshop, *Virgin Teaching Christ, Five Joys of the Virgin, Fitzwilliam Hours*, Cambridge, Fitzwilliam Museum, MS 62, fol. 145v, *c.*1418–30. Reproduction by permission of the Syndics of the Fitzwilliam Museum, Cambridge (© Cambridge, Fitzwilliam Museum)

Yolande of Anjou's social roles as a duchess, wife and mother would also have rendered her sensitive to the levels of meaning in another miniature in the *Fitzwilliam Hours*, the *Purification of the Virgin* that illustrates the hour of Nones (figure 17). Following her pregnancy and lying-in period, Yolande would almost certainly have attended a churching ceremony. It was noted above that late-medieval illustrations of Mary's Purification are often conflated with those of the Presentation of Christ in the Temple and this is the case for the *Fitzwilliam Hours*. That this is both Christ's Presentation and Mary's Purification is indicated by Mary handing Christ to the High Priest and by the presence of a female attendant holding a basket of two doves, Mary's sacrificial offering for her purification.

By the fifteenth century, as Chapter 3 demonstrated, the purificatory aspect of churching was less important than its function as a way for new mothers, their companions and family to give thanks for a successful birth, or at least the safe deliverance of the mother. The ritual provided an excuse for celebration across the social strata, the most lavish displays coming from the aristocracy for whom it offered another occasion to assert their status and authority. The extant accounts of late-medieval churching analysed earlier showed that an aristocratic woman like Yolande would be accompanied by male and female members of the court and by her assistants and that, as for the lying-in, special fabrics were purchased for the duchess to wear and for the room in which the celebrations were held afterwards. Furthermore, during the ceremony she may well have been led into the sacred space of the sanctuary as Rieder suggests was common in certain French rites. Thus, in the same way as Yolande's situational eye was sensitive to the images of conception, pregnancy and birth depicted at Matins and Lauds, it was also able to discern the relevance, for her own circumstances, of the *Presentation-Purification* miniature at Nones. Viewing the manuscript during her pregnancy or her lying-in, Yolande could have imagined herself like the Virgin, dressed in a sumptuous blue and gold robe, approaching the priest at the altar accompanied by a female assistant who holds her sacrifice. This miniature, like the others of holy mothers in the *Fitzwilliam Hours*, thus provided a model through which Yolande could ask for blessing and assistance in executing her social role and through which she could look forward, beyond what would be a physically demanding time, to the safe delivery of her child and her own appearance in church.

The interpretations of the *Fitzwilliam Hours* offered thus far, through the methodological strategy of the situational eye, are intended to suggest how the two likely first owners of the manuscript received and understood its imagery from the social positions that they occupied as aristocratic lay women. The readings have been intended to take account of the expectations placed upon such women but, at the same time, to propose how they could read the images in a positive and 'active' fashion. As Randolph noted in his interpretations of the *dovizie* and *deschi da parto* discussed in Chapter 1, such readings, which stress the fulfilment of the maternal function for a patriarchal society, risk 'short-circuiting for the female viewer even the possibility of contemplation, desire, and intellection'.[84] The risk lies in ascribing to Yolande and her daughter a set of hypothetical responses to a series of maternal and dynastic images that, as the critical approaches of Butler and Aers and Staley suggest, simply reasserts the patriarchal hegemony rather than offering an instance of women's 'agency'.

However, by focusing on the positions from which these two women read the *Fitzwilliam Hours* in conjunction with the evidence from devotional and material culture, it has been possible to propose how these women could have actively engaged with the manuscript in so far as it was first a bespoke, personalised, commission and then a family gift. Through the manuscript, these two duchesses were able to deal with the performance of their roles as aristocratic wives, (future) mothers, and educators. In a similar way, the use of prayers for labour and participation in the rituals of lying-in and churching were also a means to better perform these roles since they were intended to facilitate labour and childbearing and to acknowledge the woman's role. Thus the intertextualities and intervisualities between images and material culture came together through the situational eye in ways that did not necessarily reduce the woman to the role of passive recipient but instead allowed her to harness the images and practices available to her for the better management of her life.

That the types of maternal and dynastic themes found in the *Fitzwilliam Hours* were not destined solely for female viewers but could also be of interest to male viewers is demonstrated by considering three other manuscripts related to the house of Anjou through patronage, workshop and ownership: the *Rohan Hours*, and the two *Hours of René of Anjou*. Whereas the discussion has so far suggested how female viewers engaged with narratives of holy motherhood and blessed lineage, the following section considers how such imagery was understood by the two men who owned these manuscripts: first, Charles of Ponthieu, the future Charles VII, Yolande of Aragon's protégé, and husband of her daughter Marie of Anjou; and, second, René of Anjou, Yolande's second son who inherited the titles of his brother Louis III after the latter's early death. In showing how the situational eye can be applied to male as well as female agents, the following analysis is further informed by James Marrow's interpretation of the unusual stylistic and liturgical contents of the duke of Berry's *Très Belles Heures*, which allude to, or quote from, other manuscripts owned by the duke of Berry and his Capetian and Burgundian relatives.[85]

The *Très Belles Heures*, Marrow argues, are thus 'linked to a group of related Books of Hours made for the duke's forebears and members of his immediate family, and in ways that bind the owners individually and dynastically'.[86] As such, the *Très Belles Heures* offered the duke a symbolic image of stability and continuity in troubled and disruptive times: 'These continuities thus embody a particular kind of historical consciousness, one immediately bound to the time, place, patronage, and circumstances of the commissions.'[87] By turning first to the *Rohan Hours* and then to the *Hours of René of Anjou*, it will be shown that a similar kind of historical and dynastic consciousness contributed to the cognitive habits of the viewers discussed here. The stylistic relationships between these manuscripts and the *Fitzwilliam Hours* imply that together they embodied a collective Angevin interest in self-promotion that derived part of its authority from the historical and contemporary dynastic connections between the houses of France and Anjou. Viewed through the Angevin situational eye, the features and the provenance of the manuscripts functioned to strengthen the resolve of the family, including its associated member, the Dauphin Charles, by providing both symbolic coherence in a time of uncertainty and encouragement to ensure the continuation of the Franco-Angevin *beata stirps*.

A manuscript fit for a king: Charles VII and the *Rohan Hours' Bible moralisée*

The *Rohan Hours* were produced by the Rohan workshop, certainly in the first third of the fifteenth century. It is a luxury manuscript, measuring 290 x 210 mm and is profusely illustrated with full-page miniatures and a marginal cycle of part of the *Bible moralisée*, from Genesis to the Book of Numbers.[88] Attempts to identify the manuscript's original owner are complicated by the presence of an unfinished coat of arms on folio 26v. These arms show, on the dexter side (the viewer's left), those used by Alan IX of Rohan, who died in 1461.[89] The sinister side has a gold ground but nothing more. Some scholars have argued that these arms are part of the original campaign of illumination and that the manuscript was commissioned around 1430, either by the Rohan family, or by Yolande of Aragon for a projected marriage that never took place between Yolande's youngest son, Charles of Maine, and a daughter of Alan IX.[90] The latter proposition, maintained by Avril, is difficult to justify since the Rohan arms appear on the dexter side of the shield, reserved for the male party of the union, whereas Charles was from the house of Anjou.[91] Other critics have followed A. de Laborde's contention that the arms are not original, thus making the manuscript much earlier.[92]

Working on the basis that the arms are not original and following a suggestion by Meiss, the next section proposes that the *Rohan Hours* was commissioned by Yolande of Aragon for her protégé and son-in-law Charles VII. It is first argued that the manuscript's relationship to the *Fitzwilliam Hours* and to other manuscripts associated with Yolande of Aragon place it within her patronage and that for Yolande the manuscript was a way for her not only to assert her protection of the dauphin but also, at the same time, to continue to promote the Angevin dynasty, whose ascendance she hoped to assure through the marriage of Charles and her daughter Marie. It then suggests how Charles viewed the *Rohan Hours* as a gift from his mother-in-law, one which was intended to bolster his contested claims to the French throne and to help him execute his duties as monarch.

The marginal *Bible moralisée* cycle included in the *Rohan Hours* is key to the interpretations offered here since it not only serves to link the manuscript with the Angevin court and with the *Fitzwilliam Hours*, which also contains a marginal cycle, but it also suggests a royal recipient for the manuscript. Furthermore, the extract from the *Bible moralisée* contained in the *Rohan Hours* includes many unusual *in partu* images of the births of Old Testament children in which the mothers are all represented naked from the pelvis upwards and the children are delivered by another woman from beneath a blanket which just about maintains the mother's modesty.

Although this type of representation is a feature of other *Bibles moralisées*, the *Rohan Hours'* images have sometimes been taken out of context to illustrate studies of the history of childbirth. For example, as noted in the Introduction, the *Birth of the Male Children of Israel* was used as the front cover for Laurent's book on childbirth in the middle ages (figure 7). However, considering these images in their original context of both the *Bible moralisée* and the *Rohan Hours* helps to answer some of the questions posed at the beginning of this book about the historical value of images of childbirth. Like the Book of Hours in the John Rylands Library, owned by an Augustinian canon, the *Rohan Hours* is associated with a male reader, which implies that men were certainly not excluded from receiving this kind of imagery and suggests that gender alone is not sufficient a category to understand the appeal and meanings that these images held for different viewers. Here it is shown how the situational eye of Charles of Ponthieu, as a son of France, was informed by cognitive habits that rendered him sensitive not only to the *Rohan Hours* as a whole, but also to the *Bible moralisée* and to its emphasis on holy childbearing.

Evidence for an Angevin provenance for the *Rohan Hours*, specifically for Yolande of Aragon's involvement in the commission, is indicated by the manuscript's connections to several sources known at the Angevin court, or in Yolande's possession. The first of these is the striking dependence of the *Rohan Hours'* marginal *Bible moralisée* on a fourteenth-century Neapolitan copy of this text, now in Paris.[93] This manuscript may have been brought back to France in an Angevin entourage returning from one of Louis II of Anjou's campaigns to reclaim the kingdom of Naples.[94] The compositional similarity between the manuscripts is unmistakeable and Jean Porcher has claimed that the Neapolitan manuscript must have served as a direct exemplar for the *Rohan Hours'* cycle since the Rohan illuminators copied a faint note from the original into their manuscript.[95]

Further evidence for Yolande of Aragon's patronage is found in the *Rohan Hours'* visual quotations from the duke of Berry's *Belles Heures*, which Yolande acquired after the duke's death in 1416. A note in an inventory of the duke's estate indicates that Yolande (*la royne de Secille*) purchased the *Belles Heures*, which she had long admired (*elle ot longeuement veues et advisees icelles heures*), for the sum of 300 *livres tournois*.[96] The Rohan workshop's borrowings from the Limbourg brothers' masterpiece can be seen at many places throughout the manuscript. For example, the figure lying on a sheaf of grain in the *Rohan Hours' Flight into Egypt* (fol. 99r) is modelled on that of the *Belles Heures'* miniature representing the labours for the month of July (fol. 8r), and in another example, the sower from the October calendar page in the *Belles Heures* (figure 28) is repeated in the miniature for September in the *Rohan Hours* (figure 29).[97] Furthermore, the *Rohan Hours* also shows an awareness of another of the duke's manuscripts, the *Très Riches Heures*, and Porcher does not exclude the possibility that Yolande also acquired this manuscript on the settlement of the duke's estate.[98] Parallels can be found, for example, in the horsemen of the *Rohan Hours' Flight into Egypt* which derive from a king and his retinue in the *Très Riches Heures' Meeting of the Magi*.[99] It appears, then, that Yolande made the *Belles Heures*, and possibly the *Très Riches Heures*, available to the Rohan workshop. Given her knowledge and acquisition of the duke's manuscript(s), Yolande's situational eye would have been aware of the quotations from and allusions to her recent purchase in the *Rohan Hours*.

The commission of the *Rohan Hours* consolidated Yolande's interest in illuminated manuscripts and it established a link, through style and

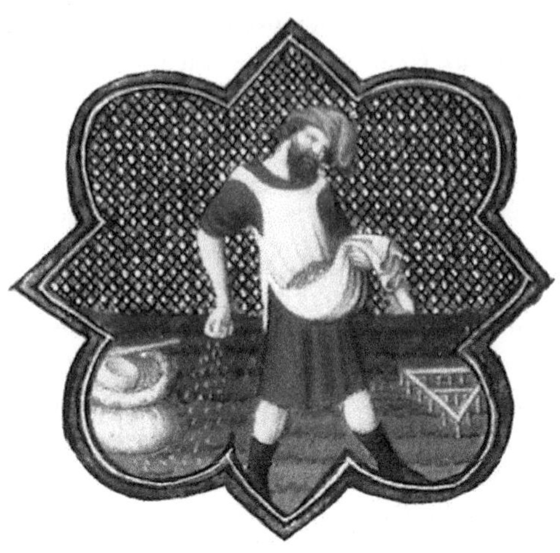

28   Limbourg Brothers, *Sower*, calendar (detail from October), *Belles Heures*, New York, The Cloisters, fol. 11r, *c.*1405–08. The Metropolitan Museum of Art, The Cloisters Collection, 1954 (54.1.1) (Image © The Metropolitan Museum of Art)

contents, to other manuscripts known to or commissioned by her. For instance, the same long-limbed, scrawny figure of Christ is depicted at the beginning of the *Seven Requests* prayer in both the *Fitzwilliam Hours* and the *Rohan Hours* (figures 30–1). The blue sky peppered with tiny gold clouds or stars that appears in many *Rohan Hours'* miniatures, as on the calendar page for September (figure 29), is also found in the *Fitzwilliam Hours*, for example in the sky behind the *Annunciation* scene at Matins, and in the *Paris Hours of René of Anjou*, in the *Nativity* illustrating the hour of Prime (plates 3 and 5). The latter image features the stable and wattle fencing also seen in the *Nativity of Christ* in the *Fitzwilliam Hours* (plate 10) where the figure of St Joseph is, in turn, reminiscent of the white-haired, bearded figure of Adam in the *Rohan Hours' Birth of Cain and Abel* (figure 32). Whereas these stylistic similarities are features of the Rohan workshop, they also gave coherence to Yolande's commissions, drawing on the cognitive habits of her situational eye, just as Marrow argued for a 'historical consciousness' in the duke of Berry's reception of the *Très Belles Heures*.[100]

The *Rohan Hours* were also intrinsically linked to Yolande's own manuscript, the *Fitzwilliam Hours*, through the inclusion of the marginal cycles. The cost of including a marginal cycle and the choice of texts

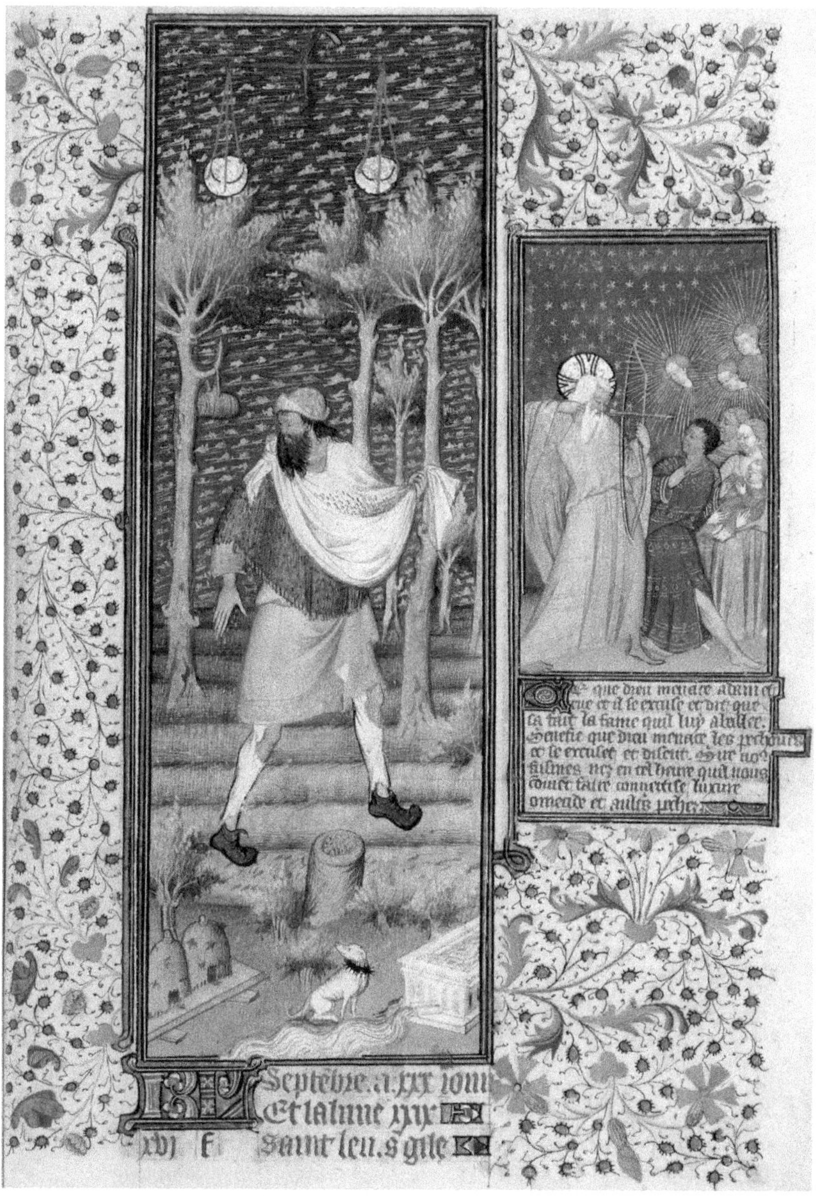

29   Rohan Workshop, *Sower*, calendar (September), *Rohan Hours*, Paris,
Bibliothèque nationale, fonds latin, 9471, fol. 13r, *c.*1420 (© Paris, BnF)

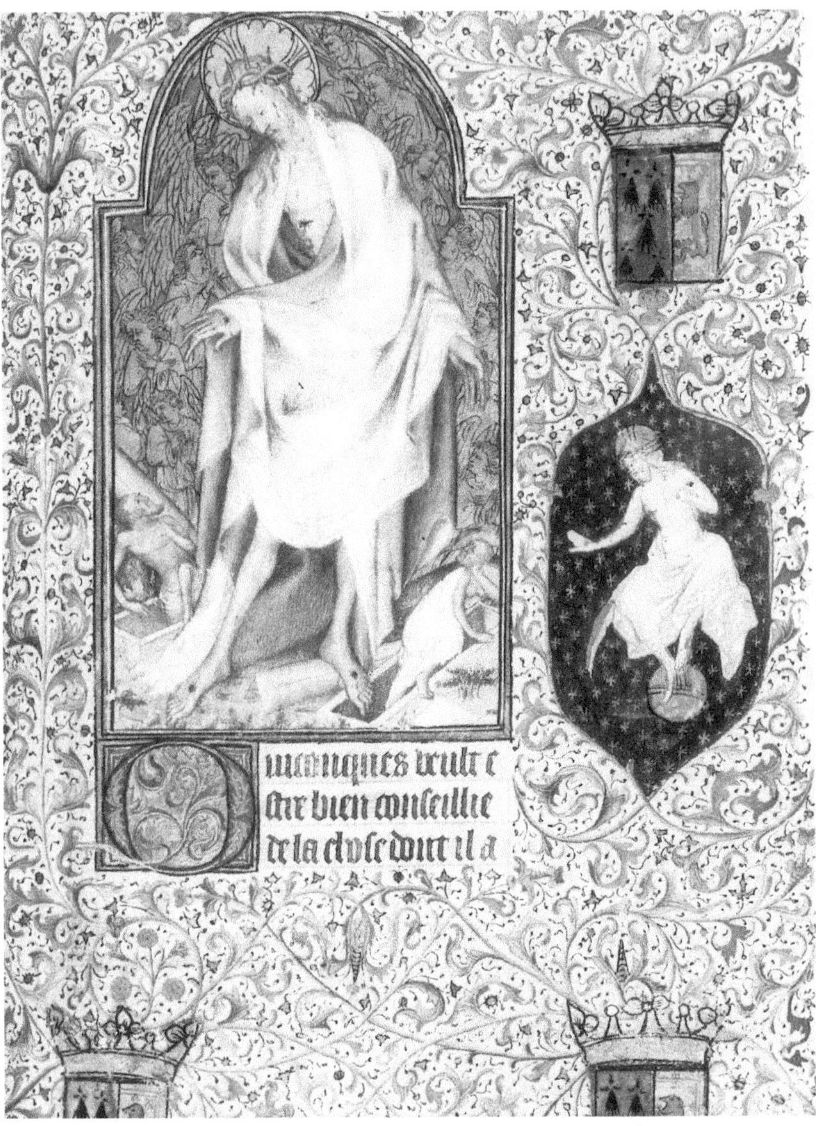

30   Rohan Workshop, *Christ with Crown of Thorns* (text) and *Christ in Judgement* (border), *Seven Requests*, *Fitzwilliam Hours*, Cambridge, Fitzwilliam Museum, MS 62, fol. 199r, *c.*1418–30. Reproduction by permission of the Syndics of the Fitzwilliam Museum, Cambridge (© Cambridge, Fitzwilliam Museum)

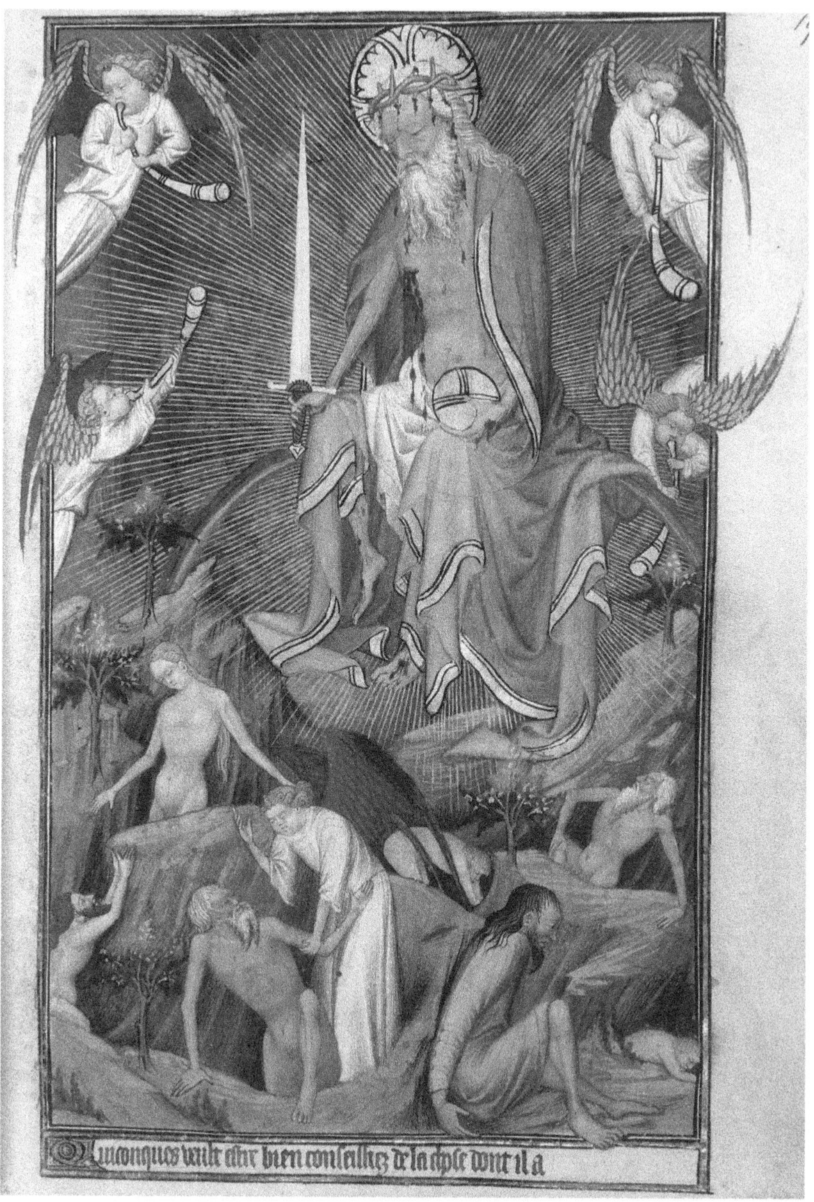

31   Rohan Workshop, *Christ in Judgement, Seven Requests, Rohan Hours,* Paris, Bibliothèque nationale, fonds latin, 9471, fol. 154r, *c.*1420 (© Paris, BnF)

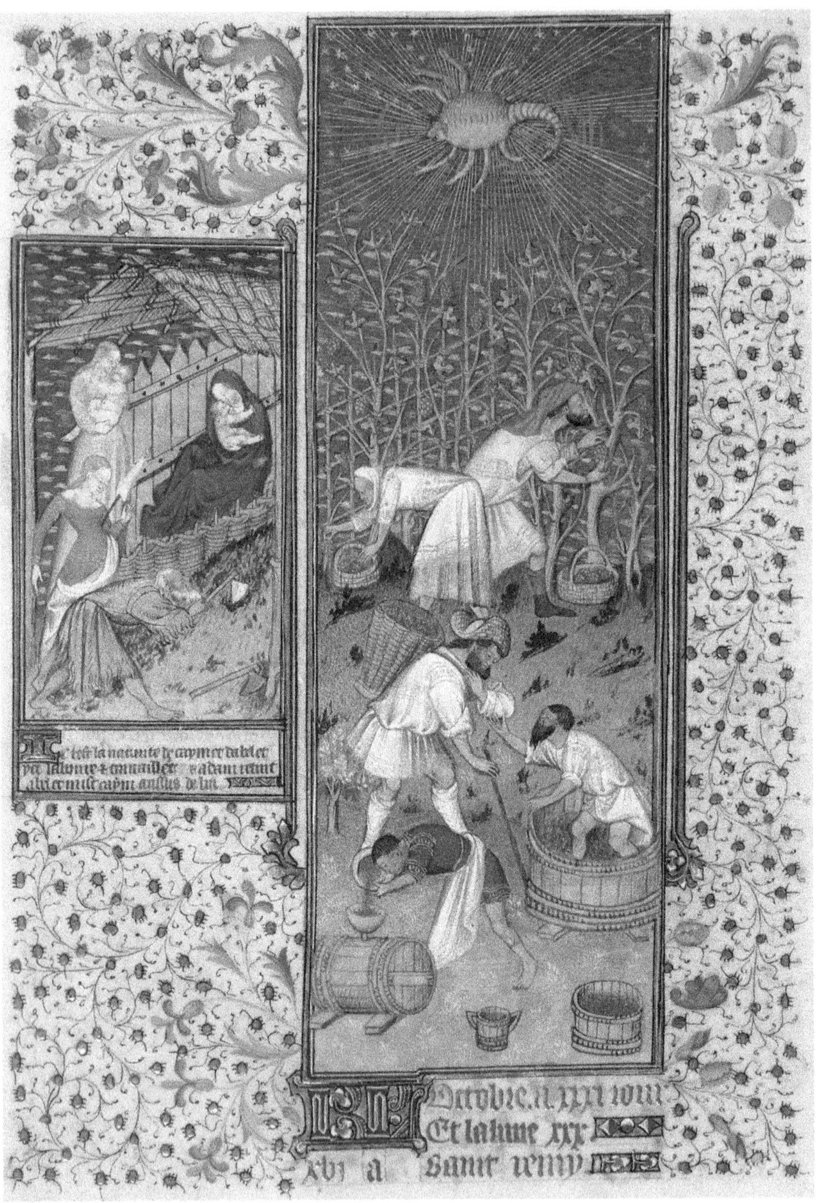

32   Rohan Workshop, *Birth of Cain and Abel*, *Bible moralisée* marginal cycle, *Rohan Hours*, Paris, Bibliothèque nationale, fonds latin, 9471, fol. 14v, *c.*1420 (© Paris, BnF)

indicate that both manuscripts were bespoke commissions that were intended to speak to a particular viewer. Whereas the *Fitzwilliam Hours'* *Pilgrimage* and *Apocalypse* cycles related to contemporary reading interests within Yolande's circle at the Angevin court, the *Bible moralisée* cycle in the *Rohan Hours* specifically implied a royal reader. Yolande of Aragon's association with the Rohan workshop and the reliance of the *Rohan Hours* on manuscripts to which she had access make her a strong candidate for being the manuscript's commissioner. Furthermore, her mentoring of the young dauphin, Charles, who was engaged to her daughter Marie, makes it reasonable to suppose that she commissioned the manuscript for her son-in-law, for whom the *Bible moralisée* cycle would have provided a fitting marker of royal status.

The *Bible moralisée* was primarily a luxury picture book in which a series of biblical stories were paired together, often Old Testament with New Testament, and explained by a series of moralising commentaries or glosses that relate to the everyday lives of Christians. The sheer number of types and antitypes made *Bibles moralisées* extremely expensive to produce, with some books containing over 5,000 images.[101] As a result, nearly all extant copies of the *Bible moralisée* were commissioned by nobility and it came to serve, like the *Mirror of Princes* (*Speculum Principis*) genre of writing, as a way 'to advise lay rulers on the proper ways of governing'.[102] The *Bible moralisée* was associated in particular with Capetian rulers of the late twelfth and thirteenth centuries.[103] A copy owned by St Louis IX may have been commissioned for him by his mother, Blanche of Castile, during the early years of her regency (*c*.1226–34).[104] King John II (the Good) of France (1319–64) also owned a copy, which ended up in the duke of Burgundy's collection.[105] The decision to incorporate a marginal cycle of this text into the *Rohan Hours* was thus not a casual choice on the part of the commissioner. Not only was the cost of producing such a profusely illuminated manuscript enormous but the connotations of the *Bible moralisée* itself implies that the patron was of, or was aligning themselves with, the status and luxurious patronage of the French royal household. By commissioning the *Rohan Hours* for Charles VII, Yolande would have created, as she had done in the *Fitzwilliam Hours*, another tangible embodiment of the Anjou family's royal connections and aspirations. Whereas the *Fitzwilliam Hours* celebrated Yolande's own status and the illustrious Franco-Hungarian history of the house of Anjou, the *Rohan Hours* indicates her immediate interest in the house of France. At the same time as it symbolised her support for the dauphin and bolstered the legitimacy of his position, the manuscript also represented her hopes for the future of the duchy of Anjou through the alliance of her daughter Marie with the future Charles VII.

As the third son of Charles VI and Isabeau of Bavaria, Charles of Ponthieu had not initially been destined for the crown. However, following the death of his two older brothers, Louis and John, in 1416 and 1417 respectively, he suddenly found himself dauphin at the age of fourteen. Charles's position was, nevertheless, increasingly unstable: his father was mentally ill and neither he, nor Isabeau, were willing to support their son's claims to the throne in the face of the threat from the English king, Henry V. Isolated from his own family, Charles found refuge and counsel with the family of his fiancée, Marie of Anjou, to whom he had been engaged since 1414 as a means to strengthen the links between the ducal and royal houses.[106] When Charles fled Paris in 1418, his new power-base became the Loire region, including Saumur, where Yolande of Aragon's own castle was situated.[107] Yolande's support and promotion of her son-in-law meant that he gradually became 'the symbolic, as well as the tangible, alternative to the coalition which was forming between Burgundy and Henry V of England'.[108] Yolande's protection became particularly important from 1420 onwards when Charles's parents, Charles VI and Isabeau of Bavaria, and his rivals Henry V and duke Philip of Burgundy signed the Treaty of Troyes, which disinherited the dauphin and proclaimed Henry V, married to Charles's sister Catherine, and his children, the successors of Charles VI.[109]

As a member of the French royal house, Charles would have been aware of the *Bible moralisée* as a book with royal associations and he would have understood that its presence in the *Rohan Hours* bolstered his position as divinely-appointed heir of France. Furthermore, Charles may also have appreciated the allusions to the duke of Berry's manuscripts, now in the possession of his mentor, that were included in the *Rohan Hours*. The duke of Berry was Charles's great uncle and when he died without any surviving male heirs, his territories reverted to the Crown. Charles thus inherited the duchy of Berry at the same time as he became heir to the French Crown. Therefore, he could have seen quotations from the duke's manuscripts in the *Rohan Hours* as a reference to his own family and status.

In the same way that Marrow suggested the duke of Berry saw the *Très Belles Heures* as embodying a 'historical consciousness', so it might be claimed that Charles would have viewed the *Rohan Hours* as a sign of his own dynastic history as well as his future as king of France with the support of, and in alliance with, the house of Anjou. The manuscript could have functioned in this way at one of either of two distinct points in Charles's life, both of which allow for the discrepancies in dating the manuscript.

If the manuscript had been executed at an early date, from around 1418 up until the death of Charles VI in 1422, Charles would have received it while still dauphin. Symbolically then, the regal associations of the manuscript would have served to legitimate Charles's position as heir apparent. A later date of execution, perhaps 1429 or 1430, means the manuscript could have been made to celebrate Charles's eventual victory over the supporters of his English nephew, Henry VI, and his official accession to the throne: his coronation took place in Rheims cathedral in 1429. Either way, the marginal *Bible moralisée* cycle referred to Charles's regal status, legitimated his claim to rule, and offered a moralistic guide to leading a good life.[110] In order to elucidate the importance of the *Bible moralisée* further, the discussion turns now to the *Bible*'s many birth scenes. Doing so also reveals that the situational eye of a male, aristocratic viewer was able to understand nuances in images of holy, miraculous childbirth, in a way that takes them beyond the 'bastion of female solidarity and omnipotence' described by Greilsammer.[111]

In the *Rohan Hours*, the *Bible moralisée* starts right at the beginning of the book with the calendar, and runs from the Book of Genesis to the Book of Numbers. The moralisations, several of them told through the pairings of images of childbirth, draw parallels or stress the differences between the Old and the New Testaments, Jews and Christians, and the need to keep one's faith and to ensure the continuation of the Christian Church. Thus, through the image of the *Birth of Male Children of Israel* (figure 7), paired with an image of Ecclesia and Synagogue (labelled *la vieille loy*), it is explained that just as Israelite women raise their male children and do not kill them, so the Holy Church raises all male children who are fruits of the Gospels. Viewed through Charles's situational eye, the birth scenes conflated the macrocosm and the microcosm, speaking to his need to procreate legitimately in order to ensure not only the succession of God's law but also his own prestigious lineage.

The first of the *Bible moralisée* birth scenes is the image on folio 14v in the margins of the calendar page for October; it combines the birth of Cain and Abel with Adam and Eve labouring after the Fall (figure 32). In the foreground, Eve stands spinning while Adam toils with an axe. In the background, seated against a fence beneath a stable-like structure, Eve holds a child close to her. This representation of Eve and the way she is dressed in a blue robe evokes images of her anti-type, the Virgin-Ecclesia, found throughout the *Bible moralisée* images. This visual connection between the old and the new Eve thus emphasises the redemptive nature of the Fall. Next to Eve stands another female figure also holding a child: this could be interpreted either as another depiction of Eve, holding her second son, or perhaps as a female assistant helping Eve with both her children. The rubric notes how Adam favours Abel over Cain, which is interpreted on the following folio as an allegory of Christ who keeps the Christians with him while driving the Jews out of Holy Church: the miniature shows God the Father meeting figures at the door of a church-like building (fol. 15r). Advice to Christians to remain faithful to God's law and to respect Holy Church is continued in the moralisations on the births of Esau and Jacob, and Perez and Zerah. However, in contrast to the post-partum scene of the *Birth of Cain and Abel*, these two scenes follow the *in partu* style of representation, already seen in the *Birth of the Male Children of Israel*, showing the actual moment of the birth.

In the miniature of the *Birth of Esau and Jacob* (figure 33), Rebecca is depicted sitting on a chair with a red cushion, under a stable-like structure similar to that in the *Birth of Cain and Abel*. Her hands are raised in an attitude of prayer; a blue cloth with gold trim covers the lower part of her body. Two babies emerge from her pelvic area beneath the cover, one following on the heels of the other. Another female figure, seated on the floor in front of Rebecca, takes hold of the first child. Above her, on the right-hand side, a male figure is shown in the act of hunting with a bow and arrow. The rubric accompanying the image informs the reader that Rebecca has two children, Jacob and Esau, but whereas Jacob stays with his mother and does her bidding, Esau goes into the woods to hunt animals and quarrels with his household. The significance of this biblical story is explained by the antitype on the following page. Showing a miniature of the Madonna of Mercy standing in front of a church while men attack her with swords, the rubric explains that Rebecca stands for Holy Church who gives birth to two types of people: those Christians who do her will, represented by Jacob who stays with his mother, and those miscreants who abandon her, symbolised by Esau who leaves her.[112] The image thus served as a warning to the reader to behave in a Christian manner and to follow God's teachings.

In addition to its moralised explanation, the story of Rebecca and her sons is also one of miraculous conceptions. Rebecca was married to Isaac, who was himself conceived by Sarah and Abraham after years of sterility. Rebecca conceived the twins Jacob and Esau after Isaac entreated God for His help because Rebecca was barren.[113] Charles may, therefore, have viewed this image of the *Birth of Esau and Jacob* and its antitype as an example of God granting children to his deserving subjects in order that they might continue His Law. As such, the pair of images functioned as a reminder of Charles's duty as a Christian king not only to protect Holy

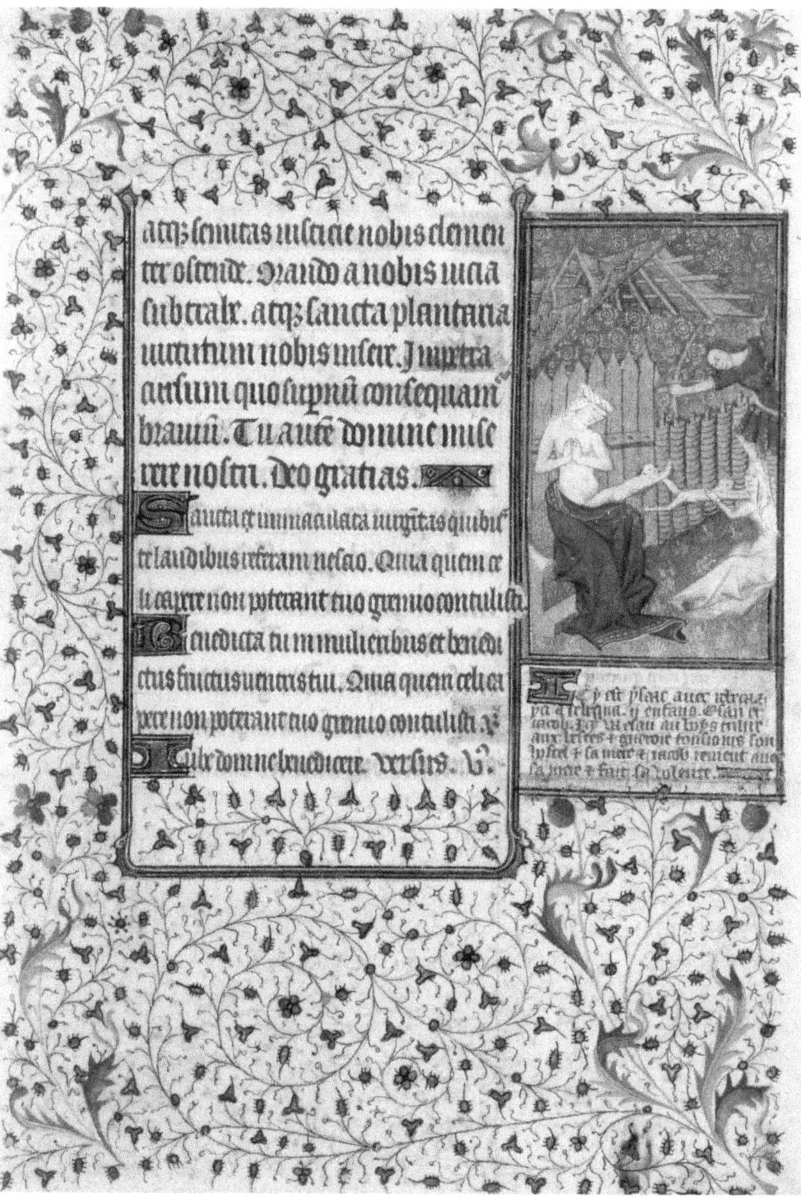

33   Rohan Workshop, *Birth of Esau and Jacob*, *Bible moralisée* marginal cycle, *Rohan Hours*, Paris, Bibliothèque nationale, fonds latin, 9471, fol. 55r, *c*.1420 (© Paris, BnF)

Church but also of the need to bear children to ensure the continuation of his and, by extension, God's dynasty since, as discussed below, French kings associated themselves with Christ's ancestor, King David.

The theme of holy lineage is reinforced through the story of Tamar in the *Birth of Perez and Zerah* (figure 34). In the Book of Genesis, Tamar's husband Er was slain by God for wickedness, and she was then promised to his brother Onan. When Onan did not give her children, his father Judah promised her to his youngest son Shelah, although this union never took place.[114] Disguising herself as a prostitute, Tamar tricked Judah into sleeping with her and she became pregnant with twins. When Judah found out he tried to have her killed but when she produced the staff, signet and cloak that she had taken from him in payment, he realised his own fault and spared her life. While delivering Tamar's twins, the midwife tied a red thread to the hand of the first child to emerge, thus marking the identity of the first-born, Zerah. Yet the child withdrew and his brother Perez came out first. It is this episode which is represented in the *Rohan Hours'* miniature. Tamar is seated, swathed in a pale pink cloak which falls open around her stomach; two children emerge from beneath the cloak. A woman kneeling in front of Tamar receives the two children, one of whom has a red thread attached to him. The miniature's pairing with an image of Ecclesia giving birth to two children (figure 35), reveals that Tamar's first child, who was identified with a red thread by the midwife, represents Christians, who are responsible for Holy Church and matrimony.

Through his situational eye Charles could have read a number of subtle references in this story. On one level the story referred to Judah's lack of responsibility in not looking after his daughter-in-law, and to the sin of fornication and illegitimate children. Following the Treaty of Troyes in 1420, Charles found himself without the support of his immediate blood family, and the fact that his mother Isabeau of Bavaria had agreed to the Treaty fuelled rumours that Charles was in fact a bastard and thus had no legitimate claim to the throne – rumours which plagued Charles during his early years as dauphin.[115] The story of Tamar and the contrasting antitype thus draw attention to the transgressions of God's law by presenting marriage, rather than adultery, as the proper context for procreation. This provided a stark contrast to the rumours circulating about Charles's legitimacy and thus, implicitly, about his mother. On another level, the story of Tamar also shows how good can come out of a transgressive relationship since, through the episode of his adultery, Judah took responsibility for his actions and, importantly, the royal line of King David was descended from the child Perez, the line from which Christ himself was born.[116]

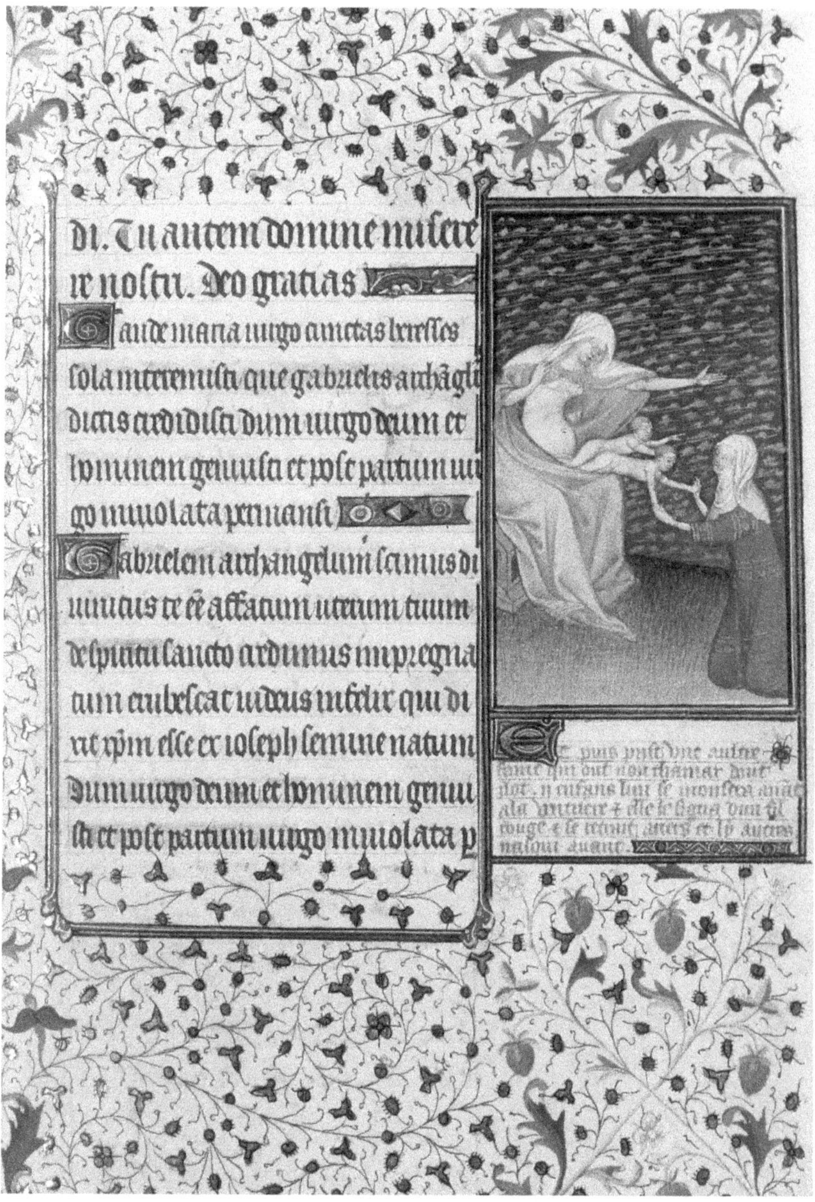

34   Rohan Workshop, *Birth of Perez and Zerah, Bible moralisée* marginal cycle, *Rohan Hours*, Paris, Bibliothèque nationale, fonds latin, 9471, fol. 67r, *c.*1420 (© Paris, BnF)

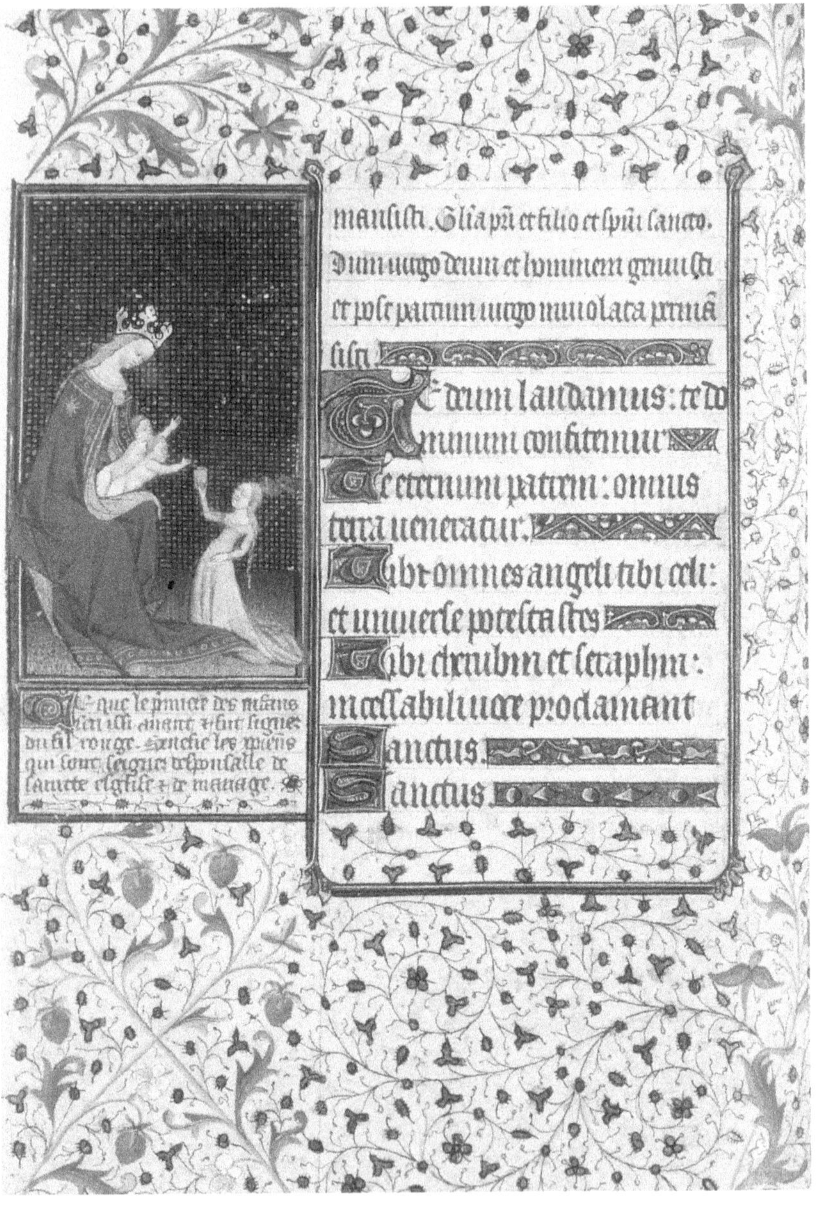

35   Rohan Workshop, *Ecclesia, Bible moralisée* marginal cycle, *Rohan Hours*, Paris, Bibliothèque nationale, fonds latin, 9471, fol. 67v, *c.*1420 (© Paris, BnF)

Furthermore, Charles, like Perez, was not the first-born son yet he was still the head of, and could hope to engender, an illustrious lineage.

As Charles's counsellor and as the commissioner of the *Rohan Hours*, Yolande of Aragon may therefore have been playing to Charles's particular interests and sensitivities just prior to, or during the early part of, his reign. In particular, by choosing to include the beginning of the *Bible moralisée* in the *Rohan Hours*, Yolande was able not only to warn Charles of the need to secure his own lineage with legitimate heirs but also to draw out the well-established practice of allying French kings with biblical ancestors like King David.[117] As Daniel H. Weiss notes, by the time of Louis IX, 'the assimilation was so complete that in 1239 Pope Gregory IX was led to characterize the French as the new chosen people' by noting how, '"just as [Judah's tribe] was taken up to receive special blessing, so the kingdom of France is distinguished above all other peoples . . . by being singled out for honor and grace by the Lord" '.[118] For Charles, the *Bible moralisée* brought the biblical and the contemporary worlds together by alluding to the conjunction of Old Testament genealogical narratives with those of the house of France.

Two more birth scenes in the *Rohan Hours*, the *Birth of Moses* and the *Nativity of Christ*, contain other elements that served to bring the secular, regal and divine worlds closer together, this time through references to the material culture of contemporary childbearing. It has already been shown that in the *Fitzwilliam Hours' Birth of the Virgin*, for example, the opulent bed in which St Anne receives her child and the presence of another woman alluded to the experiences or expectations of the manuscript's aristocratic female readers. Although the proposed owner of the *Rohan Hours* was a man, he, too, would have been sensitive to the decorations and furnishings of royal bedrooms and this may have extended to the particular preparations made for royal childbirths. The accounts of King Edward IV of England discussed in chapter 3, showed how the king's household ordered special fabrics to decorate the bedrooms used to receive its Burgundian visitors, and other accounts from France and Anjou suggest that rich draperies and special bedroom furniture were also appreciated by aristocratic men.[119] Therefore, in viewing the *Rohan Hours'* miniatures of the *Birth of Moses* and its antitype the *Nativity of Christ* (plates 11–12), Charles could have used his cognitive habits to discern the air of high estate given to these holy births and thus to draw further parallels between the biblical stories and his own status as dauphin and the king of the blessed Frankish dynasty.

The *Birth of Moses* shows the mother in a large canopied bed, rather like the one in which St Anne sits in the *Fitzwilliam Hours* (plate 3). As noted previously, the canopied bed was a clear marker of a household's estate and here the rich blue and gold covers and curtains reveal that this is no ordinary birth. A similar note of luxury is given to the *Nativity of Christ* scene where, despite the traditionally poor, outdoor setting, the Virgin is depicted wearing an opulent cloak and is covered in a blue and gold cloth. This representation of the *Nativity of Christ* is, in fact, an interesting image which contains a number of conflicting features. On the one hand, such an *in partu* depiction of the Nativity might be seen as contradicting the uniqueness of the Virgin birth by showing Mary apparently undergoing a normal, physical childbirth. On the other, it serves to emphasise the human aspect of Christ as someone who was literally born of a woman. Yet, the depiction of the Virgin as fully-clothed not only marks her difference from Moses' mother and from her other Old Testament predecessors but also reinforces her conflation with the figure of Ecclesia who appears, fully-clothed and giving birth to two children, as the antitype to the *Birth of Perez and Zerah* (figure 35). Thus whereas the *in partu* representations clearly locate Christ's ancestry in the human, physical world and bring the secular and the divine closer together, the difference in the mothers' state of undress serves to maintain a distinction between the Virgin-Ecclesia and her Old Testament predecessors, and between the Virgin and ordinary women. Yet the depiction of the Virgin dressed in, and surrounded by, opulent fabrics reminiscent of those commissioned for royal bedrooms and lying-ins suggests that Charles could have interpreted these images as a reinforcement of the proximity between Christ's *beata stirps* and his own Frankish lineage, which God had chosen to favour.

So far in this chapter it has been suggested how the iconographic programmes of the *Fitzwilliam Hours* and the *Rohan Hours* were designed to express the dynastic and political interests of the manuscripts' patron, Yolande of Aragon and, in the case of the *Rohan Hours*, those of the intended recipient Charles VII. In particular, it has been shown that the social situations of Yolande of Aragon, her daughter Yolande of Anjou, and the dauphin rendered them sensitive to the themes of *beata stirps*, holy motherhood and miraculous childbirth, and that they could have interpreted the representations of these themes in their manuscripts as an encouragement to generate their own lineage and to ask for God's help in doing so. Viewed through their situational eye, these themes served to promote both the house of Anjou and the dauphin whose inheritance of the French crown was far from certain. By turning to two Books of Hours belonging to Yolande's son René of Anjou, it is possible to show how this Angevin duke also celebrated his family's connections to the house of

France and used manuscripts with symbolic coherence to create a sense of stability at a time plagued by war, contested lands and untimely deaths. René's *Hours* also show that an aristocratic but not necessarily female, situational eye was sensitive to images of holy motherhood and could interpret them as markers of dynastic ambition.

Recycling, relics and *rois morts*: the *Paris* and *London Hours of René of Anjou*

René of Anjou was born in 1409, the second son of Yolande of Aragon and Louis II of Anjou. In addition to the County of Guise, René added the duchies of Bar and Lorraine to his territories through his marriage to Isabel of Lorraine in 1420. Following the death of his elder brother Louis III, in 1434, René went on to inherit the duchy of Anjou and, a year later, the kingdom of Naples. In the absence of children of her own, Joan II of Naples (1373–1435) had adopted Louis III as her heir and after his death she transferred these rights to René before she died. René's territories and his political affiliations to the king of France thus made him an important figure in French politics in the first half of the fifteenth century. However, René's titles were not uncontested and his support for Charles VII at the battle of Bulgnéville in 1431 landed him in the captivity of the Philip the Good, duke of Burgundy, for two long periods between 1431 and 1434.

Throughout his lifetime, René was an avid patron of the arts and many of the manuscripts and paintings commissioned by him, such as the image of him at prayer in his *Paris Hours*, served to demonstrate and assert both his piety and his social status in the face of opposition (figure 36). Although there is no space here to discuss René's literary interests and artistic acquisitions in their entirety, the two Books of Hours on which this section focuses, nevertheless, reveal that René took great interest in the quality and provenance of his manuscript collection.[120] He could well have inherited such taste from his mother's patronage of the Rohan workshop and her interest in the duke of Berry's manuscripts. René's acquisition of his *London* and *Paris Hours*, and the additions he made to them, indicate that the manuscripts functioned for him as markers of his status and aspirations, and that they provided material and symbolic links between him and other members of his family. The calendar in the *Paris Hours*, for example, was used to record important dates relating to members of the Anjou family until 1446, including René's own marriage, the births of his children, and his involvement in the conflicts that became the Hundred Years' War.[121] Furthermore, after his accession to the duchy of Anjou in 1434, René had extra miniatures

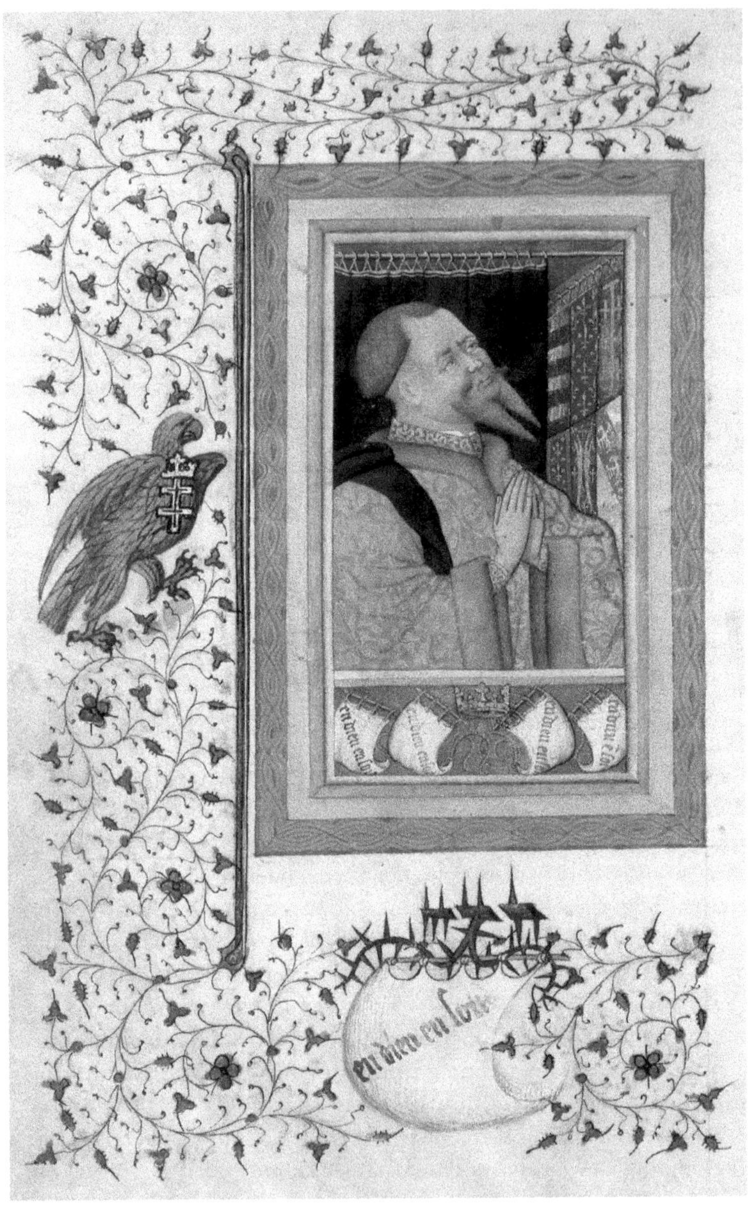

36   Rohan Workshop, Portrait of René of Anjou, Hours of Christ, *Paris Hours of René of Anjou*, Paris, Bibliothèque nationale, fonds latin, 1156A, fol. 81v, *c.*1434, added after 1434 (© Paris, BnF)

added to both the *London* and *Paris Hours*. These miniatures, it will be shown, reveal René's interest in the relics of the Passion, an interest that demonstrated and strengthened his kinship with the house of France.

René's *London Hours* are the earlier of the two manuscripts and were not originally made for him. They were produced by the Egerton workshop with assistants from the Boucicaut Master's workshop around 1410. The liturgical arrangements together with the vast number of offices and suffrages included in the manuscript suggest that they were made for a religious, rather than lay, person.[122] The Egerton and Boucicaut workshops were under royal patronage in the early fifteenth century and the manuscript's connection with the Valois court and the Passion relics of the Sainte-Chapelle is suggested by the inclusion of the feast of Charlemagne in gold in the calendar (28 January), and the feast of the Finding of the True Cross (3 May).[123]

Through his acquisition of the *London Hours*, René was able to enjoy a level of decoration and devotion associated with French royalty and to exploit, as his mother had done in the *Fitzwilliam Hours*, the Angevin connection to the Capetian-Valois dynasty. Therefore, although the majority of the decorative programme was not commissioned by or for René, he could still have viewed the manuscript's references to holy motherhood in relation to his dynastic heritage. The suffrages, for example, contain a miniature of the *Meeting at the Golden Gate* accompanying the prayer in honour of the conception of the Virgin (fol. 81v) and a miniature of the Holy Kinship illustrating the prayer to St Anne (fol. 97r). There are also miniatures depicting the births of Christ and the Virgin. In the *Nativity*, Mary lies in a canopied bed hung with blue curtains, a gold cover and white sheets; another woman stands to one side holding the swaddled Christ who is haloed (figure 37). Representing Christ's birth without the stable, St Joseph and the animals, serves to give His birth a more secular aspect, bringing it into the realm of the aristocratic viewer. The miniature of the *Birth of the Virgin* several folios later (fol. 101v), in which St Anne lies in a blue and green canopied bed and is presented with the swaddled Virgin by a female assistant, also has an aristocratic aspect.

The *Paris Hours*, like the *London Hours*, were probably not originally made for René. The *Paris Hours* were produced by the Rohan workshop for the house of Anjou but the date of execution and original owner are a matter of debate since the arms included in certain of the initials 'cannot yet be connected definitively with any member of the [Anjou] family'.[124] Another feature of the manuscript which has complicated attempts to identify the original owner is the portrait of Louis II in the suffrages, opposite

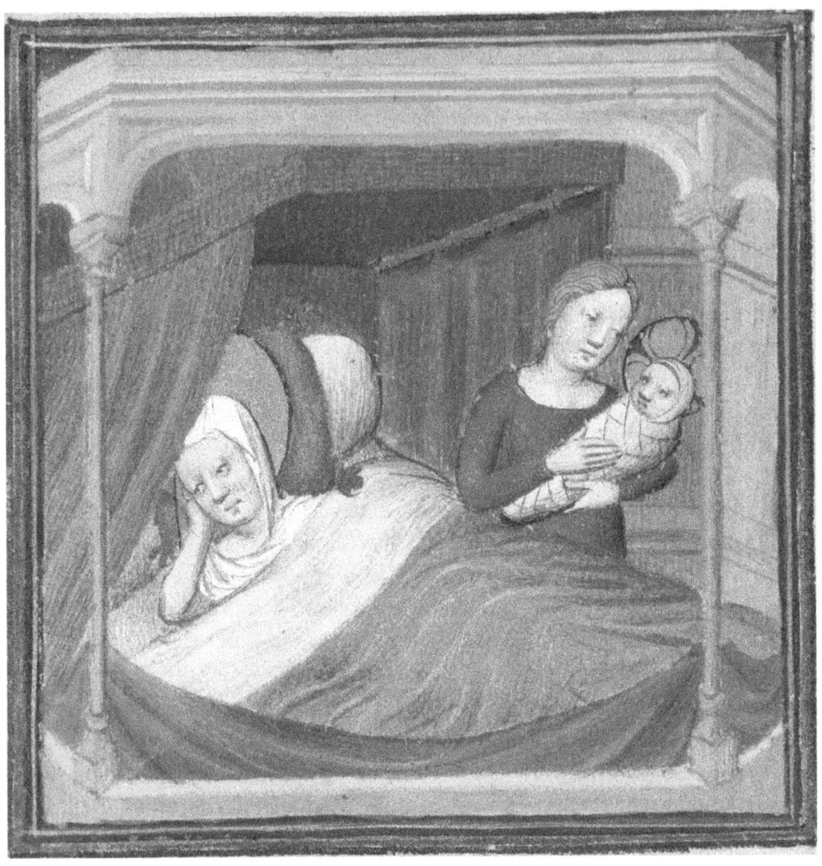

37   Egerton Master, *Nativity of Christ* (detail), suffrages, *London Hours of René of Anjou*, London, British Library, Egerton MS 1070, fol. 82r, *c.*1410 (© London, British Library)

that of St René, René's own patron saint (figure 38). The manuscript was, however, certainly in the possession of René after 1434 on account of the coats of arms included on two inserted folios (figures 36 and 39). These arms refer to those titles acquired by René after his marriage to Isabel of Lorraine, and to those following the death of Joan II of Naples in 1435, including the kingdoms of Hungary and Jerusalem.[125] It has been suggested, therefore, that the manuscript was originally started for Louis II of Anjou, or for his son Louis III, in memory of his father, but was definitely finished for René.[126]

172

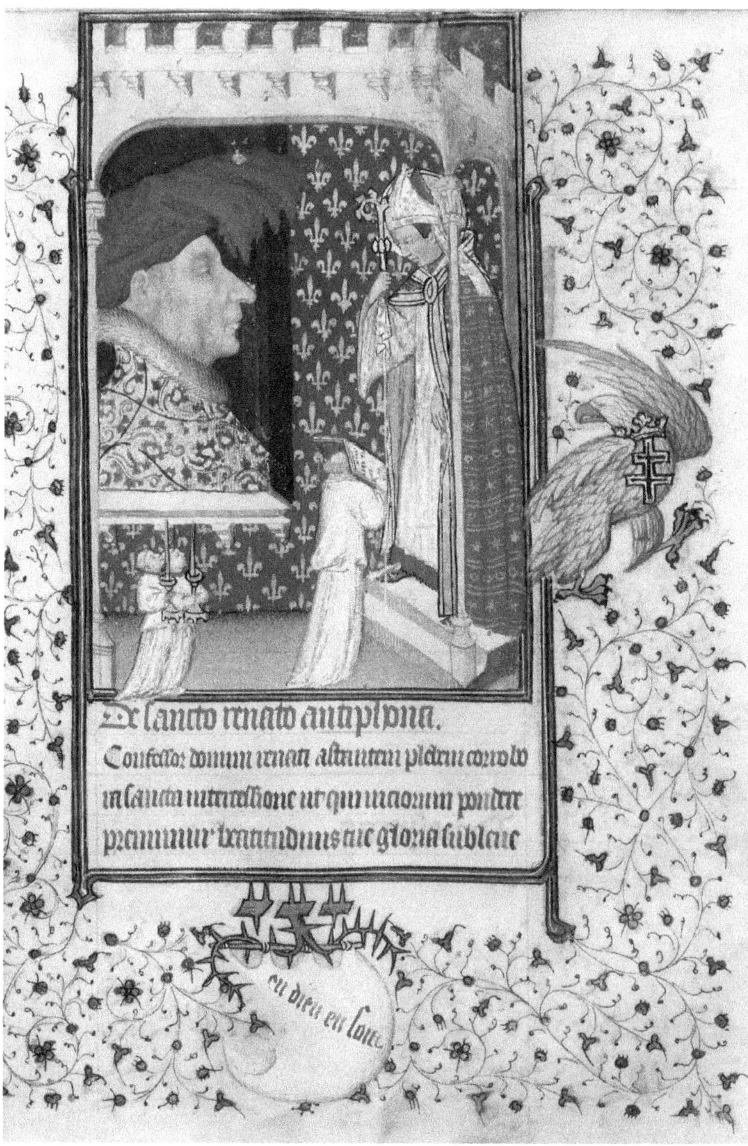

38   Rohan Workshop, Portrait of Louis II of Anjou with St René, suffrages,
Paris Hours of René of Anjou, Paris, Bibliothèque nationale, fonds latin,
1156A, fol. 61r, *c*.1434 (© Paris, BnF)

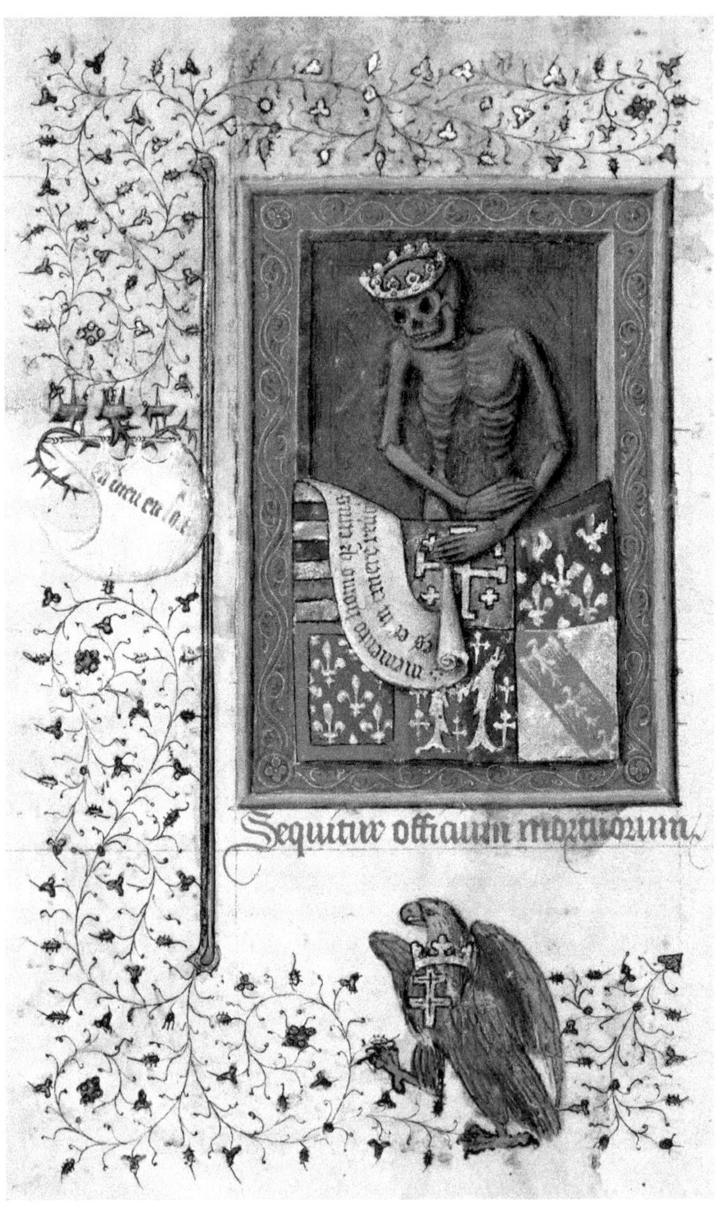

39   Rohan Workshop, *Roi Mort*, Office of the Dead, *Paris Hours of René of Anjou*, Paris, Bibliothèque nationale, fonds latin, 1156A, fol. 113v, *c.*1434, added after 1434 (© Paris, BnF)

Since they were produced by the Rohan workshop, the *Paris Hours* are closely related stylistically to the *Fitzwilliam* and *Rohan Hours*. In addition, René's *Paris Hours* and the *Rohan Hours* share exactly the same saints in their calendars.[127] To a discerning patron of the arts like René, such similarities between manuscripts with familial connections would have been immediately evident. For instance, the miniature of the Virgin and Child on a crescent moon with Saints Peter and Paul at the opening of the *Creator celi* prayer in the *Fitzwilliam Hours* is repeated, without the saints, at the opening of the *Obsecro te* in René's *Paris Hours* (figures 40–1). The kneeling figures that lean backwards in the *Paris Hours'* Pentecost miniature are also repeated in the *Rohan Hours'* miniature of the same subject (figures 42–3). The miniature accompanying the Office of the Dead in the *Paris Hours*, with a monk praying in a cemetery, shows a dependence on the *Belles Heures*, which, as we have seen, was also used as a model for the *Rohan Hours*.[128] The figure of the Virgin weaving at a loom in the bas-de-page miniature of Matins (figure 44) in the *Paris Hours* is also a feature found in the *Fitzwilliam Hours' Doulce Dame* prayer and in the borders at Matins (plate 3). Finally, the *Nativity* miniature accompanying the hour of Prime in the *Paris Hours* also recalls the birth scenes in the *Rohan Hours*, and the *Nativity of Christ* in the *Fitzwilliam Hours*, through the stable with a pitched roof, wattle fencing, a dark blue sky peppered with tiny gold clouds, and the inclusion of a female assistant (plates 5 and 10; figure 7). In René's *Hours*, the female assistant prepares a bath for the Christ-Child; Mary, who is breastfeeding Christ, places her hand in the water to test the temperature. Joseph looks on, leaning on his staff, and the ox, the ass and an angel watch the scene. The outdoor, stable setting, acknowledges the poverty of Christ's birth but, in addition to the preparation of the child's bath, the inclusion of a fireplace, with pot hanging over the fire, in the background, gives the stable a further comfortable, domestic note. Moreover, as in the *Rohan Hours'* miniature of the *Nativity of Christ*, the dominating richness of the Virgin's blue cloak and the gold of the haloes indicate the special status of this mother and child.

By the time René had his manuscript adjusted (after 1434), he was not in need of encouragement to procreate per se: his marriage to Isabel of Lorraine was fertile and by 1434 had produced at least four surviving children.[129] However, given his brother's early demise, the death of several of his own children, and his involvement in the war between France and England, René was aware that the succession of titles was precarious and open to challenge.[130] Since his defeat at Bulgnéville in July 1431, René had been held prisoner by the duke of Burgundy, Philip the Good. The duke

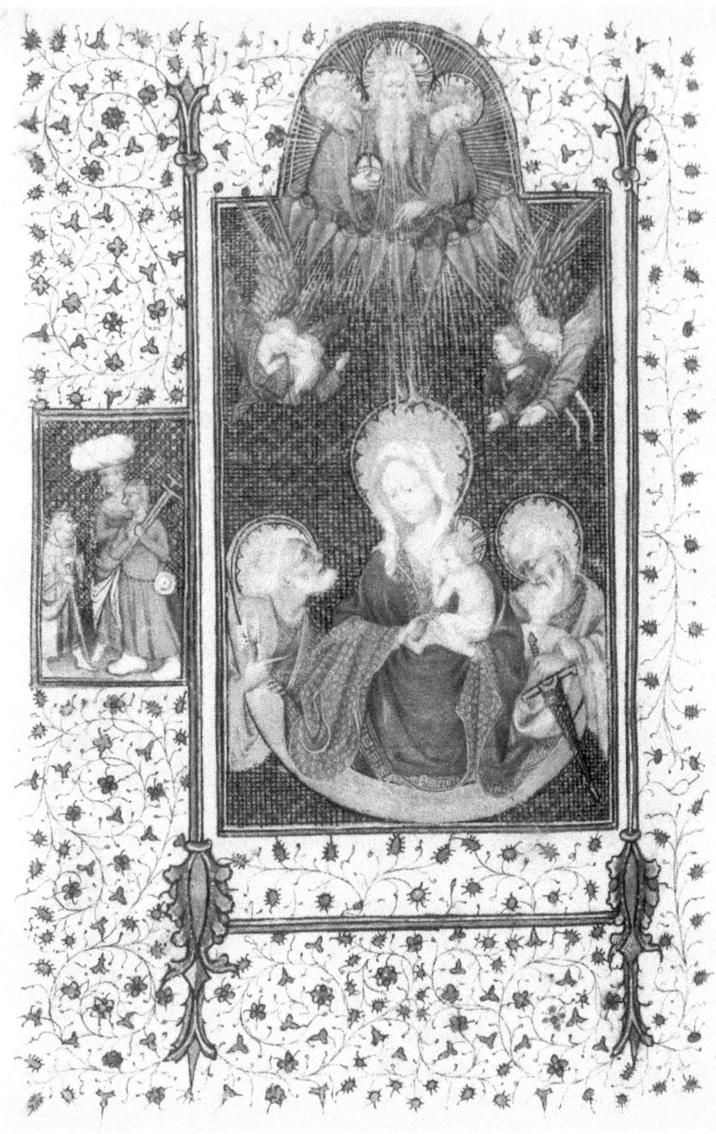

40   Rohan Workshop, *Virgin and Child on a Crescent Moon with Saints Peter and Paul, Creator celi, Fitzwilliam Hours*, Cambridge, Fitzwilliam Museum, MS 62, fol. 136v, *c*.1418–30. Reproduction by permission of the Syndics of the Fitzwilliam Museum, Cambridge (© Cambridge, Fitzwilliam Museum)

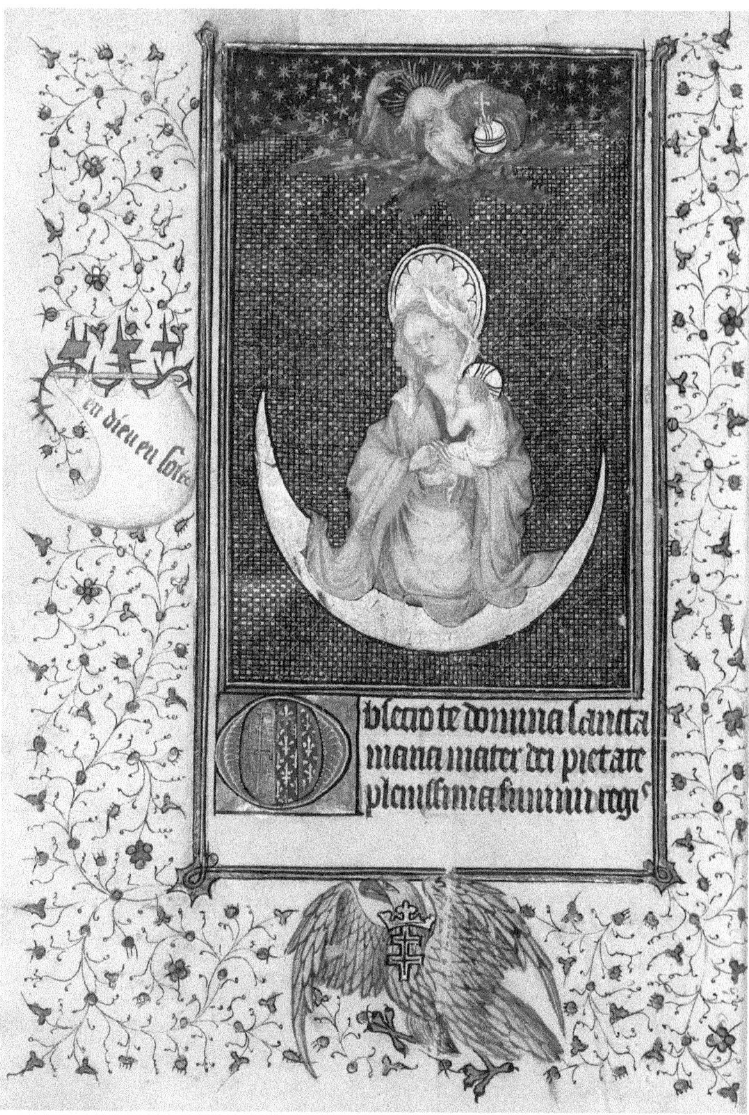

41   Rohan Workshop, *Virgin and Child on a Crescent Moon, Obsecro te,
Paris Hours of René of Anjou*, Paris, Bibliothèque nationale, fonds latin,
1156A, fol. 18v, *c.*1434 (© Paris, BnF)

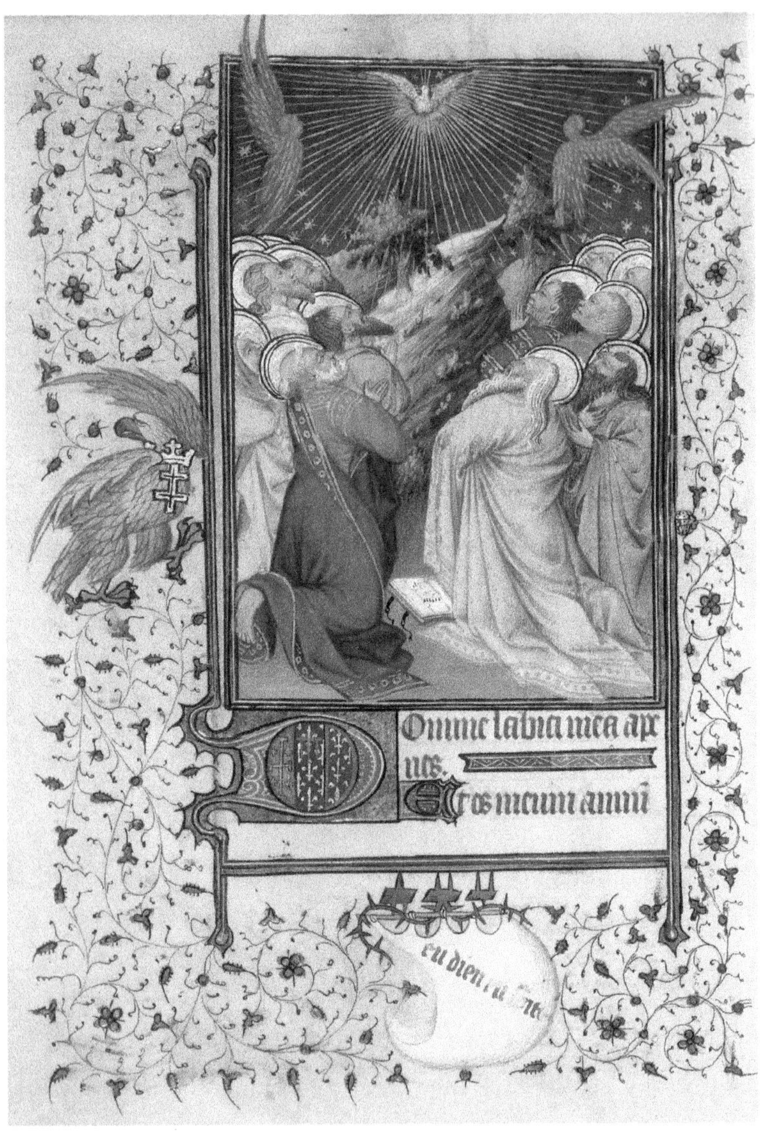

42   Rohan Workshop, *Pentecost*, Hours of the Holy Spirit, *Paris Hours of René of Anjou*, Paris, Bibliothèque nationale, fonds latin, 1156A, fol. 87v, c.1434 (© Paris, BnF)

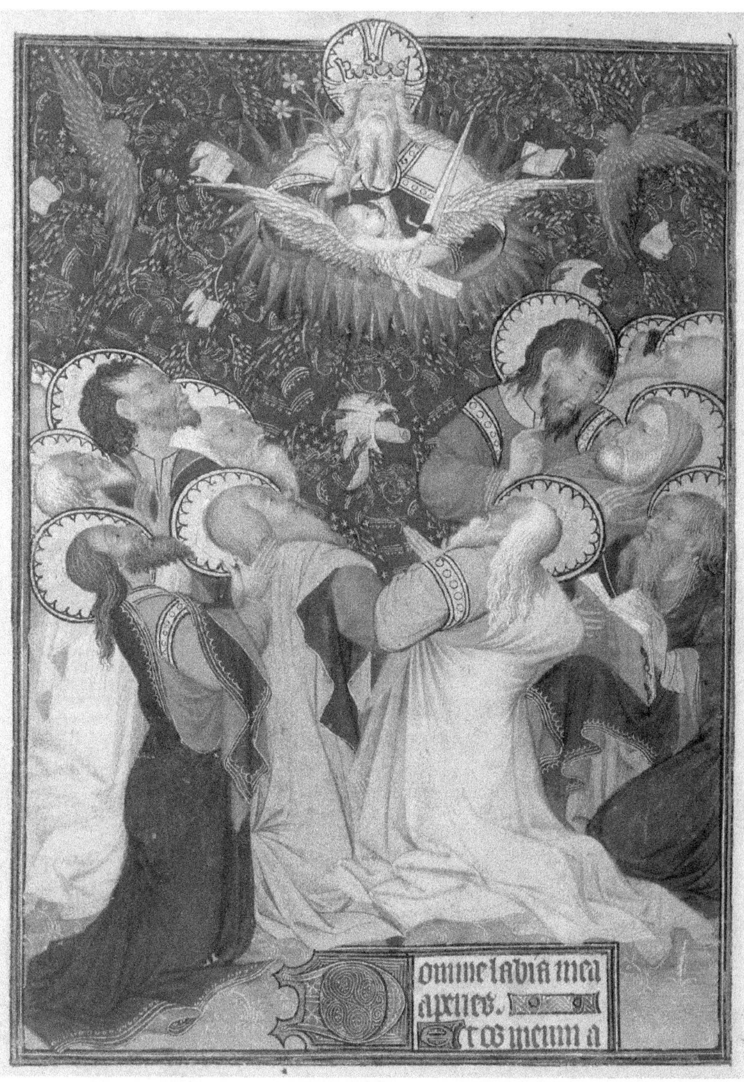

43   Rohan Workshop, *Pentecost*, Hours of the Holy Spirit, *Rohan Hours*,
Paris, Bibliothèque nationale, fonds latin, 9471, fol. 143v, *c.*1420
(© Paris, BnF)

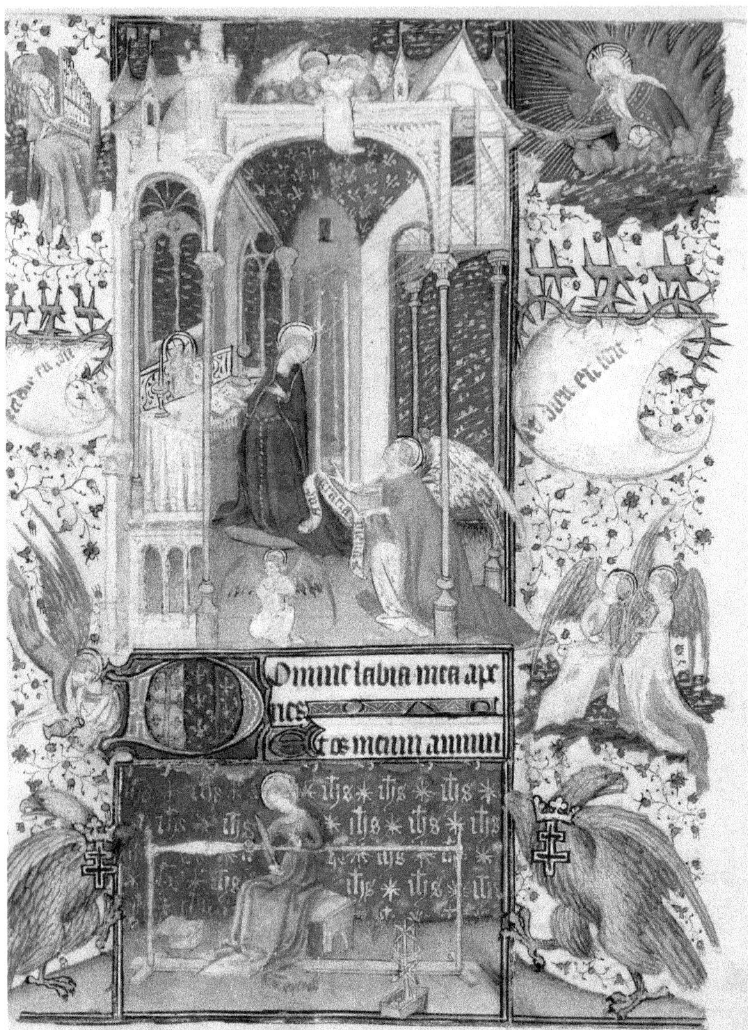

44   Rohan Workshop, *Annunciation with Virgin Weaving*, *Paris Hours of René of Anjou*, Paris, Bibliothèque nationale, fonds latin, 1156A, fol. 23r, c.1434 (© Paris, BnF)

temporarily released him in May 1432 but he had to leave his two young sons behind as hostages. Following a further breakdown in relations between the two dukes over the succession of the duchy of Lorraine, Philip the Good ordered René to return to prison in Dijon in March 1435 where he remained until his release in November 1436.[131] Therefore, on his accession and in the first few years of his reign, René was often far from his family and his new duchy. The intimate image of the *Nativity* in his *Paris Hours*, which included his arms in the initial, could thus have functioned as a reminder of René's own family and offered a means to ask God for His continued protection, especially of his young sons held by the duke of Burgundy. As God protected His own holy family, in the stable, in their time of need, so too could He help the house of Anjou, which itself had a holy provenance.

After his accession to the duchy of Anjou in 1434, René had extra miniatures added to both manuscripts.[132] René's deliberate personalising of both manuscripts, and with similar images, served to link the two Books of Hours together as his property and to promote his acquisition of new territories. The view of the city of Jerusalem for example, added at the beginning of the *London Hours* (fols 4v–5r) refers to René's new title of king of Jerusalem that he inherited, along with the throne of Naples, from Joan II. René's claim to Jerusalem and, by association, his royal and holy lineage, was further made apparent in the image of King David receiving homage that was added to the *London Hours* (fol. 139r). The image has the title, *Tres fortes attulerunt regi David aquam de cisterna Beethleem*, which refers to an episode in the second book of Samuel when David, king of Jerusalem, being held prisoner by the Philistines yearned for some water from Bethlehem, which was fetched for him by three strong men. According to Pächt, this added miniature drew a parallel between René, prisoner of the duke of Burgundy, and the biblical David, type of Christ and original king of Jerusalem.[133] Furthermore, additional prayers were also inserted into the *London Hours*, including a version of the *Commendatio animae* which asks God to free René from all confinement: *Libera me Renatum de omnibus angustiis*.[134] Thus the reference to the imprisoned David who, like Christ and René was isolated from his allies, has led Harthan to associate the manuscript's second campaign of illumination and texts directly with René's imprisonment by the duke of Burgundy, calling them René's 'prison' Hours.[135]

René's titles are also evoked through the coats of arms that accompany two paintings of a *roi mort* that were added to the Office of the Dead in the *London* and *Paris Hours* (figures 39 and 45). In both images a crowned skeleton stands behind a cloth displaying René's arms; each holds a scroll inscribed with a phrase beginning *memento homo* that trails over the cloth. These images of the *roi mort* suggest that at the same time as René was thinking of his terrestrial titles, symbolised in the skeletons' crowns and

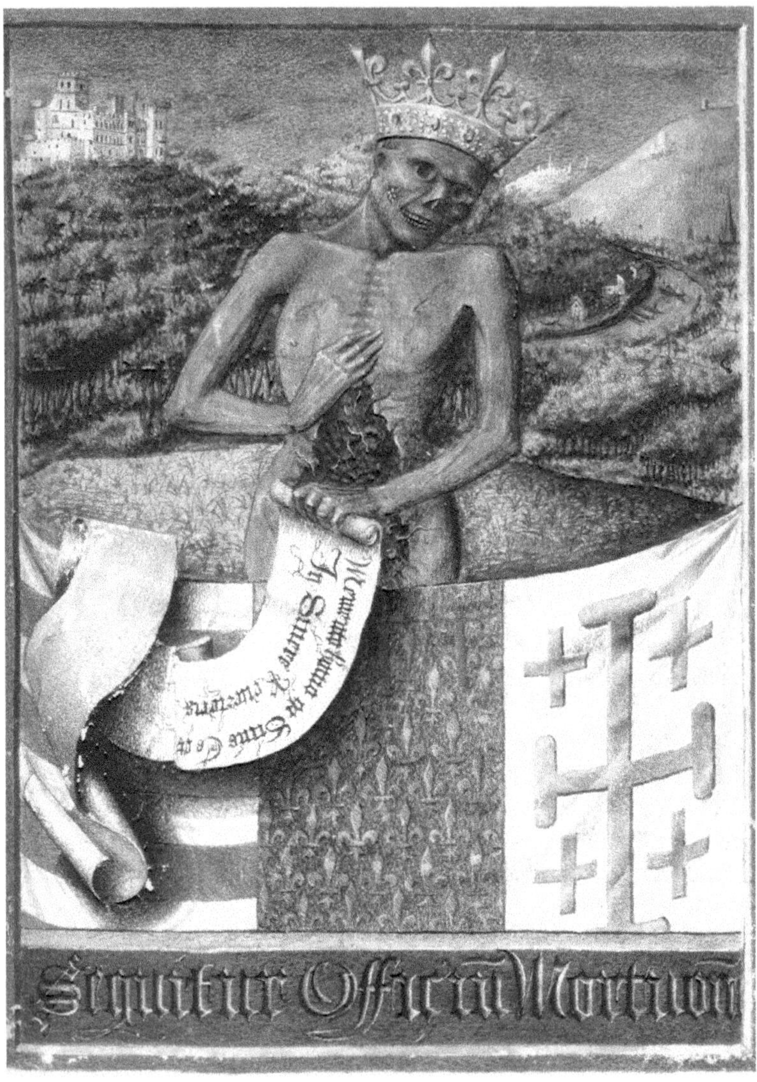

45   Egerton Master, *Roi Mort*, Office of the Dead, *London Hours of René of Anjou*, London, British Library, Egerton MS 1070, fol. 53r, *c.*1410, added after 1434 (© London, British Library)

René's coat of arms, he was also aware of the transience of earthly life and the need to prepare for the life to come.[136] In addition, these images may have provided another link between René's manuscripts and his mother's patronage of the Rohan workshop since, as Châtelet has pointed out, the skeleton in the *London Hours* recalls the image of the man in front of his judge in the *Rohan Hours* (fol. 159r).[137] Châtelet argues for René's familiarity with the *Rohan Hours* on the basis that it was commissioned for Alan IX of Rohan who frequented the court of Charles VII. The idea that René was familiar with, and even alluded to, the *Rohan Hours* in his own manuscripts is supported further by the suggestion that the manuscript was in fact commissioned by Yolande of Aragon for Charles VII.

Further images added to René's Books of Hours reveal that he drew on the specific devotional interests of his Capetian predecessors and these helped to give a sense of coherence to his manuscripts as well as to assert his position as duke and *prince de sang*. For example, miniatures of the angels holding up the host appear in both the *London* and the *Paris Hours* (figures 46–7). In discussing the miniature in the *London Hours* Pächt has noted that it depicts the 'Sainte Hostie miraculeuse', a relic that was given to René's adversary duke Philip the Good of Burgundy by Pope Eugenius IV in 1431.[138] Philip deposited the relic in the Bar Chapel of the Ste-Chapelle in Dijon, a chapel which served as René's personal oratory during his time as Philip's prisoner.[139] René was particularly devoted to this relic and he founded a perpetual mass in its honour, just before he was released in 1436.[140] In both the images from the London and *Paris Hours*, the host held up by the angels carries the figure of Christ showing his wounds and surrounded by the instruments of the Passion. Furthermore, the host is placed against a Cross, at the top of which hangs a Crown of Thorns. Thus, in addition to evoking the miraculous host of Dijon, the image also refers more generally to Christ's Passion, to which the dukes of Anjou were especially devoted: René himself possessed three fragments of the True Cross.[141] In fact, the Angevin dukes revered the most prestigious of the relics venerated by the house of France, those of the True Cross and the Crown of Thorns, which St Louis IX had acquired and placed in the Sainte-Chapelle.

The portrait of René (figure 36) in the *Paris Hours* also indicates his devotion to the Passion of Christ, being placed opposite an image of Christ as Man of Sorrows (fol. 82r). Supported by an angel, a bleeding Christ wearing the Crown of Thorns has been taken down from the Cross. As in the image of the miraculous host which shows the Cross and the Crown of Thorns (figure 46), the background of this image also shows the

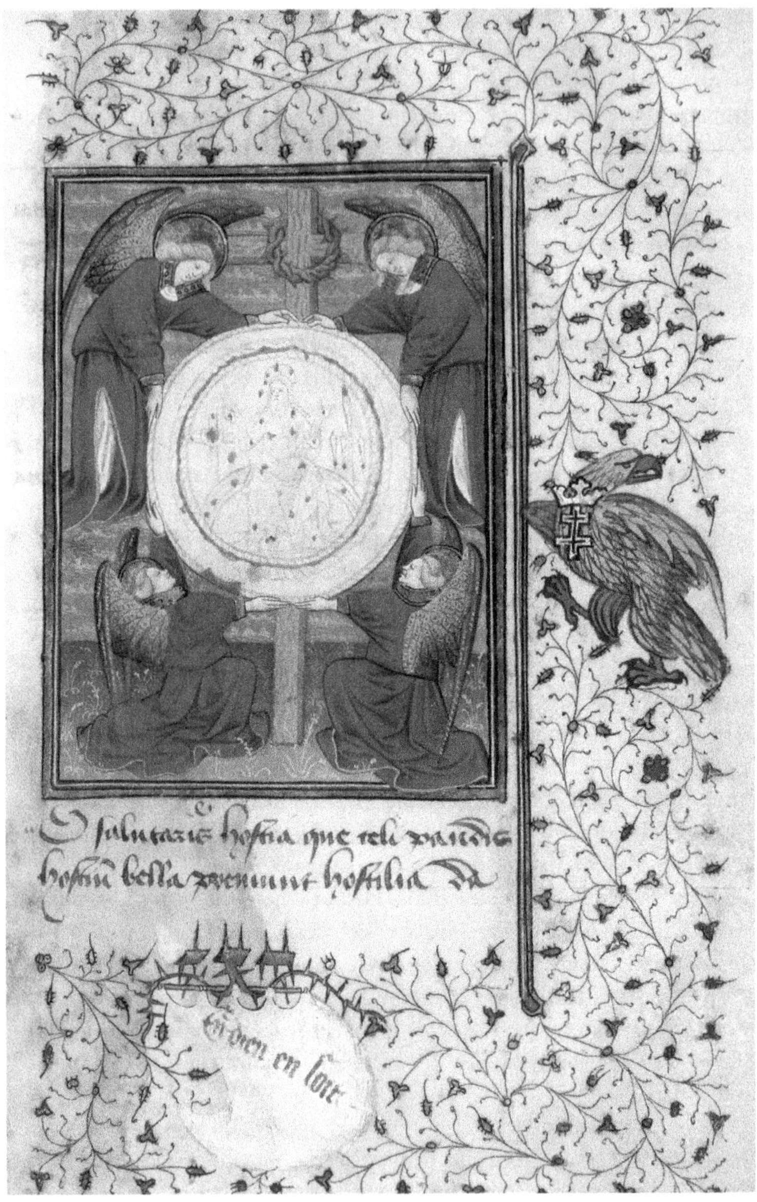

46   Rohan Workshop, *Angels Displaying the Host*, *Paris Hours of René of Anjou*, Paris, Bibliothèque nationale, fonds latin, 1156A, fol. 22v, *c.*1434, added after 1434 (© Paris, BnF)

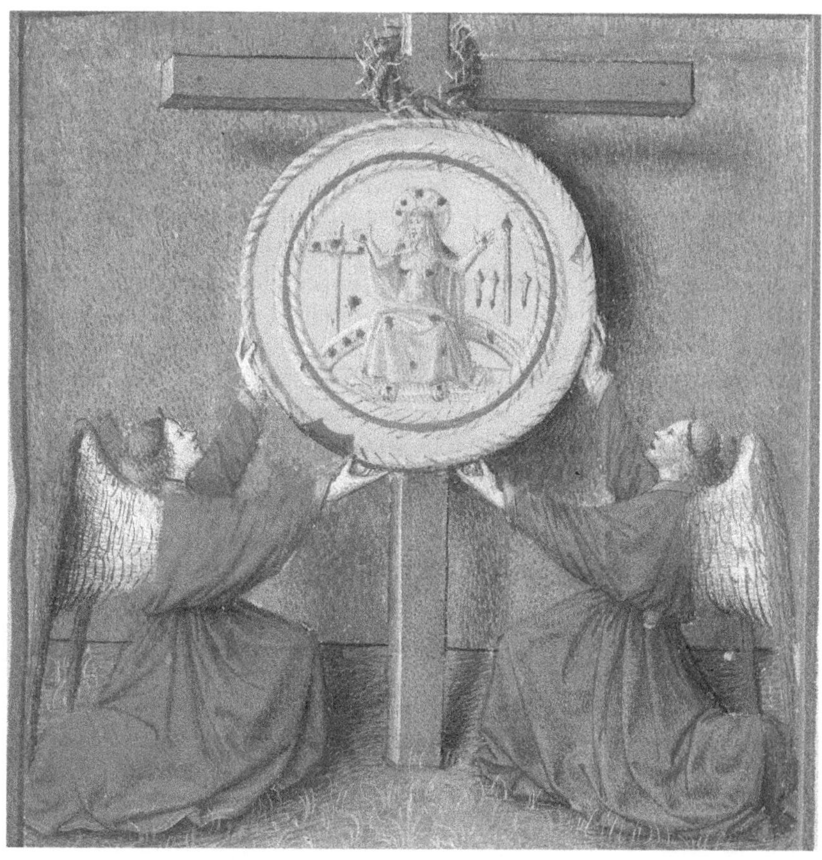

47 Egerton Master, *Angels Displaying the Host, London Hours of René of Anjou*, London, British Library, Egerton MS 1070, fol. 110r, *c.*1410, added after 1434 (© London, British Library)

instruments of the Passion, including the Cross, the nails and the scourge with which He was whipped. René's devotion to the Passion of Christ and to the miraculous host of Dijon, linked so closely to his captor Duke Philip the Good, involves a complex interplay of meanings. By venerating the relic recently acquired by the duke of Burgundy and by contributing to the cult of this object through the commissioning of a mass in its honour, and the inclusion of images in his Books of Hours, René was on the one hand paying homage to his anti-French, pro-English, captor. On the other, he was also appropriating the object, which provided a fitting complement to the Franco-Angevin Passion devotion, for himself. The insertion of images of the miraculous host into his Books of Hours pulled a Burgundian relic into the Angevin camp and thus asserted René's position as new duke of Anjou, reinforcing his familial and devotional ties with the house of France in the face of Burgundian opposition.

René's devotion to the Passion also led him to venerate the two saints Mary Salomé and Mary Jacobi, who were described, along with Mary Magdalene, as being present at the Crucifixion, and who went to Christ's tomb on the third day to find it empty.[142] Canonical and non-canonical sources, as well as the ways they have been translated, have led to confusion over the exact identity of these women but in the fifteenth century they were often conflated with the two daughters of St Anne, Mary Cleophas and Mary Salomé, sisters of the Virgin. René may, therefore, have conflated the Mary Jacobi and Mary Salomé that he venerated with the mothers of the Holy Kinship who were frequently represented with their sons, as they were in his mother's manuscript, the *Fitzwilliam Hours*. Legends that circulated after Christ's death and resurrection claimed that Mary Magdalene sailed to France, disembarking at Marseille. In 1448, René followed up another source that claimed that the two other Maries had come with her and that their bodies had been buried in the church of Notre-Dame-de-la-Mer in Provence.[143] René ordered a search to be carried out, which resulted in the finding of three bodies, and he obtained the Pope's permission to have the remains authenticated. In 1449 the relics were transferred to the church itself amid great ceremony. Around the same time René commissioned a *Légende* of the Maries, which he distributed to various prelates and influential people.[144]

According to Robin, René's interest in the Maries around 1447–50 coincided with his return from Italy and his desire to make his presence more visible and to assert his reputation in Provence.[145] Through the association of two of the three Maries with those of the Holy Kinship, René's devotion to these saints allowed him to focus not only on Christ's Passion but also on His dynastic heritage. Thus, as a cognitive habit informing his situational eye, René's knowledge of and veneration for Mary Salomé and Mary Jacobi may well have nuanced his reading of the births of Christ and the Virgin represented in his Books of Hours by providing a wider, dynastic, context in which to situate these birth narratives.

However he acquired both his *London* and *Paris Hours*, René evidently took a close interest in their contents. The additions he made to the manuscripts had a personal significance for René and enabled him to express his particular interests and loyalties around the time of his inheritance of the duchy of Anjou and the lands of Joan II of Naples. These two inheritances came about in difficult circumstances, when France was still at war with England and the throne of Naples was being contested. The miniatures René had added to the *London* and *Paris Hours* both asserted his new titles and served to link the two manuscripts together. The *Paris Hours*, in turn, were closely related to the *Rohan* and *Fitzwilliam Hours* and it is likely that René viewed both his manuscripts as markers of his family's patronage, dynastic heritage and political affiliations. Through his situational eye, then, René could have interpreted the maternal imagery and birth scenes in his manuscripts as reminders of his illustrious lineage, its holiness and proximity to that of Christ, and his social obligation to engender heirs for the survival of his family and duchy.

This chapter has explored how images of holy motherhood and narratives of dynastic saints functioned for a group of viewers in manuscripts associated with the house of Anjou and in particular with Duchess Yolande of Aragon. In suggesting how different viewers received these related manuscripts, a viewing position has emerged for images and narratives of holy childbearing, which is in many ways related as much to class as to gender, if not more so. The *Fitzwilliam Hours* functioned, for example, as marker of the status of the widowed Yolande of Aragon and her family in the early decades of the fifteenth century. Within the manuscript, the references to dynastic saints and holy motherhood disclose the importance of offspring and kinship ties to an aristocratic family, revealing the parallels that they were able to establish between themselves and the family of Christ. In commissioning this lavish manuscript, Yolande drew on the cult of St Anne and the Holy Kinship, which allowed her to promote herself as a mother and an educator, roles she was assigned as part of her class and status but ones which she developed and manipulated to serve political and dynastic interests. She also supplemented Christ's holy family with other 'family' saints from the blessed lineages of the houses of France, Hungary and Anjou, so allowing her to further assert her position as matriarch of the Angevin *beata stirps* and protector and mother-in-law of the dauphin.

The themes of holy motherhood and dynastic sanctity also informed the situational eye of her daughter Yolande who probably received the manuscript on her marriage to Francis of Brittany. The cognitive habits acquired by the younger Yolande, first as duchess of Anjou and daughter of Yolande of Aragon, and then as the wife of the heir to the duchy of Brittany, meant that she too would have been sensitive to the inclusion of model saints like St Radegund, St Elizabeth of Hungary, St Louis IX and St Louis of Toulouse. Furthermore, the manuscript's suffrages and Marian imagery, especially the way the marginal cycle and miniatures coincided to emphasise Mary's motherhood, provided pertinent examples of God's blessing of women in childbirth as Yolande started her married life as wife and potential mother to the heirs of Brittany. It has been argued that, in the details of its miniatures, the narratives they represent, and the way they draw parallels between the secular and the biblical worlds, the *Fitzwilliam Hours* and its imagery spoke to Yolunde's situational eye as means to help her perform her role as duchess and manage her own childbearing, both anticipated and experienced. For example, the fabrics depicted in the *Birth of the Virgin* miniature, and the presence of a female assistant, not only evoked the type of lying-in that Yolande, as a duchess, could expect to receive, but it also signified an acknowledgement of the value of her role through the attention that it demanded from the court in which she would be placed at the centre of attention.

Consideration of the *Rohan Hours* as a commission by Yolande of Aragon for her son-in-law, has further shown how this female patron was able to use patronage and birth narratives to consolidate her political interests. By commissioning an expensive manuscript with a marginal cycle of the first part of the *Bible moralisée*, Yolande could demonstrate to the dauphin Charles both her support for his somewhat beleaguered position as well as the need for him to execute his God-given position in the right way. The birth scenes in the *Rohan Hours*, far from offering a glimpse of actual medieval childbearing practices, are based on a *Bible moralisée* iconographic tradition in which the aim was to counsel the (regal) reader on how to live a moral life, ensure God's faith, and govern well. Viewed by Charles VII, it has been argued that the *Rohan Hours'* birth scenes alluded to his role as king, to his own heritage, and to his immediate lineage, which he was morally obliged to ensure. The two *Hours of René of Anjou* also demonstrate the importance of family relationships and dynastic stability in the way René personalised the two manuscripts with themes that showed both his loyalty to the houses of France and Anjou and his claims to other titles.

Analysing the *Fitzwilliam Hours*, the *Rohan Hours*, and the *Paris* and *London Hours of René of Anjou* as a group, has shown how images of holy motherhood and childbearing were relevant to both lay aristocratic men and women: an interest in dynastic heritage informed their situational eye and was part of the performance of the social roles which they played as wives, husbands, mothers and fathers, duchesses, dukes and monarchs. By situating the images within the context of their manuscripts and the circumstances of their commission, it has been possible to reveal the subtleties of miniatures of St Anne, the Virgin's birth, the Holy Kinship and other dynastic saints. For the female readers in particular, these images functioned as more than straightforward injunctions to submit to patriarchy and procreate, offering instead a means to think through their social roles and negotiate their expectations. Such a reading might carry the charge of reasserting the double bind explored in the first part of this book but it is important to stress that it is intended to show more how women could use available imagery and devotional paradigms to manage their roles within patriarchal society rather than naively to suggest that images and tropes offered them complete resistance or empowerment.

In Chapter 5, the discussion moves on to the reception of the *Fitzwilliam Hours* first by Francis I of Brittany's second wife, Isabel Stuart, and then by her daughter Marguerite of Brittany. It also considers two more prayer books owned by later Breton duchesses that contain images of holy motherhood and prayers for childbirth. These analyses will further demonstrate how aristocratic lay women drew on narratives of miraculous birth and motherhood to manage the roles expected of them as wives and potential mothers.

Notes

1 *Fitzwilliam Hours* (Cambridge, Fitzwilliam Museum, MS 62); *Hours of Marguerite of Foix* (London, Victoria and Albert Museum, Salting MS 1222); *Prayer Book of Anne of Brittany* (Chicago, Newberry Library, MS 82).

2 For an overview of the house of Anjou and its patronage, see *L'Europe des Anjou: aventure des princes angevins du XIIIe au XVe siècle*, exhibition catalogue (Paris: Somogy, 2001); and *Les Princes Angevins du XIIIe au XVe siècle. Un destin européen*, ed. by Noël-Yves Tonnerre and Élisabeth Verry (Rennes: Presses Universitaires de Rennes, 2003).

3 *Rohan Hours* (Paris, Bibliothèque nationale, fonds latin, 9471); *London Hours of René of Anjou* (London, British Library, Egerton MS 1070); *Paris Hours of René of Anjou* (Paris, Bibliothèque nationale, fonds latin, 1156A).

4 For full discussion of the Rohan workshop style and oeuvre, see Millard Meiss, *French Painting in the Time of Jean de Berry*, 3 vols (London and New York: Thames & Hudson, 1967–74), III, *The Limbourgs and their Contemporaries*, pp. 256–77; Meiss and Marcel Thomas, *The Rohan Hours: Bibliothèque nationale, Paris (ms lat. 9741)* (London: Thames & Hudson, 1973); Adelheid Heimann, 'Der Meister der "Grandes Heures de Rohan" und seine Werkstatt', *Städel Jahrbuch*, 7–8 (1932), 1–61; Erwin Panofsky, 'Reintegration of a Book of Hours Executed in the Workshop of the "Maître des Grandes Heures de Rohan"', in *Medieval Studies in Memory of A. Kingsley Porter*, ed. by Wilhelm R. W. Koehler, 2 vols (Cambridge, MA: Harvard University Press, 1939), II, pp. 479–99; Grete Ring, *A Century of French Painting* (London: Phaidon, 1949), pp. 202–4; and

Avril and Nicole Reynaud, *Les Manuscrits à peintures en France 1440–1520* (Paris: Flammarion-Bibliotheque Nationale, 1993), pp. 25–9.

5 The *Fitzwilliam Hours* measure approximately 245 x 175 mm. A full description together with a list of all the illuminations is given in *Cat. Fitz.*, pp. 156–74.

6 Michael Camille claims that the 'scraped-away outline of the previous [*obsecro te*] figure [*of Yolande*] is visible under light as is the very different, more opaque pigment', adding that 'Isabella's *cotte* is in a crimson found only in the added arms of the margins'. See Camille, 'The Illustrated Manuscripts of Guillaume de Deguileville's "Pèlerinages" 1330–1426' (unpublished doctoral thesis, University of Cambridge, 1985), pp. 228; 255–6; nn. 34–5. Caution should be exercised in using Camille's thesis: although, as discussed below, the arguments for Yolande of Aragon's ownership are compelling, the 'scraped-away' figure is not visible with the naked eye in good light and I found no evidence of his remark (p. 228; n. 35) that the 'rubbed-out shape' of the arms of Brittany impaling Anjou are visible behind the square arms of Brittany-Scotland, although these have clearly been added on top of the border foliage. I have not, however, examined the manuscript under UV light.

7 On Yolande's association with the workshop see Meiss, p. 270; Avril and Reynaud, pp. 25–9; Camille, pp. 227–30; Paul Durrieu, 'Le Maître des "Grandes Heures de Rohan" et les Lescuier d'Angers', *Revue de l'art ancien et moderne*, 2 (1912), 81–98 and 161–88; Jean Porcher, 'Two Models for the "Heures de Rohan" ', *Journal of the Warburg and Courtauld Institutes*, 8 (1945), 1–6.

8 More tentative proposals have been suggested for the manuscript's ownership, but not pursued. Referring to the figure of the nun in the *Creator celi* prayer, Durrieu suggested that Marie of Brittany (1424–77), the daughter of Richard of Brittany, Count of Estampes, may have been the owner, since she became Abbess of Fontevrault in the diocese of Angers in 1457. This interpretation was dismissed by Margaret R. Toynbee who claimed that 'the nun's figure hardly seems sufficiently prominent to warrant such an inference'; see Durrieu, p. 177; and Toynbee, 'The Portraiture of Isabella Stuart, Duchess of Brittany (*c.*1427– after 1494)', *Burlington Magazine*, 88 (1946), 300–6 (pp. 303–4). Meiss suggests the manuscript may be that bought by Marie of Anjou with the 200 *écus* given to her in 1418 by her father-in-law, Charles VI, for the purchase of a Book of Hours, see Meiss and Thomas, p. 14. Camille's disagreement on the basis that Marie would only have been five years old in 1417 is erroneous since Marie was born in 1404; see Camille, p. 256; n. 35.

9 Marrow, and Avril and Reynaud date the manuscript to the 1430s and thus to the latter part of the Rohan Master's oeuvre. See Marrow's entry in *The Cambridge Illuminations: Ten Centuries of Book Production in the Medieval West*, ed. by Stella Panayotova and Paul Binski (London: Harvey Miller, 2005), pp. 202–4 (no. 88); and Avril and Reynaud, pp. 25; 178. James suggests a date of 1445–50 for the manuscript but also confusingly states that 'it is not clear that these arms [of Isabel] were not inserted after the book had been bought by or for Isabel'. Given the number of arguments for the manuscript's production around or prior to the 1430s, James's dating can be considered erroneous: see *Cat. Fitz.* p. 157.

10 Early datings of *c.*1415–18 are proposed by Harthan, p. 117; Ring, p. 204; Heimann, p. 10; Meiss, p. 401; Camille, pp. 227–8. See also *Illuminated Manuscripts in the Fitzwilliam Museum*, ed. by Phyllis M. Giles and Francis Wormald (Cambridge: Fitzwilliam Museum, 1966), p. 30; no. 68.

11 See Camille, p. 228; n. 36; Legaré, 'La réception du *Pèlerinage de Vie humaine* de Guillaume de Digulleville dans le milieu angevin d'après les sources et les manuscrits conservés', in *Religion et mentalités au Moyen Âge: Mélanges en l'honneur d'Hervé Martin* (Rennes: Presses universitaires de Rennes, 2003), pp. 543–52 (p. 545); and Richard K. Emmerson, 'A "Large Order of the Whole": Intertextuality and Interpictoriality in the Hours of Isabella Stuart', *Studies in Iconography*, 28 (2007), 53–99. I am extremely grateful to Richard Emmerson for sharing a copy of his article with me prior to its publication.

12 Françoise Robin, *La Cour d'Anjou-Provence: la vie artistique sous le règne de René* ([no place]: Picard, 1985), p. 32.

13 The history of these four kingdoms is too complex to discuss in detail here but, put simply, until the death of Joan II of Naples in 1435, Naples and Jerusalem were ruled by the senior house of Anjou and Anjou-Duras, descendants of Charles II of Anjou, nephew of St Louis IX. The cadet house of Anjou began with Louis I, great-great grandson of Charles II, who claimed the kingdom of Naples after the death of Joan I, who had adopted him as her heir. Louis did not succeed in taking Naples, however, which was taken over by Joan's cousin Charles III of Anjou-Duras (d. 1386) and his children Ladislas (d. 1414) and Joan II. Louis I's descendants, Louis II and Louis III, continued to campaign for control of the kingdom and still claimed the titles king of Naples and Jerusalem. René of Anjou took control of Naples from 1435 to 1442 after he inherited it as Joan II's heir but he was then deposed by Alphonse V of Aragon. See Élisabeth Verry, 'L'impossible héritage: la deuxième maison d'Anjou et l'Italie (1380–1480)', in *L'Europe des Anjou*, pp. 255–7.

14 Robin, pp. 8; 30.

15 Robin, p. 8.

16 On the proposed marriage between Louis and Isabella, see M. G. A. Vale, *Charles VII* (London: Eyre Methuen, 1974), p. 36.

17 Robin, p. 71.

18 Robin, p. 29; see also Chevalier, pp. 82–3.

19 Helen E. Maurer, *Margaret of Anjou: Queenship and Power in Late Medieval England* (Woodbridge: Boydell, 2003), p. 23.

20 Klaniczay, p. 226.

21 Klaniczay, p. 227.

22 See the genealogical tables in Klaniczy, pp. 435–9.

23 Klaniczay, pp. 298–300.

24 Klaniczay, p. 300.

25 In addition to being taken up by Charles I of Anjou, the trope was also used by later kings of France, including Charles VI and Charles VII who used the idea to promise a victorious end to the conflict with England. In the late fifteenth century the trope was also applied to Charles VIII whose queen, Anne of Brittany, became

assimilated with the new Virgin. See the discussion below and Didier Le Fur, *Anne de Bretagne: Miroir d'une reine, historiographie d'un mythe* (Paris: Librairie Édition Guénégaud, 2000), pp. 81–2.

26 P.-E. de Riant, 'Déposition de Charles d'Anjou pour le canonisation de S. Louis', in *Notices et documents publiés par la Société de l'Histoire de la France, à l'occasion de son 50ᵉ anniversaire* (Paris: [no pub.], 1889), pp. 155–80 (p. 175). Robert of Artois 'died a martyr's death fighting the Saracens' and Alphonse of Poitiers 'was manifestly also prepared to suffer martyrdom for the faith'. See Klaniczay, p. 301. The original Latin printed by de Riant reads: 'sancta illa anima solute est, unde sancta radix sanctos ramos protulit, non solum regem sanctum, sed et comitem Atrebatensem, martirem gloriosum, et comitem Pictavemsem, affectu . . .' It is possible, as Klaniczay implies (p. 301), that *sancta illa anima soluta est* (that holy soul died) can be translated as 'that soul died holy', i.e. a saint, if 'sancta' is taken as a predicate.

27 James I of Aragon was Yolande's great-great-great-great-grandfather. Jolantha was born of Andrew II's second marriage to Jolantha, daughter of the Latin emperor of Constantinople. See the Arpad family tree in Klaniczy, pp. 438–9.

28 The suffrage begins: *Felix anna quedam matrona legitima beato ioachim promeruit generare felicem filiam nomine mariam.*

29 The identity of this figure is not clear. In James's catalogue entry (*Cat. Fitz.*, p. 173) he is described as 'a cripple following' but given his advanced age it is also possible that he represents one of St Anne's husbands, perhaps St Joachim.

30 The rubric to the prayer names the women as Mary Jacobi and Mary Cleophas. Mary Salomé was also known as Mary Jacobi, a name acquired on account of her being the mother of St James the Great.

31 Camille, p. 228.

32 Giselle de Nie, ' "Consciousness Fecund Through God": From Male Fighter to Spiritual Bride-Mother in Late Antique Female Sanctity', in *Sanctity and Motherhood: Essays on Holy Mothers in the Middle Ages*, ed. by Anneke B. Mulder-Bakker (New York and London: Garland, 1995), pp. 101–61 (esp. pp. 139–51); and Véronique P. Day, 'Recycling Radegund: Identity and Ambition in the Breviary of Anne de Prye', in *Excavating the Medieval Image: Manuscripts, Artists, Audiences: Essays in Honor of Sandra Hindman*, ed. by David S. Areford and Nina A. Rowe (Aldershot: Ashgate, 2004), pp. 151–77. In considering a breviary made for Abbess Anne de Prye, Day shows how the cults of St Anne and St Radegund functioned together to emphasise the female owner's regal heritage.

33 Day, p. 161; Nie, p. 145.

34 Day, p. 160.

35 Day, p. 160.

36 Nie, p. 144.

37 Day, pp. 160–1; Nie, p. 140.

38 On the 'anti-English spirit' of St Radegund, see Day, pp. 160–1.

39 On Charles's devotion to St Radegund, see Vale, p. 23; and Avril, p. 261. Charles's daughter-in-law, Charlotte of Savoy, also appears to have had a special devotion for this saintly queen. A copy of her *vita*, belonging to Charlotte, was later invento-

ried in the library of her daughter, Anne of France; see Chazaud, p. 243; and Avril, 'Un portrait inédit de la reine Charlotte de Savoie', in *Études sur la Bibliothèque nationale et témoignages réunis en hommage à Thérèse Kleindienst* (Paris: Bibliothèque nationale, 1985), pp. 255-62.

40 Anja Petrakopoulos, 'Sanctity and Motherhood: Elizabeth of Thuringia', in *Sanctity and Motherhood*, ed. by Mulder–Bakker, pp. 257-96 (p. 263).

41 Petrakopoulos, p. 264.

42 Adrian S. Hoch, 'Beata Stirps, Royal Patronage and the Identification of the Sainted Rulers in the St Elizabeth Chapel at Assisi', *Art History*, 15 (1992), 279-95 (p. 279).

43 Klaniczy, p. 233. For example, several decades after her death, St Elizabeth seems to have served as a model for Charles I of Anjou's second wife and widow, Margaret of Burgundy (1248-1308), who founded a hospital in 1293, where she was to work for the rest of her life. See Petrakopoulos, p. 278.

44 Klaniczy, p. 232.

45 For further information about these dynastic saints see Klaniczy, pp. 208-9.

46 Abbé Petin, *Dictionnaire hagiographique ou vies des saints et des bienheureux*, 2 vols with supplement (Paris: Ateliers Catholiques du Petit-Montrouge, 1850), II, col 282.

47 Pétin, II, cols 280; 285.

48 See Anne-Marie De Gendt, 'Aucuns petis enseignemens: "Home-Made" Courtesy Books in Medieval France', in *Centres of Learning and Location in Pre-Modern Europe and the Near East*, ed. by Jan Willem Drijvers and Alisdair MacDonald (Leiden: Brill, 1995), pp. 279-88 (p. 280). On medieval conduct more generally see *Medieval Conduct*, ed. by Kathleen Ashley and Robert L. A. Clark (London and Minneapolis: University of Minnesota Press, 2001).

49 See De Gendt and Chazaud.

50 Georges Minois, *Charles VII: un roi shakespearien* ([no place]: Perrin, 2005), pp. 128-33 and see the discussion below.

51 He is also known as St Louis of Marseille and St Louis of Anjou.

52 Hoch, pp. 279-80.

53 Hoch, p. 280.

54 Klaniczy, p. 307; emphasis original.

55 Chevalier, p. 83.

56 Emmerson, 'A "Large Order" of the Whole', p. 56.

57 There is not space in this study to offer an in-depth consideration of the *Apocalypse* and *Pilgrimage* texts and their artistic traditions. For further analysis of the *Apocalypse* see Emmerson, 'The Apocalypse Cycle in the Bedford Hours', *Traditio*, 50 (1995), 173-98; see also *The Apocalypse in the Middle Ages*, ed. by Emmerson and Bernard McGinn (Ithaca: Cornell University Press, 1992). For the *Pilgrimage* series see Emmerson, 'A "Large Order" of the Whole', and 'Translating Images: Image and Poetic Reception in French, English, and Latin Versions of Guillaume de Deguileville's *Trois Pèlerinages*', in *Poetry, Place and Gender: Studies in Medieval Culture in Honor of Helen Damico*, ed. by Catherine E. Karkov (Kalamazoo: Medieval Institute Publications, 2008).

58 Carole Meale has noted the 'apparent popularity of apocalypses amongst women' in fourteenth- and fifteenth-century England, a popularity which may have extended to the continent. See her article, ' ". . . alle the bokes that I haue of latyn, englisch, and frensch": Laywomen and their Books in Late Medieval England', in *Women and Literature in Britain*, ed. by Meale, pp. 128–58 (n. 40).

59 George Henderson, 'The Manuscript Model of the Angers "Apocalypse" Tapestries', *Burlington Magazine*, 127 (1985), 208–19 (p. 219); and Fabienne Joubert, 'L'Apocalypse d'Angers et les débuts de la tapisserie historiée', *Bulletin Monumental*, 139 (1981), 125–40 (p. 125). The manuscript lent by Charles V is Paris, Bibliothèque nationale, fonds français, 403.

60 Legaré, 'La réception du *Pèlerinage*', pp. 543–4.

61 See Legaré, 'La réception du *Pèlerinage*', p. 546; n. 19. A secretary of Yolande of Aragon, and a 'conseiller et chambellan' of René both owned copies, see Legaré, 'La réception du *Pèlerinage*', pp. 545–6.

62 Legaré, 'La réception du *Pèlerinage*', pp. 544–7; 551 and n. 17.

63 Emmerson, 'A "Large Order" of the Whole', p. 63.

64 Camille, pp. 232–3.

65 Minois, *Anne de Bretagne* (Lille: Fayard, 1999), pp. 18–24.

66 Emmerson, 'A "Large Order" of the Whole', p. 64.

67 See Gibson, 'Scene and Obscene: Seeing and Performing Late Medieval Childbirth', *Journal of Medieval and Early Modern Studies*, 29 (1999), 7–24; Penny Howell Jolly, 'Learned Reading, Vernacular Seeing: Jacques Daret's *Presentation in the Temple*', *Art Bulletin*, 82 (2000), 428–52 (p. 446).

68 Musacchio, pp. 40–1.

69 de Voragine, II, p. 152.

70 de Voragine, II, p. 152.

71 Smith, pp. 256–60 (p. 259).

72 See Toynbee, p. 304 and figure E. The fact that Francis remarried in 1442, the year of his succession, suggests that the newly-crowned Duke was hoping to secure another heir. A portrait of the child was included in a miniature for the feast of Corpus Christi in the *Missal of the Carmelites of Nantes* (Princeton, University Library, Garrett Collection, MS 40, fol. 131v), which shows him with Francis I (depicted as heir to the duchy of Brittany) with Yolande of Anjou. On the right-hand side of the miniature Francis appears as the duke of Brittany, accompanied by his second wife Isabel and their two daughters Marguerite and Marie.

73 Paviot, p. 101.

74 Eames, pp. 74; 77.

75 Paviot, p. 99.

76 Cited by Laurent, p. 210: 'la chambre fut toute tendue d'un surciel, tant qu'elle avoit de long et comprenait tout les deux litz, et tout le devant estoit frangié de franges noires blanches et rouges . . . et tout estoit de damas bleu et la courtine qui estoit tout au long de la chambre estoit de taffetaz bleu'.

77 That noblewomen took an interest in the childbearing of their peers is suggested by the fact that 'Madame de Savoye' sent Yolande of France hangings for her bedroom made of crimson velvet embroidered with figures, pearls, rubies and dia-

monds. See Laurent, pp. 210–11. She does not state which 'madame de Savoye' sent these items but it would presumably have been a member of her husband's family, perhaps her mother-in-law, Anne of Lusignan (1419–62), since Yolande of France was married to Amadeus IX, duke of Savoy.

78 See Robin, pp. 145–6.

79 On the use of images in meditative devotion, see for example, Sixten Ringbom, 'Devotional Images and Imaginative Devotions: Notes on the Place of Art in Late Medieval Private Piety', *Gazette des Beaux-Arts*, 73 (1969), 159–70. Popular texts like the *Meditationes vitae Christi* by pseudo-Bonaventure encouraged lay people to 'participate' at holy events like the Nativity or the Crucifixion. See *Meditations on the life of Christ: an illustrated manuscript of the fourteenth century, Paris, Bibliothèque nationale, MS. Ital. 115*, trans. by Isa Ragusa, ed. by Ragusa and Rosalie B. Green (Princeton: Princeton University Press, 1961).

80 Wieck, p. 94; and Joan Naughton, 'A Minimally-Intrusive Presence: Portraits in Illustrations for Prayers to the Virgin', in *Medieval Texts and Images: Studies of Manuscripts from the Middle Ages*, ed. by Margaret Manion and Bernard J. Muir (Chur: Harwood Academic Publishers, 1991), pp. 111–25 (p. 113).

81 See Camille, pp. 228; 255–6; nn. 34–5; and note 6 above.

82 Meiss erroneously described the *Five Joys* (fols 141v–146r) as the *Fifteen Joys*, p. 265. The *Five Joys* were traditionally said to be the Annunciation, the Nativity, the Resurrection, the Ascension and the Assumption. The *Doulce Dame* (fols 192r–198v) was a French text which expanded the five joys to fifteen.

83 A miniature of the Virgin educating Christ also appears in a Book of Hours belonging to another aristocratic woman who drew on the symbolism of holy mothers educating their children, Anne of Brittany. The image is in her *Grandes Heures* illuminated by Jean Bordichon around 1500–8 (Paris, Bibliothèque nationale, fonds latin, 9474, fol. 222v). The manuscript also shows St Anne educating her three daughters, fol. 197v. See L'Estrange, 'Le mécénat d'Anne de Bretagne', in *Patronnes et mécénes*, ed. by Wilson-Chevalier, pp. 169–93.

84 Randolph, 'Renaissance Household Goddesses', p. 174.

85 Marrow, p. 2. Prayers and texts from the *Très Belles Heures* were also found in the Duke's *Petites Heures*, and in a now-lost manuscript that belonged to John's father, John the Good. The *Très Belles Heures* and the *Petites Heures* also had textual and iconographic similarities with the *Savoy Hours* made for Blanche of Burgundy, subsequently owned by John of Berry's older brother King Charles V. The *Très Belles Heures* originally consisted of two volumes. The first volume, the *Très Belles Heures de Notre-Dame* illuminated by, among others, the Limbourg brothers, is now conserved in Paris (Bibliothèque nationale, nouvelle acquisition latine, 3093). The second volume (the so-called *Turin-Milan Hours*), on which Jan Van Eyck worked, was acquired by the University Library in Turin where it was partly destroyed by fire in 1904. The surviving section is conserved in Turin (Museo Civico d'Arte Antica, Inv. No. 47).

86 Marrow, p. 2.

87 Marrow, p. 2.

88 For a full catalogue description see Abbé Victor Leroquais, *Les Livres d'heures*

manuscrits de la Bibliothèque nationale, 3 vols (Paris: Bibliothèque nationale, 1927), I, pp. 281–90; see also Avril and Reynaud, p. 26. Certain folios are, however, missing, including what must have been a *Nativity* miniature for Prime and an *Adoration of the Magi* miniature for Sext in the Hours of the Virgin.

89   Meiss, p. 267; n. 76.

90   Believing the arms to be original, Durrieu (pp. 161–2) identified the manuscript's owner as either Alain IX, viscount of Rohan (d. 1461) and his wife Marie of Lorraine, or his son Alain of Porhoët (d. 1449) and his wife Yolande of Laval (the arms of each woman being on gold ground). This identification was taken up by Leroquais (I, p. 290) who followed a similar dating. Meiss (p. 270) proposes that another possible recipient for the *Rohan Hours* was Louis III of Anjou.

91   Avril and Reynaud (p. 26) date the manuscript to 1430–35. Avril reiterated this date and an execution for the marriage of Charles of Maine in the 2004 Bibliothèque nationale exhibition catalogue, *Paris 1400: les arts sous Charles VI* (Paris: Fayard, 2004), pp. 371–3.

92   See A. de Laborde, *Étude sur la Bible moralisée illustrée*, 5 vols (Paris: Société française de reproductions de manuscrits à peintures, 1911–27), V, pp. 117–22 (p. 118). Ring, Porcher and Meiss all agree that the arms are not original and argue for a date between *c.*1419 and the later 1420s: see Ring, p. 203; Meiss, pp. 267–70; n. 76; and Porcher, pp. 2–3. Porcher argues that the manuscript could have passed easily to the house of Rohan via René of Anjou who may have handed over the manuscript as part of a ransom to buy his freedom from Antoine de Vaudémont, who was holding him prisoner. Antoine's daughter was the second wife of Alan IX of Rohan; see Porcher, pp. 2–3.

93   Paris, Bibliothèque nationale, fonds français, 9561.

94   See Porcher, p. 4; and Meiss and Thomas, p. 13 who claim that f. fr. 9561 was not the one found in Louis II's inventory but was instead a copy owned by an Angevin duke. Avril and Reynaud suggest that another fourteenth-century *Bible moralisée* (Paris, Bibliothèque nationale, fonds français, 166) was also known at the Angevin court. This manuscript has generally been accepted as an early work of the Limbourg brothers; see Rob Dückers, ' "In the Beginning": The *Bible Moralisée* in the Work of the Limbourg Brothers', in *The Limbourg Brothers: Nijmegen Masters at the French Court, 1400–1416*, ed. by Rob Dückers and Pieter Roelfs (Nijmegen: Ludion, 2005), pp. 85–95.

95   Porcher, p. 4 and figures 8a and 8c (fol. 2r in the *Rohan Hours*; fol. 2v in the *Bible moralisée*). The parity of the two image cycles was established by Heimann.

96   For the complete note see Porcher, p. 1; n. 3; and Léopold Delisle, *Mélanges de paléographie et de bibliographie* (Paris: Champion, 1880), p. 284; n. 1. The *Belles Heures* are conserved in New York, Metropolitan Museum of Art, The Cloisters Collection, MS 54.1.1.

97   See Meiss, pp. 268–9; and Porcher, pp. 1–3.

98   See Porcher, pp. 3–4; see also Buettner, p. 15. The *Très Riches Heures* are conserved in the Musée Condé in Chantilly, France, MS 65.

99   See Meiss, p. 267; figures 571 and 870.

100 Marrow, p. 2.

101 Dückers, p. 85.

102 Gerald B. Guest, *Bible Moralisée: Codex Vindobonensis 2554, Vienna, Österreichische Nationalbibliothek* (London: Harvey Miller, 1995), p. 26.

103 See Guest, and Sara Lipton, *Images of Intolerance: The Representation of Jews and Judaism in the* Bible moralisée (Berkeley, Los Angeles, and London: University of California Press, 1999), p. 5.

104 Most of the manuscript is in Toledo, Cathedral Library, MS 1; several pages were removed and are conserved in the Pierpont Morgan Library, MS. M. 240. On the commission, see Daniel H. Weiss, 'Architectural Symbolism and the Decoration of the Ste-Chapelle', *Art Bulletin*, 77 (1995), 308–20 (p. 316). The queen is depicted instructing her son on folio 8r.

105 King John's copy is Paris, Bibliothèque nationale, fonds français, 167 and served as the exemplar from which BnF f. fr. 166, one of the *Bible moralisée* known at the Angevin court, was copied. See Dücker, p. 87 and note 95 above.

106 Vale, pp. 21–2.

107 Vale, pp. 22–5; Meiss, p. 269.

108 Vale, p. 25.

109 Minois, *Charles VII*, pp. 128–33. The treaty effectively punished Charles for the murder of the duke of Burgundy, John the Fearless, in 1419 in which he was implicated.

110 Guest, p. 3.

111 Greilsammer, p. 321.

112 Genesis 25. 27–34.

113 Genesis 25. 21.

114 Genesis 38.

115 Minois, *Charles VII*, pp. 133–5. Minois also notes that letters patent were issued by Isabeau of Bavaria condemning her son for crimes including parricide and lèse-majesté, which rendered him unworthy to be king. See Minois, *Charles VII*, p. 129.

116 See Matthew 1.1–16.

117 Weiss, p. 317.

118 Weiss, p. 317.

119 See p. 84; n. 47 above and Eames, pp. 73–93.

120 On René's book collection see Avril and Reynaud, pp. 233–7.

121 See Robin, pp. 169–70. A later Book of Hours belonging to René (Paris, Bibliothèque nationale, fonds latin, 17332) also includes an Angevin family chronicle in its calendar; see Avril and Reynaud, p. 233.

122 BL, Egerton MS 1070; Harthan, pp. 92–3; Avril and Reynaud, p. 227; Meiss, pp. 328–9.

123 See Harthan, pp. 92–3.

124 The arms are those of Jerusalem, *Anjou-ancien* and *Anjou-moderne*, see Meiss, p. 346.

125 Robin, p. 170.

126 Durrieu, p. 165. Meiss associated the eagles with patriarchal crosses and the sail with the motto *en dieu en soit* that occur on every single page of the manuscript,

solely with René. However, he also claims that these were part of the original campaign of illumination, which would conflict with the idea that the manuscript was originally executed for another member of the house (see Meiss, pp. 266; 346). Robin has shown that these symbols can in fact be traced back to René's father, and even his grandfather, and that they could thus have formed part of the original campaign, retaining their significance when the manuscript was adapted for René; see Robin, pp. 168–70.

127 Durrieu, p. 165.

128 Meiss, p. 347.

129 John I (1425–70); Louis (1427–43); Yolande (1428–83); Marguerite (1429–82).

130 In addition to the children noted above, René and Isabel lost six children at a very young age including their firstborn, René (b. 1426) and four other children born between 1431 and 1437.

131 Robin, p. 33 and nn. 32–3.

132 Meiss, p. 346–7. Châtelet attributes the miniatures added to the *London Hours* to Jean de Pestinien, a painter in the service of Philip the Good. See Châtelet, 'Jean de Pestinien au service de Philippe le Bon et de son prisonnier le Roi René', *Artibus et Historiae*, 20 (1999), 77–88.

133 II Samuel 23. 14–16; Otto Pächt, 'René d'Anjou et les Van Eyck', *Cahiers de l'association internationale des études françaises*, 8 (1956), 41–67 (p. 44).

134 Prayers were added at fols 14r–v; 23v; 43v–44r; the *Commedatio animae* occurs on fols 43v–44r.

135 Harthan, p. 93; see also Pächt, p. 44.

136 Pächt (p. 48) notes that René also used this theme of the *roi mort* on his tomb.

137 Châtelet, 'Jean de Pestinien', p. 84.

138 Pächt, p. 49.

139 Pächt, p. 49.

140 Pächt, p. 49. René inherited the duchy of Bar through his marriage to Isabel of Lorraine, but he also claimed it through his mother, Yolande of Aragon, who was the granddaughter of Robert of Bar.

141 Pächt, p. 49 and Robin, p. 33.

142 Matthew 27. 55–6; Mark 15. 40 and 16. 1–8; Luke 23. 49–56 and 24. 1–11; John 19. 25. They are described in St Matthew's Gospel as 'Mary Magdalen and Mary the mother of James and Joseph and the mother of the sons of Zebedee'; in St Mark's as 'Mary Magdalen and Mary the mother of James the Less and of Joseph and Salome [i.e. the wife Zebedee, mother of James the Greater and John the Evangelist]'; and in St John's as 'his [Christ's] mother's sister, Mary of Cleophas, and Mary Magdalene'.

143 Robin, p. 56.

144 Robin, p. 56.

145 Robin, p. 56.

5

Steriles fecundas fecisti: viewing and reading holy motherhood in the manuscripts of four duchesses of Brittany

In 1442, Isabel Stuart, daughter of James I of Scotland, married Francis, the heir to the duchy of Brittany. As a result of this marriage, Isabel acquired the *Fitzwilliam Hours*, which had previously been in the possession of Francis's first wife, Yolande of Anjou. Isabel evidently took a great interest in this manuscript since, as noted in the previous chapter, it is personalised with her coat of arms throughout and her portrait was added at the beginning of the *Obsecro te* prayer (plate 7). Another, later, portrait of a woman at prayer at the beginning of the *Omnis te virtus decorat* prayer, suggests that Isabel passed this book on to her eldest daughter, Marguerite of Brittany (1443–69) who, in 1455, married her cousin, the future Duke Francis II of Brittany (1435–88) (plate 13).

Whereas Chapter 4 showed how the *Fitzwilliam Hours* were originally designed to express Angevin interests in *beata stirps* and to exploit Yolande of Aragon's connections with the French royal family, this chapter begins by considering how the *Fitzwilliam Hours* and its emphasis on holy motherhood and dynastic saints were interpreted by these two later owners. It considers how the situational eye of Isabel and Marguerite, informed by the cognitive habits discussed in the first part of this book, was also nuanced by the specific context in which they inherited the manuscript. The discussion then moves on to consider two more devotional books owned by the successors of Isabel and Marguerite, Marguerite of Foix and her daughter Anne of Brittany (1477–1514). The analysis focuses on how these duchesses of Brittany and, in Anne's case, this twice queen of France, used narratives of holy motherhood and miraculous conception to negotiate the difficulties they encountered in conceiving and giving birth to heirs.

A key aspect of the interpretations offered involves considering the place occupied by the four duchesses in the Breton ducal house and how this contributed to their situational eye, making the narratives of holy motherhood pertinent to their individual positions. As the second wife of Francis of Brittany who had yet to produce an heir, Isabel Stuart would have been expected to play a pivotal role in securing the future of the duchy. Thus, it is likely that knowledge of the duke's previous fruitless marriage nuanced further Isabel's reception of the dynastic and maternal themes already evident in her predecessor's manuscript. During their eight-year marriage, Isabel gave birth to two children who survived into adulthood, Marguerite (1443–69) and Marie (1444–1507). Following Breton inheritance laws, these girls could not ensure Francis's direct succession although the eldest daughter, Marguerite, did eventually come to reign as duchess of Brittany through her marriage to Francis II. However, this union was also marred by a lack of male heirs, which some contemporaries attributed to the duke's high profile extra-marital affair that resulted in at least two sons and a daughter. It is suggested that Marguerite's reading of the *Fitzwilliam Hours*, inherited from her mother, probably around the time of her marriage, was influenced by an awareness of the duchy's previous succession problems and the importance of male children to ensure the new ducal line.

After Marguerite died without providing an heir for Francis II, the duke continued to be plagued by fertility problems in his second marriage to Marguerite of Foix. Marguerite was probably particularly attuned to the importance of male heirs since, as shown in Chapter 2, the counts of Foix had suffered from succession problems and her father, Gaston IV, had commissioned a medical treatise to help ensure his own marriage would be fertile. Furthermore, the prayer for childbirth and the decorative cycle included in Marguerite's Book of Hours indicates that she used biblical narratives of holy motherhood and miraculous conception as models with which she could identify during her own period of sterility. After six years, Marguerite gave birth to two girls, Anne and Isabeau. Anne of Brittany's own name would have reminded her of her own long-awaited birth and her patron saint played an extremely important role in her own devotions, especially where children (or lack of them), were concerned. St Anne appears throughout her commission manuscripts in the guise of blessed mother and wise educator. Since Anne's artistic patronage constitutes a large field in its own right, the discussion here focuses mainly on a little-known prayer book belonging to Anne, and dating from her second marriage, which includes a prayer for successful childbearing.[1]

Like her mother's, Anne's prayer book demonstrates that aristocratic women drew on stories about holy and miraculous childbirth when asking God to help them conceive and give birth. The fact that Anne's prayer also refers to the story of the Frankish queen, Clothilde, who was helped to deliver a child through the prayers of St Leonard, shows that Anne, like Yolande of Aragon, exploited her connections to the royal house of France, situating herself in a dynastic line going back to the first queen of the Franks. The examples of Marguerite's and Anne's prayer books provide a fitting conclusion to this study since they bring together elements of all the material discussed in the previous chapters and demonstrate how prayer, images and remedies relating to holy motherhood and blessed dynasties could come together as aids for aristocratic women whose social roles required them to produce healthy male children. As the case of Anne of France has already demonstrated, that of Anne of Brittany will also show how aristocratic women could manipulate patriarchal society's need for male heirs to try to protect their own interests: in Anne's case, to retain Brittany's independence. Thus these women's recourse to examples of holy motherhood can be considered less a passive subjugation to the demands of patriarchal society and more a way for them to manage their roles within that society.

From duchess to duchess: Isabel Stuart and the *Fitzwilliam Hours*

Two years after the death of his first wife, Yolande of Anjou, Francis of Brittany married for a second time. His union with Isabel Stuart took place in the same year as his accession to the duchy (1442) and was most likely motivated by the need to secure an heir. Records have left little trace of the child Rohan born of his marriage to Yolande and the child may well have died around the same time as his mother, or soon after. In order to ensure Francis's succession, Isabel would need to give birth to a boy since the first Treaty of Guérande, signed in 1365 to end the inheritance dispute between the two factions of the Breton ducal house, prevented the duchy passing through the female line while there was a male heir elsewhere in the house.[2] This section explores how the history of Isabel's predecessor and the need for a male heir informed Isabel's situational eye and thus her reading of the *Fitzwilliam Hours*, both as the first wife's possession and as a source of references about holy motherhood and dynastic saints.

Isabel's acquisition of the *Fitzwilliam Hours* provided her with an opportunity to assert her position as duchess of Brittany. In addition to the modification of the *Obsecro te* portrait showing Isabel at prayer, the rectangular arms of Brittany impaling those of Scotland, many topped with the ducal coronet, were added throughout the manuscript, often in the four corners of the page or within opening initials. The symbolic (re)placement of Isabel's heraldic body in her predecessor's manuscript signified that Isabel's real body was under pressure to succeed where Yolande's had failed, by producing heirs for the duke. Thus, the manuscript with its images of St Anne and her daughters, and the nativities of the Virgin and Christ, became a symbol of the potential of the marriage and the future of the house of Brittany.

Evidence of Isabel's presence in front of the *Fitzwilliam Hours* occurs at the beginning of the manuscript, where her arms appear in the border of the extract from St John's Gospel. This is the point where the marginal cycle of Deguileville's *Pilgrimage of Jesus Christ* also begins and, as noted in Chapter 4, the visual and textual arrangement of the *Pilgrimage* series in the *Fitzwilliam Hours* encouraged the reader to make a connection between the Gospels and Deguileville's texts. For example, the coinciding of a marginal image of Christ's *Nativity* with the opening of the extract from St Luke's Gospel made maternity a prominent feature right at the start of the manuscript. The fact that Isabel's arms were added to the borders of this page suggests that she participated in this interaction between text and miniature and that she too would have noted the prominence of the story of Christ's conception and birth and may have related it to her situation as the new duchess. Following the Gospels, Isabel's interaction with the manuscript is most strongly indicated by her portrait, which was added to the opening of the *Obsecro te*. The miniature shows her presented by St Catherine to the Virgin and Child (plate 7). With one hand the Christ-Child grasps the end of the banderol signifying Isabel's prayer; with the other he reaches out for a rosary lying on the desk in front of a book: both the rosary and the book, like the manuscript itself, are important means of achieving a state of meditative devotion.

Whereas the *Obsecro te* and its miniature have already been discussed in terms of how they related to the manuscript's previous owners, their significance for Isabel warrants further analysis. The image is complex and embodied many layers of interpretation. On one level, it represents Isabel in a state of personal prayer and devotion to the Virgin. As for Yolande of Aragon and her daughter, a donor portrait opening this prayer that celebrates Mary's motherhood, offered Isabel a point of connection between herself and the ultimate mother, Mary, and provided a stimulus to a divine vision. On another level, the portrait reinforced Isabel's ownership of the manuscript as well as her social status. By modifying the previous owner's portrait, Isabel signified her presence both within the manuscript and within the duchy of Brittany. Holding the book in her hands, Isabel saw an image of herself as duchess of Brittany, crowned and dressed in ducal insignia. The four crowned coats of arms placed in the corners of the page reinforce Isabel's status and, by dominating the page, they provide a Breton-Scottish alternative to the gold fleur de lys on the Virgin's blue cloak, whose original function was perhaps to signify the French origins of the manuscript's previous Angevin readers. The new image thus ensured that it was Isabel who could enjoy this privileged vision of the Virgin and Child and that it was her petition, symbolised in the scroll, which came to the Virgin's ears.

The French fleur de lys may not, however, have been entirely irrelevant to Isabel. In 1436, her sister Margaret Stuart (1424–45) married Charles VII's son and heir, the Dauphin Louis XI. The dauphine was brought up by the sister of Isabel's predecessor, Marie of Anjou, queen of France and the two sisters met at the French court prior to Isabel's marriage.[3] Margaret died a few years after Isabel's own marriage in 1442 but the alliance still provided Isabel with a link both to the French court and to the family who had commissioned the manuscript she now owned. Furthermore, knowledge of her sister's apparently unhappy, politically-motivated, marriage to the king of France could only have reinforced Isabel's awareness of the political and generational expectations of her own.[4] Since Isabel gave birth to her two daughters within two years of her marriage, she may have used the modified *Obsecro te* miniature to give thanks for her fertility, for the Virgin's protection, and for the safe delivery of her two children. By showing Isabel in the presence of the Virgin and her Son, the miniature also offered her the possibility of petitioning God for the birth of a male heir to safeguard the duchy.

Isabel was also able to envisage a close relationship between herself and Mary as a mother through the opening miniature at Matins. As already discussed, the page is decorated with a central *Annunciation* surrounded by marginal scenes recounting the story of St Anne and St Joachim and the Virgin's early life. Isabel's coat of arms was added in the centre of the letter D which opens the text, 'O Lord, open my lips' (*Domine labia mea aperies*). The enclosing of her arms within the initial letter forged a connection between Isabel, the manuscript and the prayer: she begins the prayer both vocally and visually. The images on the page also acted as a visual stimulation to her petition and, like Yolande of Anjou, Isabel's situational eye would have been tuned to the narrative of miraculous conception and in particular to the roundel of the *Birth of the Virgin*, which recalls the rich furnishings and assistance that accompanied aristocratic births, such as those described in Eleanor of Poitiers's *Honneurs de la Cour*.

Although there are no documents for Brittany comparable to Eleanor's treatise, surviving fragments of the ducal accounts still show that the duchesses of Brittany, including Isabel Stuart and her daughter Marguerite, had a discerning eye when it came to material furnishings, a discernment that would have extended to the decoration of the childbirth chamber.[5] Whereas Isabel's accounts indicate purchases for clothes, tailoring and embroidery, those for Marguerite of Brittany are more detailed and show purchases such as three and a half ounces of fine twisted silk (*trois oncez et demye de fin soye retorse*), and ten ells of the widest purple ribbon (*x aulnes de ruban voile de plus large*).[6] Some of the purchases made by Marguerite and Francis II include those specifically for bedrooms, such as a conical tent to place in a bedroom in the ducal castle in Nantes (*ung pavillon a server en une chambre en nostre chasteau de Nantes*), the linen for which cost 13 *livres* 6 *soldi*, plus another sum of 7 *livres* 13 *soldi* 9 *denarii* for the fringing of the canopy.[7] Duchess Marguerite also ordered two ells of black velvet to make bed covers, some black damask to line them, and several lengths of Syrien silk (*soille de souraine*) for a couch and bolster, plus the feathers to stuff them with.[8]

Such purchases, especially the canopied bed bought by Francis and Marguerite, and a general familiarity with the furnishings of estate would have allowed Isabel and her daughter to recognise allusions to the tastes and practices of the nobility in the *Birth of the Virgin* scene where St Anne lies in a canopied bed covered in blue material embroidered and fringed with gold. In this way the Matins page, especially the *Birth of the Virgin* roundel, became a space through which the duchesses could use these devotional images to pray for, and look forward to, a successful pregnancy and birth, after which they would become the woman 'on top' at court, and lie-in with all the assistance and trappings of their of estate.

Isabel could have drawn a connection between her own situation and the comfortable, successful image of the Virgin's birth in the *Fitzwilliam Hours* only a year or so into her marriage, since she gave birth to Marguerite in 1443 and Marie in 1444. On the one hand, the border image of the *Birth of the Virgin* provided an example of God's intervention in the birth of a female child but it also served as a prelude to the *Annunciation* scene in which God ordained that a woman should conceive a son. Therefore, as time went on and a son was still needed to ensure Francis's lineage it is possible that Isabel came to view this page as a way to direct her devotions towards the conception of a son. Viewed through Isabel's situational eye, the Matins page offered the possibility of a parallel to Isabel's own life in which a blessed female child would be followed by an equally, if not more, blessed son. The discussion below shows that Isabel's daughter Marguerite would also have been sensitive to the narratives of the Matins page but for slightly different reasons since, during her fourteen-year marriage to Francis II of Brittany, she gave birth to only one child who died after just a few months.

The suffrages in the *Fitzwilliam Hours* offered examples of holy motherhood and a blessed lineage to which the female Angevin readers could relate. For Yolande of Aragon and her daughter Yolande of Anjou, St Radegund and St Elizabeth of Hungary alluded to their own noble status and dynastic connections with the houses of France and Anjou. Like Yolande of Aragon, Isabel Stuart was the daughter of a king and, during the first years of her marriage at least, she was also connected to the house of France through her sister, the dauphine. Thus, although these and the other Angevin saints in the suffrages were not directly related to Isabel Stuart's own family nor to that of her husband, their aristocratic connotations as well as their associations with motherhood and parenting, both biological and social, mean that Isabel could have interpreted them as models for the creation of her own family and *beata stirps*. In fact, the Franco-Angevin saints paralleled the sainted forebears of the Breton dukes who were privileged in some of Isabel's other manuscripts (discussed below). Moreover, a portrait of Isabel from one of these manuscripts suggests that she became a member of the Franciscan tertiary order, linking her with the Franciscan sympathies of St Elizabeth, St Louis IX and St Louis of Toulouse. The dynastic saints in the *Fitzwilliam Hours*' suffrages were also complemented by the texts and images referring to Christ's own lineage, especially the suffrages to St Anne and to her daughters St Mary Salomé and St Mary Cleophas, and the images accompanying Matins and the Lauds. The *Visitation* miniature at Lauds, where the Virgin, pregnant with Christ, greets her cousin St Elizabeth, pregnant with St John the Baptist, offered Isabel, and later her daughter, another example of a woman who conceived a son through the grace of God. This page, like that at Matins, could thus have functioned as a space through which they could envisage and pray for the fulfilment of their social roles with the minimum of pain and God's protection.

The opening of Lauds, like the *Obsecro te* miniature, includes Isabel's coats of arms, as does the *Purification* at Nones (figure 17) and the beginning of the *Five Joys* prayer, where they appear on the gable-ends of the architectural setting, between the statues of prophets emphasising the

Virgin's fulfilment of Old Testament prophecies (figure 26). Placed at these points in the manuscript, the coats of arms reinforce the connection between the narratives of holy childbirth and the female viewer holding the manuscript – both Isabel Stuart and Marguerite of Brittany. In forming a collective of women blessed in childbirth that included the viewer, the *Fitzwilliam Hours'* many images of holy motherhood also served as a visual analogy to the widely available childbirth prayers with which these women would have been familiar. Thus, in addition to functioning as exemplars for identification, the images also served as a reminder of the prayers available during labour itself and how God could intervene to facilitate women's childbearing. A further reminder of the specific assistance available during labour appears in the form of St Margaret, patron saint of childbirth, who is depicted twice in the *Fitzwilliam Hours'* suffrages. Although a common feature of many Books of Hours, whether made for female readers or not, St Margaret was the patron saint of women in childbirth and therefore a popular figure in maternal devotion. She is discussed in more detail when considering Marguerite of Foix's Book of Hours and Anne of Brittany's prayer book, since the saint features in both manuscripts in the dual role of protector of women in childbirth and Marguerite of Foix's patron saint.

After the death of Duke Francis I in 1450, the duchy passed to Francis's brother, Peter II (1418–57). Isabel, who did not remarry and who lived until at least 1494, remained in Brittany and continued to assert her status as dowager duchess and as a mother of the future duchess, Marguerite.[9] Her apparent affection for her adopted country is evidenced through several manuscript commissions that honoured her late husband and demonstrated hers, and her daughters', piety. The three manuscripts known to have been commissioned by Isabel are two Books of Hours and a copy of *Somme le roi*. These books reveal not only a certain financial independence but also an interest in her responsibilities – practical and devotional – as a mother, daughter of Scotland, and dowager duchess of Brittany. By turning to these manuscripts it is possible to reveal more of the cognitive habits informing Isabel's situational eye and thus to suggest how she read the *Fitzwilliam Hours*, especially its maternal imagery, both during and after her marriage.

Isabel's copy of *Somme le roi*, now in Paris, is dated 1464.[10] As a moral and religious guide originally written by Laurent du Bois in 1279 for King Philip III of France, the manuscript bears witness not only to Isabel's piety but also, perhaps, to her royal background, in the same way that Yolande of Aragon used the French saints and the *Bible moralisée* to promote the royal connections of the house of Anjou. The *Somme le roi* also demonstrates

Isabel's interest in setting a good example for her daughters, since the manuscript's frontispiece shows her before a *Pietà*, her two daughters standing behind her. Isabel is presented by St Francis, Marguerite by St Peter Martyr and Marie by St Mary Magdalene (figure 48). In the *Somme le roi* miniature the aristocratic status of the three women and their affiliations through marriage are indicated by their heraldic skirts and by the crowns worn by Isabel and Marguerite. Isabel wears the arms of Brittany and Scotland as she does in the *Fitzwilliam Hours' Obsecro te* miniature; Marguerite's arms are just those of Brittany, which she held both before and after her marriage to Francis II in 1455, but her crown indicates that she already holds the title of duchess of Brittany.[11] Marie's skirt shows Brittany's ermine impaling the *mascles* of Rohan since she married John II of Rohan 1461. All three women wear the collar of the *Ordre de l'Épi*, a chivalric order that was founded by Francis I around 1448 and attached to the *Ordre de l'Ermine*, founded by his predecessor Duke Jean IV (1345–99) in 1364. In addition to being presented by her husband's patron saint, St Francis, Isabel also wears the knotted cord of his order, the Franciscans, a motif which implies that she was a member of the Franciscan tertiary order.[12] With her daughters, Isabel is likened to the miniature of St Anne in the *Fitzwilliam Hours*, as a guiding figure for her daughters and it has in fact been suggested that the artist who painted this miniature and he who painted one of Isabel's Books of Hours were followers of the Rohan Master.[13] The employment of artists using a similar style could thus have been intended to reveal Isabel's discerning taste and to link her own commissions with the lavish *Fitzwilliam Hours* that she had already acquired and adapted.

The duchess's devotion to her deceased husband and his patron saint continues in two Books of Hours belonging to her that are now in Paris. These manuscripts are much smaller and the illumination far inferior to the *Fitzwilliam Hours*. Yet, they are both spaces in which Isabel affirmed her identity as dowager duchess of Brittany. The later of the two manuscripts (Paris, Bibliothèque nationale, nouvelle acquisition latine, 588), dates to 1461 at the earliest because of the inclusion of St Catherine of Siena, canonised in that year, in the suffrages. Isabel's arms are found throughout the manuscript at all the main divisions and they signify Isabel's presence in front of the manuscript, offering a means to connect her supplications with those written in the book. Just before the opening of Matins, Isabel is depicted crowned and dressed in a heraldic skirt. She is presented by St Francis of Assisi to an *Annunciation*, which appears on the opposite folio (figure 49). Her arms, complete with ducal coronets, also appear in all four corners of the *Annunciation* page and in the letter D of *Domine*. As in the

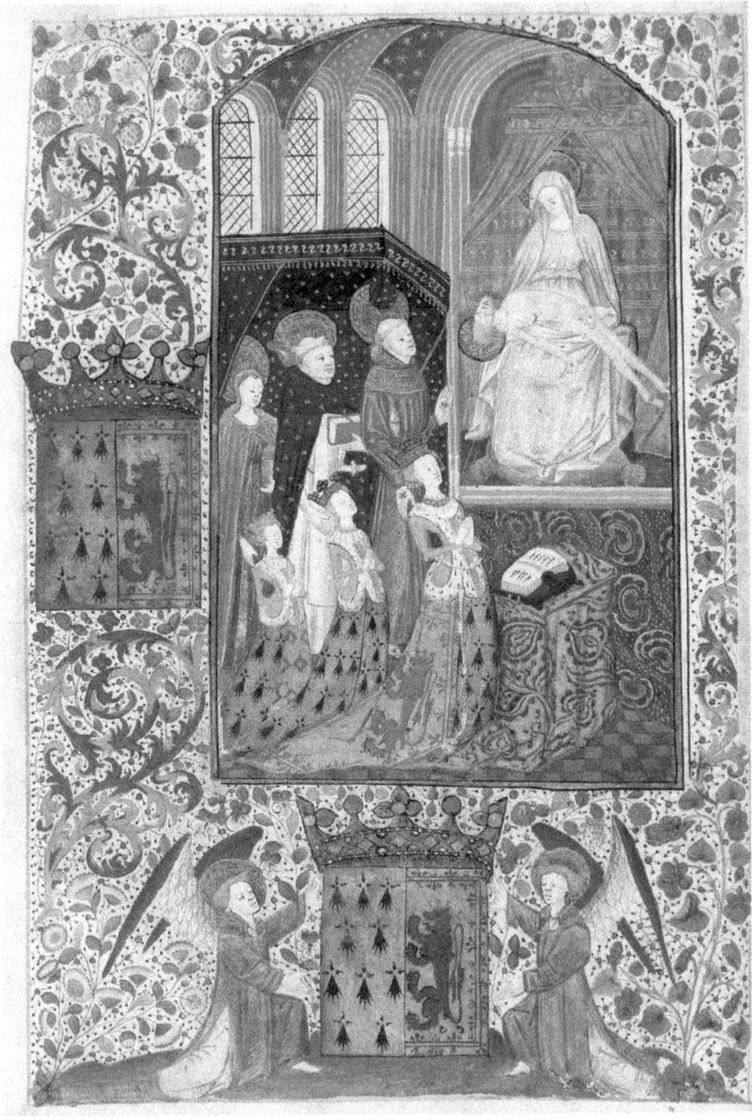

48 *Pietà*, with Isabel Stuart, Marguerite of Brittany, and Marie of Brittany presented by patron saints, *Somme le roi*, Paris, Bibliothèque nationale, fonds français, 958, fol. Fv, 1464 (© Paris, BnF)

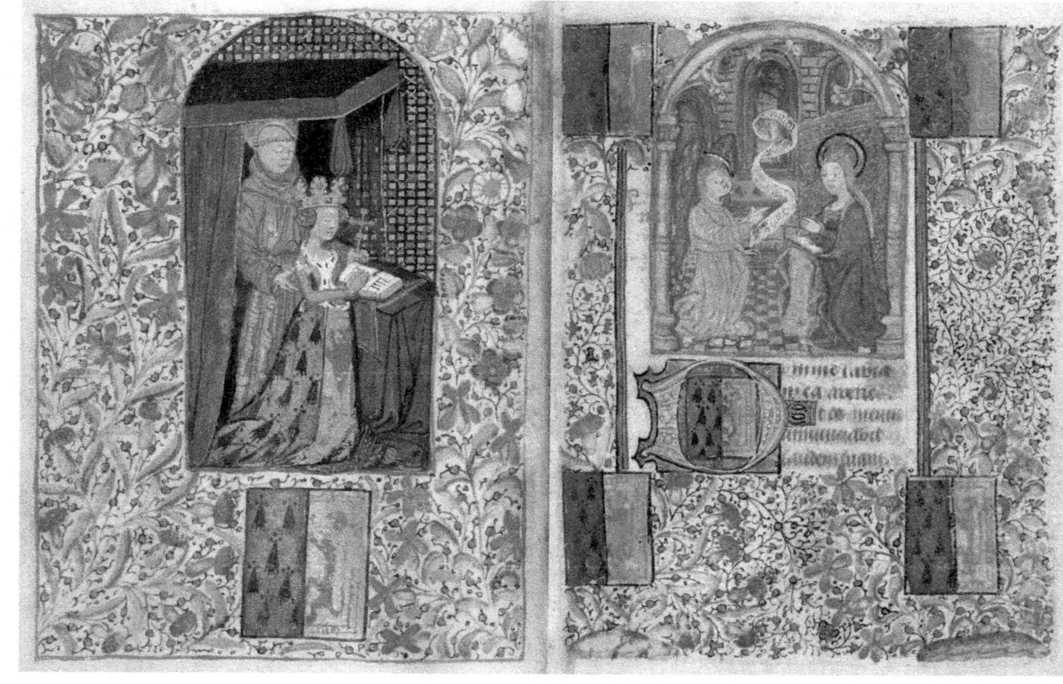

49   *Annunciation*, with Isabel Stuart presented by St Francis, *Hours of Isabel Stuart*, Paris, Bibliothèque nationale, nouvelle acquisition latine, 588, fols 33v–34r, after 1461 (© Paris, BnF)

Fitzwilliam Hours, the inclusion of Isabel's arms in the opening letter of the opening word of Matins forges a connection between the opening of the Hour and the opening of Isabel's lips in prayer. Furthermore, like the *Obsecro te* image, this image shows Isabel in a privileged encounter with the mother of God, here at the moment where she agrees to the Incarnation. Although the manuscript dates from her widowhood, Isabel's portrait here allowed her to continue to privilege her role as a Breton duchess and mother to her two daughters.

With this in mind, it is interesting to note that to this Book of Hours was also added, in a different hand, a small treatise offering advice for young girls on how to live a pious Christian life.[14] As seen previously, conduct manuals were a popular way of educating children and were often addressed to young women by their parents, such as the *Book of the Knight of the Tower* written by a knight for his three daughters, Anne of France's *Enseignements* for her daughter Suzanne, and St Louis IX's treatise for his daughter Isabel. Such personalised texts could actually reach well beyond their original audiences, thanks to the printing press, allowing other parents to use them to instruct their children.[15] Although it is not clear at what point these *Enseignements* were added to the manuscript, Isabel's apparent awareness of this genre of treatise further implies that she may have seen herself as an educator for her daughters, perhaps in the role of the wise widow St Anne, whose example was readily available to her in the *Fitzwilliam Hours*. That Isabel took an interest in her daughter's spiritual education is also evidenced by the fact that she not only passed on the *Fitzwilliam Hours* to Marguerite but also bequeathed another Book of Hours, now also in Paris (Bibliothèque nationale, fonds latin, 1369), to her youngest daughter Marie.

Several elements indicate Isabel's commission of BN lat. 1369. In addition to a miniature of Isabel at prayer, a text was added in a different hand which ends by asking for five *Our Fathers* and five *Hail Maries* to be said for her soul (*pour l'amme de la duchesse Ysabeau v fois pater noster et ave maria*).[16] Isabel also appears to have written her name on the bottom of many pages in the manuscript and her portrait appears, as it does in BN n.a.l. 588, just before the opening of Matins, although the title page that would have shown an *Annunciation* is now missing (figure 50).[17] The borders are decorated with rectangular, crowned shields, displaying, on the left, the arms of Brittany alone and, below, the arms of Brittany and Scotland together.

As in the *Somme le roi* miniature and the *Fitzwilliam Hours*, the arms complement the crown and heraldic skirt worn by Isabel in the miniature.

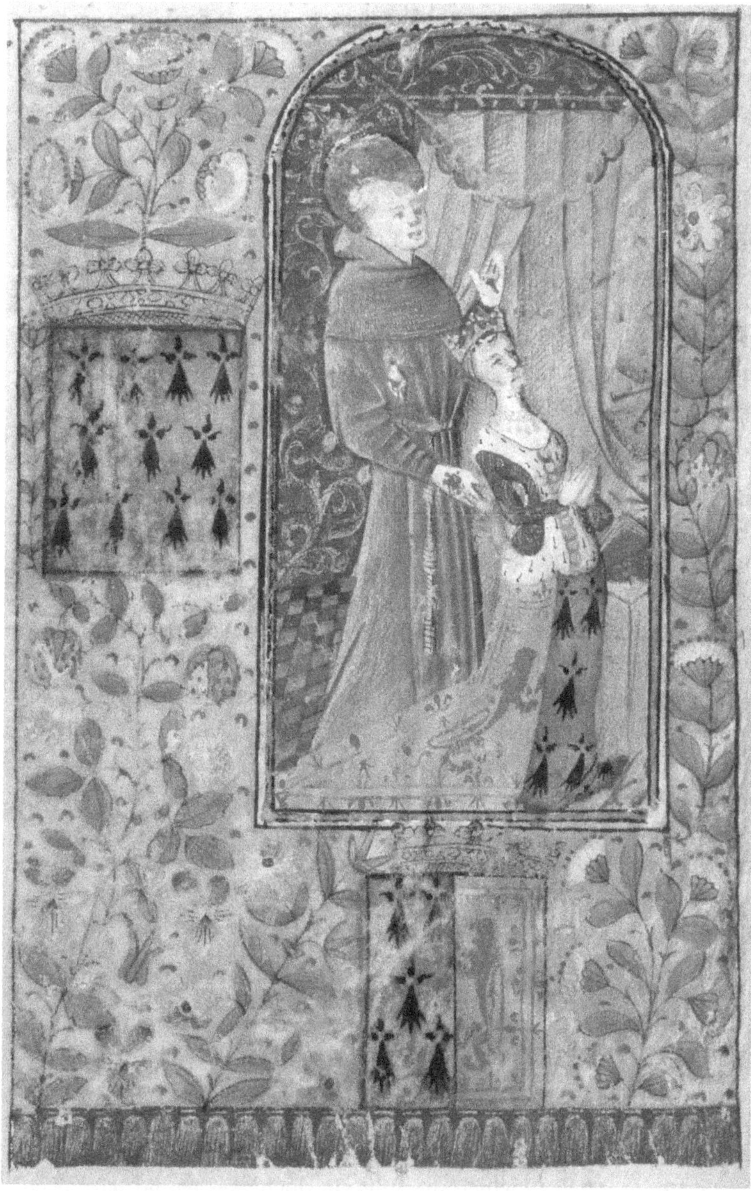

50   Portrait of Isabel Stuart (*Annunciation* missing), *Hours of Isabel Stuart*, Paris, Bibliothèque nationale, fonds latin, 1369, p. 56, after 1455 (© Paris, BnF)

She kneels at a prie-dieu on which a book lies and, presented by St Francis of Assisi, she gazes upwards and across the page to where the *Annunciation* would have been, her hands clasped in prayer. St Francis's stigmata are clearly evident on both his hands and on his side. He wears the thrice-knotted belt that Isabel was depicted wearing in the *Somme le roi* miniature, creating a link between the saint, the duchess's personal devotion, and that of her husband who, dressed in full ducal regalia, is also presented by St Francis, opposite a miniature of the Virgin and Child at the beginning of the *Obsecro te* (figure 51).

This portrait must, however, be a posthumous depiction of Francis who died in 1450, since St Vincent Ferrer (d. 1419), who was canonised in 1455, is included in the manuscript's suffrages. As in Isabel's portrait, the borders are decorated with the arms of Brittany and Scotland and the arms are also painted in the centre of the O of *Obsecro*. By including her deceased husband's portrait in her personal prayer book, and by placing his and her own arms at the beginning of the prayer, as she had done in the *Fitzwilliam Hours* and BN n.a.l. 588, Isabel was able to pray for Francis's soul by keeping him continually in her prayers. As in the *Somme le roi* miniature, in BN lat. 1369 she wears the collar of Francis's *Ordre de l'Épi*, further promoting the memory of her deceased husband and her adoption of Brittany as her home. Following Francis's death, Isabel wished to remain in Brittany and resisted her brother's attempts to bring her back to Scotland on the premise that Duke Peter II was treating her badly.[18] Thus here, as in BN n.a.l. 588 and the *Somme le roi* manuscript, Isabel was demonstrating her continued social role as a devout widow and her commitment to Brittany as its dowager duchess.

Isabel's devotion to her husband's patron saint adds to our understanding of how she received the *Fitzwilliam Hours*. Three of the most important saints in the *Fitzwilliam Hours* were St Elizabeth of Hungary, St Louis of Toulouse, and St Louis IX. Both St Elizabeth and St Louis IX became members of the Franciscan tertiary order and St Louis of Toulouse took the order's vows. Isabel's familiarity with the *Fitzwilliam Hours* and its Franciscan saints not only complemented, but may even have triggered or consolidated, her own devotion to St Francis since her possession of the *Fitzwilliam Hours* dates from before her other manuscript commissions. St Elizabeth, St Louis of Toulouse and St Louis IX formed part of the Angevin *beata stirps* to which the Angevin duchesses would have been receptive, but the Scottish Isabel could still have appropriated them for her own purposes. In fact, the inclusion of St Louis of Toulouse and St Elizabeth in the suffrages of BN lat. 1369 creates a link between Isabel's own

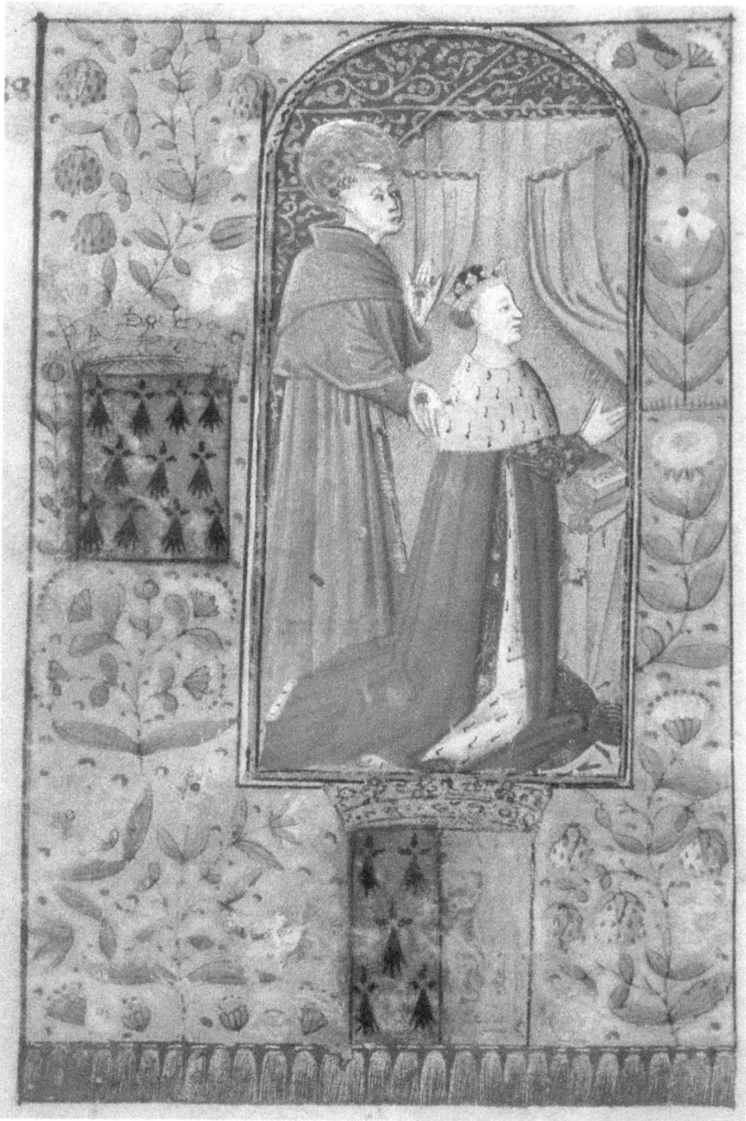

51   Portrait of Francis I of Brittany, *Obsecro te, Hours of Isabel Stuart*,
Paris, Bibliothèque nationale, fonds latin, 1369, p. 38, after 1455
(© Paris, BnF)

commission and the one she inherited from her predecessor. Furthermore, BN lat. 1369 dates from after 1455, the year in which her daughter Marguerite of Brittany married Francis II. Since Isabel probably passed the *Fitzwilliam Hours* to Marguerite, it is possible that BN lat. 1369 came to serve as a link between Isabel and her daughter by replicating the saints, with their connections to St Francis as well as to blessed lineage, from the *Fitzwilliam Hours*.

Other saints included in BN lat. 1369 reveal Isabel's interests in her adopted Breton heritage. The calendar, although now incomplete, indicates that it was for the liturgical Use of Nantes, where the ducal castle was situated.[19] Those saints whose feasts were marked in gold include two early Breton bishops, St Similien and St Clair, the translation of St Yvo (1253–1303), a Breton priest much revered by John V of Brittany, and the Presentation of the Blessed Virgin Mary, a feast that was instituted at Nantes after 1421.[20] In the suffrages, the inclusion of St Vincent Ferrer not only helps to date the manuscript but also relates to the devotion of the Breton ducal house. Ferrer was a travelling Dominican preacher, originally from Spain, who travelled widely in Western Europe in the late fourteenth and early fifteenth century. He was championed by the dukes of Brittany, especially by John V of Brittany and his wife Joan of Navarre (1370–1437), who sought his advice on account of his reputation as a miracle worker.[21]

The Breton saints Donatien and Rogatien also appear in the suffrages, dressed in the arms of Brittany (p. 357). These two brothers, known as the 'sons of the Count of Nantes' were born into a noble family in Nantes in the third century; they were tortured and murdered for their Christian beliefs under the emperor Diocletian.[22] Their presence in the calendar thus referred to Brittany's holy, aristocratic, ancestors and created a link between the current family and its illustrious past, rather like the way the *beata stirps* saints functioned in the *Fitzwilliam Hours* for the Angevin readers. When discussing the childbirth prayer contained in Marguerite of Foix's Book of Hours it will be demonstrated how the inclusion of St Rogatien, St Donatien, St Clarus, St Yvo and St Vincent Ferrer along with other Breton-specific saints also created a sense of Breton identity and support for the duchess in her supplication for a son.

Two further aspects of BN lat. 1369 suggest Isabel's interest in familial connections and indicate that her manuscripts were a place in which these were commemorated. First, an elegy on the death of her sister, the dauphine Margaret Stuart, was added in another hand at the end of the manuscript.[23] A number of works were written mourning the dauphine's demise and although the one added to Isabel's manuscript, in which the dying Margaret bids goodbye to the people of her court, has sometimes been attributed to the duchess herself, this seems unlikely.[24] Nevertheless, the fact that the elegy was added after the manuscript's completion, at least eight years after the dauphine's death, implies that Isabel was still thinking of her sister and wished to remember her in her prayers. Second, another inscription, from the seventeenth century, states that the manuscript belonged to Renée of Rohan, a direct descendant of Marie of Brittany, suggesting that Isabel passed BN lat. 1369 on to this daughter.[25] Thus, in addition to asserting Isabel's place within the duchy of Brittany, BN lat. 1369 may also have come to symbolise for Marie, as the *Fitzwilliam Hours* mostly likely did for her sister Marguerite, a tangible reminder of her mother and of her own place in the house of Brittany.

Isabel's manuscripts, commissioned after death of her husband Francis, suggest that she took her place within the Breton dynasty seriously, and saw herself as an adviser to her daughters. In particular, through these later manuscripts, she appears to have actively demonstrated her commitment to Brittany and her wish to remain in her adopted country. It is likely that the responsibilities Isabel felt after her husband's death were also important during her marriage, as she read and personalised the *Fitzwilliam Hours*. Thus, before she handed the *Fitzwilliam Hours* on to her daughter, its images of the pious widows and model parents, St Anne, St Elizabeth, St Radegund, and St Louis IX, surrounded now by the arms of Brittany and Scotland, provided a means for her to execute the role of wife, duchess, and mother to the best of her abilities.

Duchess to duchess, mother to daughter: Marguerite of Brittany's ownership of the *Fitzwilliam Hours*

When Francis I died in 1450, his two daughters could not ensure his direct and legitimate succession so the duchy passed first to their uncle Francis's brother, Peter II, then to their great-uncle Arthur III (1393–1458), and then to their cousin, Francis II. In 1455, three years before his succession, Francis II married Isabel and Francis's daughter, Marguerite. At the time of the marriage, Duke Peter II's thirteen-year marriage to Frances of Amboise was still childless and Francis was no doubt already expecting to succeed both his cousin and his older uncle who, despite three marriages, also had no legitimate successor. Through this alliance, Francis was able to silence supporters of the ancient Breton inheritance laws who refused to recognise the Treaty of Guérande and claimed Marguerite as the rightful heir. Given the improbability that the house would pass through Peter or Arthur's line, Marguerite was probably also being prepared – and preparing herself – for her eventual role as duchess, right from the time of her marriage. As with her mother before her, the succession of the duchy and her husband's line lay with her ability to produce a male child. The fact that her mother had given birth to two daughters, resulting in Francis I's inheritance being passed to other members of the house before coming back to her, through her marriage, must have made her need to conceive a male heir all the clearer. Considering in more detail the circumstances in which Marguerite inherited the *Fitzwilliam Hours* reveals that she could have viewed the manuscript and its images not only as an encouragement to her maternal role but also as a symbol of dynastic continuity and of the difficulties of her role within the house of Brittany.

It has already been noted that Marguerite's ownership of the *Fitzwilliam Hours* is inferred by a female donor portrait at the beginning of the *Omnis te virtus decorat* prayer, which shows a woman kneeling at a prie-dieu covered in the arms of Brittany (plate 13).[26] The style of this miniature is later than both the original campaign and the alterations to the *Obsecro te* made for Isabel Stuart, which imitate the Rohan style, and it probably dates from around 1450.[27] Although the arms of Brittany were those of both Isabel's daughters before marriage, they remained Marguerite's arms after her marriage to Francis II and an inventory made after Marguerite's death in 1469 provides additional evidence that Isabel did pass the *Fitzwilliam Hours* to this daughter. The inventory describes a large Book of Hours decorated with the arms of Duchess Isabel, without clasps, and for the Use of Paris (*unes grandes Heures armoyees aux armes de la duchesse Ysabeau, qui n'ont nulz fermouers et sont à l'usaige de Paris*).[28] It is likely that this entry refers to the *Fitzwilliam Hours*, since Isabel's two other Books of Hours discussed above are both for the Use of Rome and are small in comparison to the Cambridge manuscript, which is for the Use of Paris.

The addition of Marguerite's portrait in the *Fitzwilliam Hours* offered her the opportunity to see herself, like her mother, at prayer in front of the Virgin. Furthermore, since Isabel's own additions were not altered, Marguerite would also have been confronted with her mother's arms throughout the book and with her mother's portrait at the *Obsecro te* – one of the manuscript's most important prayers. Marguerite saw herself, symbolically and literally, within the history of the house of Brittany, the house into which her mother had married, and which her marriage to Francis had been intended to strengthen. However, whereas it is possible to suggest

216

that, like Isabel, Marguerite would have been sensitive to the manuscript's images of maternity and used them to pray for the heir so desperately required by the duchy, an analysis of the nature of this sensitivity can be taken one stage further.

By 1459, Francis was engaged in an affair with Antoinette of Maignelais, *Madame de Villequier*.[29] Antoinette occupied a prominent position at Francis's court and her presence was the object of much criticism, not least from Francis's aunt, Frances of Amboise (1427–85), wife of the late Peter II. Frances wrote to the duke, referring to his affair as 'your sin, so great, so scandalous, and so detestable' (*votre péché si énorme, si scandaleux et pestiféré*) and accusing him of bringing shame upon the duchess and her family.[30] One member of the Breton household even accused Antoinette of having prevented Francis from having children with the duchess (*l'empeschoit d'avoir des enfants de la duchesse*).[31] Such was Francis's affection for his mistress that 'he cherished her overmuch, keeping her in high estate, even more so than his own wife' (*[la] cherissoit outre mesure, la tenant en grand estat et plus que sa femme mesme*): the annual accounts for 1468, for example, show that Antoinette received more than double Marguerite's allowance.[32]

In 1462 Antoinette gave birth to a son, Francis of Avaugour, *Seigneur de Clisson* (d. after 1494).[33] Surviving records show a discharge by Francis II in 1468 for a payment of 100 écus to the wet-nurse of this child in respect of her marriage (*A la nourrice du sire de Cliczon [Clisson] . . . au bien et avancement de son marriage, 100ec.*).[34] A year after Francis's birth, and after an eight-year wait, Marguerite also gave birth to a child, but it lived only three months (29 June–25 August 1463).[35] After the child's death, Francis offered 2.9 kg of gold to the Carmelites at Nantes, which may have represented the weight of the dead child.[36] This act of piety indicates how important the birth of a legitimate heir was to Francis although the gesture did not help his cause: Marguerite died six years later without bearing any more children and later chroniclers such as Bertrand d'Argentré claimed that Marguerite died of grief and sorrow due to Antoinette's presence.[37]

Viewed with Marguerite's situational eye, the historical provenance and the maternal imagery of the *Fitzwilliam Hours* symbolised a number of facts and meanings that related to Marguerite's position as an aristocratic lay woman. On one level, she was equipped with the social training and cognitive habits to read the narratives of holy motherhood and the images of childbirth in ways similar to those already suggested for Yolande of Anjou and Isabel Stuart. For instance, the mothers of the Holy Kinship demonstrated God's blessing of women in childbirth and the role of women in educating their children. Like her mother, Marguerite would have been sensitive to the details of bedroom furnishings and post-partum care alluded to in the *Birth of the Virgin* miniature. In addition, the suffrage to the patron saint of childbirth, St Margaret, may have taken on a further significance as Marguerite's own patron saint and on whom she could call during labour. Thus it is possible to suggest that Marguerite, during her essentially childless marriage, saw in the manuscript evidence of the way God could intervene unexpectedly for couples, and especially women, suffering from infertility. The *Fitzwilliam Hours*, with its references to blessed lineages and as a tangible symbol of her own family history, could have provided a source of hope and expectation.

However, as noted in previous chapters, an interpretation that aims to recover instances of women's agency within the context of their social roles might still be accused of reinforcing the appropriation of women's bodies by, and for, patriarchal society. The example of Marguerite, who suffered the presence of her husband's mistress and their children, lost her only child and died young, can nevertheless be used to suggest an alternative interpretation of the images that does not necessarily exclude other meanings, didactic or otherwise. Rather than assuming that Marguerite always saw these images in a positive way, it is important to consider how her experiences could have led her to read the *Fitzwilliam Hours* as symbolising the *difficulties* of carrying out her social duties, and her failure to receive the blessing that God had bestowed upon other women. Marguerite, holding her mother's manuscript, would have been mindful of the fact that Isabel, like Yolande, had not been able to secure the future of the duchy. Unable to inherit her father's title, Marguerite had only become duchess of Brittany through her marriage to Francis II: her own failure to produce a male child would replicate the situation experienced by her mother.

The *Fitzwilliam Hours*, therefore, embodied the political importance of Marguerite's marriage, her duty to her husband and to the state, and was physically marked with reminders of the fortunes of her predecessors and the difficulties of her own position: problems with conception, infant mortality, the presence of a mistress, and illegitimate children. Thus, through her situational eye, Marguerite's interpretation of the *Fitzwilliam Hours* oscillated between several meanings. In particular, instead of seeing the manuscript and its images of holy motherhood as a simple encouragement to the execution of her ducal duties and the possibility of obtaining God's blessing, as time went on she may also have viewed it as a reminder of her inability to execute the role which society had assigned to her. That an aristocratic woman did acknowledge the difficulties of her position through examples of holy motherhood is demonstrated most clearly by turning to the Book of Hours belonging to Marguerite's successor, Francis II's second wife, Marguerite of Foix.

New duchess, Old Testament mothers: holy motherhood in the *Hours of Marguerite of Foix*

In 1471, two years after the death of Marguerite of Brittany, Francis II married Marguerite of Foix (*c.*1449–87). Marguerite was the third daughter of Gaston IV, Count of Foix and Viscount of Béarn, and Eleanor, queen of Navarre. At the time of his second marriage, the duke had not yet fathered any surviving children within the sanctity of marriage and this union provided him with another opportunity to produce the much-needed male heir to ensure his succession. The union also had a further, political goal. It was designed to unite Marguerite's father, the count of Foix, with the duke of Brittany, Charles the Bold of Burgundy, and some other allies against Louis XI of France.[38] This section explores how the circumstances of Marguerite's marriage, the continued presence at court of the duke's mistress, Antoinette, and an awareness of the fertility problems in her own family and in those of her peers, contributed to Marguerite's situational eye and thus to her interpretation of the references to holy motherhood in her Book of Hours. The conjunction of a childbirth prayer that draws on the examples of Old Testament mothers with images of the birth of the Virgin, St Elizabeth and St Anne, reveals in the most compelling way yet that the situational eye of aristocratic wives and mothers was trained to be sensitive to images of holy motherhood and that these women drew on them as exemplars in the execution of their social duties. Marguerite's Book of Hours thus exemplifies the visual and textual interrelationships between prayers for childbirth, the images in Books of Hours and the official liturgy of the church that were explored in Chapter 2.

Marguerite's manuscript was produced in France, possibly in Rennes. The basic manuscript text with its border illuminations is of high quality but it was probably bought 'off the shelf'. These pages were then passed to another workshop where the main miniatures were added and the manuscript personalised before being bound. The miniatures are of excellent quality and echo innovative styles appearing in France with the influence of Jean Fouquet.[39] Thus, although the manuscript was not bespoke in the same way as the *Fitzwilliam Hours*, the main miniatures 'set it apart and make it fitting for an aristocratic patron'.[40] That the manuscript was made for Marguerite of Foix is established by faint traces of erased arms and the personalised prayer at the end of the manuscript. The arms appear in the

Gospel sequences (fol. 21v), in the *Visitation* in the Hours of the Virgin (plate 4), and at the end of the suffrages (fol. 222r).[41] Close examination of the manuscript still reveals miniscule traces of arms that are visible with the naked eye.[42] For example, on the dexter side of the shield held by two angels on folio 21v there are traces of the black ermine of Brittany, and the parchment is stained dark, indicative of oxidised silver, used for the ground of Brittany. To the bottom and top right of the sinister side, there are traces of red and gold vertical stripes, found in the second quarter of the later Foix arms. Similar traces are found on the shields held by angels in both the *Visitation* image and at the end of the suffrages. Towards the bottom right of the latter shield are also traces of blue which may have formed part of the blue ground of the arms of *Évreux ancien*, which Gaston IV added to his coat of arms in 1455 when he inherited the kingdom of Navarre.

Additional evidence that the manuscript was destined for Marguerite is found in the prayer on folios 223–225v (see Appendix 1). The prayer, written in a female, first-person voice, invokes a series of holy mothers whom God made fertile and who were granted sons; it also refers to the shame of sterility being lifted from the female speaker. It calls upon a number of Breton saints, St Anthony of Padua and St Margaret to ask God to grant Francis, duke of the Bretons and his wife, Marguerite, a son. Marguerite and Francis waited six years for the birth their first child, Anne of Brittany, and the prayer appears to confirm Marguerite's possession of the book and place the supplication for a child that it contains, in her mouth. The question remains, of course, as to Marguerite's involvement in both the manuscript's and the prayer's commission. However, given the value of St Anne, St Elizabeth and the Virgin as models for miraculous and successful childbearing, it seems reasonable to suppose that Marguerite found the references to unexpected births granted to infertile women that were included in her prayer as suitable models during the early, infertile, years of her marriage. As discussed in Chapter 2, the lack of male heirs in the Foix family had resulted in a series of succession problems and had caused Marguerite's father to commission the *Golden Apple* treatise to ensure the fertility of his marriage to Eleanor of Navarre. The fact that Marguerite and Francis's first daughter Anne was named after the Virgin's mother further suggests that devotion to this saint played an important part in the couple's hopes for a child. Furthermore, Marguerite's near contemporary and, later, her daughter's sister-in-law, Anne of France, also turned to St Anne, as well as to medical treatises, in her own hopes for an heir. This evidence implies Marguerite's awareness of the importance of male heirs as well as the means that could be used to achieve this. Therefore, looking at the contents of the prayer and the hopes that it expresses in relation to Marguerite's circumstances sheds light on how she, and perhaps other, aristocratic lay women engaged with stories of miraculous birth and how they received the depiction of such stories in their personal prayer books.

Nobisque famule tue obprobrium sterilitatis abstulisti: thanksgiving and a prayer for a son

The prayer in Marguerite's book was written out by a different scribe to but in the same *lettre bâtarde* and with the same page rulings as the rest of the manuscript, suggesting that it is more or less contemporaneous with the book as a whole. The prayer is not, however, illuminated, apart from a decorated initial D in brushed gold on a red ground at the beginning of the text, which can be 'associated with the last third, at least, of the fifteenth century'.[43] Rowan Watson, assuming the prayer to be a plea for the *end* of the couple's sterility, has proposed a *terminus antequam* of 1477, the year in which their first child, Anne of Brittany, was born.[44] The *Burlington Catalogue* entry states that in the prayer Francis and Marguerite 'implore God for a son' and that it is 'implied that their famous daughter, Anne of Brittany, was already born, so that this prayer must have been added to the book between 1476 [*sic*] and 1487', the year of Marguerite's death.[45] Since the manuscript is in its original leather binding, it is difficult to see how the prayer could have been added more than a short time *after* the execution of the manuscript, unless it remained unbound for a time or was very quickly rebound.[46] Based on these facts, the only things that can be said with certainty are that the entire Book of Hours cannot be dated earlier than Marguerite and Francis's marriage in 1471, and that the prayer, despite being a complex plea, definitely indicates that Marguerite's infertility had been lifted. Although a precise date cannot be proffered here, close attention to the wording of the prayer reveals a number of possibilities for the circumstances of the prayer's production. In particular, it could date from and refer to the conception or birth of Anne of Brittany in 1477, or it could date from the years following Anne's birth, perhaps referring specifically to Marguerite's second pregnancy.

The prayer begins by invoking a God who has created the world out of nothing and who has not failed anyone who prays to Him (fol. 223r). It then continues with a list of barren women whom God made fertile (fol. 223r–v). These holy, Old Testament women, Sarah, Hannah, Manoah's wife, and St Elizabeth are the same as, or recall, those who feature in the childbirth prayers discussed in Chapter 2. However, whereas in the prayers these women functioned as precedents for successful and, in the case of the Virgin, pain-free birth, here the emphasis is firmly on the overturning of sterility and on the granting of sons. The first example is Sarah who, unable to conceive, persuaded her husband Abraham to have a child with their slave Hagar in order to continue the Covenant. However, God eventually blessed the couple with their own son, the patriarch Isaac, born to them when they were in their nineties.[47] The prayer then takes the example of Hannah from the first book of Samuel, who shed tears over her barrenness and who promised to dedicate any male child He might grant her to God.[48] Hannah, as already noted, gave birth to the prophet Samuel and her song of thanksgiving was interpreted as a type of the Virgin's Magnificat.

The prayer's next example, from Judges, is that of Manoah's wife who was visited by an angel who told her that although she was sterile and without children she would conceive and bear a son.[49] This son was Samson, of phenomenal strength, who delivered Israel from the Philistines. St John the Baptist, as has already been discussed, was born to the old and infertile St Elizabeth, as proof of the Virgin's conception of Christ. In all these stories, women were unexpectedly granted sons who went on to have exceptional qualities or important roles during their lives: strength, deliverance, prophet, judge. They are, therefore, especially pertinent to a woman expected to provide a male heir for a rich and powerful duchy that practised Salic law and thus needed sons to ensure succession. Marguerite may have identified in particular with Sarah, the wife of Abraham, since by the time of her marriage the duke had had a natural son by his mistress Antoinette de Maignelais. Thus both Francis and Abraham had sons by another woman before their legal wives finally became pregnant by the grace of God. Moreover, Francis's ability to father a male child with Antoinette increased the onus of conceiving a legitimate son on Marguerite. It is discussed below how Marguerite's inclusion of herself at the end of this list of barren women made fertile, strongly implies that she was trained to view narratives of holy childbirth as a space through which she could manage her childbearing concerns and her role as duchess of Brittany. However, before analysing this part of Marguerite's supplication in detail, there are further references that need to be considered: a second reference to St John the Baptist, and others to Jeremiah, Moses and to the Virgin's conception of Christ.

After the list of barren women made fertile, the prayer refers to God's sanctifying of both Jeremiah and St John the Baptist in their mother's wombs (fol. 223v–224r: *Jeremiam et Johannem in utero sanctificasti*). This is important since it was shown in Chapter 2 that there is a close link between Jeremiah and St John in church liturgy: the Office of the Nativity of St John includes verses from the first book of Jeremiah, which refer to the prophet's birth. Furthermore, Jeremiah and his mother, Celica, also appear in one of the prayers for assisting labour.[50] Given the liturgical association between Jeremiah and St John the Baptist, as well as the references to birth in the Book of Jeremiah, it was argued that Jeremiah's inclusion in prayers for labour led to an interplay of text and image for listener-viewers who might recall images of St John's birth when hearing the words of his office. This association between the two prophets may also have led participants in the childbirth chamber to think about images of the Visitation where St Elizabeth and the Virgin greet each other and the two unborn children recognise each other's holiness. The stories included in Marguerite's prayer, relating to Old Testament mothers and to St John and Jeremiah, are thus the same as those recited in the childbirth chamber.

The next reference, to Mary as predestined mother of Christ (fol. 223v), again emphasises God's blessing of women with sons and is also linked to the following mention of Moses whom God set free from Pharoah so that he could liberate the people of Israel (fol. 223v: *Moysem ut populo Israel preesset a Pharaonis decreto liberasti*). As a type of Christ, Moses' role as liberator prefigures Christ's liberation of humanity, but there is a further significance in this context. In some of the prayers for childbirth discussed previously, Christ's birth, which set people free from death, was used as a parallel for the liberation of the woman suffering in labour. Here the inclusion of Moses, as someone who sets people free, reinforces the idea of successful delivery and adds to the prayer's efficacy as a remedy and supplication for conception and birth.

It is in the line *nobisque famule tue obprobrium sterilitatis abstulisti* (fols 223v–224r), which ends the prayer's first section on holy mothers and prophets, that the key to reinterpreting this prayer lies. It is important to note that both the female speaking subject, 'your servant woman' (*famule tue*) and the perfect tense 'you have taken away' (*abstulisti*) indicate that God has removed the shame of sterility (*obprobrium sterilitatis*) from this woman. The fact that this woman, whom we can presume to be Marguerite, included herself at the end of a list of women blessed by God after years of sterility and, more specifically, rewarded with sons, implies that, after a six-year wait, she no longer considered herself to be barren. Furthermore, the end of the prayer indicates that Marguerite was hoping that God would grant her and her husband a son who could continue to safeguard the duchy (fol. 225r–v: *quatinus nobis Francisco Britannorum duci et Margarite eius uxori natum*). Several readings are possible. For example, the prayer could refer to Marguerite's first pregnancy, the outcome of which would result in the birth of Anne of Brittany; alternatively she may already be pregnant with her second child, Isabeau, and hoping that this time the child would be a son. More generally, Marguerite could have given birth to either or both of her daughters and the prayer might express her hopes that any future pregnancy would produce a son.

Since it is impossible to date the prayer precisely, these interpretations must remain speculative but it is clear that the prayer offers thanks to God for taking away Marguerite's infertility and entreats Him, who 'knows the future as well as the past', for a son. In fact, the multiplicity of the prayer's potential meanings need not be mutually exclusive as Marguerite read and re-read the prayer at different times in her life, in the same way that the miniatures in the *Fitzwilliam Hours* oscillated in meaning for the different viewers. It is important, however, that the prayer be understood not as a plea to *end* the sterility of the couple but as one in which the speaker gives thanks for conception, possibly a successful birth, and in which a male heir is prayed for. The interpretation offered here is important when considering the illuminations in Marguerite's manuscript. Before turning to these, however, the central section of the prayer also needs to be considered since it calls on the intercession of a host of local saints, creating a specifically Breton context for the prayer, suitable for the request of the duchess of Brittany.

Many of the saints referred to in the middle of the prayer were associated with the founding of the duchy of Brittany and its conversion to Christianity. They, thus, provide a link to the historical past of Duke Francis and his family. For example, the fifth-century cousins, St Paul (fol. 225r; *Pauli*), bishop of Saint-Pol-de-Léon, and St Samson, bishop of Dol (fol. 225r; *Sansonis*), were two of the seven founding saints of Brittany.[51] Two other founding saints are also mentioned, St Corentin (fol. 225r; *Corentini*), first bishop of Quimper in the fifth century, and St Malo (fol. 225r; *Maclovii*).[52] The inclusion of St Malo (b. late fifth century) is particularly important in the context of a childbearing prayer since he was said to have been born while his mother was on a pilgrimage to the monastery of Llancarfan in Wales, where the abbey's bishop, St Brendan, baptised the child and later educated him.[53] In addition to the founding saints, others in the prayer emphasise the duchy's illustrious churchmen, including St Clair (fol. 225r; *Clarii*), the first bishop of Nantes in the third century, St Guillaume (fol. 225r; *Guillermi*), thirteenth-century bishop of Saint-Brieuc (named after another founding saint) who gave a great deal of alms to the poor, and St Melaine (fol. 225r; *Melani*) bishop of Rennes in the early sixth century.[54] Another ecclesiast, St Yvo, is also mentioned: this saint was highly regarded by John V of Brittany who built a magnificent tomb for the saint in his home town of Tréguier.[55] St Yvo's legal training and his charity made him patron saint of lawyers and also of poor people, widows and orphans. Although Francis and Marguerite might not have wanted financially, they would not have felt themselves immune from the possibility of being widowed or leaving their own children orphaned at an early age. Invoking St Yvo in the prayer, therefore, offered a way to ask for the heirs, actual or hypothetical, of the Breton ducal house to be protected. Overall, by calling on saints related to the founding of the state of Brittany and on the region's holy ecclesiasts, the speaker of the prayer was able to give her supplication for an heir a historical context that emphasised God's blessing of the duchy.

Other saints mentioned in the prayer sharpen the Breton context even further by stressing the holiness of Brittany's ruling families, creating a kind of Breton *beata stirps*. Two of these, St Donatien and St Rogatien, the 'sons of the Count of Nantes' (fol. 224v–225r: *Donaciani et Rogatiani martirum comitis Nannetensij filiorum beatorum*) have already been noted in relation to one of Isabel Stuart's Books of Hours where they appear dressed in the arms of Brittany. St Gicquel (d. 685) and St Salomon (d. 875) were both kings of Brittany (fol. 224v: *Gicquelli Salomonis martirum Britannie regum*). St Gicquel gave up his throne to take religious orders but after the death of his successor he took back the responsibility of the crown. St Salomon, betrayed by his own counts, was killed and hailed as a martyr.[56] All the Breton saints mentioned in the prayer demonstrate the owner's interests in the duchy of Brittany and, more specifically, in the same way that St Radegund, St Louis of Toulouse and St Elizabeth of Hungary spoke to the *Fitzwilliam Hours'* aristocratic readers, they also established a link between the current rulers of Brittany, its illustrious, holy past, and its hopes for the future. A more contemporary link with the ducal house was created by the inclusion of St Vincent Ferrer (fol. 225r: Vincentii) who, as noted above, was much venerated by the Breton dukes and was included in one of Isabel Stuart's Books of Hours (BN lat. 1369). Ferrer was, in fact, a very recent saint and although he was of Spanish origin, Brittany and its dukes could lay particular claim to him since he died in Brittany and his relics were preserved in the cathedral of Vannes. His inclusion in Marguerite's prayer implies that this tangible saint and his connections with Brittany would allow him to take special care of the current duke and duchess.

Personal protection and intervention were offered for the duke and duchess through the last two saints mentioned in the prayer: St Anthony of

Padua and St Margaret. St Margaret was, of course, Marguerite of Foix's patron saint as well as the patron saint of women in childbirth. Just as St Anne functioned as both a patron saint and an example of a blessed mother for Anne of France and Anne of Brittany, so St Margaret offered Marguerite double protection. In addition, the Franciscan saint, Anthony of Padua (1195–1231), was also known for his protection of pregnant women.[57] The passage in which St Marguerite and St Anthony occur is difficult and two interpretations are possible, depending on how the genitive *Francisci gloriosissimi* is read in the phrase *quorum reliquie et venerationes hoc in ducatu complectuntur Francisci gloriosissimi confessoris Anthonius Paduani Margarite virginis et martiris*. On the one hand, it may refer to St Anthony's status as a Franciscan, rendering the passage as 'and of all the male saints and female saints whose remains and cults are embraced in this dukedom, of Anthony of Padua, follower *of the most glorious Francis* [*i.e. St Francis*], and of Margaret, virgin and martyr'. Alternatively, the *Francisci gloriosissimi* may refer to Duke Francis, translating as 'and of all the male saints and female saints whose remains and cults are embraced in this dukedom *of the most glorious Francis* [*II of Brittany*], of the confessor Anthony of Padua and of Margaret the virgin and martyr'. The first reading allows for the inclusion of St Francis of Assisi, Francis's patron saint, which would complement the inclusion of St Marguerite, his wife's. Like his predecessor, Francis I of Brittany, Francis II showed great devotion to St Francis and the saint's suffrage in a Book of Hours associated with the duke is surrounded with the ermine of Brittany.[58] The second reading stresses the status of Duke Francis himself as ruler of the duchy of Brittany, after the fashion of its illustrious saints. Neither reading, however, alters the fact that the prayer ends not only with the duchess's patron saint, but with two saints effective for the protection of pregnant women. This analysis of the prayer and its place in Marguerite's life provides a context in which to discuss Marguerite's reception of the visual representations of holy motherhood that precede the prayer in her manuscript.

Visualising God's blessing: reading the
miniatures in Marguerite's *Hours*

The miniatures in the Gospels, calendars and suffrages of Marguerite's *Hours* are conventional enough but, as already noted, it is the manuscript's innovative, full-page miniatures which give it a bespoke quality.[59] The illustrations for the Hours of the Virgin follow the established Infancy Cycle, apart from at the hour of Prime. This is decorated with scenes from Christ's Passion rather than the expected *Annunciation to the Shepherds*.[60] The

Annunciation scene opening Matins is, as in the *Fitzwilliam Hours*, surrounded by episodes depicting events from the story of St Anne and St Joachim and the early life of the Virgin. Given that the *Annunciation* page is one of the bespoke illuminations, it is likely that these scenes were a conscious choice on the part of the commissioner, perhaps Marguerite herself. On the left-hand side, St Joachim and St Anne are turned away from the temple.[61] In the right-hand upper panel is the *Annunciation to Joachim*, in which St Joachim is standing among a group of shepherds; in the lower right-hand panel is the *Meeting at the Golden Gate* and in the *bas-de-page* the *Birth of the Virgin* (plate 6).

Like the *Fitzwilliam Hours*, the decorative cycle shows how the humiliation endured by St Joachim and St Anne at being expelled from the Temple for their lack of offspring was reversed in the joy of the Virgin's miraculous, immaculate, conception and birth. Since the prayer at the end of the manuscript suggests that the book was made for Marguerite during the early years of her marriage, if not specifically around the time of one of her pregnancies, Marguerite's situational eye would have been extremely receptive to the narrative of the Virgin's conception and birth on this *Annunciation* page. Likewise Marguerite's *obprobrium sterilitatis* was removed by the conception of her daughter Anne.

Marguerite's association of herself in the prayer with holy mothers whom God made fertile, strongly implies that she viewed this page as a parallel to her own life and a visual 'thanksgiving' to God for lifting the curse of sterility, in the same way that Fina Buzzacarini gave thanks for the birth of her son through the *Birth of St John the Baptist* fresco in Padua's baptistery. The conception and birth of the Virgin was the first stage in the Incarnation of Christ, the birth of a male child, symbolised in the *Annunciation*. Furthermore, this page also looks forward to a successful outcome and, like the same page in the *Fitzwilliam Hours*, alludes to the childbearing practices in which a woman of high estate participated and which placed her at the centre of attention. How, then, having given birth to her own daughter(s) and following the steps of the narrative in her prayer book, did Marguerite use the images to help envisage herself on the right path for the birth of a male child to ensure the duchy's succession? Did she simply use them to pray for a male child without questioning the way her body was expected to perform for the duchy? Or did she see the images and the narratives they represented as a way to negotiate this performance by asking for God's protection in the execution of her duties, and by looking forward to her own post-partum celebrations that would signify a successful birth and acknowledge the life-threatening process she had undergone?

In the *Birth of the Virgin* scene St Anne lies in bed, turned away from the people that have crowded into the room; the top half of her body is uncovered and despite the white turban on her head her hair flows loose down her back. St Anne's nakedness, as in the *in partu* representations in the *Rohan Hours*, highlights the mother's humanity and serves to place this holy birth in the 'real' world. Behind the bed stand three women and St Joachim. As noted in the Introduction, in many miniatures depicting the births of the Virgin or St John the Baptist, St Joachim and St Zacharias are absent, or else positioned outside the room. St Joachim's presence in this *Birth of the Virgin* scene may, therefore, be significant since he provided a model for the duke that paralleled the duchess's identification with St Anne. For Marguerite, regardless of whether or not the duke engaged with her manuscript, the presence of St Joachim in the birth scene may have functioned as an indication that he too was responsible for the birth of his heirs and that he should perhaps join her in her devotions: after all, Francis was included in the prayer at the end of the manuscript.

The bathing of the child, the number of visitors gathered in the room, and the rich fabrics decorating the bed also give this divine birth a secular aspect by alluding to the type of post-partum care and celebration enjoyed by aristocratic women. As with the accounts of Isabel Stuart and her daughter Marguerite of Brittany, the records of Marguerite of Foix's wardrobe and expenses are fragmentary but there is still evidence of the fabrics and furnishings with which the duchess was familiar. For example, the accounts relating to Marguerite's tailor in 1475 show that he delivered an ell of canvas and an ell of green satin to make a bolster as well as five pounds of feathers with which to fill it (*pour une souylle une aulne de canevaz, pour l'ampliz cinq livres de pleumes, et pour le couvriz une aulne de satin vert*), and eighteen ells of white blanket cloth (*xviii aulnes de blanchet*).[62] He also supplied some gold cloth and crimson satin to make the bodice and sleeves of little tunic (*pour faire le hault du corps et les manches d'une petite cotte de draps d'or, deux tiers de satin cramoissi*).[63] Marguerite's eye would have been receptive to the fabrics shown on this page: the blue fabric edged with gold used for Anne's bed, for her cloak in the *Meeting at the Golden Gate*, and for the Virgin in the *Annunciation*, and the red and gold embroidered fabric that hangs behind her in the same scene.

Luxurious fabrics are also alluded to in the Virgin's cloak in the *Visitation* miniature accompanying Lauds, and for the backdrop to the scene of St Anne teaching the Virgin at the bottom of the same page (plate 4). The miniatures on this page also add further to the examples of holy motherhood depicted at Matins and referred to in the prayer. Given the couple's long wait for a child as well as knowledge of her own father's concerns about infertility, the depiction of St Elizabeth, as well as St Anne, offered Marguerite the possibility to identify with two women blessed with children after a period of sterility. The bas-de-page image of St Anne and her daughter reinforces the narrative of St Anne begun on the Matins page. St Anne, haloed and dressed as widow, offers a book to her daughter, pointing out the letters; the Virgin, haloed but also crowned, follows the text with her finger. Viewed by Marguerite after the birth of her own child, Anne, this miniature demonstrated the role that Marguerite could assume for her daughter, a trope which Anne herself later exploited in her own manuscripts. Furthermore, the crown that the Virgin Mary wears here and in the birth scene at Matins, not only alludes to her future status as Queen of Heaven but also functions as a sign of wealth and nobility, emphasised in the miniatures' rich fabrics, and thus her suitability as a figure with whom a young aristocratic woman like Marguerite could identify. The crown also forges a link between the biblical narratives of divine childbearing and the earthly, but divinely-appointed, families to which Marguerite and her husband belonged, thus helping to legitimate their appeals to God's intervention in their desire for a child.

At Lauds, the main image of the *Visitation* provided a visual example to complement the reference to St Elizabeth in the prayer. In contrast to St Anne, St Elizabeth, like Sarah and Hannah, was blessed with a male child after years of sterility, something for which the prayer indicates Marguerite was also hoping. The Virgin and St Elizabeth greet each other in a rocky landscape and St Elizabeth bends down and brings her hand towards the Virgin's stomach. Although St Elizabeth was already six months pregnant at the time of the Visitation, it is significant that it is the Virgin who is shown visibly pregnant since it meant the viewer could align herself with both the older woman whose infertility was taken away and with the younger woman, also pregnant with a son. As Marguerite went through the early years of her marriage and childbearing, she could thus have used the *Visitation* miniature to look forward to a future pregnancy – perhaps one which would provide the male heir who would safeguard the duchy. That Marguerite did, or was expected to, identify with this image is further suggested by the inclusion of her arms, in miniature, on a shield held by an angel on the left-hand side: the angel and the arms point towards the image of St Anne teaching the Virgin. Through the arms, Marguerite could make a connection between herself, the image, the prayers and her own role as mother and educator to two daughters, in the same way that the arms of Isabel Stuart served to symbolise the duchess's appropriation of the manuscript, its prayers and her role as duchess of Brittany, in the *Fitzwilliam Hours*.

The illuminations for Matins and Lauds, showing St Anne, St Elizabeth and the Virgin form a collective of holy women, replicating those invoked both in the commonplace prayers for labour and in Marguerite's own, personalised, petition. This group of saintly mothers was complemented further by another image of St Anne in the suffrages with the Virgin seated on her lap with Christ between them (plate 14). The open book on the Virgin's knee implies not only St Anne's instruction of the Virgin, already seen at Lauds, but also the Virgin's instruction of her son, a theme which appears in the *Fitzwilliam Hours* (figure 27). Marguerite's situational eye, informed by the contemporary tendency to humanise narratives about the relationship between the Virgin and Christ, could have allowed her to mitigate the mother–daughter theme that was an important part of St Anne's cult and to privilege instead the mother–son relationships that pertained to St Elizabeth and the Virgin, to the Holy Kinship in general, as well as to the other biblical women rewarded with sons who were noted in her prayer.

As noted above, the theme of Mary teaching Christ to read also appears in the *Grandes Heures* of Marguerite's daughter, Anne of Brittany, who drew heavily on the cult of her patron saint not only in relation to her daughters but also as a means of focusing her devotions towards the conception of a son.[64] The stories of St Anne, St Elizabeth and the Virgin provided a number of associations with sterility, miraculous conception, felicitous births and the education of children, which could have come in and out of focus during Marguerite's marriage, as she looked for signs of conception, felt the child move within her, and gave birth.

In addition to the collective of holy mothers that appears in the illuminations of her Book of Hours, Marguerite would have found another image to complement her prayer and to offer protection: that of her own patron saint and patron of women in childbirth, St Margaret. From its inception, Wendy Larson notes, the legend of Margaret's miraculous escape from the belly of a dragon was gradually 'modified and the connection with childbirth made more explicit, [and] the image of the mother being delivered whole from the belly of the beast came to represent a mother's hope for a similar fate for her child'.[65] Certain clerical sources tried to dismiss the dragon-swallowing element of St Margaret's legend but that this aspect persisted is perhaps due to the patronage of mothers themselves.[66] The standard image of St Margaret in late-medieval art, therefore, came to be that of the saint emerging intact from the body of the dragon and this is no less true of the image in the *Hours of Marguerite of Foix* (figure 52). The saint rises up through the back of the beast, hands clasped in prayer around a cross, just as the last of her red dress is disappearing into its mouth. Although St Margaret was a very common

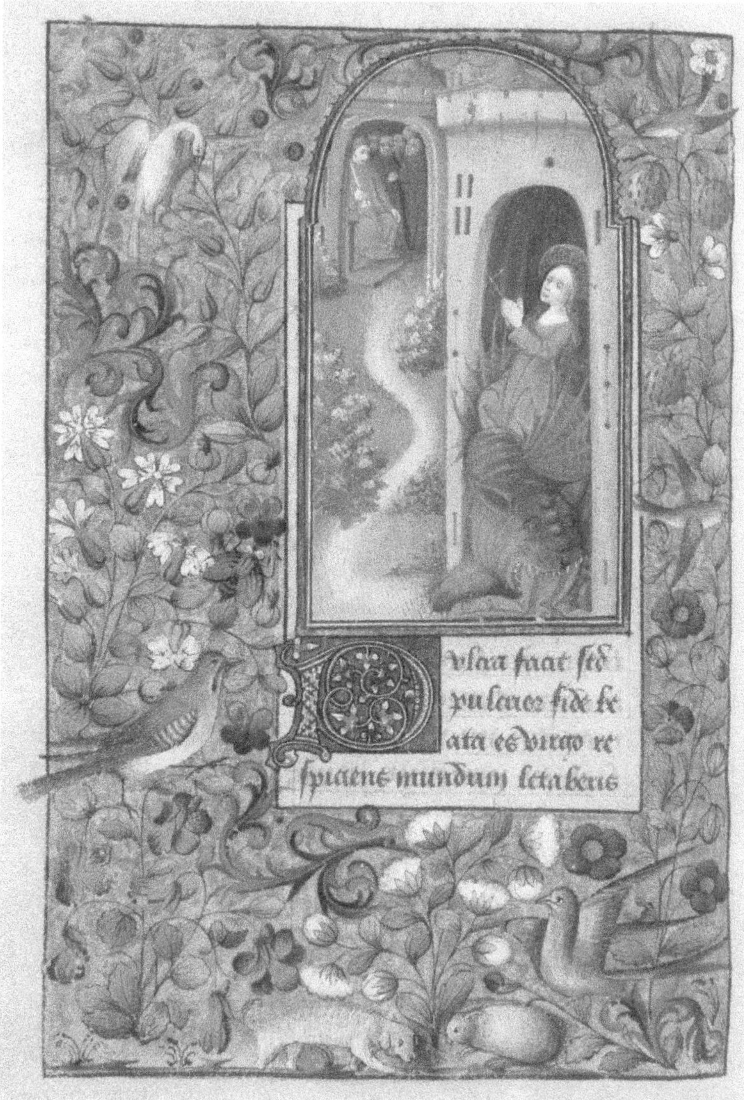

52   *St Margaret*, suffrages, *Hours of Marguerite of Foix*, London, Victoria and Albert Museum, Salting MS 1222, fol. 215v, *c.*1477. Published by kind permission of the Board of Trustees of the V&A (© V&A Images/Victoria and Albert Museum)

Roman martyr saint, as Marguerite of Foix's patron saint she signified the hope that the saint would intervene for Marguerite's own delivery, physical and spiritual, as well as that of any child she might bear.

The *Purification* scene at Nones complements those episodes of the Virgin's motherhood already discussed and refers to another stage of the childbearing process (figure 18). The Virgin's Purification in the Temple, forty days after Christ's birth, was the precursor of the churching ceremony undergone by Christian women in the middle ages. In Chapter 3 it was shown that the rite provided an opportunity for new mothers, their assistants and relatives to give thanks for a successful birth and it was suggested that women could have viewed their own 'purification' or 'thanksgiving' as a continuation of the Virgin's own churching, drawing them closer to the Mother of God. Furthermore, it was argued that in some ways the rite could have been perceived as a continuation of the disruption of normalised gender roles that the lying-in ceremony entailed by privileging a woman in a liturgical ceremony and, in particular, in the most sacred part of the church. From the duchess's point of view, the *Purification* page followed the *Annunciation* page in the same way that churching would follow birth, thus adding to the way in which the manuscript as a whole offered God's protection to Marguerite and helped her to look forward to the celebrations that would accompany a successful birth.

In Books of Hours, images of the Purification usually accompanied the hour of Nones and were often conflated with the episode of the Presentation of Christ in the Temple. This is the case in Marguerite of Foix's manuscript (figure 18).[67] The Temple is depicted as an elaborate architectural structure with flying buttresses, statues on plinths, and an audience of angels peering over the gable end. On the left-hand side, the Holy Family arrives: St Joseph and an angel lead the procession and Mary, haloed and dressed in blue, follows, carrying the Christ-Child. She is accompanied by two serving women, the one in the foreground holding a basket containing Mary's sacrifice. In the main miniature, the family and servants crowd around the altar where the high priest reaches out to receive Christ. As with the other narratives of miraculous birth depicted in her manuscript, Marguerite could easily have associated this image of the *Purification* with her own experiences. Viewing the dual episode of the Virgin's Purification and the Presentation of her son in the Temple, Marguerite had another opportunity to associate herself with the Virgin and her miraculous conception of a son through her situational eye, which was informed by knowledge of the churching ceremony. Prior to her own churching, the image, like that of the *Birth of the Virgin*, offered Marguerite an idealised version of the experiences she expected to undergo: lying-in, visitors, attendance at church, the making of an offering and, perhaps eventually, the presentation of her own son to her family and friends.

It is possible that Marguerite saw churching, and her participation in it, like that of the lying-in ceremony, as a ritual that validated her position as duchess and celebrated her long-awaited pregnancies, resulting in a ducal family that mirrored the image of the Holy Family represented in the bas-de-page of the *Purification* scene itself. Here the Holy Family are represented in a cosy domestic interior. St Joseph is seated in an armchair and the Virgin and Child sit before him, in front of a flaming hearth. An angel peers out from behind Joseph's chair and two more stand behind the Virgin on the right. A serving woman is cooking before the fire. Whereas the image alludes to the special domestic arrangements that were made for the birth of a child, including the continual burning of a fire and the preparation of special food, the presence of the angels also indicates the holy nature of the family. A similar scene of holy domesticity was depicted in the *Nativity* at Prime (fol. 6ov) where the Virgin is surrounded by three angels and two serving women. The *Nativity* and the Holy Family miniature thus draw attention to the new family and lineage that results from a successful birth, an idea to which Marguerite, as duchess, would have been especially receptive.

In the fifteenth century, the Virgin's Purification was not only remembered in the churching of individual women but was also celebrated in the popular feast of Candlemas, a major event in the liturgical calendar. In Marguerite's manuscript the feast itself is highlighted in gold in the calendar (*la Chandeleur*, 2 February). Accounts from Marguerite's time as duchess show that she and the duke took part in the community celebrations of Candlemas, the duke paying for some black velvet to decorate his and his wife's candle holders for the feast (*pour garnir les poignees des cierges de nous et de nostredicte compaigne pour le jour de la Chandeleur, ung tiers de veloux noir tiers poil*).[68] Marguerite, as a married woman and member of the aristocracy who participated in both Candlemas and the ceremony of churching, would have been equipped with the cognitive habits that allowed her to perceive how the female body and childbearing were controlled by the Christian religion and fifteenth-century patriarchal society. These skills allowed her to read images of the *Purification* and other examples of holy motherhood not only as evidence of this control but also as ways in which to manage that control from her own point of view.

By 1480, despite the birth of two daughters, Marguerite's petition for a son had still not been answered. In the same year, King Louis XI attempted to strengthen his claims on the duchy by purchasing the inheritance rights of the Penthièvre branch of the ducal family, to whom the duchy would revert if Francis and Marguerite failed to produce a son. In 1485, increasingly aware of the French threat to his duchy and still without a male heir, Francis set about naming his daughters Anne and Isabeau as his heirs.[69] In order to justify this likely female succession, a treatise was composed by Pierre Le Baud and addressed to Marguerite of Foix in which it was recalled that the Bretons were former inhabitants of Troy where women could inherit the kingdom through default of male heirs (*à default de hoir masle en leurs lignés royalles, les femmes succedroient en celuy royaume*).[70] In 1487, the year of Marguerite's death, Francis effectively reversed the Treaty of Guérande and his daughters became the sole heirs to the Duchy of Brittany. His illegitimate son by Antoinette de Maignelais, Francis of Avaugour, had declared that he was not interested in inheriting the dukedom.[71] Thus, on Francis II's death in 1488 his eldest daughter Anne became duchess of Brittany and she was crowned in Rennes the same year.

Anne was an important pawn on the political chessboard of Europe. She was married three times, including to two successive kings of France who also wished to incorporate Brittany into the French crown. Turning to Anne's manuscript commissions, it is clear that motherhood and childbearing had an important part to play in her life, as she attempted to retain Brittany's independence from France. Analysing one particular prayer book that dates from her marriage to Louis XII (1462–1515) and which includes a prayer for successful childbearing indicates that Anne, like her mother and the other aristocratic wives discussed in this study, possessed the culturally relative equipment and training that rendered her sensitive to stories and images of holy childbirth and that she used them to help her execute her social duties and to fulfil her own political interests as sovereign duchess of Brittany and queen of France.

Motherhood and queenship: the devotions of Anne of Brittany

Anne of Brittany was a great bibliophile and built up a substantial library during her time as duchess of Brittany and, twice, queen of France. Although her numerous commissions are too extensive to discuss in great detail here, a few examples serve to show Anne's devotion to her patron saint St Anne, both as a woman blessed in childbirth and as an educator of her children. These examples also reveal that Anne drew on other narratives associated with holy motherhood during her lifetime. The Chicago *Prayer Book* belonging to her, and considered here, dates from after her third marriage, to

King Louis XII, which took place on 7 January 1499.[72] Prior to this, in 1490, Anne had first been married by proxy to the widowed Emperor Maximilian of Austria (1459–1519). However, the Treaty of Vergers (1488) prohibited Brittany's heiress from marrying without the knowledge or consent of the French king and when news of this union reached Charles VIII he responded by invading Brittany.[73] In order to resolve the situation and to try to safeguard Brittany, Anne agreed to marry Charles. Her marriage to Maximilian, which had never been consummated, was annulled and in 1491 she was crowned queen of France. That Anne would have been immediately aware of her role as the potential mother of both France and Brittany's heirs is evidenced by the fact that, prior to her marriage to Charles, she underwent a physical examination, completely naked, in front of the king's envoys, an examination intended to ascertain her ability to procreate.[74]

Like his ancestors Charles I of Anjou and his grandfather Charles VII, Charles VIII assimilated himself with the prophecies noted in Chapter 4 concerning the coming of the new Charlemagne. These prophecies took on a new dimension with the approach of the year 1500 and made of Charles VIII a kind of messianic emperor who would reform the church. Anne of Brittany's place in this prophetic schema was one of the ideal queen, the woman divinely chosen to bear the heir to the Empire promised to Charles VIII.[75] The prophecies' emphasis on Anne's appointment as the mother of the new 'saviour' conjured up notions of the Virgin and quickly hailed Anne of Brittany as the new Mary.[76] This assimilation is evident in Anne's *Très Petites Heures*, a miniscule volume that probably dates from her marriage to Charles VIII of France, which asserts her role as both sovereign and bearer of God-given children.[77] The union between Brittany and France is emphasised throughout the manuscript where the borders are frequently decorated with Brittany's ermine and the gold fleur de lys of France.[78] A shield showing Anne's arms also appears, held by two angels, below the *Visitation* scene at the opening of Lauds where the two holy, pregnant women Mary and St Elizabeth greet each other (plate 15). Later, at the opening of the hour of Compline, the arms of France and Brittany appear on the columns flanking the image of the *Coronation of the Virgin* (fol. 73v). The placement of Anne's arms at these two points in the *Très Petites Heures* is crucial since it draws attention both to her coronation as the queen of France and to her role as the new Virgin and mother of future kings. In this role, Anne was expected to produce the living sons that would perpetuate the new Carolingian era.

Anne became pregnant at least four times during her marriage to Charles but only the dauphin Charles-Orlando (1492–95) lived long enough to have entered the historical record in any detail.[79] With the birth of this child, the new 'holy' family was established. The child's name, Charles-Orlando, was particularly significant: Orlando, the Italianate form of Roland, the heroic nephew of Charlemagne, was a choice intended to reinforce both the heritage and the future of the dauphin and the French dynasty.[80] A Primer-type manuscript illuminated for Anne by Jean Poyet was probably intended for the dauphin, who appears as an adolescent at the end of the book, illustrating a prayer specially composed for him.[81] The manuscript also contains images of Anne of Brittany at confession and of St Anne instructing the Virgin and her two other daughters Mary Salomé and Mary Cleophas. These miniatures indicate the hopes Anne had for the child's future and in particular her interest in serving as his educator, as St Anne had done for her children. Charles-Orlando would never use the book, however, since he died when he was just three years old from a childhood illness.[82] The tomb commissioned by Anne for her children and carved with effigies of Charles-Orlando and his brother Charles who died at only a few weeks old in 1496 bears witness to the precarious nature of childbearing even for those of the privileged classes. The fact, noted previously, that Anne borrowed the relic of the Virgin's belt from the church of Puy-Notre-Dame in September 1495, three months before the death of Charles-Orlando, is certainly an indication that more than one child was deemed necessary to ensure the royal succession and that if conception was not easy, divine intervention was one source of hope.[83]

Anne's marriage to Charles VIII was cut short when the king died suddenly in 1498 and under her marriage contract Anne regained the duchy of Brittany. In order to maintain the duchy's independence, it needed an heir but Anne's marriage contract had also stated that should Charles die before her, any remarriage should be to the king of France or his successor.[84] Anne did in fact marry the new king, Charles's cousin Louis XII of Orléans, and in 1499 she was crowned queen of France for a second time.[85] Anne's reasons for complying with this clause in her marriage contract were probably political and intended to secure the future independence of the duchy. Anne, now older and wiser than at her first marriage, negotiated her own terms for this union, securing the devolvement of the duchy of Brittany onto a second, albeit hypothetical, son.[86]

During her first marriage Anne had spent a great deal of time with her sister-in-law, Anne of France, whose own desire to secure an heir was, as noted, also driven by a political ambition to establish an independent duchy of Bourbon, an ambition which was given expression in her commissioning of the *Moulins Triptych* (figure 12). Anne of France drew not only on the cult of St Anne but also on the advice of the court doctor, Bernard de Chaussade, who wrote for her the treatise on conception and generation of children discussed above. The experience of staying with her sister-in-law would have made clear to Anne how an heir, especially a male one, was a means of exercising political power: if Anne could give birth to two sons, not only would the kingdom of France be safe, but the duchy of Brittany would retain its independence. The contents of Anne's *Prayer Book*, now in the Newberry Library in Chicago, celebrate her position as queen of France and also reveal that childbearing would have an important part to play in this second marriage. Through the book's prayers, Anne could, like her mother, draw on historical and biblical examples to help her negotiate this need both physically and devotionally.

A manuscript fit for a queen: Anne of Brittany's *Prayer Book*

The Newberry Library *Prayer Book* is not a Book of Hours but a collection of psalms, litanies, suffrages and prayers and, unlike the manuscripts considered so far in this study, it is decorated with only three miniatures. These show King David, Christ displaying his wounds, and a Crucifixion.[87] Anne's possession of the manuscript is determined by a number of factors including the female prayer forms and the highlighting of her name in red with a capital letter in two of the prayers.[88] Furthermore, a prayer at the end of the manuscript asks that this little book (*huic libello*) might contribute both to the health of the queen of France and to her salvation.[89] The highlighting of St Louis IX, ancestor and namesake of Anne's husband Louis XII, with a capital letter in the litany (fol. 25r), and the inclusion of a miniature of King David also emphasise the royal connections of this manuscript and its reader, as did the images of and prayers to these figures in both the *Fitzwilliam Hours* and in the *Paris Hours of René of Anjou*.

The most significant of the manuscript's prayers for this study is that said by St Leonard for a queen of France to help her in childbirth (fols 49v–52v, see Appendix 2). However, before considering this prayer in detail, it is first worth noting that it is framed by other prayers relevant to childbearing and to general health. For example, it is preceded by a prayer commemorating the conception of the Virgin (fols 49r–v). Although the prayer itself offers protection against the plague (*contra pestem*), it was seen in Chapter 2 that certain remedies or amulets promised protection in childbirth as well as against sudden death and diseases like the plague. Thus, given the prayer's dedication, Anne might also have considered it efficacious in childbearing. More generally, a reference to the Virgin's conception would also have evoked the story of St Anne. Therefore, despite explicitly offering protection against the plague, this prayer constituted a reference to miraculous childbirth and to Anne of Brittany's patron saint, who also appears in the suffrages (fol. 56r).[90]

Immediately following St Leonard's prayer is the suffrage to St Margaret. St Margaret was doubly suitable for inclusion in a manuscript that offered assistance in childbearing since she was both the patron saint of childbirth and the patron saint of Anne's own mother, Marguerite of Foix. As shown above, St Margaret had a special mention in Marguerite's own prayer for childbirth and in Anne's manuscript the saint's name is singled out in the litany by the capitalisation and decoration of the initial letter (fol. 16r). This suggests that Anne was honouring not only the patron saint of childbirth but also her own mother. Having lost several children in her previous marriage it was essential that Anne now provide the heirs that France so desperately needed. Thus, the special attention given to St Margaret and St Anne served as models to help and protect Anne, as they had also been intended to help and protect her mother, in this privileged role. This assistance was bolstered by the inclusion of St Leonard's prayer, the introductory words explaining that he had previously recited it to help a French queen who was not only suffering during labour but who had also experienced several stillbirths (fol. 49v: *Qua liberata fuit Regina Francie. Que in partu deficiebat nec parare poterat iam desperate*).

As noted in Chapter 2, the queen whom St Leonard helped was probably Clothilde, the wife of Clovis, and first queen of the Franks.[91] The queen of France being helped to deliver a live child by the intercession of St Leonard is thus both Clothilde and Anne of Brittany, the *regine francie*, mentioned in book's final prayer. Through the implied conflation of the two queens, Anne of Brittany could situate herself in a historical line going back centuries to the time of the conversion of the Franks to Christianity, in a kind of *beata stirps*. This notion is strengthened further by the presence, already noted, of Louis IX and King David, who provided holy, royal precedents for the current king and queen of France.

Like the prayer in the *Hours of Marguerite of Foix*, St Leonard's prayer invokes an omnipotent God who has created everything out of nothing (fol. 50r: *Qui totum mundum creasti ex nihilo*). It then refers to the wonders of creation and describes how Adam was formed from the clay of the earth and how a woman was made for him as a helper (fol. 50v: *Qui adam de limo terre plasmasti deque eius latere mulierem formans pro adjutorio et in coniugium sociasti*). The prayer notes how God joined them in lawful marriage in order that they might engender descendants (fols 50v–51r: *Quibus ad propagandam posterum sobolem. Per legitimam coniugij copulationem per-petuam dedisti benedictionem . . .*). There is thus an emphasis on the inter-connected roles of marriage and the engendering of heirs, roles which Anne's circumstances, as queen of France for the second time, would have rendered her very aware.

The prayer's examples of Sarah and Abraham to whom God gave Isaac (fol. 51r: *Qui abraam patriarcham coniugemque eius Saram licet provectos maturiori etate fecundasti insperate prolis novitate*), and the miracle of Christ's conception and birth (fols 51r–v), complement the book's other allusions to St Anne's unexpected and divine conception of the Virgin. Again, the prayer reinforces the idea of marriage as the legitimate context in which to procreate: we saw above that a similar connection between mar-riage and legitimate heirs, for both the kingdom and for Christendom, was alluded to in the *Rohan Hours*, made for a previous sovereign of France, Charles VII. Sarah's conception of Isaac was, moreover, mentioned in Marguerite of Foix's prayer: Sarah thus appears to have been a pertinent example for women wishing to conceive and, if Anne was familiar with her mother's Books of Hours, this reference would also have forged a tangible connection between Anne's devotions and those of her mother.[92] Both women found it difficult to conceive and give birth to healthy children and, as duchess of Brittany rather than as queen of France, Anne was, like her mother, looking to produce an heir to safeguard the future independence of the duchy.

St Leonard's prayer concludes with a supplication that God might assist the woman suffering because of a difficult birth in order that she might be released from danger and give thanks to God (fols 52r–v: *Ut huic pre angus-tia pariendi ingemiscenti mulieri superveniat tue pietatis auxilium. Quatenus ab instanti periculo liberata possit nobiscum glorificare nomen tuum.*) As a prayer for actual labour, this idea of liberation is directly related to another aspect of St Leonard's cult, since he was the patron saint of prisoners and those who were in chains or bonds.[93] Like the reference to Moses in Marguerite of Foix's prayer, it forms a link with the commonplace prayers for delivery, which also guarantee the woman's liberation or 'delivery' through Christ's own role as a liberator. The expectation that St Leonard's prayer will allow Anne to be able to praise the Lord's name implies her full recovery and, eventually, attendance at the rite of churching in the same way as one of the scrolls discussed in Chapter 2 promised to deliver the woman safely from labour so that 'the chylde shall have crystendome and the mother puryfycatyon'.[94] Familiarity with St Leonard's ability to help women in childbirth may also have reminded

Anne of St Remigius, St Leonard's godfather who was not only responsible for baptising Clovis after his conversion by Clothilde but who, as discussed above, also appeared with his mother in common prayers for labour. Thus the prayer, like that in Marguerite's manuscript, alluded in a variety of ways both to widely available childbirth remedies and to specific narratives relevant to the aristocratic woman in question. In the same way as the *peperit* and other prayers offered women involved in childbirth a way to manage the birth, so this personalised prayer helped a specific woman, the queen of France, to manage her own childbearing.

St Leonard's prayer, like the manuscript in which it is found, was extremely personal. Not only had the prayer been said by the saint on behalf of the first queen of France but it was now intended to be repeated for the current queen of France. Kamerick suggests that, since the manuscript has been dated from 1499, this prayer was included as a mark of gratitude, since Anne's first surviving child from this marriage was born in this year.[95] Whether or not the prayer refers to a specific pregnancy, the prayer and those surrounding it would also have offered Anne protection during any future pregnancies, in the same way that her mother's prayer could have continued to have significance beyond the specific pregnancy for which it may have been composed. Having lost other children at birth or in infancy, Anne was aware that she could expect many more pregnancies in order to guarantee the heir to the French kingdom. This heir was, however, never forthcoming, and of at least four pregnancies from this union only two daughters survived. Claude was born in October 1499, nine months after her marriage to Louis, and Renée was born eleven years later in October 1510. Anne never lost her devotion to her patron saint, however, a devotion which appears to have become more intense as time went on. The *Primer* she had made for her daughter Claude (*c.*1505) and now in Cambridge shows, at the beginning, St Anne presenting Claude and the Virgin Mary to St Claude of Besançon (p. 1); at the end of the manuscript, Claude is presented by her patron saint to St Anne, who is reading with the Virgin (plate 16). The figures of St Anne and Anne of Brittany are conflated, implying that it is both the saint and the mother (the provider of the *Primer*) who offer models of learning, comportment and protection to the young Virgin-Claude.[96]

Anne's inability to produce an heir for the kingdom was not only a blow to Louis's lineage but also meant that Anne's own duchy was at risk of being subsumed once and for all into the kingdom of France. Anne's hopes of retaining Brittany's independence by devolving the duchy onto a younger son came to nothing and Claude remained her only hope. In the meantime, Louise of Savoy (1476–1531) had been grooming her son, Francis of

Angoulême (1494–1547), and cousin of Louis XII to succeed to the crown should Anne fail to produce a son.[97] In hope of retaining Brittany's independence, Anne fiercely resisted a marriage between Claude and Francis, one that was supported by Louis XII and Louise.[98] However, just over a year after Anne's death in 1514 the marriage took place. Louis XII lived another year and in a vain attempt to secure his own heir he married Mary Tudor, daughter of Henry VII of England, but died a year later. Francis of Angoulême succeeded him as Francis I of France and Duke Francis III of Brittany: kingdom and duchy were united permanently.

The evidence presented in this final chapter has demonstrated how women of the late medieval French nobility possessed the social experience and cultural training through which they could perceive the relevance of holy childbirth narratives for their individual situations. In particular, these duchesses of Brittany were interested in the execution of the social roles assigned to them as wives, mothers, educators and even rulers. It is likely that they saw the textual and visual representations of successful, comfortable, and holy maternity in their manuscripts as a way to manage, if not to gain some control over, those duties, especially concerning the difficulties of conception and the risk of maternal and infant mortality that they expected to, and did, face. Isabel Stuart's appropriation of the *Fitzwilliam Hours*, and the adaptation of its images, meant that the manuscript took on other meanings that complemented, or were additional to, those meanings that it had had for her predecessor Yolande of Anjou and for her mother, Yolande of Aragon. The manuscript provided a platform through which Isabel, as the duke's second wife, could assert her position as the new duchess and potential mother to the duchy's heirs.

The manuscript was recycled again when it came into the possession of Isabel's daughter Marguerite, whose reception of it was conditioned not only by the histories of its previous owners but also by her own circumstances, which found her unable to provide the male heir that her openly unfaithful duke required for the succession of his duchy. Thus, consideration of Marguerite's ownership suggests how the manuscript and its images of holy motherhood were multivalent, oscillating between symbols of proper conduct, encouragement, failure and expectation.

An important aspect of this chapter has been the demonstration of the particular interrelationship between the childbirth prayers in Marguerite of Foix's *Hours* and Anne of Brittany's *Prayer Book* and those sources discussed in the first part of this book. That the saintly mothers found in the popular childbirth remedies were repeated in these personalised prayers further suggests that the stories of these holy women had a significant role to play in the devotions of lay women. The relationship between biblical narratives, childbirth prayers, and the practical preparations for childbearing, which have been teased out in this chapter came together through the situational eye to construct the viewing position of aristocratic women immediately involved in the birth or implicated in the need for an heir. While the types of sources discussed here cannot necessarily, in themselves, constitute evidence of women's negotiation of a space or active role within patriarchal society, they do help the critic to suggest how certain female viewers received and interpreted the images in their prayer books in a positive way in relation to the demands placed upon them and their bodies.

Notes

1 For an overview of Anne's patronage of books see Michael Jones, 'Les Manuscrits d'Anne de Bretagne', *Mémoires de la Société d'Histoire et d'Archéologie de Bretagne*, 55 (1978), 43–81. For her most famous commission, the *Grandes Heures* painted by Jean Bourdichon, see Delisle, *Les Grandes Heures de la Reine Anne de Bretagne et l'atelier de Jean Bourdichon* (Paris: D. Morgand, 1913); see also L'Estrange, 'Anne de Bretagne', and Cynthia Brown, 'Le mécénat d'Anne de Bretagne et la politique du livre', in *Patronnes et Mécènes*, ed. by Wilson-Chevalier, pp. 195–224.

2 Minois, *Anne de Bretagne*, esp. pp. 18–24.

3 Frédérique Chauvenet, 'Le tombeau de Marguerite d'Écosse', in *Autour de Marguerite d'Écosse*, ed. by Contamine and Contamine, pp. 73–80 (p. 78); and Priscilla Bawcutt and Bridget Henisch, 'Scots Abroad in the Fifteenth Century: The Princesses Margaret, Isabella and Eleanor', in *Women in Scotland, c.1100–1750*, ed. by Elizabeth Ewan and Maureen M. Meikle (East Linton: Tuckwell, 1999), pp. 45–55 (p. 46).

4 The Scottish-Valois alliance was forced on Louis XI by his father Charles VII in an attempt to constitute another alliance against the continued English threat. Neither Louis nor Margaret seem to have relished the union. See Chauvenet, p. 78 and Minois, *Charles VII*, pp. 395–6.

5 A summary of some of the surviving ducal accounts is listed in Jones, *Catalogue sommaire des archives du fonds Lebreton, Abbaye Sainte-Guénolé, Land Évennec* (Nottingham: University of Nottingham, 2006), pp. 74–100. I am grateful to Michael Jones for sharing his findings from the archives with me.

6 For Isabel's accounts see Abbaye Saint-Guénolé, Land Évennec, Fonds Lebreton, liasse 4A, no. 85 – Fragments of accounts of the treasurer of Isabel Stuart 1444–45; and no. 90 – Payments made by the treasurer of Isabel Stuart, 1447. Some of Marguerite of Brittany's accounts are preserved in Archives départementales d'Ille-et-Vilaine (hereafter ADIV), Financial Accounts from John IV-Francis II, 1 F 657, Fragment of household accounts for Francis II and Duchess Marguerite

(January–March 1459–69); and Letters of Discharge of Marguerite, duchess of Brittany, for her treasurer Jamet Bonamy, 2 September 1460–5 February 1461.

7   ADIV, 1 F 657, Household Accounts, January–March 1459–69, item 1.

8   ADIV, 1 F 657, Household Accounts, January–March 1459–69, items 13 and 15.

9   Toynbee, p. 300.

10 Paris, Bibliothèque nationale, fonds français, 958. The text is also known as the *Livre des vices et des vertus* or the *Livre des commandements de Dieu*. The inscription on the final page names Isabel as the commissioner and gives the date 1464: *Ysabeau aisnee fille de Roy descoce duchesse de bretaigne contesse de montfort et de Richemond fist faire ce livre qui le trouvera le luy rende et le fist escripre a sa devotion de la main de Jehan Hubert en lan mil quatre cent soixante quatre.*

11 Francis II succeeded to the duchy in 1458, several years before the miniature was painted.

12 See Toynbee, p. 305; and Avril and Reynaud, pp. 178–9.

13 See Meiss, p. 404. Avril and Reynaud (pp. 177–8; no. 94) also note that the style of this miniature has affinities with a Book of Hours made for Peter II of Brittany (Paris, Bibliothèque nationale de France, fonds latin, 1159) and with the artist of Isabel's other *horae* discussed below.

14 *Ci ensuit enseignement pour les pucelles et pour aultres* (fols 206r–213r).

15 See the article by De Gendt.

16 The added prayer occurs at pp. 15–20. Pagination follows that established by Leroquais.

17 *Ysabeau* appears at pp. 299, 301, 303, 305, 307, 312, 316, 318, 320, 346, 348, 382.

18 Toynbee (p. 300) states that a hearing in Rennes recorded that Isabel did not wish to leave Brittany where she had passed so much time, had received so many honours, and was so loved by her people. Isabel's own letter to the king of France stated that, contrary to the opinion of some, she had been honorably and favourably treated by Peter II and never had cause for complaint (*Ne jamais ne m'a été fait chose dont je me dois douloir*). See Dom P. H. Morice, *Mémoires pour server de preuves à l'Histoire Ecclésiastique et Civile de Bretagne*, 3 vols (Paris: Osmont, 1968), II, cols. 1646–7.

19 Leroquais, I, p. 185.

20 For St Similien, St Clair and St Yvo (or Ivo, sometimes of Kermatin), see Pétin, II (Supplement), col. 1571 ; I, col. 610; and II, col. 1515 respectively. On the feast of the Presentation, see Leroquais, I, p. 185.

21 Pétin, II, col. 1266.

22 Pétin, II, col. 896.

23 The account of her sister's death appears on pp. 446–50 but the script is difficult to read due to deterioration of the manuscript.

24 Bawcutt and Henisch, p. 47.

25 Fol. Bv: *Ces heures sont à Renée de Rohan, c'estoit Renée de Rohan femme de Jean de Coetquen comte de Combour*; see also Toynbee (p. 303), who states that 'Renée was related to Mary of Brittany through the marriage of the latter's younger daughter to Louis de Rohan IV, seigneur de Guémené, Renée's great-grandfather'.

26 For Margaret's ownership see Toynbee, p. 303 and Legaré, 'La réception du *Pèlerinage*', p. 545.

27 That the portrait is a later addition is noted by James in the *Cat. Fitz.*, p. 159, by Toynbee, p. 303, and Legaré, 'La réception du *Pèlerinage*', p. 545. It would appear to be a repainting or a completion since the text is already worked around the space of the miniature.

28 The inventory was published by A. de la Borderie, 'Inventaire des meubles et bijoux de Marguerite de Bretagne, Première femme du duc de Bretagne François II', *Bulletin de la société archéologique de Nantes et Loire-inferieure*, 4 (1864), 45–60; item 73 (p. 53).

29 Minois, *Anne de Bretagne*, p. 19; and *Charles VII*, p. 696. Prior to becoming the duke's mistress, Antoinette was the mistress of Charles VII after the death of her cousin Agnès Sorel in 1450.

30 G. Durville, 'Une demi-sœur inconnue d'Anne de Bretagne', *Bulletin de la société archéologique de Nantes et de la Loire-Atlantique*, 57 (1917 for 1915), 1–26 (pp. 2–3).

31 Durville, p. 4; and Émile Gabory, *Anne de Bretagne, Duchesse et Reine* (Paris: Plon, 1941), pp. 6–7.

32 According to Minois (*Anne de Bretagne*, p. 21), Antoinette received 18,391 *livres* compared to 7,000 *livres* for Marguerite.

33 The letters of Francis II creating his son baron of Avaugour on 24 September 1480 refer to him as *notre fils Francois de Bretagne, seigneur de Clisson*, see Morice, III, cols 368–70. Thanks to Michael Jones for this reference.

34 Fragments of accounts for the reign of Francis II are preserved in the Archives départementales de la Loire-Atlantique, série B, non classés: Discharge by Francis II, 1468, 25 items, no. 7.

35 Minois, *Anne de Bretagne*, p. 21.

36 Minois, *Anne de Bretagne*, p. 21.

37 Gabory, p. 7.

38 See Harthan, p. 135; Minois, *Anne de Bretagne*, p. 22; and Gabory, p. 4.

39 Rowan Watson, 'The Marguerite of Foix Book of Hours', *The V&A Album*, 2 (1983), 45–50 (esp. pp. 49–50).

40 Watson, p. 49.

41 A guide to the Salting Collection published in 1926 states that the 'armorial insignia of Brittany impaling the quarterings of the later counts of Foix are still traceable in two shields which have been almost obliterated': *A Guide to the Salting Collection* (London: published under the authority of the board of education, 1926), p. 40. The arms were also established as those of Brittany and Foix when the manuscript was displayed at the Burlington Fine Arts Club in 1908: see *Exhibition of Illuminated Manuscripts* (London: Burlington Fine Arts Club, 1908), pp. 106–7, no. 217. Thanks to Richard Emmerson for tracking down a copy of this latter reference.

42 According to Watson, 'neither ultra-violet nor infra-red light is of help in reconstructing the arms' (p. 45). See also the entry on the manuscript in Harthan, p. 124.

43 Watson, p. 45.

44 Watson, p. 45. He actually gives Anne's year of birth as 1476 but since she was born on 25 January this refers to the old year system.

45 Harthan follows the *Burlington Catalogue* in his comments on the prayer, pp. 124; 182.

46 So far the binding has only been dated rather broadly, to the second half of the fifteenth century, see Watson, p. 45.

47 Genesis 16–17.

48 I Samuel 1. 10–11.

49 Judges 13. 2–3.

50 BL, Royal 12 B xxv, fols 61v–62r.

51 For St Paul and St Samson see Pétin, II, cols 673–4 and 944–5, respectively. The others founding saints were: St Malo, St Tudwal, St Brieuc, St Patern and St Corentin.

52 For St Malo (also known as Maclou, Maclovius), see Pétin, I, cols 356–7; for St Corentin (Corentinus), see Pétin, I, col. 658.

53 Pétin, I, col. 356.

54 For St Clair (Clarus), see Pétin, I, col. 610; for St Guillaume see Pétin, I, col. 1286; and for St Melaine (Melanius) see Pétin II, col. 435.

55 Pétin, II, col. 1515.

56 For St Gicquel (also Giguel or Judicaël) and St Salomon, see Pétin, II, cols 172–3; and 940–1.

57 *The Oxford Dictionary of the Christian Church*, ed. by F. L. Cross (London: Oxford University Press, 1957), p. 66.

58 Paris, Bibliothèque nationale, fonds latin, 1385, identified by Avril and Reynaud as Francis II's *Hours*, p. 300. They also note that the manuscript has had many of its miniatures removed (the remaining decoration is mainly foliage). Leroquais notes that the *Hours* are for the (Breton) Use of Saint-Pol-de-Léon but he dates them to the beginning of the sixteenth century and does not note a connection with Francis II, who died in 1480. See Leroquais, I, pp. 210–11.

59 Although the main miniatures were not painted on singletons, which were then bound and inserted into an otherwise 'off-the-shelf' purchase, the personalised aspects of the manuscript still suggest that the patron was involved in the design of the manuscript from the start.

60 The origin of this anomaly remains unclear. According to Watson (p. 49) it might indicate a local tradition or reflect the customer's wishes, further suggesting the bespoke aspect of the miniatures.

61 Given the priest's raised hand and the way the figures turn away from the altar I am of the opinion that this scene represents an *Expulsion from the Temple*, rather than their marriage, as identified by Watson. As noted for the *Fitzwilliam Hours*, both Anne and Joachim were sometimes depicted at this event.

62 ADIV, 1 F 657, Financial Accounts from John IV–Francis II, Accounts of Olivier Boucher, Marguerite of Foix's tailor, for January–March 1475, item 5.

63 ADIV, 1 F 657, item 9.

64 BN lat. 9474, fol. 222v. See also L'Estrange, 'Le mécénat d'Anne de Bretagne'.

65 Larson, p. 97.

66 See Larson, pp. 97–100.

67 The painting has been rubbed and some of the colours smudged.

68 ADIV, 1 F 657, Fragments of Ducal Accounts, *c*.1460–70, item 12.

69 Le Fur, p. 12.

70 *Généalogie des très anciens roys, ducs et princes de Bretagne, qu'au temps passé ont régy et gouverné ceste royale principauté*, Genève, Bibliothèque publique et universitaire, ms fr. 131. See also Le Fur, pp. 13–14 for the quotation.

71 Minois, *Anne de Bretagne*, pp. 99–101.

72 For the dating of the manuscript after the marriage of Anne and Louis, on 7 January 1499, see Paul Saengar, *A Catalogue of the Pre-1500 Western Manuscripts at the Newberry Library* (Chicago and London: University of Chicago Press, 1989), pp. 155–7.

73 Harthan, p. 129; and Minois, *Anne de Bretagne*, pp. 326–8.

74 Cluzel, p. 118.

75 Le Fur, p. 84.

76 Le Fur, p. 84.

77 Paris, Bibliothèque nationale, nouvelle acquisition latine, 3120. It measures just 66 x 46mm. Avril and Reynaud (pp. 266–7) note that Porcher dated it to 1492 but that Charles Sterling placed it later, suggesting that Anne commissioned it during her widowhood, but that it was finished in 1499 after her marriage to Louis XII when she was once again pregnant, whence the arms at the *Visitation*.

78 See for example fols 55r–v and 57r.

79 A son, Francis was born in 1494, a still-born girl probably in 1495, and the dauphin Charles who lived only a few weeks (8 September–2 October 1496). For further details on Anne's childbearing and on the dauphin, Charles-Orlando, see L'Estrange, 'Le mécénat d'Anne de Bretagne'.

80 The name was apparently chosen by Francis de Paule (1416–1507), founder of the Franciscan order of Minims, who was revered at the French court for his gift of prophecy and later canonised. See Minois, *Anne de France*, p. 123.

81 New York, Pierpont Morgan Library, MS M. 50, fol. 13r. Images from this manuscript are available online: www.themorgan.org/collections/swf/exhibOnline.asp?id=355 (Accessed 28 March 2007). See also Wieck and K. Michelle Hearne, *The Prayer Book of Anne de Bretagne* (Luzern: Faksimile Verlag, 1999), pp. 49–51.

82 Wieck and Hearne, p. 23.

83 Legaré, 'Charlotte de Savoie's Library', p. 39.

84 Minois, *Anne de Bretagne*, p. 327.

85 Minois, *Anne de Bretagne*, p. 327.

86 Kathleen Kamerick, 'Patronage and Devotion in the Prayer Book of Anne of Brittany, Newberry Library MS 83', *Manuscripta*, 39 (1995), 40–50 (p. 45).

87 See Saengar, pp. 155–7; and Kamerick, p. 45.

88 The speaker of two prayers is referred to as Anne and the name written in red on fols 29r and 38r.

89 Fols 59v–60r: *Deus alpha et omega. Omnium rerum principium et finis huic libello ad salvationem regine francie finem imponat; et qui eam primum in terris reginam constituit eam in celis post longam vitam dignetur recipere. Amen.*

90 Kamerick, p. 44.

91 Réau, III, p. 799.

92 Although Marguerite's Book of Hours is not listed among the manuscripts that were in Anne's possession, she did inherit other books belonging to her mother and it is reasonable to suppose that she could have been familiar with her mother's *Hours*. On books that Anne inherited from her parents, see Jones, 'Les manuscrits d'Anne de Bretagne'.

93 Réau, III, p. 800; and Voragine, II, pp. 245-6.

94 Wellcome 632, verso side.

95 Kamerick, p. 47.

96 See Myra D. Orth, ' "Madame Sainte Anne": The Holy Kinship, the Royal Trinity, and Louise of Savoy', in *Interpreting Cultural Symbols*, ed. by Ashley and Sheingorn, pp. 199-227.

97 See Orth, esp. p. 203.

98 See Cluzel, p. 204.

Conclusion

This book began with two images of holy childbirth in a fifteenth-century Book of Hours made for a male reader-viewer in holy orders (figures 1–2). It finished with a prayer for safe delivery in childbirth included in a manuscript made for Anne, duchess of Brittany and twice queen of France. Despite differences, not only in terms of content but also in terms of the lifestyle, gender and class of their reader-viewers, these manuscripts have helped mark out a space in which the reception of images and narratives of holy motherhood and their value for historical analysis has been explored. The intimate post-partum representations of the *Birth of the Virgin* and the *Birth of St John the Baptist* from the Book of Hours in the John Rylands Library call into question the idea that such images of childbirth depict a 'feminine' space through which the (art) historian can gain access to the otherwise largely silent birth chamber: the images are not only generic and holy but they are also found in a manuscript owned by a male cleric. These miniatures, therefore, complicate any assumption that images depicting holy motherhood are necessarily indicative of childbearing practices in the fifteenth century or of 'women's' tastes as viewers and patrons. Nevertheless, the selection of images referred to in the Introduction, taken from historical and liturgical manuscripts, panel paintings, monumental frescoes and works in sculpture and print, would appear to supply a number of details about childbearing in the later middle ages through their depiction of the visitors, the attention to furnishings, the food on offer, and the care of the mother and child.

Certain examples of this female-dominated iconography can be related to female patrons and viewers and in some cases, like Fina Buzzacarini's commission of the St John the Baptist cycle in Padua (figure 3), was ordered by them on a monumental scale. Furthermore, the popularity of

St Anne and the cult of the Holy Kinship, to which these images relate, would seem to suggest that late medieval devotional and artistic practices celebrated and validated women's reproductive abilities, offering them positive role models. However, when considered in the light of women's relative social and economic exclusion in the patriarchal society of the later middle ages and the inferior status ascribed to the female sex by medical and ecclesiastical thinkers, the value of these generic, holy images as indicators of women's tastes and viewing habits becomes more difficult to discern. Increasingly complex debates about what the terms 'masculine' and 'feminine' signify and thus what it means to 'gender' images and viewers mean that the little-studied post-partum scenes and related images of holy mothers were ripe for a more subtle analysis than had hitherto been carried out. Thus, instead of using these images to illustrate a history of childbirth in the middle ages, as has been done in previous studies, the aim here has been to bring visual, textual, and historical sources into play with each other in order show how depictions of blessed mothers and holy childbirth were commissioned, viewed, interpreted and recycled. Doing so has, nevertheless, allowed another historical interpretation of childbearing in the middle ages to be proposed, one which stresses its cultural and social, rather than medical, aspects.

Any attempt to interpret, historically, images of women and the meanings they held for female viewers within a patriarchal society encounters a methodological double bind. Critics who have explored how female readers engaged with images of birth and maternity have often fallen into an empowerment–disempowerment binary that emphasises women's subjugation to patriarchy. In some cases, this has occurred perhaps unwittingly, as in the early work of Bynum and reiterated more theoretically in the work of Kristeva, whose essentialist approaches identify a subversive, reproductive desire in all women yet fail to acknowledge the cultural construction of that desire. In others, a subjugation of the female sex within patriarchy has wittingly been emphasised in order to demonstrate the constraints on, if not impossibility of, women's agency. Maternal desire, as Butler has claimed, might be 'a social practice required and recapitulated by the exigencies of kinship' and identification with the 'natural' role of motherhood is only ever disempowering.[1] Both approaches leave the art historian seeking to understand how women viewed and responded to images with little room for manoeuvre. However, as critical analyses have shifted since the 1970s from 'women's history' to 'gender studies' and beyond, critics like Butler have rightly called the very category of 'women' into question.

Harnessing the performativity and constructedness that Butler ascribes to gender roles and maternity, which appear on one level to define and restrict certain 'bodies', has actually offered the possibility of a way out of this impasse. Thus, focusing on how viewers performed their social roles as wives, duchesses, queens, mothers and educators not only helps to acknowledge the didactic or prescriptive impetus behind the images but also shows that such intentions were not automatically accepted or passively replicated by the women receiving them. Even if lay women in the fifteenth century had relatively little choice over the roles they played or had little power to commission works of art, it should not be assumed that they were not able to harness the themes and ideas in the images they encountered as ways of best negotiating and managing those roles. The variety of material presented here and the analysis employed, demonstrate the potential scope for reception and interpretation even within the hierarchical structure of late-medieval society.

A social approach to viewing and reception required a methodology that could draw out the interpretative skills and experience acquired by viewers and brought to bear on the pictures. As an adaptation of Baxandall's period eye, the situational eye serves as a way to explore the different or additional cognitive habits and culturally-relative equipment that were acquired by, or available to, viewers who do not fit Baxandall's original mercantile, masculine, model. An insistence on the relationship between viewers and their social, rather than simply gender, roles, shows that whereas lay women would be likely to acquire the cognitive habits that rendered them sensitive to images of childbirth, lay men interested in the continuation of their dynastic line and in the welfare of their wife and children would not be a priori excluded from this situational eye. In fact, as an interpretative strategy, the situational eye proves to be a flexible concept, extendable and adaptable according to whichever combination of viewers and sources are under consideration: husbands, wives, fathers, mothers, rich, poor, religious, lay. This potential holds true but since the aim here has been to explore images of holy motherhood and how far they can be indicative of gendered reception, the cognitive habits explored in Chapters 2 and 3 related specifically to the cultural and devotional practices of childbearing in the fifteenth century, including treatises for conception, prayers said during labour, furnishings and preparations for the birth, and the ceremony of churching.

From a broad perspective, the evidence from material culture adds to our understanding of childbearing in the later middle ages. The remedies for conception and birth, together with the attention paid to the details of the lying-in and churching ceremonies, reveal both the social and political importance attached to childbirth as well as the advice and care available to the men and women involved. More specifically, examined together, these sources reveal connections between them that have hitherto not been explicitly analysed, such as the way narratives of miraculous, holy, childbirth permeated images, texts and popular devotional practices like pilgrimage as a means for people to try to ensure successful conception, birth and future protection. For example, when considered in the light of the popular *peperit/exi* prayers for labour that invoke St Anne and other biblical and saintly mothers, the equally popular images representing certain of these women at the visitation or at birth of St John or the Virgin take on an additional dimension, becoming another way to manage the physical, social, and spiritual aspects of conception and childbirth.

The material practices of childbirth predominantly involved lay women and, therefore, reveal the kinds of knowledge and experience that wives and mothers would have brought to their viewing of images of holy motherhood. Furthermore, certain of these cognitive habits refer chiefly, but not exclusively, to those skills acquired by aristocratic lay women, especially those who were members of three of the leading families in fifteenth-century France and for whom the conception of (male) heirs was their main social role. This refinement of the situational eye is partly due to the fact that it is much easier to pinpoint evidence about childbearing practices and artistic patronage in the fifteenth century that relates to the nobility than to those from the less privileged end of society. Such a bias means, inevitably, that it is more difficult to suggest how the vast majority of women, and indeed men, understood their social roles as parents and managed the events surrounding childbearing. The aim, however, was to avoid a generalising of 'women viewers', collapsing them under one category of spectatorship. Of course, a focus on the cognitive habits of a small group of aristocratic readers might still carry the charge of creating yet another 'subgroup' of female viewers united by the common theme of maternity. Nevertheless, this is mitigated by close attention to the historical context in which the Angevin and Breton duchesses received their exceptional manuscripts. Furthermore, attention to how male readers also encountered images of holy motherhood and maternity shows that they too were implicated in the social exigency of parenting and that, like their female counterparts, they could also draw on narratives of holy motherhood and blessed dynasties to negotiate and assert their positions. In fact, it appears that class – and the possibilities for identification with holy figures that it entailed – is often a more important category than gender when it comes to suggesting how images of holy motherhood were received.

The survival of aristocratic dynasties depended largely on their ability to provide a number of male heirs to inherit lands and titles and to make marital matches that would strengthen kinship and political ties. The evidence from the Angevin and Breton manuscripts demonstrates how the commissioners and later owners of these books exploited their provenance from, or connections to, the houses of France, Anjou and Brittany. The likely commissioner of the *Fitzwilliam Hours*, Yolande of Aragon, drew on her own and her husband's association with the Hungro-Angevin *beata stirps* and the sainted lineage of the house of France to assert her position as matriarch of the house of Anjou. The inclusion of the saints Elizabeth of Hungary, Louis IX, Louis of Toulouse, Radegund, Anne, Mary Salomé and Mary Cleophas, who occupied positions as monarchs, parents and educators, made explicit, and gave a holy aspect to, the various roles that Yolande performed as dowager duchess of the sainted Angevins: daughter of a king, queen herself (albeit in name only), mother of a large family, educator and adviser, and supporter of the future Charles VII.

When the *Fitzwilliam Hours* came into the hands of her daughter Yolande of Anjou, its emphasis on Angevin *beata stirps* cannot have failed to escape the young duchess's notice. The *Fitzwilliam Hours* thus embodied not only the illustrious history of Yolande's family, but also alluded to the achievements of her mother, offering a model for her own life. In particular, Yolande, newly-married to the heir to the duchy of Brittany would have acquired the cognitive habits to make her sensitive to the narratives of holy mothers and to the allusions to the material practices of childbirth in the manuscript's decorative cycle. Such sensitivity meant that the manuscript could function for Yolande, as it did for the later owners Isabel Stuart and Marguerite of Brittany, not only as a place through which social roles were constructed and reasserted but also through which they could be managed and performed. In so far as they showed examples of divine intervention for successful childbearing and dynastic continuity, the duchesses could have discerned in the images a means whereby they could ask God to look favourably upon their own situation, especially their physical and spiritual health, as they carried out the duties expected of them as duchesses.

The *Rohan Hours* reveal how images of holy motherhood and childbirth were also important to male viewers as markers of dynastic ambition and of God's protection. It appears that the *Bible moralisée* included in the *Rohan Hours*, with its emphasis on Old Testament births as moralising messages for government, was deliberately chosen by the likely commissioner, Yolande of Aragon, to inform and influence the political development of the young Charles VII. Thus, in addition to showing how a male aristocratic viewer could have responded to images of child-bearing, the *Rohan Hours* also demonstrate how a lay woman like Yolande of Aragon could exercise commissioning power to manipulate and support the French crown for her own political purposes. Charles VII's accession to the throne in the face of English threats would not only ensure that Yolande's own daughter, Marie, became queen, but it would also strengthen the position of the house of Anjou, as *princes de sang*. This, in turn, would support, indirectly or otherwise, the duchy's ongoing claims to the kingdoms of Sicily and Naples, part of Yolande's own heritage.

The two Books of Hours belonging to René of Anjou show how Angevin family history, particularly its connections to France, was impor-tant to the duke as he attempted to assert his position at the head of the Angevin dynasty during an uncertain time. The stylistic similarities, espe-cially in the maternal imagery, between René's *Paris Hours*, and the *Fitzwilliam* and *Rohan Hours*, helped to create a sense of family identity that gravitated round the patronage of his mother, Yolande. René's per-sonalising of his *Paris* and *London Hours* with his coats of arms and with miniatures of the *roi mort* and the angels holding the host was a means for him to demonstrate his power, reinforce his claims to territories in Italy and beyond, and assert his allegiance to France in the face of Burgundian opposition.

The two manuscripts belonging to two later duchesses of Brittany, Marguerite of Foix and her daughter Anne of Brittany, exemplify perhaps most strongly the importance of childbearing in the life of an aristocratic woman and the steps that she could take not only to execute, but also to protect herself, in this role. The personalised prayer for a son in the *Hours of Marguerite of Foix* that draws on, and places the speaker in direct com-parison with, examples of biblical mothers rendered fertile suggests that the duchess, who waited six years for her first child, was not only acutely aware of the duchy's need for a legitimate male heir, but that she situated her viewing of the manuscript's images of holy motherhood in relation to this need. Furthermore, the fact that Marguerite and Francis II's first child was named after St Anne indicates the importance of this saint in the couple's devotions to resolve their infertility.

The emphasis in Anne of Brittany's *Prayer Book* on St Anne as well as on St Louis IX, patron saint and ancestor of Anne's second husband Louis

XII, and on St Margaret, her mother's patron saint and protector of women in childbirth, show that family connections, dynastic history and child-bearing played an important part in this queen's life and devotions. This fact is reiterated by the inclusion of the prayer with which St Leonard delivered the first Frankish queen, Clothilde. Anne's little manuscript, despite not containing any images of childbirth, provided a way for her to try to ensure that, following the death of all her children from her first marriage, her second would be more fruitful and that she would, like Clothilde, be able to secure the future of the kingdom of France. Successful childbearing during this second marriage would also, Anne hoped, allow her to guarantee the independence of her own duchy of Brittany from the grasp of her husband's family.

The question remains, however, as to how far the critic can go in assigning agency to female viewers in the middle ages, both in the reception of images and in the execution of their social roles. On one level there is the question of evidence: short of the discovery of new documents, many of the interpretations regarding manuscript commissions and ownership must remain as hypotheses. For instance, despite compelling internal and circumstantial evidence relating the *Fitzwilliam Hours* to Yolande of Aragon, scholars are still divided over the date of the manuscript, as they are for the commissioners and dating of the *Rohan Hours* and the *Hours of René of Anjou*. Furthermore, it is possible that the duchesses discussed in this book were either indifferent to, or fiercely resisted, attempts to encourage them to procreate: Isabel's refusal to leave Brittany after the death of Francis I may have been a strategy to avoid remarriage and the attendant risks of further childbearing rather than a specific interest in her duty to her husband's memory and his territories. Similarly, it could be argued that the centrality of the female sex in the images and narratives of Christ's genealogy, also discernible in the cultural practices of lying-in and churching, led to the inevitable reassertion of patriarchy, rather than a reversal or disruption, by suggesting that women's only weapon against hierarchical gender roles is biological capacity, a capacity that, according to Butler, is always already appropriated by patriarchy.

Nevertheless, it is precisely the idea of maternity as social practice that has been important here since analysing the images and their reception in terms of binary oppositions that oppose men to women, masculine to feminine, resistance to submission, and power to subjection, is not always a helpful strategy. It is a subtle distinction to make but, viewed from the duchesses' socially-constructed, situational eye informed by an awareness of the place and roles occupied by women in fifteenth-century society, the images of, and practices surrounding, childbirth become multivalent, symbolising instances of the disruption that childbirth could entail, of the benefits that lying-in and churching held for the new mother, and of patriarchy's dependence on the sex it had appropriated.

Such dependence must have been only too clear to women like Anne of Brittany and her sister-in-law Anne of France. Anne of France's ability to rule as regent but not actually to succeed to the throne of France eventually led her to shift her political interests away from the Crown towards her own 'holy family'. The lack of a male heir, however, risked thwarting Anne's plans for the future and she turned not only to St Anne as the matriarch of the Holy Kinship but also to the court physician in the hopes of engendering a son who would be able to ensure the ambitious strategy she had defined for the duchy of Bourbon. Likewise Anne of Brittany, instead of contenting herself with her regained sovereignty over her duchy following Charles VIII's death, chose to fulfil the clause in her marriage contract that jeopardised Brittany's independence from France at the same time as it offered the possibility for her to ensure its autonomy by engendering an heir. Although her marriage to Louis XII did not produce the wished-for son on whom the duchy could be devolved, Anne's Chicago *Prayer Book* and other commissions like the *Très Petites Heures*, the *Grandes Heures* and the *Primer of Claude of France* show that she actively used the mothers of the holy kinship, St Anne, St Elizabeth and the Virgin, to pray for a son, as well as to serve as models for her two surviving daughters, Claude and Renée.

A critical practice that seeks to recover the history of women's lives can inevitably lead the over-enthusiastic scholar to seek out instances of 'feminine' identification or subversion without considering the implications of such an analysis. The images of all-female, post-partum confinement in fifteenth-century manuscripts do not offer a direct window on to late-medieval childbearing practices and must be considered as cultural constructs that, in many ways, reinforced the marginalisation of women in fifteenth-century society. Yet, at the other extreme, the images were extremely popular and allude sufficiently to other sources to suggest that lay women encountered in them ways to negotiate their social roles. Images of holy motherhood and miraculous childbirth should, therefore, be considered multivalent, altering or oscillating in meaning for different viewers at different times in their lives, rather than as inherently prescriptive or empowering. By looking at the experiences and circumstances informing the situational eye of certain viewers in particular, this study has shown how images of holy motherhood could function not only as depictions of patriarchy's appropriation of the female sex but also as zones through which women's, and men's, concerns and interests about childbearing, parenting and dynasty could be expressed.

Note

1 Butler, p. 115.

Appendix 1: prayer and translation from the *Hours of Marguerite of Foix* (London, Victoria and Albert Museum, MS 1222)

[fol. 223r][1] Domine deus omnipotens cuius sapientia conditi sumus ac pietate conservati qui tua bonitatis plenitudine cuncta de nichilo creasti tantorumque mirabilium operum tuorum orbem decorasti nec ulli poscenti te toto corde defuisti, steriles fecundas fecisti: Sarre Ysaac patriarcham sterili constituisti, Anne uxori Helcane Samuelem prophetam [fol. 223v] lacrimanti condonasti, Sansonem fortissimum uxori Manne angelo nunciante infecunde tribuisti, Johannem batistam Elizabeth adornate senectute dedisti, Jeremiam et Johannem in utero sanctificasti et, quod in oculis cunctorum mirabile, Mariam Christi matrem et virginem predestinasti, Moysem ut populo Israel preesset a Pharaonis decreto liberasti: nobisque[2] famule [fol. 224r] tue obprobrium sterilitatis abstulisti, humili[3] deprecor parte: Fateor te futura ut preterita nosse cognitione cuius cuncte carent creature. Quid de futuro postulare velim ignaram me quasi penitus reddo. Si tue tamen videatur providentie rei publice ac petende personne honestum et utile totis mentis nisibus et affectu supplico hoc in modo mitissime Deus, aures [fol. 224v] tue pietatis nostris precibus accommoda: meritis unigeniti filii tui ac virginis sacratissime matris eius, totius curie celestis angelorum patriarcharum prophetarum apostolorum martirum confessorum virginum penitentium contemplativorum activorum singularique presidio sanctorum Gicquelli Salomonis martirum Britannie regum, Donaciani et Rogatiani martirum [fol. 225r] comitis Nannetensij filiorum beatorum, Sansonis, Melani, Maclovii, Clari, Vincentii, Guillermi, Corentini, Yvonis, Pauli, et omnium sanctorum et sanctarum quorum reliquie et venerationes hoc in ducatu complectuntur Francisci gloriosissimi confessoris Anthonii Paduani Margarite virginis et martiris: quatinus nobis Francisco Britan[fol. 225v]norum duci et Margarite eius uxori natum

qui viriliter ad honorem dei viventis et salutem presideat[4] subditorum sub-
sidium utilitatis et honoris concedas per eundem dominum nostrum
Ihesum Cristum filium tuum qui tecum vivit et regnat in secula seculorum.
Amen.

God almighty, by whose wisdom we have been created and by whose goodness we have been preserved, you who created everything from nothing by
your full measure of goodness and who embellished the circle of your so
great wonderful works and who failed no one begging you with all his heart,
you who made the barren fertile: to the barren Sarah you assigned as a son
the patriarch Isaac, to [H]Anna[h] in her tears, the wife of Elkannah, you
presented the prophet Samuel, to the infertile wife of Manoah through the
announcement of the angel you assigned the very strong Samson, to
Elizabeth distinguished by her old age you gave John the Baptist; you made
Jeremiah and John holy in the womb and, something remarkable in the eyes
of all, you appointed in advance Mary, mother of Christ and virgin; you set
free Moses from the dictate of the Pharaoh in order that he might be in charge
of the people, Israel, and you have taken away from us [i.e. me] your servant
the disgrace of barrenness, I in my humble position earnestly pray: I
acknowledge that you know the future as you know the past, the knowledge
of which all living creatures lack. I, as it were, completely hand myself over,
not knowing what I would like to ask about the future. However, if it should
seem honourable and advantageous to your forethought for the state of
Brittany and to your person that must be prayed to I earnestly request with
all the efforts and will of my mind in the following manner: O most gentle
God, apply the ears of your goodness to our [i.e. my] prayers: through the
services of your only begotten son and the most holy virgin his mother, of the
whole heavenly court consisting of angels, patriarchs, prophets, apostles,
martyrs, confessors, virgins, penitents, contemplative monks, active monks,
and through the unique protection of the holy martyrs Gicquel and Salomon
the kings of Brittany, Donatien and Rogatien the martyrs, [i.e.] the blessed
sons of the Count of Nantes, of Samson, of Melaine, of Maclou, of Clair, of
Vincent, of Guillaume, of Corentin, of Yvo, of Paul, and of all the male saints
and female saints whose remains and cults are embraced in this dukedom,[5]
of Anthony of Padua, follower of the most glorious Francis [i.e. St Francis],
and of Margaret, virgin and martyr: I earnestly pray that in the name of the
same Lord our Jesus Christ your son who lives and reigns with you for ever
and ever you grant to us, Francis Duke of the Bretons and Marguerite his
wife, a son who may direct the support consisting of advantage and honour
for the honour of the living God and for the safety of his subjects. Amen.

Notes

1 Punctuation and capitalisation have been added.

2 The first person ablative plural *nobisque* – 'from us' – is here read as an instance of the 'royal we', used to mean the first person singular. The same applies to *nostris precibus*, fol. 224v.

3 Abbreviation, usual for 'us', follows *humili*; *humilius* would make sense and would be an adverb of the comparative degree giving the sense 'rather humbly'. However, this would leave *parte* without any adjective; therefore, the reading *humili* has been retained. The presence of other difficulties in the text means it is not unlikely that this is a mistake on the part of the scribe or composer.

4 Watson at the V&A and I both read 'presidentis' with contraction over the 'e'. However, a subjunctive verb is needed at this point and 'presideat' would seem appropriate in this context.

5 Alternative reading: '. . . whose remains and cults are embraced in this dukedom of the most glorious Francis [i.e. the Duke], namely of the confessor Anthony of Padua and of Margaret the virgin and martyr . . .'.

Appendix 2: prayer and translation from the *Prayer Book of Anne of Brittany* (Chicago, Newberry Library, MS 83)

[fol. 49v][1] Oratio habita per beatum Leonardum. Qua liberata fuit Regina Francie. Que in partu deficiebat nec parare poterat iam desperate. Et est maxime virtutis quoties devote legitur [fol. 50r] et attente auditur cum mulier est in partu. Oratio: Deus omnipotens solus sine fine et initio. Qui totum mundum creasti ex nihilo. Ad cuius imperium in stabile volvitur celum. Terra autem immobilis persistit in eternum. Cuius luce illuminantur sydera celi. Cuiusque nutu luna noctem. Sol occupat tempus diei. Cuius inmensa et inenarrabilis claritas abissi profundas irradiat tenebras. Cuius [fol. 50v] precepto mare constringitur: dum ultra terminos numque progreditur. Qui ex eodem mari flumina producis et flamma ventorum in cavernis terre concludis. Qui etiam inextimabili potentia tua ex durissimo lingo molha deducis femina. Qui adam de limo terre plasmasti deque eius latere mulierem formans pro adiutorio et in coniugium sociasti. Quibus ad propagandam posterum sobolem. Per [fol. 51r] legitimam coniugij copulationem perpetuam dedisti benedictionem dicens: Crescite et multiplicami et replete terram et dominamini piscibus maris et volatilibus celi, quin etiam bestijs totius diversitatis. Qui abraam patriarcham coniugemque eius Saram licet provectos maturiori etate fecundasti insperate prolis novitate. Qui etiam cooperante spiritu sancto de sinu tuo misisti filium tuum ad intemerate virgi[fol. 51v]nis uterum. ut in ea [ds][2] Deus fieret homo et humana lege impregnatis lateret divina. Atque etiam post novem mensium legitimum numerum matre virgine pariente de thalamo procedens nascendo virginis relinqueret uterum. In cuius nomine te deus pater. Cum spiritu sancto invoco. Et ad exaudiendam vocem deprecationis mee. Solita clementia qua me semper exaudis. Quatenus velox et exaudibi[fol. 52r]lis adsis. Suppliciter obsecro. Intret in conspectu tuo oratio mea. Inclina aurem

260

tuam pijssime ad preces meas. Tu enim per sacratissimum os filij tui domini nostri iesu Christi. Duodecim apostolis ceterisque fidelibus Christianis inquiens promisisti. Quodcumque petieritis patri in nomine meo dabitur nobis. Peto itaque omnipotens pater per unicum filium tuum. Simulque etiam per spiritum sanctum. Ut huic pre angustia pariendi ingemiscenti mu[fol. 52v]lieri superveniat tue pietatis auxilium. Quatenus ab instanti periculo liberata possit nobiscum glorificare nomen tuum. Qui est bene-dictus in secula seculorum. Amen.

Prayer made by the blessed Leonard by means of which the queen of France was released. She was not succeeding in bringing to full term and was not able to produce children, being at that stage beyond hope. And the prayer is of very great power whenever it is read piously and listened to attentively when a woman is in course of bearing children. Prayer: 'Only and almighty God without end and without beginning, who created the whole universe from nothing, at whose command the changing sky is turned, while the earth continues unmoving for ever, by whose light the stars of the sky are lit up and at whose nod the moon takes over the night, the sun takes over the day time, whose vast and indescribable brightness shines upon the deep darkness of the bottomless pit, by whose command the sea is controlled to the point that it never advances beyond its bounds, who brings forth the rivers from the same sea and who shuts up the blasts of the winds in the caves of the earth, who also by means of your incon-ceivable power draws soft thighs out of the hardest timber, who formed Adam from the clay of the earth and, forming from his flank a woman as helper to him, associated them in marriage. To them for the purpose of engendering issue in terms of descendants through the lawful coupling of marriage you gave an everlasting blessing, saying "Increase and multiply and fill the earth and rule over the fishes of the sea and the flying creatures of the sky, even over the beast of every varied type." God, who made fertile with the strange phenomenon of un-hoped-for offspring Abraham the patriarch and his wife Sarah, though well advanced in old age, who also, with the holy spirit working alongside, sent forth from your bosom your son into the womb of a pure virgin in order that God might be made man, and in order that the divine law of the begetter might lie hidden by the human law and in order that also, when his virgin mother gave birth after the lawful number of nine months, he, coming forth from the chamber, might by being born leave the womb of the virgin. In His [i.e. Christ's] name I call upon you, O God the father in company with the holy spirit, and I call upon you to listen favourably to the words of my earnest prayer with the customary mercy with which you always listen favourably to me. I earnestly beg that you be present swiftly and attentively. Let my prayer enter into your sight. Bend your ear, O most holy one, to my prayers. For you made a promise through the most holy mouth of your son our Lord Jesus Christ when you said to the twelve apostles and to the other faithful followers of Christ: "Whatever you will have asked from the father in my name will be given to you." Therefore I ask, almighty father through your one and only son and at the same time too through the holy spirit, that the assistance of your holiness may come upon this woman who is groaning because of the difficulty of giving birth in order that she, having been released from immediate danger may be able along with us to praise your name – you who are blessed for ever and ever. Amen.'

Notes

1 Some punctuation and capitalisation have been added, and a number of letters (mainly i and o), probably serving as line-fillers, have been removed.
2 End of the line: justification abbreviation for Deus, which appears on the following line.

BIBLIOGRAPHY

Archive, manuscript and incunable sources cited

Archives départementales d'Ille-et-Vilaine
1 F 657, Financial Accounts from John IV of Brittany – Francis II of Brittany
Archives départementales de la Loire-Atlantique
Série B, non classés, fragments of Accounts for the reign of Francis II
Archives du Fonds Lebreton, Abbaye Saint-Guénole, Land Évennec
Liasses 4A and 4B, Bretagne: Comptes et mandements ducaux et lettres royales, 14ᵉ–17ᵉ
    siècles
Cambridge, Fitzwilliam Museum
MS 62, *Fitzwilliam Hours (Hours of Isabel Stuart)*
MS 48, *Carew-Poyntz Hours*
MS 159, *Primer of Claude of France*
Chantilly, Musée Condé
MS 65, *Trés Riches Heures of the Duke of Berry*
Chicago, Newberry Library
MS 83, *Prayer Book of Anne of Brittany*
Geneva, Bibliothèque publique et universitaire
MS français 131, *Généalogie des très anciens roys, ducs et princes de Bretagne, qu'au temps
    passé ont régy et gouverné ceste royale principauté*
London, British Library
Egerton MS 1070, *Hours of René of Anjou*
Egerton MS 2781, *Neville of Hornby Hours*
Harley MS 585, Anglo-Saxon remedies (*Lacnunga*)
Harley MS 1260, Liturgical collection
Harley MS 2897, *Burgundy Breviary*
Rotulus Harley 43 A 14, Devotional scroll
Royal MS 2 B vii, *Queen Mary Psalter*
Royal MS 12 B xii, Medical tracts
Royal MS 12 B xxv, Medical tracts and recipes
Royal MS 15 E iv, Jean Wavrin, *History of England*
Royal MS 17 A viii, Medical collection in English
Royal MS 18 E vi, Jean Mansel, *Fleur des histoires*
Sloane MS 3160, Homilies and medical recipes
Sloane MS 3564, Medical recipes
London, The Wellcome Trust, Wellcome Library
MS 632, Devotional scroll

London, National Art Library, Victoria and Albert Museum
Salting MS 1222, *Hours of Marguerite of Foix*
Manchester, John Rylands University Library of Manchester
Latin MS 39, Book of Hours
Inc 12018.1, Jacobus de Voragine, *The Golden Legend*, translated and printed by William
    Caxton, Westminster, 1497
S15444, Book of Hours in French and Latin, printed by Thielman Kerver, Paris, 1498
New York, Metropolitan Museum of Art, The Cloisters Collection
MS 54. 1 1, *Belles Heures of the Duke of Berry*
New York, Pierpont Morgan Library
Glazier MS 39, Devotional scroll
M1092, Devotional scroll
MS M. 50, *Prayer Book of Anne of Brittany*
MS M. 700, *De Bois Hours*
MS. M. 240, *Bible moralisée*
Oxford, Bodleian Library
Douce MS 208, *Commentaires de César*
Paris, Bibliothèque nationale de France
Fonds français, 91, Prose *Merlin*
Fonds français, 166, *Bible moralisée*
Fonds français, 167, *Bible moralisée*
Fonds français, 403, *Apocalypse*
Fonds français, 958, *Somme le roi*
Fonds français, 1327, Medical miscellany
Fonds français, 1802, Collection of prayers
Fonds français, 9561, *Bible moralisée*
Fonds latin, 1156A, *Hours of René of Anjou*
Fonds latin, 1159, *Hours of Peter II of Brittany*
Fonds latin, 1369, *Hours of Isabel Stuart*
Fonds latin, 1385, *Hours of Francis II of Brittany*
Fonds latins, 6992, Pierre Andrieu, *Pomum Aureum (The Golden Apple)*
Fonds latin, 7064, Bernard de Chaussade, *Tractatus de conceptione et generatione prae-*
    cipue filiorum (On Conception and Generation, Especially of Male Children)
Fonds latin, 9471, *Rohan Hours*
Fonds latin, 9474, *Grandes Heures of Anne of Brittany*
Fonds latin, 17332, *Hours of René of Anjou*
Nouvelle acquisition latine, 588, *Hours of Isabel Stuart*
Nouvelle acquisition latine, 3039, *Très Belles Heures of the Duke of Berry* (see also Turin,
    Museo Civico d'Arte Antica, Inv. No. 47)
Nouvelle acquisition latine, 3120, *Très Petites Heures of Anne of Brittany*
Nouvelle acquisition latine, 3231, *Châtillon Hours*
Princeton, University Library
Garrett Collection MS 40, *Missal of the Carmelites of Nantes*
Toledo, Cathedral Library
MS 1, *Bible moralisée*

Turin, Museo Civico d'Arte Antica

Inv. No. 47, *Très Belles Heures of the Duke of Berry* (*Turin-Milan Hours*, see also Paris, nouvelle acquisition latine 3039)

Printed sources cited

Anne of France, *Les Enseignements d'Anne de France duchesse de Bourbonnois et d'Auvergne à sa fille Susanne de Bourbon*, ed. by A.-M. Chazaud (Moulins: Desroisiers, 1878)

Aers, David and Lynn Staley, *Powers of the Holy: Religion, Politics and Gender in Late Medieval Culture* (Pennsylvania: University of Pennsylvania Press, 1996)

Ashley, Kathleen and Pamela Sheingorn, eds, *Interpreting Cultural Symbols: Saint Anne in Late Medieval Society* (Athens, GA and London: University of Georgia Press, 1990)

—— and Robert L. A. Clark (eds) *Medieval Conduct* (London and Minneapolis: University of Minnesota Press, 2001)

Avril, François, 'Un portrait inédit de la reine Charlotte de Savoie', in *Études sur la Bibliothèque nationale et témoignages réunis en hommage à Thérèse Kleindienst* (Paris: Bibliothèque nationale, 1985), pp. 255–62

—— and Nicole Reynaud, *Les Manuscrits à peintures en France, 1450–1520* (Paris: Flammarion-Bibliothèque nationale, 1993)

—— and Sylvie Lisiecki, 'Le livre d'heures de Jacques II de Châtillon', *Chroniques de la Bibliothèque nationale de France*, 17 (2002), 7–10

Aymar, A., 'Le sachet accoucheur et ses mystères: Contribution a l'étude du folklore de la Haute-Auvergne', *Annales du Midi*, 38 (1926), 273–347

Baskins, Cristelle L., *Cassone Painting, Humanism, and Gender in Early Modern Italy* (Cambridge and New York: Cambridge University Press, 1998)

Bawcutt, Priscilla and Bridget Henisch, 'Scots Abroad in the Fifteenth Century: The Princesses Margaret, Isabella and Eleanor', in *Women in Scotland, c.1100–1750*, ed. by Elizabeth Ewan and Maureen M. Meikle (East Linton: Tuckwell, 1999), pp. 45–55

Baxandall, Michael, *Painting and Experience in Fifteenth-Century Italy: A Primer in the Social History of Pictorial Style*, 2nd edn (Oxford: Oxford University Press, 1972; repr. 1986)

——, *The Limewood Sculptors of Renaissance Germany* (London: Yale University Press, 1980)

Bell, Susan Groag, 'Medieval Women Book Owners: Arbiters of Lay Piety and Ambassadors of Culture', in *Women and Power in the Middle Ages*, ed. by Mary Erler and Maryanne Kowaleski (London and Athens: University of Georgia Press, 1988), pp. 149–87

Benedek, Thomas G., 'The Changing Relationship between Midwives and Physicians During the Renaissance', *Bulletin of the History of Medicine*, 51 (1977), 550–64

Bennett, Judith M., 'Medieval Women, Modern Women: Across the Great Divide', in *Culture and History 1350–1600: Essays in English Communities, Identities and Writing*, ed. by David Aers (Hemel Hempstead: Harvester, 1992), pp. 147–75

—— and Amy Froide (eds), *Singlewomen in the European Past, 1250–1800* (Philadelphia: University of Pennsylvania Press, 1999)

Benton, John, 'Trotula, Women's Problems and the Professionalization of Medicine in the Middle Ages', *Bulletin of the History of Medicine*, 59 (1985), 30–53

Berdini, Paolo, 'Women under the Gaze: A Renaissance Genealogy', *Art History*, 21 (1998), 565–90

Biddick, Kathleen, 'Genders, Bodies, Borders: Technologies of the Visible', *Speculum*, 68 (1993), 389–418

Biller, Peter, 'Childbirth in the Middle Ages', *History Today*, 36 (1986), 42–9

Blumenfeld-Kosinski, Renate, *Not of Woman Born: Representations of Caesarean Birth in Medieval and Renaissance Culture* (Ithaca and London: Cornell University Press, 1990)

Bodman, Herbert L., 'The Sator-Formula: An Evaluation', in *Laudatores Temporis Acti: Studies in Memory of Wallace Everett Caldwell*, ed. by Mary Francis Gyles and Eugene Wood Davis (Chapel Hill: University of North Carolina Press, 1964), pp. 131–41

The Book of the Knight of La Tour-Landry, ed. by Thomas Wright, Early English Text Society, extra series 33 (London: N. Trüber, 1868)

de la Borderie, A., 'Inventaire des meubles et bijoux de Marguerite de Bretagne, Première femme du duc de Bretagne François II', *Bulletin de la société archéologique de Nantes et Loire-inferieure*, 4 (1864), 45–60

Bozóky, Edina, 'From Matter of Devotion to Amulets', *Medieval Folklore*, 3 (1994), 91–107

Braekman, W. L., 'Notes on Old English Charms II', *Neophilologus*, 67 (1983), 605–10

Brandenbarg, Ton, 'St Anne and Her Family', in *Saints and She-Devils: Images of Women in the Fifteenth and Sixteenth Centuries*, ed. by Lène Dresen-Coenders (London: Rubicon Press, 1987), pp. 101–27

Brown, Cynthia, 'Le mécénat d'Anne de Bretagne et la politique du livre', in *Patronnes et mécènes en France à la Renaissance*, ed. by Kathleen Wilson-Chevalier (St-Étienne: Université de St-Étienne, 2007), pp. 195–224

Buettner, Brigitte, 'Women and the Circulation of Books', *Journal of the Early Book Society*, 4 (2001), 9–31

Bühler, Curt F., 'Prayers and Charms in Certain Middle English Scrolls', *Speculum*, 39 (1964), 270–8

Butler, Judith, *Gender Trouble: Feminism and the Subversion of Identity* (New York: Routledge, 1990; repr. 1999)

Bynum, Caroline Walker, *Jesus as Mother: Studies in the Spirituality of the High Middle Ages* (Berkeley, Los Angeles and London: University of California Press, 1982)

——, *Holy Feast and Holy Fast: The Religious Significance of Food to Medieval Women* (Berkeley and Los Angeles: University of California Press, 1986)

——, *Fragmentation and Redemption: Essays on Gender and the Human Body in Medieval Religion* (New York: Zone Books, 1991)

Camille, Michael, 'The Illustrated Manuscripts of Guillaume de Deguileville's "Pèlerinages" 1330–1426' (unpublished doctoral thesis, University of Cambridge, 1985)

Cadden, Joan, *Meanings of Sex Difference in the Middle Ages: Medicine, Science and Culture* (Cambridge: Cambridge University Press, 1993)

Carolus-Barré, Louis, 'Un nouveau parchemin amulette et la légende de sainte Marguerite patronne des femmes en couches', *Comptes Rendus de l'Académie des Inscriptions et Belles-Lettres*, (1979), 256–75

Cassidy, Brendan, 'A Relic, Some Pictures and the Mothers of Florence in the Late Fourteenth Century', *Gesta*, 30 (1991), 91–9

Castillon, H., *Histoire du comté de Foix, depuis les temps anciens jusqu'à nos jours*, 2 vols (Toulouse: Cazaux, 1852)

Caviness, Madeleine H., 'Patron or Matron? A Capetian Bride and a *Vade Mecum* for Her Marriage Bed', *Speculum*, 68 (1993), 333–62

Châtelet, Albert, *Jean Prévost: le Maître de Moulins* (Paris: Gallimard, 2001)

——, 'Jean de Pestinien au service de Philippe le Bon et de son prisonnier le Roi René', *Artibus et Historiae*, 20 (1999), 77–88

de Chauliac, Guy, *Inventarium sive Chirurgia magna*, 2 vols, ed. by Michael R. McVaugh with Margaret S. Ogden, Studies in Ancient Medicine 14 (Leiden: Brill, 1997)

Chauvenet, Frédérique, 'Le tombeau de Marguerite d'Écosse', in *Autour de Marguerite d'Ecosse: Reines, princesses et dames du XVe siècle, Actes du colloque de Thouars (23 et 24 mai 1997)*, ed. by Geneviève and Philippe Contamine (Paris: Honoré Champion, 1999), pp. 73–80

Chevalier, Bernard, 'Marie d'Anjou, une reine sans gloire, 1404–1463', in *Autour de Marguerite d'Ecosse: Reines, princesses et dames du XVe siècle, Actes du colloque de Thouars (23 et 24 mai 1997)*, ed. by Geneviève and Philippe Contamine (Paris: Honoré Champion, 1999), pp. 81–98

Cluzel, Jean, *Anne de France: fille de Louis XI, duchesse de Bourbon* (Paris: Fayard, 2002)

Coletti, Theresa, 'Purity and Danger: The Paradox of Mary's Body and the En-gendering of the Infancy Narrative in the English Mystery Cycles', in *Feminist Approaches to the Body in Medieval Literature*, ed. by Sarah Stanbury and Linda Lomperis (Philadelphia: University of Pennsylvania Press, 1993), pp. 65–93

Coster, William, 'Purity, Profanity, and Puritanism: The Churching of Women, 1500–1700', *Woman and the Church*, Studies in Church History 27 (Oxford: Basil Blackwell, 1990), pp. 377–87

Cressy, David, 'Purification, Thanksgiving and the Churching of Women in Post-Reformation England', *Past and Present*, 141 (1993), 106–46

——, *Birth, Marriage, and Death: Ritual, Religion, and the Life-cycle in Tudor and Stuart England* (Oxford: Oxford University Press, 1997)

Cross, F. L. (ed.) *The Oxford Dictionary of the Christian Church* (London: Oxford University Press, 1957)

Cullum, Patricia and Jeremy Goldberg, 'How Margaret Blackburn Taught her Daughters: Reading Devotional Instruction in a Book of Hours', in *Medieval Women: Texts and Contexts in Late Medieval Britain: Essays for Felicity Riddy*, ed. by Arlyn Diamond, Rosalynn Voaden and Jocelyn Wogan-Browne (Turnhout: Brepols, 2000), pp. 217–36

Cunnington, Phillis and Catherine Lucas, *Costume for Births, Marriages and Deaths* (London: Adam & Charles Black, 1972)

Davis, Whitney, 'Gender', in *Critical Terms for Art History*, ed. by Robert S. Nelson and Richard Shiff, 2nd edn (Chicago and London: University of Chicago Press, 2003), pp. 330–1

Day, Véronique P., 'Recycling Radegund: Identity and Ambition in the Breviary of Anne de Prye', in *Excavating the Medieval Image: Manuscripts, Artists, Audiences: Essays in Honor of Sandra Hindman*, ed. by David S. Areford and Nina A. Rowe (Aldershot: Ashgate, 2004), pp. 151–77

Delisle, Léopold, *Mélanges de paléographie et de bibliographie* (Paris: Champion, 1880)

——, *Les Grandes Heures de la Reine Anne de Bretagne et l'atelier de Jean Bourdichon* (Paris: D. Morgand, 1913)

Dilling, W. J., 'Girdles: Their Origin and Development, Particularly with Regard to their Use as Charms in Medicine, Marriage, and Midwifery', *Caledonian Medical Journal*, 9 (1912), 337–57 and 403–25

Driver, Martha W., 'Mirrors of a Collective Past: Re-considering Images of Medieval Women', in *Women and the Book: Assessing the Visual Evidence*, ed. by Lesley Smith and Jane H. M. Taylor (London and Toronto: The British Library and Toronto University Press, 1996), pp. 75–93

Duffy, Eamon, *Marking the Hours: English People and their Prayers 1240–1570* (New Haven and London: Yale University Press, 2006)

Durrieu, Paul, 'Le Maître des "Grandes Heures de Rohan" et les Lescuier d'Angers', *Revue de l'art ancien et moderne*, 2 (1912), 81–98 and 161–88

Durville, G., 'Une demi-sœur inconnue d'Anne de Bretagne', *Bulletin de la société archéologique de Nantes et de la Loire-Atlantique*, 57 (1917 for 1915), 1–26

Dückers, Rob, '"In the Beginning": The *Bible Moralisée* in the Work of the Limbourg Brothers', in *The Limbourg Brothers: Nijmegen Masters at the French Court, 1400–1416*, ed. by Rob Dückers and Pieter Roelofs (Nijmegen: Ludion, 2005), pp. 85–95

Eames, Penelope, *Furniture in England, France and the Netherlands from the Twelfth to the Fifteenth Century* (London: Furniture History Society, 1977)

Elsakkers, Marianne, 'In Pain You Shall Bear Children: Medieval Prayers for a Safe Delivery', in *Studies in the History of Religions*, ed. by Anne-Marie Korte (Boston, Leiden and Cologne: Brill, 2001), pp. 179–209

Emmerson, Richard K., 'A "Large Order of the Whole": Intertextuality and Interpictoriality in the Hours of Isabella Stuart', *Studies in Iconography*, 28 (2007), 53–99

——, 'The Apocalypse Cycle in the Bedford Hours', *Traditio*, 50 (1995), 173–98

——, 'Translating Images: Image and Poetic Reception in French, English, and Latin Versions of Guillaume de Deguileville's *Trois Pèlerinages*', in *Poetry, Place and Gender: Studies in Medieval Culture in Honor of Helen Damico*, ed. by Catherine E. Karkov (Kalamazoo: Medieval Institute Publications, 2008)

—— and Bernard McGinn (eds) *The Apocalypse in the Middle Ages* (Ithaca: Cornell University Press, 1992)

L'Europe des Anjou: aventure des princes angevins du XIIIe au XVe siècle, exhibition catalogue (Paris: Somogy, 2001)

Exhibition of Illuminated Manuscripts (London: Burlington Fine Arts Club, 1908)

Finucane, Ronald C., *The Rescue of the Innocents: Endangered Children in Medieval Miracles* (New York: St Martin's Press, 1997)

Forbes, Thomas, *The Midwife and the Witch* (New Haven and London: Yale University Press, 1966)

Foster, Marjory Bolger, 'The Iconography of St Joseph in Netherlandish Art, 1400–1550' (unpublished doctoral dissertation, University of Kansas, 1978)

Franz, Adolph, *Die kirchlichen Benediktionen im Mittelalter*, 2 vols (Freiburg: Herder, 1909; repr., Graz: Akademischer Druck U.-Verlagsanstalt, 1960)

Gabory, Émile, *Anne de Bretagne, Duchesse et Reine* (Paris: Plon, 1941)

De Gendt, Anne-Marie, 'Aucuns petis enseignemens: "Home-Made" Courtesy Books in Medieval France', in *Centres of Learning and Location in Pre-Modern Europe and the Near East*, ed. by Jan Willem Drijvers and Alisdair MacDonald (Leiden: Brill, 1995), pp. 279–88

Gibson, Gail McMurray, *The Theater of Devotion: East Anglian Drama and Society in the Late Middle Ages* (Chicago: Chicago University Press, 1989)

——, 'Blessing from Sun and Moon: Churching as Women's Theater', in *Bodies and Disciplines: Intersections of Literature and History in Fifteenth-Century England*, ed. by Barbara A. Hanawalt and David Wallace (London and Minneapolis: University of Minnesota Press, 1996), pp. 139–54

——, 'Scene and Obscene: Seeing and Performing Late Medieval Childbirth', *Journal of Medieval and Early Modern Studies*, 29 (1999), 7–24

Giles, Phyllis M., and Francis Wormald (eds) *Illuminated Manuscripts in the Fitzwilliam Museum* (Cambridge: Fitzwilliam Museum, 1966)

Gray, Douglas, 'Notes on Some Middle English Charms', in *Chaucer and Middle English Studies in Honour of Rossell Hope Robbins*, ed. by Beryl Rowland (London: George Allen & Unwin, 1974), pp. 56–71

Green, Monica H., 'Women's Medical Practice and Health Care in Medieval Europe', *Signs*, 14 (1989), 437–3

——, 'From "Diseases of Women" to "Secrets of Women": The Transformation of Gynecological Literature in the Late Middle Ages', *Journal of the Medieval and Early Modern Society*, 30 (2000), 5–39

——, *Women's Healthcare in the Medieval West* (Aldershot: Ashgate Variorum, 2000)

——, 'Bodies, Gender, Health, Disease: Recent Work on Medieval Women's Medicine', *Studies in Medieval and Renaissance History*, 2 (2005), 1–49

——, *The* Trotula: *A Medieval Compendium of Women's Medicine* (Philadelphia: University of Pennsylvania Press, 2001)

——, *Making Women's Medicine Masculine: The Rise of Male Authority in Pre-Modern Gynaecology* (Oxford: Oxford University Press, 2008)

Green, Rosalie B., and Isa Ragusa, *Meditations on the life of Christ: an illustrated manuscript of the fourteenth century, Paris, Bibliothèque nationale, MS. Ital. 115*, trans. by Isa Ragusa (Princeton: Princeton University Press, 1961)

Greilsammer, Myriam, 'The Midwife, the Priest, and the Physician: The Subjugation of Midwives in the Low Countries at the End of the Middle Ages', *Journal of Medieval and Renaissance Studies*, 21 (1991), 283–329

Guest, Gerald B., *Bible Moralisée: Codex Vindobonensis 2554, Vienna, Österreichische Nationalbibliothek* (London: Harvey Miller, 1995)

A Guide to the Salting Collection (London: published under the authority of the board of education, 1926)

Haas, Louis, 'Women and Childbearing in Medieval Florence', in *Medieval Family Roles: A Book of Essays*, ed. by Cathy Jorgensen Itnyre (New York and London: Garland, 1996), pp. 87–99

Hahn, Cynthia, ' "Joseph Will Perfect, Mary Enlighten and Jesus Save Thee": The Holy Family as Marriage Model in the *Mérode Triptych*', *Art Bulletin*, 68 (1986), 54–66

Hale, Rosemary Drage, 'Joseph as Mother: Adaptation and Appropriation in the Construction of Male Virtue', in *Medieval Mothering*, ed. by John Carmi Parsons and Bonnie Wheeler (New York and London: Garland, 1996), pp. 101–16

——, 'Rocking the Cradle: Margaretha Ebner (Be)Holds the Divine', in *Performance and Transformation: New Approaches to Late Medieval Spirituality*, ed. by Mary A. Suydam and Joanna E. Zeigler (London: Macmillan, 1999), pp. 211–39

Hamburger, Jeffrey, *The Visual and the Visionary: Art and Female Spirituality in Late Medieval Germany* (New York: Zone Books, 1998)

Harley, David, 'Historians as Demonologists: The Myth of the Midwife-Witch', *Social History of Medicine*, 1990 (3), 1–26

Harthan, John, *Books of Hours and Their Owners* (London: Thames & Hudson, 1977)

Heimann, Adelheid, 'Der Meister der "Grandes Heures de Rohan" und seine Werkstatt', *Städel Jahrbuch*, 7–8 (1932), 1–61

Henderson, George, 'The Manuscript Model of the Angers "Apocalypse" Tapestries', *Burlington Magazine*, 127 (1985), 208–19

Henderson, W. G., ed., *Manuale et processionale ad usum insignis ecclesiae eboracensis*, Surtees Society, 63 (London: Whittaker and Co, 1875)

Hoch, Adrian S., 'Beata Stirps, Royal Patronage and the Identification of the Sainted Rulers in the St Elizabeth Chapel at Assisi', *Art History*, 15 (1992), 279–95

Hunt, Tony, *Popular Medicine in Thirteenth-Century England: Introduction and Texts* (Woodbridge: Brewer, 1990)

Jacobsen, Grethe, 'Pregnancy and Childbirth in the Medieval North: A Topology of Sources and a Preliminary Study', *Scandinavian Journal of History*, 9 (1984), 91–111

James, M. R., *A Descriptive Catalogue of the Manuscripts in the Fitzwilliam Museum* (Cambridge: Cambridge University Press, 1895)

——, *A Descriptive Catalogue of the Latin Manuscripts in the John Rylands Library at Manchester* (Manchester: Manchester University Press, 1921)

——, trans., *The Apocryphal New Testament* (Oxford: Clarendon Press, 1924)

Johnson, Geraldine A., 'Beautiful Brides and Model Mothers: The Devotional and Talismanic Functions of Early Modern Marian Reliefs', in *The Material Culture of Sex, Procreation, and Marriage in Premodern Europe*, ed. by Anne L. McClanan and Karen Rosoff Encarnación (New York: Palgrave, 2001), pp. 135–61

Jolly, Penny Howell, 'Learned Reading, Vernacular Seeing: Jacques Daret's "Presentation in the Temple" ', *Art Bulletin*, 82 (2000), 428–52

Jones, Michael, 'Les Manuscrits d'Anne de Bretagne', *Mémoires de la Société d'Histoire et d'Archéologie de Bretagne*, 55 (1978), 43–81

——, *Catalogue sommaire des archives du fonds Lebreton, Abbaye Sainte-Guénolé, Land Évennec* (Nottingham: University of Nottingham, 2006)

Jordanova, Ludmilla, *History in Practice* (London: Edward Arnold, 2000)

Joubert, Fabienne, 'L'Apocalypse d'Angers et les débuts de la tapisserie historiée', *Bulletin Monumental*, 139 (1981), 125–40

Kamerick, Kathleen, 'Patronage and Devotion in the Prayer Book of Anne of Brittany, Newberry Library MS 83', *Manuscripta*, 39 (1995), 40–50

Keiser, George R. (ed.), *A Manual of the Writings in Middle English, 1050–1500*, X (part XXV *Works of Science and Education*) (New Haven: The Connecticut Academy of Arts and Sciences, 1998)

Kempe, Margery, *The Book of Margery Kempe*, ed. by Barry Windeatt (Harlow: Longman, 2000)

Klaniczay, Gábor, *Holy Rulers and Blessed Princesses: Dynastic Cults in Medieval Central Europe* (Cambridge: Cambridge University Press, 2002)

Klapisch-Zuber, Christiane, *Women, Family and Ritual in Renaissance Italy*, trans. by Lydia Cochrane (Chicago and London: University of Chicago Press, 1985)

Kohl, Benjamin, 'Fina da Carrara, née Buzzacarini: Consort, Mother, and Patron of Art in Trecento Padua', in *Beyond Isabella: Secular Women Patrons of Art in Renaissance Italy*, ed. by Sheryl E. Reiss and David G. Wilkins (Kirksville: Truman State University Press, 2001), pp. 19–36

Kren, Thomas and Scot McKendrick, *Illuminating the Renaissance: The Triumph of Flemish Manuscript Painting in Europe* (Los Angeles and London: J. Paul Getty Museum/Royal Academy of Arts, 2003)

Kristeva, Julia, 'Motherhood According to Giovanni Bellini', in *Desire in Language: A Semiotic Approach to Literature and Art*, ed. by Leon S. Roudiez, trans. by Thomas Gora, Alice Jardine and Leon S. Roudiez (New York: Columbia University Press, 1980), pp. 237–70.

——, 'Stabat Mater', in *The Kristeva Reader*, ed. by Toril Moi (Oxford: Basil Blackwell, 1986), pp. 160–86

de Laborde, A., *Étude sur la Bible moralisée illustrée*, 5 vols (Paris: Société française de reproductions de manuscrits à peintures, 1911–27)

Lafontaine-Dosogne, Jacqueline, *Iconographie de l'enfance de la Vierge dans l'empire byzantin et en occident* (Brussels: Palais des Academies, 1964)

Larson, Wendy, 'Who is the Master of this Narrative? Maternal Patronage of the Cult of St Margaret', in *Gendering the Master Narrative: Women and Power in the Middle Ages*, ed. by Mary C. Erler and Maryanne Kowaleski (Ithaca and London: Cornell University Press, 2003), pp. 94–104

Laurent, Sylvie, *Naître au moyen âge: de la conception à la naissance: la grossesse et l'accouchement (XIIe–XVe siecle)* (Paris: Le Léopard d'or, 1989)

——, 'L'accouchement dans l'iconographie médiévale d'après les miniatures de la Bibliothèque nationale', in *Maladies, Medecines et Sociétés: approches historiques pour le présent*, 2 vols, ed. by F. O. Touati (Paris: L'Harmattan, 1993), I, pp. 144–52

Le Fur, Didier, *Anne de Bretagne: Miroir d'une reine, historiographie d'un mythe* (Paris: Librairie Édition Guénégaud, 2000)

Lee, Becky R., 'The Purification of Women After Childbirth: A Window onto Medieval Perceptions of Women', *Florilegium*, 14 (1995–96), 43–55

——, 'A Company of Women *and* Men: Men's Recollections of Childbirth in Medieval England', *Journal of Family History*, 27 (2002), 92–100

Legaré, Anne-Marie, 'Reassessing Women's Libraries in Late Medieval France: The Case of Jeanne de Laval', *Renaissance Studies*, 10 (1996), 209–29

——, 'Charlotte de Savoie's Library and Illuminators', *Journal of the Early Book Society*, 4 (2001), 32–87

——, 'La réception du *Pèlerinage de Vie humaine* de Guillaume de Digulleville dans le milieu angevin d'après les sources et les manuscrits conservés', in *Religion et mentalités au Moyen Âge: Mélanges en l'honneur d'Hervé Martin*, ed. by Sophie Cassagnes-Brouquet *et al.* (Rennes: Presses Universitaires de Rennes, 2003), pp. 543–52

——(ed.), *Livres et lectures des femmes en Europe: entre Moyen Âge et Renaissance, Lille, 24–26 mai 2004* (Turnhout: Brepols, 2007)

Lemay, Helen, 'Anthonius Guainerius and Medieval Gynecology', in *Women of the Medieval World: Essays in Honour of John H. Mundy*, ed. by Julius Kirshner and Suzanne F. Wemple (Oxford: Basil Blackwell, 1985), pp. 317–36

——, 'Women and the Literature of Obstetrics and Gynecology', in *Medieval Women and the Sources of Medieval History*, ed. by Joel T. Rosenthal (Athens, GA and London: University of Georgia Press, 1990), pp. 189–209

Lequain, Élodie, 'Anne de France et les livres: la tradition et le pouvoir', in *Patronnes et mécènes en France à la Renaissance*, ed. by Kathleen Wilson-Chevalier (St-Étienne: Université de St-Étienne, 2007), pp. 154–68

Leroquais, Abbé Victor, *Les Livres d'heures manuscrits de la Bibliothèque nationale*, 3 vols (Paris: Bibliothèque nationale, 1927)

L'Estrange, Elizabeth, 'Anna Peperit Mariam, Elizabeth Johannem, Maria Christum: Images of Childbirth in Late-Medieval Manuscripts', in *Manuscripts in Transition: Recycling Manuscripts, Texts and Images*, ed. by Brigitte Dekeyzer and Jan Van der Stock, Corpus of Illuminated Manuscripts 15 (Leuven: Peeters, 2005), pp. 335–46.

——, 'Sainte Anne et le mécénat d'Anne de France', in *Patronnes et mécènes en France à la Renaissance*, ed. by Kathleen Wilson-Chevalier (St-Étienne: Université de St-Étienne, 2007), pp. 135–54

——, 'Le mécénat d'Anne de Bretagne', in *Patronnes et mécènes en France à la Renaissance*, ed. by Kathleen Wilson-Chevalier (St-Étienne: Université de St-Étienne, 2007), pp. 169–93

Letts, Malcolm (ed.), *The Travels of Leo Rozmital: Through Germany, Flanders, England, France, Spain, Portugal, and Italy, 1465–1467*, Hakluyt Society, second series, 108 for 1955 (Cambridge: Cambridge University Press, 1957)

Lipton, Sara, *Images of Intolerance: The Representation of Jews and Judaism in the Bible moralisée* (Berkeley, Los Angeles and London: University of California Press, 1999)

Marrow, James H., 'History, Historiography, and Pictorial Invention in the *Turin-Milan*

Hours', in *In Detail: New Studies of Northern Renaissance Art in Honor of Walter S. Gibson*, ed. by Laurinda S. Dixon (Turnhout: Brepols, 2001), pp. 1–14

Maurer, Helen E., *Margaret of Anjou: Queenship and Power in Late Medieval England* (Woodbridge: Boydell, 2003)

McClive, Cathy, 'Engendrer durant les menstrues: devoir conjugal et interdit sexuel à l'époque moderne', in *Le désir et le goût: une autre histoire (XIIIe–XVIIIe siècles), actes du colloque international à la mémoire de Jean-Louis Flandrin, Saint-Denis, septembre 2003*, ed. by Odile Redon, Line Sallman and Sylvie Steinberg (Paris: Presses Universitaires de Vincennes, 2005), pp. 245–63

Meale, Carol M., ' ". . . alle the bokes that I haue of latyn, englisch, and frensch": Laywomen and their Books in Late Medieval England', in *Women and Literature in Britain 1150–1500*, ed. by Carole M. Meale (Cambridge: Cambridge University Press, 1993), pp. 128–58

Meiss, Millard, *French Painting in the Time of Jean de Berry*, 3 vols (London and New York: Thames & Hudson, 1967–74)

——, and Marcel Thomas, *The Rohan Hours: Bibliothèque nationale, Paris (ms lat. 9741)* (London: Thames & Hudson, 1973)

Miles, Margaret, *Image as Insight: Visual Understanding in Western Christianity and Secular Culture* (Boston: Beacon Press, 1985)

Minois, George, *Anne de Bretagne* (Lille: Fayard, 1999)

——, *Charles VII: un roi shakespearien* ([no place]: Perrin, 2005)

Morice, Dom P. H., *Mémoires pour servir de preuves à l'Histoire Ecclésiastique et Civile de Bretagne*, 3 vols (Paris: Osmont, 1968)

Moorat, S. A. J., *Catalogue of Western Manuscripts on Medicine and Science in the Wellcome Historical Medical Library: MSS written before 1650 AD* (London: [no pub.], 1962)

Mulvey, Laura, 'Visual Pleasure and Narrative Cinema', *Screen*, 16 (1975), 6–18

Musacchio, Jacqueline Marie, *The Art and Ritual of Childbirth in Renaissance Italy* (New Haven and London: Yale University Press, 1999)

Nash, Susie, *Between France and Flanders: Manuscript Illumination in Amiens in the Fifteenth Century* (London and Toronto: The British Library and University of Toronto Press, 1999)

Naughton, Joan, 'A Minimally-Intrusive Presence: Portraits in Illustrations for Prayers to the Virgin', in *Medieval Texts and Images: Studies of Manuscripts from the Middle Ages*, ed. by Margaret Manion and Bernard J. Muir (Chur: Harwood Academic Publishers, 1991), pp. 111–26

de Nie, Giselle, ' "Consciousness Fecund Through God": From Male Fighter to Spiritual Bride-Mother in Late Antique Female Sanctity', in *Sanctity and Motherhood: Essays on Holy Mothers in the Middle Ages*, ed. by Anneke B. Mulder-Bakker (New York and London: Garland, 1995), pp. 101–61

Ogden, Margaret S., (ed.), *The* Liber de Diversis Medicinis *in the Thornton Manuscript*, Early English Text Society, original series 207 (London: Oxford University Press, 1938)

Olsan, Lea, 'The Arcus Charms and Christian Magic', *Neophilologus*, 73 (1989), 438–47

——, 'Latin Charms in British Library Royal MS 12 B xxv', *Manuscripta*, 33 (1989), 119–28

Orth, Myra D., '"Madame Sainte Anne": The Holy Kinship, the Royal Trinity, and Louise of Savoy, in *Interpreting Cultural Symbols: Saint Anne in Late Medieval Society*, ed. by Kathleen Ashley and Pamela Sheingorn (Athens, GA and London: University of Georgia Press, 1990), pp. 199–227

Pächt, Otto, 'René d'Anjou et les Van Eyck', *Cahiers de l'Association internationale des études françaises*, 8 (1956), 41–67

Panayotova, Stella and Paul Binski (eds), *The Cambridge Illuminations: Ten Centuries of Book Production in the Medieval West* (London: Harvey Miller, 2005)

Panofsky, Erwin, 'Reintegration of a Book of Hours Executed in the Workshop of the "Maître des Grandes Heures de Rohan"', in *Medieval Studies in Memory of A. Kingsley Porter*, ed. by Wilhelm R. W. Koehler, 2 vols (Cambridge, MA: Harvard University Press, 1939), II, pp. 479–99

Paris 1400: les arts sous Charles VI, exhibition catalogue (Paris: Fayard, 2004)

Park, Katharine, 'Medicine and Magic: The Healing Arts', *Gender and Society in Renaissance Italy*, ed. by Judith C. Brown and Robert C. Davis (London: Longman, 1998), pp. 129–49

Paviot, Jacques, '*Les États de France (Les Honneurs de la cour)* d'Éléonore de Poitiers', *Annuaire-Bulletin de la Société de l'Histoire de la France*, (1996), 75–125

——, 'Les honneurs de la cour d'Éléonore de Poitiers', in *Autour de Marguerite d'Écosse: Reines, princesses et dames du XVe siècle, Actes du colloque de Thouars (23 et 24 mai 1997)*, ed. by Geneviève and Philippe Contamine (Paris: Champion, 1999), pp. 163–79

Pearson, Andrea, *Envisioning Gender in Burgundian Devotional Art, 1350–1530: Experience, Authority, Resistance* (Aldershot: Ashgate, 2005)

Penketh, Sandra, 'Women and Books of Hours', in *Women and the Book: Assessing the Visual Evidence*, ed. by Lesley Smith and Jane H. M. Taylor (Toronto and London: University of Toronto Press and the British Library, 1997), pp. 266–80

Pétin, Abbé, *Dictionnaire hagiographique ou vies des saints et des bienheureux*, 2 vols with supplement (Paris: Ateliers Catholiques du Petit-Montrouge, 1850)

Petrakopoulos, Anja, 'Sanctity and Motherhood: Elizabeth of Thuringia', in *Sanctity and Motherhod: Essays on Holy Mothers in the Middle Ages*, ed. by Anneke B. Mulder-Bakker (New York and London: Garland, 1995), pp. 257–96

Pierce, Joanne M., ' "Green Women" and Blood Pollution: Some Medieval Rituals for the Churching of Women after Childbirth', *Studia Liturgica*, 29 (1999), 191–215

de Pizan, Christine, *Le Livre des Trois Vertus*, ed. by Charity Cannon Willard (Paris: Champion, 1989)

Porcher, Jean, 'Two Models for the "Heures de Rohan"', *Journal of the Warburg and Courtauld Institutes*, 8 (1945), 1–6

Pradel, Pierre, *Anne de France, 1461–1522* (Paris: Publisud, 1986)

Randolph, Adrian W. B., 'Renaissance Household Goddesses: Fertility, Politics, and the Gendering of Spectatorship', in *The Material Culture of Sex, Procreation, and Marriage in Premodern Europe*, ed. by Anne L. McClanan and Karen Rosoff Encarnación (New York: Palgrave, 2001), pp. 163–89

——, 'Gendering the Period Eye: *Deschi da Parto* and Renaissance Visual Culture', *Art History*, 27 (2004), 538–62

Réau, Louis, *Iconographie de l'art chrétien: l'iconographie des saints*, 3 vols (Paris: Presses Universitaires de France, 1958)

de Riant, P.-E., 'Déposition de Charles d'Anjou pour la canonisation de S. Louis', in *Notices et documents publiés par la Société de l'Histoire de la France, à l'occasion de son 50ᵉ anniversaire* (Paris: [no pub.], 1889), pp. 158-80

Riddy, Felicity, ' "Women Talking About the Things of God": A Late Medieval Sub-Culture', in *Women and Literature in Britain 1150-1500*, ed. by Carol M. Meale (Cambridge: Cambridge University Press, 1993), pp. 104-27

Rieder, Paula M., 'Insecure Borders: Symbols of Clerical Privilege and Gender Ambiguity in the Liturgy of Churching', in *The Material Culture of Sex, Procreation, and Marriage in Premodern Europe*, ed. by Anne L. McClanan and Karen Rosoff Encarnación (New York: Palgrave, 2001), pp. 93-113

——, *On the Purification of Women: Churching in Northern France, 1100-1500* (New York: Palgrave Macmillan, 2006)

Rigby, S. H., *English Society in the Later Middle Ages: Class, Status and Gender* (London: Macmillan, 1995)

Ring, Grete, *A Century of French Painting* (London: Phaidon, 1949)

Ringbom, Sixten, 'Devotional Images and Imaginative Devotions: Notes on the Place of Art in Late Medieval Private Piety', *Gazette des Beaux-Arts*, 73 (1969), 159-70

Robin, Françoise, *La Cour d'Anjou-Provence: la vie artistique sous le règne de René* ([no place]: Picard, 1985)

Roettgen, Steffi, *Italian Frescoes: The Flowering of the Renaissance* (New York, London and Paris: Abbeville Press, 1997)

Rublack, Ulinka, 'Female Spirituality and the Infant Jesus in Late Medieval Dominican Convents', *Gender and History*, 6 (1994), 37-57

Rushton, Peter, 'Purification or Social Control? Ideologies of Reproduction and the Churching of Women after Childbirth', in *The Public and the Private*, ed. by Eva Gamarnikow *et al.* (London: Heinemann, 1983), pp. 118-31

Saengar, Paul, *A Catalogue of the Pre-1500 Western Manuscripts at the Newberry Library* (Chicago: University of Chicago Press, 1989)

Scott, Joan W., 'Gender: A Useful Category of Historical Analysis', *American Historical Review*, 91 (1986), 1053-75

Sheingorn, Pamela, 'The Wise Mother', *Gesta*, 32 (1993), 69-80

——, 'Appropriating the Holy Kinship: Gender and Family History', in *Interpreting Cultural Symbols: Saint Anne in Late Medieval Society*, ed. by Kathleen Ashley and Pamela Sheingorn (Athens, GA and London: University of Georgia Press, 1990), pp. 169-98

Sheldon, Susan Eastman, 'Middle English and Latin Charms, Amulets and Talismans from Vernacular Manuscripts' (unpublished doctoral dissertation, University of Tulane, 1978)

Shorr, Dorothy C., 'The Iconographic Development of the Presentation in the Temple', *Art Bulletin*, 28 (1946), 17-31

Simons, Patricia, 'Women in Frames: The Gaze, the Eye, the Profile in Renaissance Portraiture', *History Workshop*, 25 (1988), 4-30

Skemer, Don C., 'Amulet Rolls and Female Devotion', *Scriptorium*, 55 (2001), 197-227

Smith, Kathryn A., *Art, Identity, and Devotion in Fourteenth-Century England: Three Women and Their Books of Hours* (London and Toronto: British Library and University of Toronto Press, 2003)

Smith, Lesley, and Jane H. M. Taylor (eds), *Women and the Book: Assessing the Visual Evidence* (Toronto and London: University of Toronto Press and the British Library, 1997)

Sommé, Monique, 'Le Cérémonial de la naissance et de la mort de l'enfant princier à la cour de Bourgogne au XVe siècle', in *À la cour de Bourgogne: le Duc, son entourage, son train*, ed. by Jean-Marie Cauchies (Turnhout: Brepols, 1998), pp. 32-48

Soranus' Gynecology, trans. by O. Temkin (Baltimore: Johns Hopkins Press, 1956)

Stanbury, Sarah, 'Regimes of the Visual in Premodern England: Gaze, Body, and Chaucer's Clerk's Tale', *New Literary History*, 28 (1997), 261-89

Staniland, Kay, 'Royal Entry into the World', in *England in the Fifteenth Century: Proceedings of the 1986 Harlaxton Symposium*, ed. by Daniel Williams (Woodbridge: Boydell Press, 1987), pp. 297-313

Stanton, Anne Rudloff, 'From Eve to Bathsheba and Beyond: Motherhood in the Queen Mary Psalter', in *Women and the Book: Assessing the Visual Evidence*, ed. by Lesley Smith and Jane H. M. Taylor (Toronto and London: University of Toronto Press and the British Library, 1996), pp. 172-89

Stefaniak, Regina, 'Correggio's Camera di San Paolo: An Archaeology of the Gaze', *Art History*, 16 (1993), 203-28

Stoerz, Fiona Harris, 'Suffering and Survival in Medieval English Childbirth', in *Medieval Family Roles: A Book of Essays*, ed. by Cathy Jorgensen Itnyre (New York and London: Garland, 1996), pp. 101-20

Stones, Alison, 'Nipples, Entrails, Severed Heads, and Skin: Devotional Images for Madame Marie', in *Image and Belief: Studies in Celebration of the Eightieth Anniversary of the Index of Christian Art*, ed. by Colum Hourihane (Princeton: Index of Christian Art and Princeton University Press, 1999), pp. 47-64

Storms, G., *Anglo-Saxon Magic* (The Hague: Martinus Nijhoff, 1948)

Taglia, Kathryn, 'Delivering a Christian Identity: Midwives in Northern Synodal Legislation, *c*.1200-1500', in *Religion and Medicine in the Middle Ages*, ed. by Peter Biller and Joseph Zeigler (York: York Medieval Press, 2001), pp. 77-90

Thomas, Keith, *Religion and the Decline of Magic* (London: Penguin, 1973; repr. 1991)

Tonnerre, Noël-Yves and Élisabeth Verry (eds), *Les Princes Angevins du XIIIe au XVe siècle. Un destin européen* (Rennes: Presses Universitaires de Rennes, 2003)

Toynbee, Margaret R., 'The Portraiture of Isabella Stuart, Duchess of Brittany (*c*.1427-after 1494)', *Burlington Magazine*, 88 (1946), 300-6

Vale, M. G. A., *Charles VII* (London: Eyre Methuen, 1974)

Van Gennep, Arnold, *The Rites of Passage*, trans. by Monika B. Vizedom and Gabrielle L. Caffee (London: Routledge and Paul, 1960)

Verry, Élisabeth, 'L'impossible héritage: la deuxième maison d'Anjou et l'Italie (1380-1480)', in *Les Princes Angevins du XIIIe au XVe siècle. Un destin européen*, ed. Noël-Yves Tonnerre and Élisabeth Verry (Rennes: Presses Universitaires de Rennes, 2003)

de Voragine, Jacobus, *The Golden Legend: Readings on the Saints*, trans. by William Granger Ryan, 2 vols (New Jersey: Princeton University Press, 1993)

Warr, Cordelia, 'Painting in Late Fourteenth-Century Padua: The Patronage of Fina Buzzacarini', *Renaissance Studies*, 10 (1996), 139–55

Watson, Rowan, 'The Marguerite de Foix Book of Hours', *The V&A Album*, 2 (1983), 45–60

Weiss, Daniel H., 'Architectural Symbolism and the Decoration of the Ste-Chapelle', *Art Bulletin*, 77 (1995), 308–20

Weston, L. M. C., 'Women's Medicine, Women's Magic: The Old English Metrical Childbirth Charms', *Modern Philology*, 92 (1994–95), 279–93

Wickersheimer, E., *Dictionnaire biographique des médecins en France au Moyen Âge*, 2 vols and supplement (Geneva: Droz, 1979)

Wieck, Roger, *Time Sanctified: The Book of Hours in Medieval Art and Life* (New York: Brazilier and The Walters Art Gallery, 1988)

——, and K. Michelle Hearne, *The Prayer Book of Anne de Bretagne* (Luzern: Faksimile Verlag, 1999)

Wiesner, Merry E., 'Early Modern Midwifery: A Case Study', in *Women and Work in Pre-Industrial Europe*, ed. by Barbara Hanawalt (Bloomington: Indiana University Press, 1986), pp. 94–113

Wilson, Adrian, 'Participant or Patient? Seventeenth-century Childbirth from the Mother's Point of View', in *Patients and Practioners: Lay Perceptions of Medicine in Pre-Industrial Society*, ed. by Roy Porter (Cambridge: Cambridge University Press, 1985), pp. 129–44

——, 'The Ceremony of Childbirth and its Interpretation', in *Women as Mothers in Pre-Industrial England: Essays in Memory of Dorothy McLaren*, ed. by Valerie Fildes (London: Routledge, 1990), pp. 68–107

——, *The Making of Man-Midwifery: Childbirth in England 1660–1770* (London: UCL Press Ltd, 1995)

Wogan-Browne, Jocelyn, ' "Reading is Good Prayer": Recent Research on Female Reading Communities', *New Medieval Literatures*, 5 (2002), 229–97

York, William Henry, 'Experience and Theory in Medical Practice during the Later Middle Ages: Valesco de Tarenta (*fl.* 1382–1426) at the Court of Foix (France)' (unpublished doctoral dissertation, Johns Hopkins University, 2003)

Zemon Davis, Natalie, *Society and Culture in Early-Modern France* (London: Duckworth, 1975)

Electronic publications and sources

Catholic Encyclopaedia Online: www.newadvent.org (Accessed: 27 April 2007)

The Bible (Douai Rheims and Vulgate versions) www.bible.crosswalk.com (Accessed: 20 April 2007)

The Wardrobe Accounts of Edward IV: Part XXIX: www.r3.org/bookcase/wardrobe/ ward19.html (Accessed 29 March 2006)

Green, Monica H., 'Childbirth and Infancy', *Dictionary of the Middle Ages*, Supplement I: www.gale.com/pdf/samples/sp806428.pdf (Accessed 26 July 2006)

Prayer Book of Anne of Brittany: www.themorgan.org/collections/swf/exhib Online.asp?id=355 (Accessed 28 March 2007)

INDEX

Note: 'n.' after a page reference indicates the number of a note on that page;
numbers in *italics* refer to figures; 'pl.' refers to plates

EU authorised representative for GPSR:
Easy Access System Europe, Mustamäe tee 50,
10621 Tallinn, Estonia
gpsr.requests@easproject.com

www.ingramcontent.com/pod-product-compliance
Ingram Content Group UK Ltd.
Pitfield, Milton Keynes, MK11 3LW, UK
UKHW020037170726

7214IPUK00035B/145